THE IRISH AND THE IMAGINATION OF RACE

The Irish and the Imagination of Race

WHITE SUPREMACY ACROSS THE ATLANTIC
IN THE NINETEENTH CENTURY

Patrick R. O'Malley

UNIVERSITY OF VIRGINIA PRESS
Charlottesville and London

UNIVERSITY OF VIRGINIA PRESS
© 2023 Patrick R. O'Malley
All rights reserved
Printed in the United States of America on acid-free paper

First published 2023

ISBN 978-0-8139-5057-0 (cloth)
ISBN 978-0-8139-5056-3 (paper)
ISBN 978-0-8139-5055-6 (ebook)

1 3 5 7 9 8 6 4 2

Library of Congress Cataloging-in-Publication data
is available for this title.

Cover art: Scene from Mr Boucicault's New Drama at the Adelphi, the Slave Market, Sale of the Octoroon; illustration for *The Illustrated London News,* 30 November 1861. (Look and Learn / Illustrated Papers Collection / Bridgeman Images)

In memory of

Robert Edmund O'Malley Jr. (1939–2020)
Richard Leo O'Malley (1939–2020)
Jacqueline Sue Harvey (1952–2021)

CONTENTS

ACKNOWLEDGMENTS ix

Introduction 1

1. Nineteenth-Century Irishness and the Construction of Race 29
2. The Gothic Palimpsest of Black and Irish Histories 68
3. From Irish Bardicism to the White Nationalist Verse Epic 96
4. Irish American Whiteness in *The Garies and Their Friends* 130
5. John Mitchel and the Polemic of White Grievance 159
6. Performing Sympathy in *The Octoroon* 189

Coda: The Irish National Tale and Confederate Nostalgia 223

NOTES 245

BIBLIOGRAPHY 277

INDEX 301

ACKNOWLEDGMENTS

This project began with a very different argument than the one it discovered, and I have many people to thank for their guidance and critique as it found its way. At Georgetown, Tommaso Astarita, John Glavin, Nathan Hensley, Lindsay Kaplan, Lori Merish, Ricardo Ortíz, Josiah Osgood, Cóilín Parsons, Amanda Phillips, Daniel Shore, Christine So, and Kathryn Temple have been constant sources of intellectual sustenance and comradeship; Soyica Colbert, David Edelstein, and Andrew Sobanet expertly guided humanistic scholarship within Georgetown's College of Arts & Sciences. I am in awe of Melissa Jones, Georgetown's research librarian for English, and grateful to her for her archival sorcery. I thank also my graduate and undergraduate students for forging their own intellectual and personal paths and, in doing so, teaching me to see anew what I thought was familiar.

Friends and colleagues across the United States and beyond have patiently listened as I thought through the issues of this book, engaged with its ideas at conferences and presentations, asked key questions that I was ignoring and sent me scurrying back to rethink my assumptions, or supported me in writing this book in other myriad ways. There are far too many to list here, but they include Tanya Agathocleous, Gordon Bigelow, Mary Burke, Manu Samriti Chander, William A. Cohen, Kimberly A. Coles, Mary Jean Corbett, Jed Esty, Jonathan Farina, Maria Frawley, Jason Haslam, Marjorie Howes, Simon Joyce, Chanté Mouton Kinyon, David Lloyd, Amy E. Martin, Christina Morin, Olivia Loksing Moy, James H. Murphy, Sangeeta Ray, Jason R. Rudy, Talia Schaffer, John

Schulz, Martha Nell Smith, Margaret Stetz, Amy Sullivan, Rachel Teukolsky, Tara Ghoshal Wallace, Alisha Walters, and Julia M. Wright. I am particularly indebted to Sara Maurer, Mary L. Mullen, and Renée Fox, not only for their brilliance and generosity but also for their leadership in putting together two conferences—the "Referent of Ireland" conference at Villanova University in February 2020 and the "Race, Violence, and Form in 19th-Century Ireland" conference at the University of California, Santa Cruz, in January 2023—that helped me shape inchoate ideas into an argument. Samantha Pinto rode to my rescue at a discouraging time, and there are not enough milkshakes in the world to thank her sufficiently for her insights and ingenuity as well as her enthusiasm and encouragement.

At the University of Virginia, Eric Brandt has been a source of consistently sage advice and enthusiastic support for this book. I'm grateful for that, as I am for the keen insights and recommendations of the anonymous peer reviewers and the expert guidance of my copy editor, Susan Murray.

I owe a tremendous amount to those friends and family who have enriched my life with their affection and joy and support, showing me that there's a world to enjoy outside the academy even when everything seems to be falling to pieces: Timothy, Sandra, Daniel, Angie, John, Laura, Borchien, Max, Kathy, Patrick, Shaun, Rob, Brian, Jim, Joey, Walker. The years during which I was writing this book witnessed some bleak times for many, personally, professionally, and politically. It is impossible for me to express the extent of my love and admiration for my mother and brothers in sustaining our family through the loss of three close family members in quick succession.

Finally, I want to thank Leon Lai, who gives me all the reasons to wake up in the morning and to come home in the evening. I cannot imagine a better person to hole up with during the apocalypse.

Parts of chapter 1 previously appeared as "Irish Whiteness and the Nineteenth-Century Construction of Race" in *Victorian Literature and Culture* (2023), © Cambridge University Press; it is reprinted with permission.

THE IRISH AND THE IMAGINATION OF RACE

Introduction

> No pen can give an adequate description of the all-pervading corruption produced by slavery.
> —Harriet Jacobs, *Incidents in the Life of a Slave Girl* (1861)

IN THE SUMMER OF 1882, the Memphis-based *Meriwether's Weekly* interviewed the twenty-seven-year-old Oscar Wilde, then in the midst of a yearlong series of lectures across the United States and Canada. According to the newspaper, Wilde—who was reading Jefferson Davis's two-volume *Rise and Fall of the Confederate Government* during his travels—declared that "Jefferson Davis is the man I would like most to see in the United States" and expressed his wonder that it required "Northern armies numbering three million soldiers four years to whip him."[1] The article finding its way to Davis's wife, it was a sentiment that garnered Wilde an invitation to Beauvoir, in Mississippi, the estate of the seventy-four-year-old Davis, where he dined with the Davises and stayed overnight on June 27 of that year.[2]

In his account of Wilde's lecture tour, David M. Friedman observes of the *Meriwether's* report, "Several of the words in that article—especially the 'four years to whip him' part—sound much more like something an American southerner would have said rather than Wilde."[3] And it is true that *Meriwether's* makes of Wilde the sort of character that fulfills its own political interests within the postbellum American order: most particularly as an ardent admirer of Davis and the Confederacy. It was not alone in that rhetorical transfiguration of the Irish lecturer into a quasi-literary character; from a more skeptical position, the *Selma (AL) Times*, casting doubt on the upcoming visit, similarly represented Wilde—and, for that matter, Davis—as a set of caricatures rather than actual people: "The Vice-President [sic] of the Confederacy," it huffed, "is the last man in the United States we should suspect of taking an interest in the laughing stock of the day. He is so modest, retiring, elegant in his dignity that we would not have thought it possible for the self-asserting, sight-seeing, pseudo-fanatical, long haired, aesthetic humbug to have penetrated the quiet home of the grand Southerner."[4] (Davis himself came to agree, it seems, not enjoying Wilde's visit.)[5]

While the *Selma Times* flattened Wilde to a stereotypical aesthete, Wilde himself made a similar although inverse rhetorical move in his interactions with the press of the American South, casting Davis as a figure out of literature, a tragic hero, more archetype than man: to the *New Orleans Daily Picayune*, for example, he decked Davis in Romantic-inflected Miltonism, announcing, "His fall, after such an able and gallant pleading of his own cause, must necessarily arouse sympathy." In fact, he went further. For Wilde—whose mother, Jane Francesca Elgee, had in the 1840s written for the Irish nationalist newspaper the *Nation* with such anticolonial vigor that the paper was shut down by the British-aligned government—Davis's cause was cognate with Irish nationalism itself: "The case of the South in the civil war," he told the *Daily Picayune*, "was to my mind much like that of Ireland today. It was a struggle for autonomy, self-government for a people.... This is my feeling about the Southern people, as it is about my own people, the Irish."[6] And in an interview with the *Atlanta Constitution*, held on the Fourth of July, Wilde again described the Confederacy's aspirations as, explicitly, a mirror of Ireland's: "We in Ireland are fighting for the principle of autonomy against empire, for independence against centralization, for the principles for which the south fought. So it was a matter of immense interest and pleasure to me to meet the leader of such a great cause. Because although there may be a failure in fact, in idea there is no failure possible. The principles for which Mr. Davis and the south went to war cannot suffer defeat."[7] On the

American Independence Day, Wilde insisted that the correlate of the Irish quest for its own independence was not the Revolutionary War but the insurrection of the Confederacy, in the interest of the maintenance of slavery and white supremacy, against the government of the United States.

Wilde, not atypically, used the occasion of the interview to emphasize the role of literature in national identity and greatness, here figuring the states of the former Confederacy as constituting a cultural unit: "The south has produced the best poet of America—Edgar Allen [sic] Poe: and with all its splendid traditions it would be impossible not to believe that she will continue to perfect what she has began so nobly."[8] In a lecture titled "Irish Poets and Poetry of the Nineteenth Century" (or, alternatively, "The Irish Poets of 1848"),[9] delivered in San Francisco almost three months earlier, he had drawn a similar association between literature and nationhood, in that case in relation to Ireland: "Since the English occupation," he declared, "we have had no national art in Ireland at all, and there is not the slightest chance of our having it ever until we get that right of legislative independence so unjustly robbed from us; until we are really an Irish nation. . . . There is, however, one art which no tyranny can kill and no penal laws can stifle, the art of poetry—an art which is one of the supreme triumphs of the race to which we belong."[10] Identifying "Celtic poetry"—a triumph of his "race"—as "the primary basis of Irish politics, the keystone of Irish liberty,"[11] he names a group of nineteenth-century writers as the vanguard of an Irish nationalist movement, among them his mother, Thomas Moore, Samuel Ferguson, Thomas Davis, Charles Gavan Duffy, and the transported seditionist John Mitchel, whom he remembers seeing "on his return to Ireland, at my Father's table, with his eagle eye and impassioned manner."[12] The Irish nationalist poet James Clarence Mangan, he posits, is "the Edgar Allen [sic] Poe of our country."[13] Thus, in San Francisco, Wilde figured the Irish-descended Poe as the American version of the Irish nationalist Mangan; when speaking in Atlanta, he makes Poe's Americanness explicitly southern and implicitly Confederate.

Poe is not Wilde's only rhetorical hinge between the cause of Irish literary nationalism and that of American white supremacy. The radical polemicist Mitchel, the focus of chapter 5, had by the 1850s been transported to Van Diemen's Land (present-day Tasmania) for treason felony, escaped to the United States, and established a series of newspapers in enthusiastic support of the American South and, in particular, of the enslavement of Black people as the basis of that region's economy and culture; as Michèle Mendelssohn points out, "By the time Mitchel took a seat at the Wildes' table, in 1872, he had already lived in Tennessee and Virginia, owned slaves, and warred for the Confederacy."[14] It was less than a decade later that Wilde both invoked Mitchel as a key "Irish poet" of the nineteenth century and, after visiting Davis, aligned the nationalist cause of Ireland with that of the same Confederacy for which Mitchel advocated.

That alignment is the subject of this book, which analyzes the role of Irishness and Irish literary production in the nineteenth-century constructions of race and racialization. It focuses in particular on the ways in which Irish writers and Americans writing about the Irish translated the literary modes of Irish nationalism into the racial regimes of the United States. Some drew specifically upon the image of Black suffering as support for their arguments for Irish political enfranchisement, often without registering any cognizance of the differences between those fundamentally distinct forms of disadvantage. Others, like Mitchel, instead explicitly conflated Irish nationalist aspiration with the white supremacist cause of the Confederacy. In that way, Wilde's praise of the Confederacy in the terms of Irish nationalism is characteristic, offering a late instance of this nineteenth-century pattern, the endpoint of a literary and rhetorical trajectory that this book, focusing primarily on an earlier set of examples, will trace.

My critical focus is on genre, and especially on the genres that, like Mitchel's militant polemic, had become central to the Irish struggle for political and cultural enfranchisement after the Union with Great Britain at the turn of the nineteenth century. I read genre not merely as the form in which information appears but also as a central means by which thought itself is constructed, what Mark C. Jerng has identified as "fields and frames with which to organize meaning," and as "practices of worldmaking."[15] Genres, that is, not only reflect the values of a culture (as in Tzvetan Todorov's classic observation that they "reveal the constitutive traits of the society to which they belong")[16] but also produce them. By shaping the narratives that we find meaningful, genres provide contours for the ways we think, not only about literature but also about the world. They articulate but also normalize patterns of thought; in complex ways, they turn ideology into "common sense," or legend, or dream. The stories—often the lies—that these nineteenth-century writers told continue to buttress strains of white nationalism today.

The argument of this book is that what had, by the middle of the nineteenth century, become recognizable genres of the early nineteenth-century rhetorical fight for Irish rights within the polity of the United Kingdom frequently lost their liberationist drive in the new cultural and moral context of racial structures and racial oppression on either side of the Atlantic. In fact, the Irish in both the antebellum United States and the British Isles articulated and leveraged their whiteness through a set of literary and rhetorical genres, some produced by Irish and Irish American writers and others by non-Irish writers explicitly positioning the Irish in relation to Black Americans. In many of these literary examples, Irishness becomes the very test case of whiteness, the identity of an admittedly oppressed minority whose fundamental racial whiteness could come to authorize in complex ways the continued terrorism enacted against Americans of African descent, enslaved or free.

Wilde's invocation of Irish national aspiration in his praise of Davis—along with his apparent disinterest in the centuries of anti-Black violence upon which Davis's "principles" were based—might seem surprising if we are looking to nineteenth-century Irish nationalism for a history of coalitional resistance to brutality and settler-colonial domination. The *Selma Times* derogated the possibility of a meeting between Wilde and Davis according to its appraisal of their relative moral worth, the "pseudo-fanatical, long haired, aesthetic humbug" penetrating "the quiet home" of the "modest, retiring, elegant" former president of the Confederacy. We may find it repugnant for opposed but structurally similar reasons. The discomfort arising from the difficulty of accommodating Wilde's praise of Davis and the Confederacy with our sense of Wilde as a figure of progress—most notably for understandings of same-sex relationships but also for the sort of political advance that nineteenth-century Irish nationalist activism might represent—is symptomatized in many accounts of his American tour: that Wilde met twice with Walt Whitman while he was in the United States is now canonized in critical retellings;[17] the stay with Davis has been, until recently, much less reported. Richard Ellmann, in his lengthy biography of Wilde, gave it only three sentences buried in a long paragraph on Wilde's display of his Irish nationalism while in the United States.[18] It matters, though, as one point in a trajectory of a mid-nineteenth-century Irish alignment with the aesthetics and, indeed, the politics of the enslaving American South—embodied here by an Irishman lecturing on art, advocating for the rights of his "race," and lamenting Irish oppression, all while traveling through—and praising—the lands of the defeated Confederacy.

The specific language of Wilde's juxtaposition of the Confederate rebellion with Irish aspirations for national self-determination is telling. It registers its roots in a transatlantic interchange of rhetorical strategies for figuring military defeat as moral victory, particularly when that moral victory is represented as the result of cultural or racial superiority. We see that in Wilde's reliance on the language of both chivalry and loss— and the remediation of loss precisely through chivalry: Davis's fall, "after such an able and gallant pleading . . . , must necessarily arouse sympathy"; "although there may be a failure in fact, in idea there is no failure possible." To the *Atlanta Constitution,* he praised Davis's "personal[i]ty that is as simple as it is strong" and "enthusiasm that is as fervent as it is faultless."[19] (In a letter to Julia Ward Howe, he would use a different, although still admiring, idiom: "How fascinating all failures are!")[20] By the early 1880s, this is clearly recognizable as the imagery and rhetorical cadences of the so-called Lost Cause, a deliberate reimagining of the American regime of brutal, race-based enslavement as a sentimental fantasy of romantic heroism and chivalry by white southerners who might be militarily defeated but who nonetheless remain culturally superior.[21] The nomenclature of the Lost Cause stems most directly from the titles of two books by the Virginian Edward A. Pollard, published almost immediately after the Union victory: *The Lost Cause: A New Southern History of the War of the Confederates* (1866), and *The Lost Cause Regained* (1868). In *The Lost Cause* (the frontispiece of which was an image of Davis, gazing in three-quarter profile out of the frame and, apparently, into the future), Pollard insists that the enslaving South represented a uniquely chivalric culture, almost medieval in its nobility, and that the system of race-based slavery, far from a monstrous iniquity, was a key source of that nobility. A few examples represent the flavor: "Slavery established in the South a peculiar and noble type of civilization.... If habits of command sometimes degenerated into cruelty and insolence; yet, in the greater number of instances, they inculcated notions of chivalry, polished the manners and produced many noble and generous virtues"; the Confederate General John Hunt Morgan "met his death as he met his foes a thousand times before; there was no shrinking—not a quiver of a nerve.... He fell, leaving to his countrymen a testimony of Kentucky chivalry—the record of a gallant, dashing life and a fearless death"; "If the fact be that the North has produced no great General in this war; that the exhibitions of generalship, chivalry, humanity, and all that noble sentimentalism that properly belongs to the state of war have been more largely on the Confederate side; that the Northern people have exhibited gross materialism in the war, have excluded that noble spirituality common to the great conflicts of civilized nations, and worshipped the grossest types of physical power, the fault is in themselves."[22] Yes, Pollard acknowledges, the South lost the military conflict. But as Wilde said about Davis, "although there may be a failure in fact," for Pollard, "in idea there is no failure possible."

But what is that "idea" that compensatorily transforms southern military loss into moral victory? Pollard makes utterly clear that it was, from beginning to end, the celebration of white supremacist domination over the bodies and lives of Black people, explicitly understood as a continuation of the brutal racial regime of enslavement. Pollard opens his introduction to *The Lost Cause Regained* with a series of propositions that express that point directly:

> That the true question which the war involved, and which it merely liberated for greater breadth of controversy was the supremacy of the white race, and along with it the preservation of the political traditions of the country....
>
> That if [the South] succeeds to the extent of securing the supremacy of the white man, and the traditional liberties of the country—in short, to the extent of defeating the Radical party—she really triumphs in the true cause of the war, with respect to all its fundamental and vital issues.
>
> That this triumph is at the loss only of so many dollars and cents in the property tenure of Slavery—the South still retaining the Negro as a

labourer, and keeping him in a condition where his *political* influence is as indifferent as when he was a slave;—and that the pecuniary loss is utterly insignificant, as the price of "the lost cause regained."

These propositions, we believe, sum a novel, and even sublime philosophy on the political questions of the day. They contain the true hope of the South.[23]

Pollard shifts the terms of Confederate military defeat by downplaying, in Wilde's terms, "autonomy against Empire" in favor of—explicitly and forthrightly—the political, cultural, economic, and philosophical advancement, *within* the polity of the United States, of "the supremacy of the white race." Such is Pollard's "sublime philosophy"; this is the context for the assertion—in an irony of which Pollard appears utterly unaware— that it was the *North* which "worshipped the grossest types of physical power" rather than the slaveholding South.

Pollard was not alone in turning to the rhetoric of a lost cause to underpin a particular kind of nationalist argument. "White supremacy" itself is an early nineteenth-century term, emerging in the literature of the British Empire to describe an alternative means of securing the privileges of whiteness after the anticipated abolition of slavery; in 1824, T. S. Winn, in *Emancipation; or Practical Advice to British Slave-Holders: with Suggestions for the General Improvement of West India Affairs,* urged enslavers to plan ahead to ensure that "their emancipated slaves would have remained as orderly and manageable as hitherto": "Let not our colonists trust to the hazardous experiment of not acceding, or preparing for general Emancipation of their slaves, 'till they forcibly acquire it for themselves," warns Winn; "or it may be too late by any means, however wisely and honestly attempted, to reduce them to order and obedience under White supremacy."[24] Pollard's proposal for shifting the terms of debate from enslavement to white supremacist dominance through racial violence thus has transatlantic roots in an early nineteenth-century transition in which Irish enslavers were certainly not disinterested; the recipient of the largest single payment from the British government as compensation for the abolition of slavery in the West Indies (the sort of financial arrangement that Winn anticipates) was James Blair, a Scots-Irishman from Newry, where John Mitchel grew up, and an antiabolitionist member of the British Parliament who enslaved nearly 1,600 human beings.[25]

Wilde may have absorbed the particular rhetorical patterns of Confederate Lost Cause nostalgia from his reading of Davis's memoir. But while the notion of the "Lost Cause" came in the course of the nineteenth century to be grounded most deeply in the white supremacist vision that Pollard and others developed in the aftermath of the American Civil War, it actually arises earlier as an *Irish* version of the same politicized aesthetic. Some of its rhetorical cadences echo those of the eighteenth-century Anglo-Irish statesman and political philosopher Edmund Burke's famous figuration of the French Revolution as the loss of a chivalric culture to a violent and vulgar materialism:

> The age of chivalry is gone.—That of sophisters, œconomists, and calculators, has succeeded; and the glory of Europe is extinguished for ever. Never, never more, shall we behold that generous loyalty to rank and sex, that proud submission, that dignified obedience, that subordination of the heart, which kept alive, even in servitude itself, the spirit of an exalted freedom. The unbought grace of life, the cheap defence of nations, the nurse of manly sentiment and heroic enterprize is gone! It is gone, that sensibility of principle, that chastity of honour, which felt a stain like a wound, which inspired courage whilst it mitigated ferocity, which ennobled whatever it touched, and under which vice itself lost half its evil, by losing all its grossness.[26]

In its rhetorical framing, this could be Pollard. Burke's "sophisters, œconomists, and calculators" slide almost seamlessly into Pollard's "gross materialis[ts]" of the North, while Burke's "manly sentiment," "sensibility of principle," and "chastity of honour" become Pollard's "noble and generous virtues" and "exhibitions of generalship, chivalry, humanity, and all that noble sentimentalism."

Writing specifically about the Irish, Matthew Arnold would likewise draw upon these same nostalgic tropes of a lost age of chivalry in his account of the noble but doomed "Celt" in *On the Study of Celtic Literature* (1867), published almost exactly contemporaneously with Pollard's *Lost Cause* volumes. For Arnold, the sense of Irish heroism as picturesquely doomed evokes the legendary world of Ossian, the purported poet of a cycle of epics invented by the eighteenth-century Scottish writer James Macpherson: "For ages and ages the world has been constantly slipping, ever more and more, out of the Celt's grasp," Arnold declares. "'They went forth to the war,' Ossian says most truly, '*but they always fell.*'"[27] Arnold's invocation of the Ossian cycle as the exemplar of a lost national cause was echoed by Irish writers themselves; the powerful nationalist myth of eternal—and chivalric—aspiration in the face of military defeat at the hands of a more brutish conqueror is fundamental to the nineteenth-century Irish embrace of the Ossian narratives, as G. J. Watson has noted: "Defeat in battle, the subsequent systematic breaking of an old culture by military repression and by legislation, in the name of centralizing progress, the conflict between the 'Celtic' and the 'Saxon' worlds—these are the historical realities that lurk behind the cloudy imagery of *Ossian*."[28] Wilde might pick the heroic sentimentalism with which he bedecked Davis from his Lost Cause–inflected reading during his travels (or the southern newspapers that covered him might have punched up his remarks in that direction), but the chivalry-obsessed Lost Cause rhetoric itself sounds much like Irish elegiac paeans over the previous century.

In fact, the rhetoric of an Irish "lost cause" appears a decade earlier than Pollard's books in the writings of John Mitchel, Wilde's "eagle-eyed" dinner companion himself. In the introduction to *Jail Journal* (1854), a memoir of his conviction and transportation, Mitchel framed his narrative in prophetic—indeed, apocalyptic—terms: "In half a century, the carcasses are armed men, the ashes flaming fire; and an Oliver Cromwell has to come over to smite and to slay again. Ireland was conquered by Cromwell, literally and universally. The cause of Ireland—Ireland as against England—was what all men would call *lost*."[29] But precisely through loss, he envisions a resurrection of Irish racial victory against "the Anglo-Saxons"; he closes his introduction with a defiant prophecy, insisting that his "native country has not been, even this time, finally subdued; that this earth was not created to be civilized, ameliorated and devoured by the Anglo-Saxons; that Defeat is not necessarily Wrong; that the British Providence is not Divine; and that *his* dispensations are not to be submitted to as the inscrutable decrees of God" (24). For Mitchel, as for Pollard, military defeat is prologue to moral victory.

Mitchel similarly advances a "lost cause" argument for Irish nationalist politics in *The Last Conquest of Ireland (Perhaps),* serialized in 1858 and 1859 in his pro-Confederate *Southern Citizen* and dedicated to Alexander Stephens, then a US representative from Georgia and, later, the vice president of the Confederacy. In that work, he framed violent opposition to British rule as a manifestation of chivalric nobility, and he disparaged the strategies of nonviolence advocated by the late Irish nationalist—and antislavery activist—Daniel O'Connell as a betrayal of both Irish chivalry and masculinity: "He [O'Connell] had used all his art and eloquence to emasculate a bold and chivalrous nation. . . . He had helped the disarming policy of the English by his continual denunciations of arms, and had thereby degraded the manhood of his nation."[30]

Similarly, in an 1848 open letter published in the radical nationalist newspaper the *United Irishman,* Mitchel framed armed revolt as a return to the nobility of character and action that, in this vision, constitute Irish nationhood:

> It is the mighty[,] passionate struggle of a nation hastening to be born into new national life. . . . And how are we to meet that day?—*In arms,* my countrymen, in arms. Thus, and not otherwise, have ever nations of men sprung to liberty and power.—But why do I reason thus with you—with you, the Irish of Ulster, who never have denied the noble creed and sacraments of manhood? . . . You have not yet learned the litany of slaves, and the whine of beaten hounds, and the way to die a coward's death. No, let once the great idea of your country's destiny seize on *you,* my kinsmen, and the way will be plain before you as a pike-staff twelve feet long.[31]

For Mitchel, even prior to his migration to the United States, Irish nationalism earns both its heroic masculinity and its suggestive whiteness (transcending "the litany of slaves") by taking up in the nineteenth century the imagery of knightly battle, the "pike-staff twelve feet long." With ugly ramifications in terms of Mitchel's own trajectory toward vicious racial politics, Irish nationalism expresses its value here precisely as white valor. Wilde—with his first name derived from the Ossian poems and his memory of Mitchel at his family's table—perhaps inevitably draws upon this rhetorical register in his praise of Davis as well.[32] What this suggests is that Wilde's account of Davis represents but one instance of a translation of the rhetoric of Irish nationalism into the context of the American racial state,[33] established on race-based chattel slavery. That is even more explicitly the case for Mitchel's polemic a quarter century earlier.

Whereas Wilde, following Mitchel, suggests an analogy between Ireland and the Confederate States, other nineteenth-century writers found a different conceptual rhyme in the experiences of Irish and nonwhite persons: some saw in the history of Irish dispossession a motivation to forge alliances with Black antislavery activists. For example, as Christine Kinealy points out, "In the 1790s, several of the people who hosted former slave Olaudah Equiano were leaders of the republican United Irishmen, many of whom were to die or be exiled as a result of the 1798 Rising."[34] And in the early years of the next century, the Ulster poet and former United Irishman James Orr composed the abolitionist poems "The Persecuted Negro" and "The Dying African" for Belfast papers.[35] A few decades later, the Ulster-born Irish Australian poet Eliza Hamilton Dunlop, as Jason R. Rudy reveals, "open[ed] up spaces for thinking through differences across geographic spaces (Ireland, the United States, Australia) and among groups of individuals (white settlers, Native Americans, Indigenous Australians)."[36] Developing a nuanced account of similarity and difference, she both alluded to and resisted what Ronjaunee Chatterjee, Alicia Mireles Christoff, and Amy R. Wong have identified as the Eurocentric "fantasy of an unmarked universality."[37] The racial framing of Mitchel's form of Irish nationalism was certainly not the only possibility.

One important early nineteenth-century instance of Irish abolitionism, arising even within the context of British colonial administration, was offered by Richard Robert Madden, a justice of the peace in emancipation-era Jamaica, translator of Juan Francisco Manzano's *Poems by a Slave in the Island of Cuba*, biographer of Irish nationalist rebels, and poet (like Jane Francesca Wilde) for the nationalist newspaper the *Nation*. On his return from the Caribbean in 1839, Nini Rodgers observes, Madden

> travelled home via the United States where he was impressed with the political power of his countrymen and horrified at their racial prejudice. He could not understand how, in the light of their own past, they failed to sympathise

with the position of the Negro, and particularly the slaves, treated as strangers in the land of their birth. On return to Ireland he pressed the Catholic church to explain to the people that slavery was a sin, thus arming them against racial prejudice and suggesting to them that they become the van of the anti-slavery movement.[38]

An Irish compatriot who found Madden's argument convincing was O'Connell, whom Mitchel would later attack for both his nonviolence and his abolitionism. O'Connell's political activism foregrounded Catholic enfranchisement and repeal of the Union of Great Britain and Ireland, which had gone into effect in 1801, in the aftermath of the failed 1798 rebellion out of which arose the nationalist abolitionists who welcomed Equiano. But by the mid-1820s he, like Madden, explicitly argued for a broad-based politics of liberation grounded in his Irish nationalism.[39]

In a tribute to O'Connell in honor of his centenary in 1875, the white American abolitionist Wendell Phillips related the anecdote that when O'Connell entered Parliament in 1830, he was approached by "a large number of members" representing West Indian enslavers; according to Phillips, those members offered their support "on every Irish question" as long as O'Connell agreed to silence on the question of abolition. O'Connell, in the account of the antislavery MP Thomas Fowell Buxton, refused, declaring, "Gentlemen, God knows I speak for the saddest people the sun sees; but may my right hand forget its cunning, and my tongue cleave to the roof of my mouth, if to save Ireland, even Ireland, I forget the negro one single hour!"[40] It is possible that the specific quotation is apocryphal, as it appears secondhand in Phillips's speech forty-five years after the event and thirty years after Buxton's death, but the substance is accurate. An "Address from the People of Ireland to their Countrymen and Countrywomen in America," to which O'Connell was the first signatory (although not the principal author),[41] closed with a call for a politics of solidarity aligning Irish nationalist sentiment with abolition: "Irishmen and Irishwomen! treat the colored people as your equals, as brethren. By all your memories of Ireland, continue to love liberty—hate slavery—CLING BY THE ABOLITIONISTS—and in America you will do honor to the name of Ireland."[42] When the Address was read at an antislavery meeting at

Boston's Faneuil Hall, in 1842, the Quaker James Cannings Fuller reportedly echoed its juxtaposition of the Irish nationalist struggle with abolition: "Irishmen! I stood in our Irish House of Peers when Castlereagh took the bribe for the betrayal of Ireland, . . . and I know what feelings and sufferings bring an Irishman to America. . . . OPPRESSION drove you here, and you came for universal liberty. . . . I must be a radical reformer here, as I was in the old country. My Irish friends know what that means."[43] For Fuller, as for Madden and O'Connell, the causes of Irish nationalism and abolition of race-based slavery were, indeed, analogous.

That insistence upon homology, however, could threaten to obscure the fundamental differences between the cases, falling into what Frank B. Wilderson III has dubbed "the ruse of analogy."[44] One close observer of Victorian-era Irish nationalist rhetoric who witnessed—and came to critique—the implicit analogy underwriting intimations by O'Connell and Fuller of an equivalency between Irish and Black experience was Frederick Douglass, who in 1845 and 1846 lectured in Ireland as the first major stop on his travels through the British Isles.[45] Douglass did, in fact, find in that Irish rhetoric some powerfully flexible oratorical tools that might be adapted to different situations. In Dublin, he met O'Connell after hearing him give a speech in support of the repeal of the 1801 Union, "skilfully delivered, powerful in its logic, majestic in its rhetoric, biting in its sarcasm, melting in its pathos, and burning in its rebukes," as Douglass described it in a letter to the white American abolitionist William Lloyd Garrison that was published in Garrison's newspaper the *Liberator*.[46] These were, Douglass's biographer David W. Blight writes, "all the same oratorical elements Douglass had tried to master";[47] the effective rhetorical address was by no means birthed by Irish nationalist oratory, but a particular generic lineage does travel, at least imaginatively, from one side of the Atlantic to the other. As one example of that, in the years just prior to the foundation of Garrison's antislavery paper, "the Liberator" became a sobriquet for O'Connell himself, who was so dubbed for his oratorical and political activism on behalf of Catholic enfranchisement.

As Douglass wrote to Garrison, O'Connell directly took up the question of American slavery in the context of his Irish nationalist activism, asserting that

> I have been assailed for attacking the American institution, as it is called,—negro slavery. I am not ashamed of that attack. I do not shrink from it. I am the advocate of civil and religious liberty, all over the globe, and wherever tyranny exists, I am the foe of the tyrant; wherever oppression shows itself, I am the foe of the oppressor; wherever slavery rears its head, I am the enemy of the system, or the institution, call it by what name you will. I am the friend of liberty in every clime, class and color. My sympathy with distress is not confined within the narrow bounds of my own green island. No—it extends itself to every corner of the earth.[48]

Patricia J. Ferreira proposes that "Douglass's experiences in Ireland ultimately contributed to the revitalization of his energy, enabling his return to the United States and his ability to fight for slavery's end at home."[49] And Blight similarly writes that "Douglass had been deeply affected, even changed, by Ireland and her people. He had learned from and fought ideological and personal battles with them. He had found yet a new range of his powerful voice."[50] Years later, Douglass would relate of O'Connell, "In introducing me to an immense audience in Conciliation Hall, he playfully called me the 'Black O'Connell of the United States.'"[51]

Douglass had already posited a potential alignment between Irish nationalism and abolition in his *Narrative of the Life of Frederick Douglass* (1845), published in the year that he journeyed to Ireland; there he wrote of finding in one of the first books he read, Caleb Bingham's anthology *The Columbian Orator* (1797), "one of Sheridan's mighty speeches on and in behalf of Catholic emancipation": "They gave tongue to interesting thoughts of my own soul, which had frequently flashed through my mind, and died away for want of utterance.... What I got from Sheridan was a bold denunciation of slavery, and a powerful vindication of human rights. The reading of these documents enabled me to utter my thoughts, and to meet the arguments brought forward to sustain slavery."[52] The speech to which Douglass alludes here is not in fact by the Irish playwright and politician Richard Brinsley Sheridan—although Douglass continued to attribute it to him in all of his autobiographies—but by Sheridan's friend, the United Irishman Arthur O'Connor.[53] A Sheridan speech in the *British Parliament* does appear in *The Columbian Orator,* but it does not have the characteristics that Douglass identifies. The argument for the significance of Irish liberatory rhetoric to Douglass's development as a public speaker holds, though. Blight points out that "*The Columbian Orator* was much more than a stiff collection of Christian moralisms for America's youth. It was the creation of a man of decidedly antislavery sympathies, one determined to democratize education and instill in young people the heritage of the American Revolution, as well as the values of republicanism."[54] George Washington and Benjamin Franklin appear together with Cato and Cicero—and with Sheridan and O'Connor. What I want to stress here is the degree to which, even beyond the construction of *The Columbian Orator* itself, the appeal for Douglass of the affective and political power of Irish nationalist rhetoric is rooted in genre, in the conceptual categories that give form to our understandings both of art and of human history and experience, in their similarities and in their differences.

Given all of that, it is not surprising that Douglass would, at times, echo O'Connell in drawing an analogy, a sort of structural association, between Black and Irish situations. Although the title of Douglass's newspaper the *North Star*, published from 1847 to 1851, refers explicitly to the path toward emancipation, it also hints at the radical United Irish newspaper the *Northern Star* (based in Belfast and running from 1792 to 1797, when it was suppressed by the British army), as well as the Chartist newspaper named in tribute to it (founded by the Irish-born Feargus O'Connor in 1837). In 1854, almost a decade after his visit to Ireland, Douglass suggested that political abuse created similarities in physical appearance across race: of the "common people of Ireland," he declared that "the open, uneducated mouth—the long, gaunt arm—the badly formed foot and ankle—the shuffling gait—the retreating forehead and vacant expression—and, their petty quarrels and fights—all reminded me of the plantation, and my own cruelly abused people."[55] And the following year, in a now famous passage of *My Bondage and My Freedom* (1855), he reflected on the singing of enslaved people in the southern United States: "I have never heard any songs like those anywhere since I left slavery, except when in Ireland. There I heard the same *wailing notes*, and was much affected by them. It was during the famine of 1845–6."[56] Douglass, that is, opens the possibility of solidarity across race by locating points of intersection that might foster a multiracial and transatlantic coalitional politics of precarity.

But despite those suggestive parallels, Douglass himself expressed wariness about the rhetorical alignment of African Americans and the Irish under the aegis of a cognate history of suffering, even in O'Connell's terms. While open to the possibility of *similarities* between Irish and Black experience, he stringently critiqued the suggestions of an *equivalency*, offering astute accounts of what could not transfer from the genres of Irish nationalist agitation to American abolitionism as well as what could. In Limerick in November 1845, he explicitly took on and rejected any proposed correlation between Irish oppression (real though it was) and Black enslavement: "There was nothing like American slavery on the soil on which he now stood. Negro-slavery consisted not in taking away a man's property, but in making property of him."[57] And a month later, he again found himself having to make this argument in response to repeated claims to the contrary:

> Since he had come to Ireland, he had been thus accosted—"We are slaves here as well as your countrymen in America," and his answer was, "if you have slaves, they ought to be emancipated; if the people here are tyrannized over, they ought to be relieved from oppression; but let us inquire what slavery is, and see whether you are in that state." The error which people who spoke in the way he had stated fell into was, that they did not sufficiently distinguish between certain forms of oppression and slavery. Slavery was not what took away any one right or property in man; it took man himself, and made him the property of his fellow. It was what unmans man, takes him from himself, dooms him as a degraded thing, ranks him with the bridled horse and muzzled ox, makes him a chattel, a personal, a marketable commodity, to be swayed by the caprice and sold at the will of his master. . . . Had they anything like this in Ireland? Ah, no![58]

Douglass, already in 1840s Ireland, was confronted with and forced to debunk the ruse of analogy deforming Irish advocacy for political and economic relief by appropriating the language of Black enslavement.

Douglass was right to be suspicious of the eagerness of some Irish and Irish American writers to co-opt the experiences of Black Americans for their own political purposes. While assertions of analogy do a disservice to the important distinctions between Black and Irish hardship, assertions of radical difference on the basis of Irish whiteness also become central to Irish anti-Black politics and aesthetics. In fact, the insistence by such Irish nationalists as Madden and O'Connell upon a broad-based and multiracial opposition to oppression frequently went unheeded by Irish communities in the United States, a fact which speaks to a persistent Irish American adherence to the politics of racial whiteness. As David R. Roediger has emphasized, "The making of the Irish worker into a white worker was . . . a two-sided process. On the one hand, much to the chagrin of [New York Whig] George Templeton Strong, Irish immigrants won acceptance as whites among the larger American population. On the other hand, much to the chagrin of Frederick Douglass and Daniel O'Connell, the Irish themselves came to insist on their own whiteness and on white supremacy."[59] That is, I suggest, in itself a sort of translation failure: as with the development of Lost Cause nostalgia, upon arrival in the United States, what had been forms of resistance often became the basis for an explicitly white supremacist aesthetic. Analogies can go wrong in multiple ways: while Mitchel aligned Irish nationalism with the Confederate cause of white supremacist domination, the enthusiastic Irish audiences that Douglass encountered too readily appropriated his situation as their own. As Douglass repeatedly suggested, coalitional politics, while essential, need to acknowledge historical and ongoing differences as well as similarities.

Centering the years just prior to the American Civil War, this book asks how the seemingly liberationist politics of many mid-nineteenth-century Irish nationalist writers could fail to comprehend the ethical necessity of opposing both race-based chattel enslavement in the United States and the structures of white supremacy that underwrote and ultimately outlived it. The language of Lost Cause aesthetics represents only one rhetorical mode that moved in the course of the mid-nineteenth century from the arena of Irish nationalism to that of American racial violence. Wilde's romanticized description of Davis as a translocated version of Irish nationalism represents, I suggest, an appeal to what this book identifies as a putative *generic* similarity, a network of conceptual rhymes across the Atlantic. And, as will be the case for many of the book's examples, that generic alignment can undermine the need for both coalitional politics and the ethical account of difference that Douglass insisted upon.

My first chapter grounds itself in Douglass's critique of Irish appropriations of Black experience in order to analyze the nineteenth-century history of race as a structure, parsing the ways in which whiteness, by means of one of its limit cases, defined and produced itself in both Ireland and the United States. As one key instance, I trace the persistent tactical conflation of the Irish experience with race-based chattel enslavement. While Tricia Lootens has rightly maintained that the term "slavery," "even at [its] most abstract, may remain haunted by ultimately irreducible, ineffaceable, corporeal histories of transimperial human loss,"[60] many nineteenth-century Irish and non-Irish advocates for Irish rights repeatedly turned to that term to both abstract and reduce it, to rhetorically decouple it from its brutally specific historical relationship to Black bondage. In fact, their reliance on the term as a descriptor of Irish deprivation in fact frequently figured that deprivation as deplorable precisely because of Irish whiteness.

In the chapters that follow, I trace the movement of a series of early nineteenth-century Irish nationalist literary genres into the United States of the 1840s and 1850s: the gothic, the nationalist poem, the realist novel, the political polemic, and the stage melodrama. Each chapter focuses on a particular text or set of texts: Edgar Allan Poe's "The Gold-Bug" (1843); William J. Grayson's "The Hireling and the Slave" (1854) and "Chicora" (1856); Frank J. Webb's *The Garies and Their Friends* (1857); John Mitchel's *Jail Journal* and *The Last Conquest of Ireland (Perhaps)*; and Dion Boucicault's *The Octoroon* (1859), respectively. As a coda to the book, the final chapter reads Margaret Mitchell's *Gone with the Wind* (1936), set in the 1860s, as a reconstruction of the Irish national tale in the United States, transforming that genre's anticolonial potential into Lost Cause revisionism and nostalgia for Black enslavement. Irish writers did not invent these genres—in many cases, their roots go back centuries—but they reformed them into modes of nationalist aesthetics, and they often set the stage for their translation into the United States.

Genre matters to this study in its naming of a unit of analysis, a category that manifests some key common element, the necessary predicate for belonging to a particular genre. Caroline Levine has defined genres, in contradistinction to broader and less contingent "forms," as the "customary constellations of elements into historically recognizable groupings of artistic objects, bringing together forms with themes, styles, and situations of reception."[61] The *Oxford English Dictionary* gives the term's emergence into English, from the French for "kind," as occurring in the second half of the eighteenth century and meaning "a particular style or category of works of art; esp. a type of literary work characterized by a particular form, style, or purpose."[62] The designation of a group on the basis of conventional or hypothesized similarity is at the root of the situational recognitions and misrecognitions across the Atlantic that this book traces. At the same time, I do not read genres as inflexible or exclusive categories but rather as (often multiple) modal allusions and affiliations; Mitchel's *Jail Journal* might be a memoir of imprisonment, but it also partakes of the polemical tract, on the one hand, and the adventure novel, on the other; Webb's realist novel evokes in places both minstrel comedy and melodramatic sentimentality. "It is impossible," as Jerng has theorized, "*not* to mix genres."[63] The issue is one of a suggestive and often provisional literary kinship, a conceptual rhyme or cognation which offers affordances for comparison even as it opens space for dissent and transformation. Genres are, Wai Chee Dimock proposes, "fields of knowledge," a generatively messy and always fluid kinship network, a "general solvent out of which particular entities can acquire particular features."[64] That play of kinship and distinction characterizes, as well, the problematics of similarity or difference between Irishness and American Blackness; as Douglass claimed of Irish nationalists who called themselves "slaves," "they did not sufficiently distinguish between certain *forms* of oppression and slavery." That the literary genres of nineteenth-century Irish nationalism fail to account for radical differences in history and experience when translated to the United States is itself in part a function of generic association.

Genre, importantly, is not solely the naming of literary categories. Yogita Goyal reminds us that "race has always been entangled with form. Not only are all aesthetic categories deeply racialized, identity itself has a form. Race, accordingly, is never a given, but must be read."[65] And Brigitte Fielder similarly points out that "in [its] dependence upon relation, racialization is very much like literary genre," and that we might read "genre itself as a genealogy of race."⁶⁶ If genres mix, influence each other, and recombine in surprising ways,⁶⁷ race (as I will explore in chapter 1) is also far from a stable concept in the mid-nineteenth century. Literary genres themselves are, after all, structures and thus, in incomplete and incommensurate ways, they rhyme with the structures of race and racism.

Although it would have been formulated differently, this observation would not have been wholly alien to the nineteenth century, which gave rise to a racial account of cultural production, what Joseph Rezek has called "the essentializing phase" of print's racialization: "Over the course of the late eighteenth and early nineteenth centuries, the medium's racialization intensified to the point where a published book by a single author was understood as capable of representing the essential nature of an entire race of people."⁶⁸ "From its beginnings," Joep Leerssen contends, "the science of comparative linguistics was a handmaiden to ethnological history; when the spread of certain languages and language families was traced, this was automatically seen as the spread or retreat of nations and races."⁶⁹ That racialization of linguistic and literary patterns marks, for instance, Hippolyte Adolphe Taine's famous claim, in his *History of English Literature* (1863–69), that "a work of literature is not a mere play of imagination..., but a transcript of contemporary manners, a type of a certain kind of mind," produced by "the *race*, the *surroundings*, and the *epoch*" (*la race, le milieu* et *le moment*).⁷⁰ Emerging in the context of an ongoing mid-nineteenth-century consolidation of racial categories, Taine's reference to "race" is subject to the unstable significations of the term among his contemporaries,⁷¹ even as he attempts to ground it—with reference to the persistence of specifically "Aryan" traits across geography, culture, and history—in some sort of embodied essence: "What we call the race are the innate and hereditary dispositions . . . which, as a rule, are united with the marked differences in the temperament and structure of the body. They vary with various peoples."⁷² What we see in Taine is an emblematic move toward the alignment of literary culture with an increasingly essentialized racialism that differentially marks both Irishness and Blackness.

At the same time, literature transnavigates countries and cultures in a literal—even material—as well as figurative sense, as Wilde's series of

American lectures on art and literature exemplify.[73] The influence is by no means unidirectional, and—in Levine's terms—it moves beyond the nation to constitute a network.[74] Rezek has pointed out that a number of books by Black authors were published in Ireland as early as the late eighteenth century, offering "a more direct account of the experience of slavery and racism than white-authored texts": "The works of Olaudah Equiano, James Albert Ukawsaw Gronniosaw, Ignatius Sancho, and John Marrant were published in Dublin as part of that city's robust trade in unauthorised reprints—with the exception of Equiano's *Narrative,* which Equiano published himself."[75] Ferreira reports that the Dublin editions of Frederick Douglass's *Narrative,* published by the Irish abolitionist Richard Webb, were remarkably popular: "An initial run of 2,000 copies in 1845 was quickly bought up.... When the version sold out, Webb began production of 2,000 more copies for the 1846 edition."[76] Douglass was only one of many Black antislavery activists who toured Ireland, giving lectures and publishing work, in the years before the Civil War, as Christine Kinealy's *Black Abolitionists in Ireland* has recently demonstrated; there were, in addition, Charles Lenox Remond and Sarah Parker Remond, William Wells Brown, Edmund Kelly, Samuel Ringgold Ward, and others. In a different literary migration, both Dion Boucicault and John Mitchel published work in Ireland and the United States—and both arrived in person in the United States, where they continued publishing, in 1853.

The genres that I have selected here for particular attention—the gothic, the bardic epic, the stage melodrama, the political polemic, the sentimental novel, and the national tale—are far from the only ones that are relevant to a study of this kind. Perhaps most importantly, the slave narrative is a genre that, at multiple points, haunts this work; as the publication history of Douglass's *Narrative,* along with others, proves, Irish readers and writers certainly encountered it and, in many cases, learned from it, even while it stands at the limit of what they could themselves represent. The Christian sermon as well traces multiple trajectories. Along one, it moves from the anti-Catholic Irish cultural nationalist Charles Robert Maturin (Wilde's great-uncle by marriage) at the beginning of the nineteenth century to the "poet-priest of the Confederacy," Father Abram Ryan, in the years after the Civil War. In another, the gospel sermon was taken up by Black preachers to disrupt racist rhetorics within Christianity itself, to circulate, as Travis M. Foster has put it, "a resistance to white supremacy that didn't allow white supremacy to call the shots, straying far off the pathways of mere opposition."[77] The elegy is central both to the commemoration of the martyrs of the multiple Irish uprisings against British rule (in 1798, in 1803, in 1848, and further) and to the aesthetics of the Confederate Lost Cause. Less explicitly literary, the systematics of education that Richard Lovell Edgeworth and Maria Edgeworth developed in *Practical Education* (1798) themselves represent a genre that we might consider as one step in the theorization and institutionalization of learning that structured both racialized education and its resisters throughout the nineteenth century and beyond.[78]

The political ballad likewise represents an important alignment of Irish and African American genres—as well as the multivalence of that alignment. As I. J. Corfe has established, for example, the ballad "Erin go Bragh" became a persistent trope of Irish nationalism in London as well as in Ireland, associated with Irish resistance to British control *and* assimilated into unionist verse by the transformation of a political nationalism into a sentimental regionalism.[79] The mid-nineteenth-century African American ballad could likewise represent divergent ideological orientations. Laurel Hankins has demonstrated that the ballads printed in the New Orleans–based *Black Republican* in 1865 could, on the one hand, do "the work of community and identity building," while giving their "public a way of participating and becoming members without the literacy requirement." But, she further shows, particularly in cases where the *Black Republican* reprinted white-authored "dialect" ballads, they could also, on the other hand, lead to minstrelized mockery when reprinted in different journals.[80] While nineteenth-century African American songwriters and lyricists certainly did not need Irish models for their own music, the political charge of a genre like the ballad as it appeared in different contexts could echo across the Atlantic—or demonstrate its susceptibility to co-optation; although I do not dedicate a separate chapter of this book to it, the relationship between Irish music (and musicians) and the development of racialized minstrelsy in the United States does appear as context for my analysis in a number of places.

Other genres are similarly important to both Irish and Black communities and politics of the nineteenth century. While necessarily limited, though, the genres highlighted in the following chapters offered an important set of affordances to nineteenth-century Irish nationalists, and they became similarly foundational to the articulation of Irishness in relationship to race in the United States. Incomplete as they are as a comprehensive archive, I propose that the genres I center here are emblematic of a significant investment in a particular social task: the nineteenth-century insistence upon Irish whiteness precisely through the allusion to and, often, deployment of anti-Black racism.

Even as the process of investment and representation crosses eras, the historical specificity of that process's instantiations matter. I focus primarily on the literature of the 1850s for a number of reasons. For one, these years represent the beginning of a series of transformations in the material history of literary genres, as Foster—naming the steam press and the commercial paper mill as key examples—reminds us: "Through these technologies, the aesthetic conventions of popular genres entered into and influenced people's day-to-day experiences and guided how they located themselves within larger social and political organizations."[81] Secondly, as I will argue in chapter 1, they span an era in which the epistemology of race had (at least in many circles) achieved or came close to achieving the status of a scientifically validated "fact." The language that we use for race matters to the way we understand race, as do the stories we tell about it. And "the Victorians," Douglas Lorimer reminds us, "invented our language of race relations."[82] As K. Anthony Appiah has written, "by the mid-century," educated Victorians "believed . . . that we could divide human beings into a small number of groups, called 'races,' in such a way that all members of these races shared certain fundamental, biologically heritable, moral and intellectual characteristics with each other that they did not share with members of any other race."[83] Likewise in the United States, Ariela J. Gross shows, "race as a scientific category, interpreted by medical experts or others who used the new language of physiology and ethnology, began to appear in the courtroom in the late 1840s," an indication of its increasing influence by that point as a putative "truth" of human difference.[84]

Thirdly, as the decades of the Great Famine and its immediate wake, these years are marked both by significant shifts in Irish nationalist activism and by a massive increase in immigration from Ireland to the United States. Wilde's allusion to the "Irish poets of 1848" situates literature as a central vehicle for nationalist uprising in the Famine era, given 1848's significance as the year of the Young Irelander Rebellion; led by figures like William Smith O'Brien, Thomas Francis Meagher, Charles Gavan Duffy, and Mitchel, among others, Young Ireland represented a militant break from O'Connell's Repeal Association. One manifestation of that is Mitchel's 1847 resignation from the *Nation*, edited by Duffy, in order to found the still more radical *United Irishman*, named for the rebels of 1798 and appearing in 1848. As Seamus Deane maintains, "O'Connell's repeal movement died before 1848 was over. Both it and the Young Ireland movement were replaced by Fenianism, a secret, revolutionary society which was to carry on the Jacobin tradition of [Wolfe] Tone, relying now on Irish-American rather than on continental support for its success."[85]

Concurrently, spurred by the Famine, emigration from Ireland soared, creating Irish diasporic communities in the United States and around the world; Jay P. Dolan estimates that "in eleven years, from 1845 to 1855, more people left Ireland (2.1 million) than in the prior 250 years.... Of these emigrants, 1.5 million sailed for the United States."[86] Between the Famine and the transportation of convicted nationalists, as James Quinn explains, "the failure of the Irish Confederation's revolt in 1848 did not mark the end of Young Ireland but rather scattered a group of angry and articulate nationalist writers across the globe."[87] Shaped by that dissemination of ideas from Ireland, these decades stand as the culmination of a shift in the Irish American rhetorical relation to the American slave system, what Ian Delahanty has characterized as the point at which "Irish American anti-abolitionism became as much Irish as it was American, a marked change from the pre-famine era when O'Connell had emphasized opposition to all forms of oppression as a pillar of Irish identity."[88] And, more broadly, these years represent a final historical moment before the American Civil War and Reconstruction would introduce significantly altered legal, governmental, and cultural structures of racialization and citizenship.

As Douglass insists in his many reflections on Irishness and Blackness, it is important to notice conceptual dissonances as well as rhymes, obstacles to the model of generic analogy, including the explicitly racial basis of American citizenship that did not have a direct correlate in the United Kingdom. And, of course, not all nineteenth-century writers constructed a univocal or consistent relationship between Irishness and Blackness. Although white supremacy is systemic rather than primarily personal, the ways these authors understood and mobilized their genres marked the acts of individual choice that gave personalized form to the systemic. Mitchel's position, to take one obvious example, was far different from O'Connell's, even if both were marked by their white Irishness. There were contestations and transformations of generic and political expectations alike, arising clearly in Frank J. Webb's *The Garies and Their Friends* but also, more ambivalently, in Dion Boucicault's *The Octoroon*. Texts themselves sometimes work at cross-purposes to their own putative arguments and structures.

Genre, that is, provides simultaneously a structuring frame and the possibility of resistance or revision within that frame. While the majority of the literary works I read here were written by white Irish or Irish American authors, Black writers themselves spoke back to, critiqued, and refigured generic conventions. Rezek has pointed out that "hundreds of nineteenth-century writers of color harnessed print ... in the cause of their humanity, local community, mutual relief, self-determination, racial identity, diasporic consciousness, political agency and belonging, tribal sovereignty, religious affiliation, citizenship, and emancipation" and thereby "radically undermined the traditional association of print with whiteness."[89] When Harriet Jacobs writes that "no pen can give an adequate description of the all-pervading corruption produced by slavery,"[90] she not only references a long tradition of *generic* apologias for the insufficiency of writing for the representation of intense experience ("No Pen can describe, no Words can express ... the strange Impression which this thing made upon my Spirits," exclaims Daniel Defoe's Roxana, in what, in 1724, was already a familiar form of locution);[91] she also exposes the incommensurability of any language to the lived brutality of chattel enslavement, naming the necessary limitations of a project in which her own work arrives as one of the most powerful exemplars.

I therefore acknowledge that, in structuring this book around literary texts, I am centering representations that by definition cannot encompass the lived experiences of Black persons. In fact, many of the works I look at in this study were written with the express purpose of producing political and social systems that attempted to silence the expressions of those lived experiences even as they funneled them into the devastations of slavery and white supremacy. I attempt to contextualize those abusive texts with the insights and interventions of those who knew their poison all too well, writers like Douglass and Jacobs and Hosea Easton, as well as Webb, whose novel is at the center of my chapter 4, but literary representation—and its frequently damaging modes of representation—is the primary focus. Literary and cultural representation, I hold, has a powerful effect on actual lives, for good or for ill, and is therefore important to understand as clearly as we can. If I focus on what I identify as a set of *failed* transpositions of the genres of Irish nationalist activism into the United States, it is in recognition of the truth of Jacobs's claim that any literary representation of enslavement *must* fail—although to greater or lesser degrees—to accommodate its enormity. Further, though, I do so because I believe that failure holds lessons for our own continued engagements with racial difference and systemic—and often unrecognized—white supremacy. As Douglass observed, some tropes of generic similarity across the mid-nineteenth-century Atlantic Ocean are necessarily misleading, even damagingly so. That failure is the subject of this book.

1

Nineteenth-Century Irishness and the Construction of Race

> Perhaps no class of our fellow citizens has carried this prejudice against color to a point more extreme and dangerous than have our Catholic Irish fellow citizens, and yet no people on the face of the earth have been more relentlessly persecuted and oppressed on account of race and religion, than the Irish people.
> —Frederick Douglass, "This Decision Has Humbled the Nation" (1883)

IN "HATING VICTORIAN STUDIES PROPERLY," Nasser Mufti posits that "the field lacks a theory of—or even a debate about—race in the nineteenth century."¹ One of the areas in which that is not wholly true is Irish studies, where significant postcolonial scholarship has interrogated the nineteenth-century constructions of racialized Irishness, often in relation to nonwhiteness. "Given the amount of prejudice in England and Scotland against the Irish in general and Irish immigrant workers in particular," argues L. Perry Curtis Jr., "it is hardly surprising that Celtic Irishmen should have found themselves occupying a branch which was closer in some respects to the Negro limb than to the Anglo-Saxon crown of [the] tree."² Patrick Brantlinger is more explicit: "The idea of the Irish as 'the n[—]s of Europe'... goes back at least to the 1830s."³ Michael de Nie deplores "historians who have difficulty appreciating that 'race' was popularly understood and used by Victorians to explain cultural as much as biological differences" and "others who refuse to believe that the Irish received treatment any different from that of other marginalized groups."⁴ Much similar work has followed Noel Ignatiev's influential assertion that the nineteenth-century Irish "became white" upon their migration to the United States, whereas they ostensibly had not been in the United Kingdom. "To become white," Ignatiev contends, "they had to learn to subordinate county, religious, or national animosities, not to mention any natural sympathies they may have felt for their fellow creatures, to a new solidarity based on color—a bond which, it must be remembered, was contradicted by their experience in Ireland."⁵

It is important to critique the historical construction of whiteness, if only to attempt to disrupt its status as an uninterrogated norm. Yet, the claim that Irish Americans "became white" raises a significantly underexamined conceptual challenge, as David Lloyd has astutely observed: "Since even emancipation failed to allow the former slaves to escape the taint of blackness and become fully fledged citizens, this explanation clearly begs the question of how such a crossing of the ethnic/racial line would have been possible if the Irish were not already to some degree regarded as white."⁶ For Lloyd, what has frequently been described as a historical transit of Irishness into whiteness in the United States depends upon both the flexibility of whiteness to accommodate and reshape itself around Irishness *and* the amenability of Irishness to be understood as white from the start—in a way that persons of African descent could not be so understood. At least an incipient Irish whiteness must precede, rather than arise out of, the historical developments that Ignatiev details.

It is true that the relationship of racialization to legal status manifested differently in the United Kingdom than in the United States. For one thing, American citizenship was explicitly—and increasingly—the province of whiteness in the early decades of the nineteenth century; at least as early as the 1790 Naturalization Act, Peter D. O'Neill points out, "The Irish always were understood to be among those 'free white' people whom the statute was intended to benefit. . . . Yet in the same period, that legal category was utterly unavailable to persons of African and Asian ancestry—even those who were US-born."⁷ In contrast, British enfranchisement was not necessarily grounded in race: the formerly enslaved Ignatius Sancho, as a male property owner in London, voted in parliamentary elections as early as 1774 and 1780.[8] As Amy E. Martin has convincingly explained, mid-nineteenth-century racial epistemology situated Irishness "at the intersection of two contemporaneous racial formations—one relying on an epidermal logic of whiteness emerging primarily in North America and the other founded on a more fluid understanding of racial hierarchy that justified the British Empire."[9] Recognizing this multiplicity of racial epistemologies is critical. Yet despite the suggestions of some postcolonial scholarship, the construction of Irishness as whiteness was not limited to the American side of the Atlantic, nor was the notion of Irishness as a peculiar test case of that whiteness exclusive to the British Isles. In fact, an emphasis on the mobilization of racialized tropes for the depiction of Irish poverty and politics can distract us from an important truth: in nineteenth-century Britain and Ireland as well as the United States, "Celticness" was not in any serious or widespread way understood (or treated) as equivalent to Blackness, although—as I will show—that did not stop some nineteenth-century Irish advocates from drawing that misleading analogy or even arguing that Irish political and cultural disadvantage surpassed the brutality enacted against enslaved Black people in the West Indies or the United States.

Given the fundamental legal, cultural, and social distinctions, the implication that Irishness is cognate to Blackness—or the Irish experience a version of the Black experience—represents the epistemological and ethical error that Frank B. Wilderson III has called "the ruse of analogy": "a mystification, and often erasure, of Blackness's grammar of suffering."[10] It is essential to distinguish between forms of disadvantage and precarity, to acknowledge that not all manifestations of what is often identified as "racialization" were enacted upon bodies and lives in the same or even cognate ways. The fact that a number of nineteenth-century Irish writers—along with non-Irish witnesses to Irish political and economic hardship—made the argument that they were treated *as though* they were Black (and that this is particularly egregious because they were white) does not require that we take that claim at face value. This matters, because—as important as it has been to our understanding of the constructedness of racial whiteness—the critical attention paid to the putative nonwhiteness (or even "probationary whiteness," in Matthew

Frye Jacobson's evocative construction)[11] of nineteenth-century Irishness can misleadingly suggest an equivalency between the radically distinct historical experiences of Black and Irish persons.

The work of this chapter is to look more closely at the nineteenth-century understanding of Irishness, in both the United Kingdom and the United States, in relation to the production of whiteness in both anthropological and popular thought. Racial ideas, borne by persons and books and literary genres, moved back and forth across the ocean. As context for the readings that follow, this chapter will track the complexly interrelated (and sometimes opposed) terms of Irishness and Blackness by the 1840s and 1850s as the foundation for the literature that produced, wrestled with, and conflated that relationship in the years encompassing the Great Irish Famine and preceding the American Civil War.

Geraldine Heng has rightly described a "long history of race," as our term "race" itself "is attached to a repeating tendency . . . to demarcate human beings through differences among humans that are selectively essentialized as absolute and fundamental, in order to distribute positions and powers differentially to human groups."[12] "Medieval examples," she has demonstrated, "instruct us that racial thinking, in pre-modern contexts, does not require races as such to exist a priori but will *produce* races at need, in answer to specific historical imperatives and occasions."[13] Within that "long history," though, the eighteenth and nineteenth centuries witnessed the development of the racial categories (what Sebastian Lecourt calls "organically unique groups—sometimes called nations, sometimes *Völker,* and increasingly *Rasse* or races")[14] that continue to shape our modern world, along with an apparatus of putatively scientific theories that both articulated and enforced those categories. Focusing in particular on Britain, Roxann Wheeler shows that "throughout the eighteenth century older conceptions of Christianity, civility, and rank were *more explicitly* important to Britons' assessment of themselves and other people than physical attributes such as skin color, shape of the nose, or texture of the hair," and that "the assurance that skin color was the primary signifier of human difference was not a dominant conception until the last quarter of the eighteenth century, and even then individuals responded variously to nonwhite skin color."[15] Indeed, Irene Tucker has theorized that "the history of modern race"—instantiated by "the notion that racial identity might be instantly discerned by noting the color of an individual's skin"—is "intimately bound up with the emergence of modern 'anatomical' medicine" in the eighteenth and nineteenth centuries.[16] And across the Atlantic as well, as Nell Irvin Painter has pointed out, "it is in the eighteenth century that we find the more familiar, hardened boundaries of racialized American identity."[17]

An oft-cited Victorian exponent of this developing "race science" is the Edinburgh anatomist Robert Knox, who argued in his introduction to *The Races of Men* (1850) that although "the word, *race*, is of daily use, applied even to man . . . , I use it in a new sense." Rather than understanding race as contingent upon what he called "fanciful causes, such as education, religion, climate, &c.," he insisted "that race is everything in human history; that the races of men are not the result of accident; that they are not convertible into each other by any contrivance whatever."[18] Knox's "race," that is, seems to be biological and stable rather than cultural and contingent, an argument that emerged in the eighteenth century.[19] And Knox presents his racialist account as an explicit debunking of arguments for broader categories of whiteness comprising persons of European descent in general: "When the word race, as applied to man, is spoken of, the English mind wanders immediately to distant countries; to Negroes and Hottentots, Red Indians and savages. . . . But the object of this work is to show that the European races, so called, differ from each other as widely as the Negro does from the Bushman; the Caffre from the Hottentot; the Red Indian of America from the Esquimaux; the Esquimaux from the Basque" (39). For Knox, that is, "race" is not only a designation of difference between Europeans and non-Europeans but also of difference between variations within Europe; he insists that there is no umbrella category of racial "European-ness."

The Irish were by no means exempt from the nineteenth-century rise of this putatively scientific racism. As Jacobson has related, "Negative assessments of Irishism or Celtism as a fixed set of inherited traits . . . became linked at mid-century to a fixed set of observable physical characteristics, such as skin and hair color, facial type, and physique."[20] Knox was among the foremost polemicists contending that the "Celtic" Irish were fundamentally different in race from the English "Saxon": "700 years of absolute possession has not advanced by a single step the amalgamation of the Irish Celt with the Saxon-English.... If you seek an explanation, go back to France; go back to Ireland, and you will find it there: it is the race" (21). Knox continues, explicitly denying any role to geographical or cultural environment in the production of race: "The Anglo-Saxon in America is a Saxon, and not a *native:* the Celt will prove a Celt wherever he is born, wherever he is found. The possible conversion of one race into another I hold to be a statement contradicted by all history" (22; italics in original). Of what he insists is always the "failed" result of "intermarriage," he claims, "with Celt and Saxon it is the same as with Hottentot and Saxon, Caffre and Hottentot" (66).

As Knox's language suggests, some Victorian theorists of race did in fact posit parallels between Irishness and Blackness. The ethnologist John Beddoe, for example, in the 1880s developed an "Index of Nigrescence," what he designated "a ready means of comparing the colours of two peoples or localities."[21] Describing "prognathism" (the protrusion of the jaws), he asserted, "While Ireland is apparently its present centre, most of its lineaments are such as lead us to think of Africa as its possible birthplace; and it may be well, provisionally, to call it Africanoid."[22] And, Brantlinger notes, "Though of the same [Celtic] race . . . , the French, according to Knox, are very different from the Irish. The French are close to the pinnacle, whereas the Irish are the lowest dregs of civilization and seem fated to go the way of the dark races of the world."[23] (That fact itself, of course, undermines the thesis that "race" is the fundamental unit of human difference, if the racial category in this case is "the Celt," given that, for Knox, it includes both the Irish and the French.)

Perhaps the most notorious nineteenth-century rhetorical association of the Irish with people of African descent is Thomas Carlyle's, in his belligerently racist "Occasional Discourse on the Negro Question" (1849), which he wrote just after his return from Famine-era Ireland. In this essay, published anonymously under the fictional editorship of the suggestively Irish "Dr. Phelim M'Quirk," Carlyle juxtaposes enslaved West

Indians with the Irish: "If the Africans that are already there could be made to lay down their pumpkins and labour for their living, there are already Africans enough.... To bring in new and ever new Africans, say you, till pumpkins themselves grow dear; till the country is crowded with Africans; and black men there, like white men here, are forced by hunger to labour for their living? That will be a consummation. To have 'emancipated' the West Indies into a *Black Ireland;* 'free' indeed, but an Ireland, and black!"[24] Famine-era Ireland, "sluttishly starving from age to age on its act-of-parliament 'freedom,'"[25] offers Carlyle a model for his vision of enslaved Africans in the West Indies, represented as a people with no energy for work but only for complaint.[26] "Alas, look at that group of *unsold,* unbought, unmarketable Irish 'free' citizens, dying there in the ditch," he sneers, suggesting that the fact that the Irish are not enslaved makes no difference to their (un)willingness to do work.[27]

A decade earlier, in *Chartism* (1840), Carlyle had made a similar point, proposing a dichotomous set of solutions to the problem of Ireland: "The time has come when the Irish population must either be improved a little, or else exterminated.... In a state of perennial ultra-savage famine, in the midst of civilisation, they cannot continue. For that the Saxon British will ever submit to sink along with them to such a state, we assume as impossible."[28] His naming of the British as "Saxon" is emblematic of the midcentury argument for a racial difference between Ireland and England that reaches a climax in Knox's vitriol. And in "Repeal of the Union" (1848), Carlyle uses the language of chattel enslavement (which he figures as "wholesome") for the "savage" Irish: "Fruitless futile insurrections, continual sanguinary broils and riots that make his dwelling-place a horror to mankind, mark his progress generation after generation; and if no beneficent hand will chain him into wholesome *slavery,* and, with whip on back or otherwise, try to tame him and get some work out of him,—Nature herself, intent to have her world tilled, has no resource but to exterminate him."[29] Here, Carlyle gestures toward Black enslavement as rhetorical support for his critique of the putatively unproductive and nonprogressing (but bloodstained) cycles of Irish history.

Like Carlyle (with his references to "the Saxon British"), Knox would posit that the existence of different "races" within the United Kingdom was a demographic problem to be solved: "The source of all evil lies in *the race,* the Celtic race of Ireland," he writes, his near-hysterical exasperation erupting in frenzied italics. "There is no getting over *historical facts*" (253). Since Knox forecloses the possibilities of "amalgamation" or the "conversion of one race into another," the necessary solution, with reference to Oliver Cromwell's seventeenth-century military brutalities in Ireland, was—as with Carlyle—a beneficial extermination: "The race must be forced from the soil; by fair means, if possible; still they must leave. England's safety requires it.... The Orange club of Ireland is a Saxon confederation for the clearing the land of all papists and jacobites: this means Celts. If left to themselves, they would clear them out, as Cromwell proposed, by the sword; it would not require six weeks to accomplish the work" (253–54). For Knox, as for Carlyle, the failure of the Celt is a failure to develop as a race; given that lack of racial progress, annihilation by a stronger racial "confederation" is the only answer.

Sectors of the midcentury British popular press, particularly the caricaturists, reveled in the putatively "scientific" association between Black and Irish. Curtis contends that "the dominant Victorian stereotype of Paddy looked far more like an ape than a man," in a shift from both the Elizabethan representation of the "handsome features of the 'wild Irishman'... and different, too, from the brutish, slovenly faces of Irish peasants appearing in prints dating from the reign of George III." In Curtis's history of these images, "the process of simianizing Paddy's features took place roughly between 1840 and 1890 with the 1860s serving as a pivotal point in this alteration of the stereotype."[30] By 1862, in the wake of the 1859 publication of *The Origin of Species, Punch* would give this new stereotype a fashionably Darwinian spin in a short prose spoof of evolutionary discourse titled "The Missing Link":

> A gulf, certainly, does appear to yawn between the Gorilla and the Negro. The woods and wilds of Africa do not exhibit an example of any intermediate animal. But in this, as in many other cases, philosophers go vainly searching abroad for that which they would readily find if they sought for it at home.... It comes from Ireland, whence it has contrived to migrate; it belongs in fact to a tribe of Irish savages: the lowest species of the Irish Yahoo.[31]

Thereby, Curtis asserts, has *Punch*'s Irishman "devolved . . . from a primitive peasant to an unruly Caliban, thence to a 'white Negro,' and finally he arrived at the lowest conceivable level of the gorilla and the orangutan," suggesting a coherent sliding scale of difference.[32]

Despite these instances, though, the argument that this trope represents a consistent and culturally widespread understanding of the Irish as, in some way, fundamentally nonwhite can be overstated. The construction of nineteenth-century "race"—along with the place of the Irish "Celt" or "Gael" within it—is admittedly complex and often internally inconsistent or haphazardly deployed.[33] In fact, nineteenth-century scientific racialism provided conceptual tools not only for thinking about the "Celt" and the "Saxon" as distinct but also for thinking of them as variants within a broader unity. And that unity depended upon the rise of a theory, beginning in the eighteenth century and developing in the course of the nineteenth, of whiteness as a racial category simultaneously multiple and unified. In *The History of White People,* Painter traces that development to Johann Friedrich Blumenbach's *On the Natural Variety of Mankind,* which, she shows, undergoes significant revisions between its appearance as his doctoral dissertation in 1775 and its far more extensive 1795 third edition. It is in that later version that Blumenbach introduced the term "Caucasian" into racial classification: "In the interim," Painter demonstrates, "skin color, not heretofore the crucial factor for Blumenbach, had risen to play a large role. He now sees it necessary to rank skin color hierarchically, beginning, not surprisingly, with white."[34] That consolidation was not limited to racial whiteness; when, in his "Notes on the five varieties of Mankind," Blumenbach listed the "Ethiopian variety" (along with the "Caucasian variety," the "Mongolian variety," the "American variety," and the "Malay variety"), he conflates people from widely different nations, cultures, languages, appearances, and ethnicities. It is a collapse of heterogeneity into homogeneity that he acknowledges even while enacting it: "There is no character which does not shade away by insensible gradation from this variety of mankind to its neighbours, which is clear to every one who has carefully considered the difference between a few stocks of this variety, such as the Foulahs, the Wolufs, and Mandingos, and how by these shades of difference they pass away into the Moors and Arabs."[35] Here, the term "variety" comes to name the broader racial category (which he also, at points, calls "Negro"); vast differences *within* that "variety" become, in an ugly translation, "stocks."[36] A concept of large racial units containing smaller distinct but related types of people has emerged.

For Blumenbach, all racial categories derived from a single ancestral source, a theory that came to be known as "monogenism." There are, in his account, "Five Principal Varieties of Mankind, One Species" (264). While the "varieties" comprise a number of "stocks," they are themselves historical developments within the single "species." More specifically, Blumenbach describes nonwhite typologies of skin color, hair texture, and other physical characteristics as having "degenerated" over historical time from an originary "Caucasian variety" through environmental effects of climate, diet, and other factors (207–63): the Caucasian, he declares, "is white in colour, which we may fairly assume to have been the primitive colour of mankind, since . . . it is very easy for that to degenerate into brown, but very much more difficult for dark to become white" (269). (That said, he also claims that "it has been recorded that Ethiopians, when they have changed their climate in early infancy, and from that time forward have inhabited a temperate zone, have gone on getting paler by degrees" [222].) "It is well known," Blumenbach asserts, "that the national colour of their skin is not congenital even to the Ethiopians themselves, but is acquired by the access of the external air after birth" (211). Blumenbach, that is, proposes a climatic theory of racial difference in which, as Alisha R. Walters has described it, "the body and skin" are "integral, potentially changeable sites that participate physically in the production of racial markers with the environment."[37]

Becoming influential in the early nineteenth century, however, an alternative anthropology—so-called polygenism—contended that races (in numbers that varied with different authors) had completely distinct origins, in violation of the biblical narrative, and represented different biological species.[38] George Stocking Jr. writes of this claim:

> On the basis of skeletal and cranial evidence, polygenists insisted that blacks were physically distinct and mentally inferior; on the basis of the

racial representations on "ancient Egyptian monuments" they argued that races had remained unchanged throughout the major portion of human history; on the basis of the mortality of whites in tropical areas they hypothesized that different races were aboriginal products of different "centers of creation" and could never fully "acclimate" elsewhere; on the basis of anecdotal evidence they asserted that the hybrid offspring of blacks and Europeans were only partially interfertile.[39]

While polygenism underwrote a number of the most flamboyantly racist claims, both models could support the privileging of whiteness: in Blumenbach's monogenism, Caucasianness represents the peak from which other racial "varieties" degenerate, whereas for the polygenists, nonwhite persons were not even in the same species (although not all used that specific term).[40]

It is true, therefore, that our modern categories of race have not always existed; "whiteness" has, over centuries, come into being as a privileged category that includes certain human beings and excludes others, and its boundaries have not been universally stable. As Painter writes, describing American constructions of race, "Rather than a single, enduring definition of whiteness, we find multiple enlargements occurring against a backdrop of the black/white dichotomy."[41] In that way, the Irish did, at some point, "become white"; the question is not only whether that happened in the nineteenth century but also whether the Irish subsumption into whiteness was a process categorically different from that of other groups. While this chapter attends particularly to the former question, there is evidence even for the latter that the distinction has at times been overstated. *The Oxford English Dictionary* finds instances of "white" as an umbrella designation for "a light-skinned group of people, esp. one of European origin or descent" at least as far back as the sixteenth century.[42] And, in fact, as Alden T. Vaughan explains, even before the rise of scientific racism in the eighteenth and nineteenth centuries, the Irish were generally understood as white: "Despite virulent English antipathy toward the Irish during [the seventeenth century] ... the Irishman's whiteness was incontrovertible."[43] If we're looking for the date at which the Irish became white, we might look to the origin of whiteness as a category.

Knox did contend—contra Blumenbach—that there was no "Caucasian" race; he really did argue for a fundamental distinction between "Saxon" and "Celt" (and other "races"), and some allied writers similarly posited an intrawhite polygenism. In 1854, for example, the Mobile, Alabama, physician Josiah Nott asserted that "nothing short of a *miracle* could have evolved all the multifarious Caucasian forms out of one primitive stock; because the Canaanites, the Arabs, the Tartars and Egyptians, were absolutely as distinct from each other in primeval times as they are now; just as they all were then from co-existent Negroes," and, therefore, "there must have been many centres of creation, even for *Caucasian* races, instead of one centre for *all* the types of humanity."[44] But Knox—even bracketing the fact that, as Reginald Horsman puts it, he was "the anatomist who had been responsible for buying the hardly cold, murdered bodies provided by the notorious Burke and Hare in the Edinburgh of the 1820s"[45]—was a bit of a crank and not as representative as he is occasionally made to seem in present-day criticism. Stocking, while acknowledging that "the physical anthropological viewpoint was by no means without influence," calls him "marginal to the mainstream of nineteenth-century British anthropological thought."[46] (This is a far cry from Brantlinger's nomination of Knox to the status of "minor Victorian sage" and his racial theories as "hegemonic" after the 1840s.)[47] "Except for the overriding theme of the supreme importance of race," Horsman concludes, "Knox had little coherence of thought, and there was hardly any logical progression in his arguments."[48]

Importantly—and in line with Lloyd's critique—in neither of these models, at least in their most influential formulations, was it necessary for the Irish to "become white," since that phrasing suggests that there was an existing category of "whiteness" which excluded the Irish before it included them. For Blumenbach, both "Anglo-Saxon" and "Celt" are explicitly "Caucasian"; he designated these subcategories as "nations," drawing distinctions amid "the natural diversity which separates the races and the multifarious nations of men" (*hominum gentes et nationes multifarias*).[49] Although he doesn't subscribe to this model, Blumenbach does, in 1795, offer as a point of comparison Christoph Meiners's reduction of "all nations to two stocks: (1) handsome, (2) ugly; the first white, the latter dark." Blumenbach notes, as a point of interest, that for Meiners, "Celts, Sarmatians, and oriental nations" are included in "the handsome stock" (268).[50] In contrast, for Knox the Celt is not white—but neither is the Scandinavian or the Saxon; for Knox there *is* no general category of whiteness into which the Irish would or would not fall. Far too often we assume that if Knox asserts that the Celt and the Saxon are different "races" (and that the Saxon is superior in various ways to the Celt), he means that the Saxon is white and the Celt is not, but that isn't the framework he's using.

Part of the challenge for those of us working from within the context of twenty-first-century racial categories is the ambiguity of the term "race" itself for nineteenth-century writers. As the *Oxford English Dictionary* relates, the term's meaning as "any of the (putative) major groupings of humankind, usually defined in terms of distinct physical features or shared ethnicity, and sometimes (more controversially) considered to encompass common biological or genetic characteristics," arises in the later eighteenth century and comes to prominence in the nineteenth, but is "frequently overlapping with, and difficult to distinguish from" two earlier senses: "a tribe, nation, or people, regarded as of common stock," and "a group of several tribes or peoples, regarded as forming a distinct ethnic set." The fact that it continued at times to bear the older meaning of "a house, family, kindred" (as in the speaker's claim, in Alfred Tennyson's "The Sisters," that "we were two daughters of one race") only adds to the confusion.[51] When a writer describes Celts as a "race," the designation might suggest what the *OED* calls "the (putative) major groupings of mankind," but it also might suggest something more like a tribe or nation or—to use a term that had not yet taken on this meaning—an ethnicity.

The imprecision of "race" within the rhetoric of nineteenth-century race science struck even its practitioners. The French anthropologist Paul Broca, for instance, in 1860 complained, "The word *race* has thus, in the language of authors, two very different significations," since it was possible to speak of "the white races" (in the plural), including "the Arabs, the Basques, the Celts, the Kimris, the Germans, the Berbers, etc.," and "the black races," including "the Ethiopian Negroes, the Caffres, the Tasmanians, Australians, Papuans, etc.," while it was also possible to speak of each of those entire "ensembles" as themselves races.[52] Although somewhat inconsistent in his own usage, Broca tentatively—like a number of polygenists—proposed "race" for the former (small) units and "species" for the latter (larger) ones.[53] For Broca, in contrast to Blumenbach, there are multiple "species" of "the genus *Homo*." Again, the Celts appear as one of the "white races." Other theorists turned to "tribe" or "people" for the smaller subsets, sometimes using "race" for the larger ones.

In contrast to categorical distinctions between white and nonwhite, Stocking proposes that (*within* the context of what we think of as whiteness), "much of Anglo-Saxon and other forms of 'racial' nationalism" were predominantly "cultural phenomena" and "biological only in a secondary way."[54] This was the case in Britain as well as in the United States. By the late 1840s, the English physician and zoologist William Benjamin Carpenter could refer to "those nations (commonly termed Caucasian) which, in the form of their skulls and other physical characters[,] resemble Europeans."[55] And in 1849, the *North British Review* could both acknowledge and dismiss the notion of intrawhite racial distinctions by noting somewhat exasperatedly, "In practical politics it is certainly possible to push such ethnographical considerations too far, as, for example, in our own cant about Celt and Saxon, when Ireland is under discussion." For the *North British Review*, "it is only by a firm and efficient handling of this conception of our species as broken up into so many groups or masses, physiologically different to a certain extent, that any progress can be made," and it denominates the "three great types or varieties into which naturalists have divided the inhabitants of our planet": "Negro," "Mongolian," and "Caucasian." Whatever problems the "Celt" might have, he falls firmly in the Caucasian "variety"; the reviewer asserts that "every schoolboy knows" this.[56] In the United States, even the strenuously polygenist Nott, who insisted that there "must have been many centres of creation," frequently relies on categories like "Caucasian races," "white races," and other terms that suggest a fundamental distinction, and he actually approvingly quotes the *North British Review*'s description of the Saxon/Celt division as "cant."[57]

That is, an emerging "scientific" reification of whiteness as a meaningful and coherent category, notwithstanding internal variety, arises in Britain as well as in the United States, albeit in uneven ways. And it shaped understandings of how to think about what was sometimes called the Irish "race question." In 1869, the Knoxian anthropologist J. W. Jackson would, on the one hand, assert that "inferior and non-Aryan racial elements are clearly perceptible in the population of the sister isle [Ireland]." On the other hand, though, he also claimed that it is a difference of degree from the situation in England, not an opposition of kind; for geographical reasons, "Ireland, during the historic period, was imperfectly Teutonised and not at all Romanised." For Jackson, Ireland is merely at one "extremit[y] of the Caucasian area." (The other "extremity," in his account, is India.)[58] Even in the "cultural" arena, Irish racialism was inconsistent and often quickly abandoned. In 1867, in *On the Study of Celtic Literature*, Matthew Arnold had offered a similar analysis while wrestling with the question of what—if Celts and Saxons are in fact racially distinct—happened to all of those aboriginal Celts. For Arnold, as for Jackson, the solution is racial admixture, a combination of Celt and Saxon in some relative proportions to produce British whiteness: "Of deliberate wholesale extermination of the Celtic race, all of them who could not fly to Wales or Scotland, we hear nothing; and without some such extermination one would suppose that a great mass of them must have remained in the country, their lot the obscure and, so to speak, underground lot of a subject race, but yet insensibly getting mixed with their conquerors, and their blood entering into the composition of a new people."[59]

Arnold is frequently understood as drawing a firmly Knoxian line between the Celt and the Saxon.[60] In fact, despite what he posits as essential racial differences, he actually moves toward subsuming those distinctions under a larger aegis of whiteness: "Fanciful as the notion may at first seem," he proposes, the "march of science" has come to the conclusion that "there is no such original chasm between the Celt and the Saxon as we once popularly imagined, that they are not truly . . . *aliens in blood* from us, that they are our brothers in the great Indo-European family."[61] This language of the "Indo-European family" derives from the British ethnologist James Cowles Prichard, who did not invent it but who was instrumental in shepherding its shift from linguistics to race.[62] Prichard dedicated subsequent editions of his *Researches into the Physical History of Mankind* (1813) to Blumenbach, and he refers to Blumenbach's language of "Caucasian," although he finds it misleading as a designation for one of what he calls the "great departments of the human family."[63] In *The Eastern Origin of the Celtic Nations* (1831), Prichard both offered "proofs of a common origin derived from the grammatical structure of the Celtic and other Indo-European languages" and argued that "the use of languages really cognate must be allowed to furnish a proof, or at least a strong presumption, of kindred race."[64] What Arnold calls "the great Indo-European family"—including the Celt—is thus an evolution of what Blumenbach and his ethnological disciples had designated the "Caucasian." In a nuanced reading of Arnold's racialism, Lecourt posits that he "used racial polygenesis to dramatize a project of cultural hybridity," drawing "freely and unsystematically upon ... [,] on the one hand, comparative philology, which read human progress as the collaborative project of different racial families, and, on the other hand, the polygenist anthropology of Robert Knox and James Hunt."[65] When it comes to the Celt, what this results in is a type of Knoxian differentiation and racial polygenism retrofitted within a comfortable Blumenbachian assurance of a broadly understood whiteness.

Given all of this, the argument that the mid-nineteenth-century Irish were, in a general way, constructed as nonwhite frequently seems grounded in an overprivileging (and some misrepresentation) of specifically Knoxian polygenism. And, in fact, R. F. Foster has convincingly challenged Curtis's characterizations of the British caricatures of Irish simianism as, inevitably, cherry-picked. It is certainly true, Foster acknowledges, that "*Punch*'s classic characterization of the Irish remained much the same from the 1850s on; and it was by and large bestial." But, importantly, "By contrast the *Graphic* and the *London Illustrated News*, though they were far from endorsing Irish nationalist politics, showed Irish crowds as handsome, well formed and physically varied." Even in *Punch*, Hibernia (the allegorical representative of Ireland) "is pure and lovely, with classical limbs, and a pure line from forehead to chin which approximates to [Petrus] Camper's ideal ninety degrees."[66] *Punch* could certainly be anti-Irish even in its early years, Foster concedes, "but no more obsessively than it was anti-medical students, or anti-politicians, or anti-income tax. Nor were its representations of the Irish very pronouncedly different in physiognomy from the representations of English plebeians" (174).

And while midcentury *Punch* was frequently gleefully anti-Catholic, it is also not the case that the variations in its representations of Irishness were invariably sectarian, despite the frequent claim that it was really only the *Catholic* Irish who were understood as nonwhite.[67] Theodore Allen, for example, in *The Invention of the White Race* (1994), which would become a key source for Ignatiev, insists upon that point as the linchpin of the analogy he draws between the Protestant Ascendancy and white supremacy in the Americas: "If the English colonial system of racial oppression in Ireland was to be perpetuated," Allen writes, "it was essential that the people not be converted, but remain Catholic."[68] "In these details," Ignatiev asserts, "Allen reveals the essential identity of the Irish and American cases," that is, the status of the Catholic Irish under British colonial rule and people of African descent under the American regimes of white supremacy, including enslavement.[69] But the distinction between a "white" Protestant Ireland and a "nonwhite" Catholic (or Celtic) Ireland fails to hold convincingly. For instance, as Foster points out, when the Roman Catholic Daniel O'Connell appeared in *Punch*'s caricatures, "his theatrical, self-parodying, larger-than-life elements were much appreciated; foxy, sometimes brusquely ironic, and nobody's fool, but with a heart of gold, O'Connell appears in the early volumes as a sort of Irish Mr Punch" (174).

From the other side of the coin, we can see an instance of the problem even in one of *Punch*'s most famous anti-Irish cartoons of the mid-nineteenth century, the 1848 representation of the ardent nationalist John Mitchel—later convicted of "treason felony" and transported—as an "Irish monkey."[70] On the question of the basis for the ostensible racialization, Curtis hedges; he mentions the cartoon in a paragraph whose topic sentence describes a "link between anthropoid apes and Irish Celts" without acknowledging that, as an Ulster Protestant, Mitchel had a thin relationship to "Celticness" (let alone Catholicism).[71] It is true, as Bryan P. McGovern points out, that Mitchel himself, after his arrival in the United States, became "convinced that his family descended from Gaelic stock, and it is possible, although highly doubtful, that the Mitchels were once Gaelic Catholics who converted to Protestantism to save their land."[72] But Mitchel's later genealogical fantasies are largely irrelevant to *Punch* in 1848; it is his politics that *Punch* represents as bestial, not his (non-)Celticness.

Even the fact that Mitchel, notwithstanding his efforts to point out British tyranny in every aspect of Irish life, could propose that his ancestors converted from Catholicism itself undermines Allen's argument that Catholic Irishness was "analogous" to American Blackness because the Protestant Ascendancy made it virtually impossible to convert. Anti-Catholicism might be the motive behind the racial tropes in a number of representations of the nineteenth-century Irish, but it is not typically their basis.

So what accounts for the common, although by no means universal, "simian" representations of the Irish, particularly from the mid-1840s on? As Foster, taking a wider view, shows, *Punch*'s "representation of *all* working-class types was dark and brutish; all enemies, especially class enemies, tended to the monster. (French apes were a commonplace.)" (192; italics added). And, "From 1845, with an avalanche of starving Irish emigrants landing up in British cities, the attitude hardened" (176). As Amy E. Martin has detailed, the rise of a more radical Irish nationalism that *Punch* opposed inspired imagery of Fenian racial alterity.[73] "Certainly," Foster allows, "the attitude was colonial": "How *could* they not know what was good for them?" (193; italics in original). But the satirical racialization seems more the means than the end.

None of these details should obscure the fundamental point, which is that nineteenth-century caricaturists, in both prose and image, turned to racist stereotypes of Black people in order to mock *whites* who—for whatever reason—came under critique. After all, the deprecatory rhetorical alignment of the Irish with nonwhite people was frequently rather scattershot: the Irish-born (but London-based) royal physician James Johnson, giving an account of his "tour in Ireland" in the early 1840s, described Killarney guides as "an amusing race" who "swarm about the hotels like the Hindoos and Mahomedans on the beach at Madras," Cashel as "a city of wig-wams inhabited by Titanians," and the "Hibernian" as "like a Mahomedan Cadi." He declared that "the murders of this county [Tipperary] would disgrace the most gloomy wilds of the most savage tribes that ever roamed in Asia, Africa, or America."[74] For all of Johnson's racialized rhetoric, this is not a serious attempt at racial taxonomy but rather the deployment, in the interest of evocative insult, of whatever racist stereotype of nonwhite persons comes to hand. As David Theo Goldberg states more generally, "The charged atypicality of the Irish or Jews in the European context ... is comprehended and sustained only by identifying each respectively with and in terms of the conjunction of blackness, (European) femininity, and the lumpenproletariat."[75] That says far more about the largely unquestioned ideologies of anti-Black racism than about prejudice toward explicitly and deliberately disparaged subsets of whites.[76]

The centrality of Irish whiteness and its dependence upon rhetorical or corporeal racial violence emerges as well in the unapologetically racist accounts of the English historian and Liberal politician Edward Augustus Freeman, who visited the United States from 1881 to 1882, at the same time as Oscar Wilde's own American tour. His most notorious characterization of the relationship between Irish and Black Americans in the years following the Civil War and the Thirteenth and Fourteenth Amendments to the Constitution is likely his claim—which he asserted was "approved" by "very many" in the United States—that "the best remedy for whatever was amiss would be if every Irishman should kill a negro and be hanged for it." The quip appears in *Some Impressions of the United States* (1883) after a forthrightly racial representation of nineteenth-century politics that both contrasts Irish and Black electoral interests and balances them: "Men better versed in American matters than myself point out to me the fact that the negro vote balances the Irish vote. But one may be allowed to think that an Aryan land might do better still without any negro vote, that a Teutonic land might do better still without any Irish vote."[77] It does seem, at least when taken out of context, that Freeman understands the Irish as racially cognate with Black people. But that is not actually the case. What Freeman poses here as a kind of equivalency of ethnic and racial distinction is quickly refigured as fundamental difference across what Frederick Douglass would almost precisely contemporaneously designate the color line.[78] On the one hand, "the Irishman is, after all, in a wide sense, one of ourselves. He is Aryan; he is European; he is capable of being assimilated by other branches of the European stock." For Freeman, the trouble with the Irish is a political (and collective) problem, not in the end a racial one: "There is nothing to be said against this or that Irishman all by himself.... It is only when Irishmen gather in such numbers as to form an Irish community capable of concerted action that any mischief is to be looked for from them."[79] On the other hand—and in specific contradistinction to the Irish—for Freeman, Black people are fundamentally different from his "Aryan" model in a way that the Irish are not: "To the old question, Am I not a man and a brother? I venture to answer: No. The negro may be a man and a brother in some secondary sense; he is not a man and a brother in the same full sense in which every Western Aryan is a man and a brother. He cannot be assimilated; the laws of nature forbid it."[80] Freeman makes the genocidal implications of his racial politics explicit in a fantasy of what would come to be called ethnic cleansing: "The Irish difficulty is troublesome just now; it is likely to be troublesome for some time to come; but it is not likely to last for ever. But the negro difficulty must last, either till the way has been found out by which the Ethiopian may change his skin, or till either the white man or the black departs out of the land."[81] Published just over three decades after Robert Knox's pronouncement in *The Races of Men* that "the [Celtic] race must be forced from the soil; by fair means, if possible; still they must leave," Freeman's text makes clear that such eliminationist rhetoric survives in the later nineteenth century—but with the Irish, despite their troublesome politics, clearly aligned with the white masters. Even Carlyle, in "Repeal of the Union," makes the point explicit: "The Celts of Connemara, and other repealing finest peasantry, are white and not black; but it is not the colour of the skin that determines the savagery of a man."[82] The issue is habitual, dispositional, even political and historical, but not essentially racial. (Knox himself can't seem to distinguish "Celts"—a putatively racial term—from "papists and jacobites"— terms of religious and political threat.)

This certainly supports de Nie's argument that nineteenth-century race is cultural rather than biological—except that for all its fictiveness, the color line between white and Black exerted real and brutal power. In his *Latter-Day Pamphlets* (1850), for example, Carlyle repeatedly uses the trope of the chain to describe Irish disadvantage; in a fantasized "Speech of the British Prime Minister to the floods of Irish and other Beggars," he imagines "some three millions of you, as I count: so many of you fallen sheer over into the abysses of open Beggary; and, fearful to think, every new unit that falls is *loading* so much more the chain that drags the others over."[83] In a virtuosic reading of this section of the *Latter-Day Pamphlets*,

Vanessa D. Dickerson points out that "the literal and figurative chains that fetter blacks restrict only blacks even as they promote white civilization; however, the figurative chains that fetter the Irish and the British pauper are the particular concern of British Victorians because they impede white progress.... The chain the Irish wear is more than a manacle of economic depression and oppression but one of connectedness to other whites."[84] As Dickerson observes, Carlyle's racial model works through the deployment of rhetorics of similarity and difference that only seem to be mutually contradictory. On one hand, "his fellow Victorians should not perceive the condition of blacks to be particularly special or important in the greater scheme of things";[85] the spectacle of Black suffering can be mobilized as a trope for the "chaining" of Irish paupers. On the other, "he is careful to maintain the distinction 'between our Black West Indies and our White Ireland, between these two extremes of lazy refusal to work, and of famishing inability to find any work'";[86] any sympathy accruing to Irish hardship need not be extended to persons of African descent. For all of Carlyle's derogatory rhetoric, when he comes right down to it, it matters that the Celt is white.

The key aspect of these racialized portraits is the fact that Blackness is represented as its own insult while Irishness is insulted by being brought into alignment with it. The caricatures—and the scientific racists like Knox—rarely mock the Black man for being like the Irishman; far more frequently, they mock the Irishman for being like the Black man. This is true even of satire like *Punch*'s "Missing Link," which proposed that the Irish are closer to the gorilla than the African is; the putative humor arises from the assumed incongruence of using the terms *commonly* leveled against Black people for the Irishman. It is predicated upon the more virulent, the less questioned racism, directed against Black people; "The Missing Link" appeared in the context of an issue of *Punch* that, in the wake of the promulgation of Abraham Lincoln's preliminary Emancipation Proclamation, was largely given over to multiple pieces ridiculing the very idea of Black freedom and, indeed, Black humanity. The attack on the Irish, by contrast, depends upon the fact that they are white—and, therefore, that they have whiteness to lose through alignment with nonwhite people. That is, as Lloyd has proposed, under the "law of verisimilitude, which governs the metaphorical system of racism ..., the identity between ape and black is self-evident, and it is scandalized by the possibility of a conjunction between whiteness, as the outward sign of human identity, and the simian, which, as a metaphor, becomes a metaphor of nonidentity in the very structure of the human."[87] Sheridan Gilley likely clinches the case with the simple observation, "Here is the clear difference between nineteenth-century discussion of the relative merit of the so-called white races in 'intra-European' racial theory, and the racist attitude to coloured peoples: that 'miscegenation' between say Saxons and Celts was normally regarded as a source of strength and a positive good, while racial mingling between white and black was always considered the reverse."[88] For J. W. Jackson, the mismatch between relative levels of Teutonism and Celticism in England and Ireland is something to be solved not by enslavement or segregation but by gradual miscegenation. The imagined amenability of Irishness to Jackson's plan is itself telling: it is, to use a term that had not quite yet been coined, a eugenic proposal, even if not enforced through state power, but it is a fundamentally different approach than that typically advocated for Black-white relations.[89]

That racial hierarchy emerges even in a now infamous derogation of Irishness in an 1860 letter from the English clergyman Charles Kingsley to his wife, written from County Sligo in the west of Ireland: "I am haunted by the human chimpanzees I saw along that hundred miles of horrible country.... [T]o see white chimpanzees is dreadful; if they were black, one would not feel it so much, but their skins, except where tanned by exposure, are as white as ours."[90] We might read in this letter's quiver of disgust a proleptic version of Joseph Conrad's Marlow, forty years later: "We are accustomed to look upon the shackled form of a conquered monster, but there—there you could look at a thing monstrous and free. It was unearthly, and the men were—No, they were not inhuman. Well, you know, that was the worst of it—this suspicion of their not being inhuman."[91] But there's a difference: Conrad is describing Black African men; for Kingsley, the horror lies in the animalism of the (explicitly) white person, the Irish person who, *because he is white,* becomes uncanny in his degradation. The specter of Blackness haunts his description in an explicitly stated racist corollary: to imagine a Black person as a chimpanzee would not be as "dreadful"; the shock is to see the Irish as white people in that way. "If," Gilley points out, "on one occasion [Kingsley] called the Irish 'chimpanzees,' on another he has his hero express the hope that intermarriage with the Irish might revive the exhausted and degenerate South Saxon race."[92]

Across the Atlantic, a parallel racial consolidation has been more commonly analyzed. As David R. Roediger explains, "At a time when most Democratic theorists were coming to accept polygeniticist [sic] ideas regarding the separate creations of the 'black' and 'white' races, they were also defining 'white' in such a way as to include more surely the Irish and other immigrants."[93] In 1845, in his first month as a United States representative from Mississippi, Jefferson Davis—opposing attempts by the so-called Native American Party to restrict immigrant rights—simultaneously defended the rights of white immigrants to citizenship and *also* defended Black enslavement against the criticism of those same northern representatives. With no acknowledged irony, he declared that "if we admitted foreigners, and yet denied them the enjoyment of all political rights among us, we did but create enemies to our Government, and fill our country with discontented men." That, in opposition to the particular anti-Irish activism of the nativists, he specifically meant Irish immigrants to partake of what he called "happiness and liberty on the American shore" is manifest in his anecdote of "the adoption of Washington by the Irish as a son of St. Patrick, although he had no Irish blood in his veins."[94] Similarly, in an 1848 speech in the United States Senate, the South Carolinian John C. Calhoun declared, "With us [that is, in the southern United States] the two great divisions of society are not the rich and poor, but white and black; and all the former, the poor as well as the rich, belong to the upper class, and are respected and treated as equals, if honest and industrious."[95] In an 1853 Senate debate, Stephen A. Douglas of Illinois asserted that he "cannot recognize England as our mother," given that "our ancestry were not all of English origin. They were of Scotch, Irish, German, French, and of Norman descent as well as English. In short, we inherit from every branch of the Caucasian race."[96] By 1859, the Massachusetts Democrat Caleb Cushing, the former attorney general of the United States under Franklin Pierce, would in the Massachusetts House of Representatives declare whiteness a categorical type, a genre of identity, that explicitly included the Irish and excluded people of African, Asian, and Native American descent:

> Mr. Speaker, I,—you,—we,—gentlemen of the House of Representatives, belong to that excellent white race, the consummate impersonation of intellect in man and loveliness in woman, whose power and whose privilege it is, wherever they may go, and wherever they may remain, to Christianize and to civilize, to command and to be obeyed, to conquer and to reign. I admit to an equality with me, sir, the *white man*,—my blood and race, whether he be the Saxon of England, or the Celtic of Ireland. But I do not admit as my equals either the red man of America, or the yellow man of Asia, or the black man of Africa.[97]

That a defense of Black enslavement and a defense of Irish citizenship could become two sides of the same vision of American nationhood, versions of the same argument, makes clear that, at least for Davis, Douglas, Calhoun, and Cushing, the Irish were fully white. American antiabolitionism in the 1850s, that is, can come to locate itself in Irishness precisely as that Irishness has become the warrant of whiteness, earned through racial domination—rhetorical and actual—over Black persons, enslaved or free.

The interplay between sometimes unspoken assumptions of Irish whiteness and complaints that the Irish were nonetheless treated *as though* they were not white becomes a staple of Irish (and allied) grievance in the nineteenth century. What Wilderson designates the "ruse of analogy" certainly characterizes a persistent nineteenth-century rhetorical conflation, in both the United Kingdom and the United States, between the experience of Irish dispossession and political disadvantage and that of literally enslaved persons. In an 1812 speech to the House of Lords, for example, George Gordon, Lord Byron, argued in favor of what was commonly called Catholic Emancipation by juxtaposing that cause with the abolition of slavery, a juxtaposition that quickly moved toward the assertion of the putatively *greater* suffering of the Irish. In response to those opponents of Catholic enfranchisement who argued that "the Catholics have too much already," Byron asserted that "it might as well be said, that the negroes did not desire to be emancipated, but this is an unfortunate comparison, for you have already delivered them out of the house of bondage without any Petition on their part, but many from their task-masters to a contrary effect." Still further, he continued, "for myself, when I consider this, I pity the Catholic peasantry for not having the good fortune to be born black."[98]

Byron's reference here is fundamentally misleading: the 1807 Slave Trade Act and the 1811 Slave Trade Felony Act to which he seems to allude moved toward the abolition of the Atlantic slave trade, but Britain did not in fact emancipate enslaved people throughout the empire until the Slavery Abolition Act of 1833, more than two decades after Byron's speech (and, even then, there was an exception for "Territories in the Possession of the East India Company"). Further, of course, Olaudah Equiano and others had brought active campaigns against slavery to Ireland and Britain in the 1790s, rendering absurd Byron's assertion that there had been no "petition" on the part of Black people for freedom. Notwithstanding its duplicity, this tactical conflation of the Irish with enslaved people of African descent was by no means limited to Byron. In fact, it arose as a common analogy at the opening of the nineteenth century, often advanced by white liberals in the interest of political progress and, particularly, in support of Irish enfranchisement. Also speaking in support of Catholic enfranchisement, for instance, the Marquess Wellesley (a pro-enfranchisement Tory) declared, "I cannot help saying, when I hear the authority of king William quoted for the continuance of these unjust disabilities, or the deprivation of any human being of his liberty, that it reminds me of quoting the Scriptures in justification of the African Slave Trade."[99] "King William" here refers to William III, Prince of Orange, whose seventeenth-century military incursions into Ireland made him the eponym of the unionist paramilitary Orange Order, founded in 1795—what Knox would call "a Saxon confederation for the clearing the land of all papists and jacobites." And just days before Byron's speech, the liberal Charles Stanhope, Third Earl Stanhope, went still further, standing before the Lords "to call the attention of the House to a train of sufferings not exceeded, perhaps not paralleled, by those of the slave,—in all cases equally unjust, and in most equally attended with horrid and calamitous circumstances. He alluded to the state of the Irish Peasantry under the present laws, as they related to the recovery of rent."[100]

The argument is as tendentious as the analysis is shoddy, the alignment of the situation of Irish Catholics ("the recovery of rent"!) with that of human chattel made possible by a rhetorical trickery, appropriating the affective pull of Black suffering for white liberalism and thereby conflating two radically different situations in the interest of white ethnic progress. Kieran Quinlan has asserted that "it was not, of course, that the Irish in Ireland confused their own situation with that of chattel slaves in America," and that might—on a deep level—be true.[101] After all, as Joseph Rezek points out, many early nineteenth-century Irish people certainly had reason to know about the conditions of actual chattel enslavement: "Some Irish landowners held plantations in the West Indies; residents in Ireland consumed profitable slave commodities like sugar and tobacco; and small-scale, domestic slavery in Ireland itself accounted partly for the presence of a small black population."[102] But by the nineteenth century a strategic conflation of the experience of Irish persons with that of enslaved Black people was *useful* to writers about Ireland, in that it could advance a political argument.

The appropriation and metaphorization of Black chattel enslavement by Irish writers as a figure for Irish disadvantage stretches from the late eighteenth century through the nineteenth. In *Practical Education,* published in 1798, for example, Maria Edgeworth and Richard Lovell Edgeworth entertain a literal similarity between the Irish and enslaved people: the "description, which Mr. [Bryan] Edwards, in his history of the West Indies, gives of the propensity to falsehood amongst the negro slaves, might stand word for word for a character of that class of the Irish people who, till very lately, actually, not metaphorically, called themselves *slaves.*"[103] Daniel O'Connell himself was prone to falling back upon that misleading equivalency: in an 1814 speech to the Catholic Board in Dublin, O'Connell announced of Irish Catholics that "I flattered myself that we had risen in their [Protestants'] estimation; I did imagine we had ceased to be whitewashed negroes, and had thrown off for them all traces of the colour of servitude; but this correspondence has, I confess, done away [with] the delusion."[104] The patriot writer Thomas Moore, poet of the widely popular *Irish Melodies,* declared in the preface to his 1840–41 collected works, "Born of Catholic parents, I had come into the world with the slave's yoke around my neck."[105] That was not, of course, true in any literal sense. But several writers followed the lead of the Marquess Wellesley in turning to the admittedly bloody Irish seventeenth century as "proof" of the analogy. One much-cited source, reprinted in Thomas Carlyle's 1845 edition of *Oliver Cromwell's Letters and Speeches*, is a 1649 letter in which Cromwell described the brutal aftermath of the 1641–42 siege of Drogheda: "When they [the Catholic Irish rebels] submitted, their officers were knocked on the head; and every tenth man of the soldiers killed; and the rest shipped for the Barbadoes. The soldiers in the other Tower were all spared, as to their lives only; and shipped likewise for the Barbadoes."[106] Significantly, Cromwell does not here specify that the Irish resisters "shipped to the Barbadoes" were *slaves*, although it is true that they were impressed into penal servitude.[107]

But by the nineteenth century, Cromwell's letter could be read as a *suggestion* of racialized Irish enslavement mobilized in the interests of Irish political aspirations. Thus, in her 1883 historical romance *Leixlip Castle*, the Irish nationalist novelist M. L. O'Byrne would represent a seventeenth-century Catholic character lamenting that "there were a hundred thousand men transported, sold slaves, into the Barbadoes."[108] And, similarly, in the 1884 edition of his *Historical Sketch of the Persecutions Suffered by the Catholics of Ireland under the Rule of Cromwell and the Puritans*, the Irish-born archbishop of Sydney, Patrick Francis Moran, quoted the mid-seventeenth-century *Commentarius Rinuccianus* to the effect that, "To the island of St. Christopher (better known as St. Kitt's) several thousand Irish Catholics (it says), and whole colonies were transported as slaves. . . . And the Irish transported thither, are held like slaves under a cruel lash."[109] The explicit grievance articulated by these works is that the Irish nationalist opponents of British rule were putatively enslaved under Cromwell; the implicit grievance is that the enormity of this is that, unlike other enslaved people, they were white.

This analogy shapes more progressive representations of Irish poverty as well. In her 1851 *Annals of the Famine in Ireland in 1847, 1848, and 1849*, the American reformer Asenath Nicholson forthrightly argues for the salience of the rhetoric of slavery in understanding Irish impoverishment: "Never had I seen slaves so degraded; and here I learnt that there are many pages in the volume of slavery, and that every branch of it proceeds from one and the same root, though it assumes different shapes. These poor creatures are in as virtual bondage to their landlords and superiors as is possible for mind or body to be."[110] Observing a system of labor in the west of Ireland, she asserts of the managers, "Slave-owners do precisely in the same way. They employ a faithful driver, pay him bountifully, and his duty is to get the most work done in the least time, and in the best way. If a delinquent be flogged to death, the owner is always away from home or somehow engaged—entirely ignorant of the matter" (177). Indeed, she suggests—as do a number of white social observers of the nineteenth century—that this "virtual bondage" of the Irish is, at least in some ways, *worse* than that of those enslaved by the American system of chattel labor: "Well did James Tuke say, in his graphic description of Erris, that he had visited the wasted remnants of the once noble Red Man in North America, and the 'negro-quarter' of the degraded and enslaved African; but never had he seen misery so intense, or physical degradation so complete, as among the dwellers in the bog-holes of Erris" (134–35).

For Nicholson, the putative homonymy between Irish economic and cultural hardship and Black enslavement is a spur to political action on behalf of the Irish. Thus she posits, suggesting that the United States might send money to support Ireland if Britain would allow it, "though she has a right to say she will not send Ireland food to keep them strong in idleness, she has no right to say she will not send them food to give them strength for labor. She has not a heart to say it; foul as her hands may be with slavery, yet she will feed the hungry with a cheerful hand" (155). And, invoking a British abolitionist, she declares, "Where is your George Thompson? He who shook the United States from Maine to Georgia, in pleading long and loud for the down-trodden black man? Can he not, will he not lift his voice for poor Ireland?" (153–54). Nicholson, that is, figures Black emancipation as an important goal, even as she hints in places that the Irish situation is still more pressing.

As Nicholson's *Memoir* makes clear, the rhetorical invocation of putative Irish slavery (perhaps of a "virtual" nature) is not independent of allusions to the *actual* enslavement of Black persons; that is, it is not—at least in the nineteenth century—the case that the word simply meant different things, one applicable to the situation of the Irish vis-à-vis England and one applicable to the situation of chattel slaves under the race-based enslavement regimes of the United States or, earlier, the British Empire. The figure of speech that aligns the literal with the metaphorical also permits a type of thought that understands two radically different situations, both admittedly brutal, as cognate. Those distinctions, as Liam Hogan, Laura McAtackney, and Matthew C. Reilly have made clear in their analysis of Irish transportation to the New World, matter tremendously: "Colonial servitude in the Anglo-Caribbean was temporary and non-hereditary, with legal personhood, while chattel slavery was perpetual and hereditary with subhuman legal status. It is inevitable that if we refer to these two different statuses in the same historical context using the same term ('slave') these profound distinctions are erased. The refusal to differentiate often reveals a motivation to equate indentured servitude for Europeans with African chattel perpetual slavery to claim spuriously that slavery had nothing to do with race."[111] Nikole Hannah-Jones, among many others, has shown that the distinctions between chattel enslavement and forms of labor abuse that might be inflicted upon non-Black persons became absolute by the eighteenth century. It was in that century that a "brutal system of racial slavery that through the decades would be transformed into an institution unlike anything that had existed in the world before" solidified: "Chattel slavery was not conditional but racial. It was heritable and permanent, not temporary, meaning generations of Black people were born into it and passed their enslaved status on to their children. Enslaved people were not recognized as human beings but were considered property that could be mortgaged, traded, bought, sold, used as collateral, given as a gift, and disposed of violently."[112] Even abusive indentured servitude—explicitly "conditional" in all of its forms—was in no way comparable. As Vaughan puts it, "In Virginia's exploitive society, indentured servants, though sometimes treated slavishly, were never slaves."[113]

As early as 1680, the English missionary Morgan Godwyn deplored the fact that "these two words, *Negro* and *Slave*," had "by custom grown Homogeneous and Convertible."[114] And it is significant that this observation about the specific racialization of enslavement occurs, in Godwyn's treatise, in the midst of a discussion of whether the Irish, due to their barbarity, can be slaves:

> So much are they [the Irish] Degenerated, or at least so little Fruit thereof hath of late accrued to their Posterity, that the *Natives* of that Kingdom, who have been Imported hither, are observed to be, in divers respects, more Barbarous than the *Negro's* [sic]: And this in its kind is so notorious in some of them, as to fall under even the *Negro's* observation; by whom this petulent [sic] Taunt hath contemptuously, and in reproach of their doltish Stupidity, been returned upon them, *viz. That if the Irishman's Country had first lighted in the Englishman's way, he might have gone no further to look for Negro's:* That is, Slaves, such as the *Negro's* here generally are.[115]

Nonetheless, even while he argues for similarities in condition, Godwyn—in the seventeenth century—distinguishes between "Negro" slaves and "White servants," a category which he glosses as "the general name for *Europeans*."[116] The Irish might be impoverished, even "degenerated" into barbarism, but there is nevertheless a remarkably strong racial distinction—manifested in Godwyn's language itself—between them and Black people.

Vaughan points out that Godwyn's "explanation of racism's insidious emphasis on pigmentation preceded by almost a century the insights of several Revolutionary era reformers."[117] He shows as well that while anti-Black racial attitudes differed in various ways in England from those in Barbados and Virginia (where Godwyn had traveled), "By and large, Godwyn's ideas made as little headway in England as in the colonies against the tides of hostility and indifference toward Africans."[118] There were not, that is, two completely different racial regimes divided by the Atlantic: Godwyn's antiracist appeal failed to significantly influence either England or its colonies. And, despite his odd anecdote, the English *did*, of course, come to Ireland before Africa; as Friedrich Engels wrote to Karl Marx in 1856, following a trip through Ireland, "Ireland may be regarded as the first English colony and as one which because of its proximity is still governed exactly in the old way." He continues, "One can already notice here that the so-called liberty of the English citizens is based on the oppression of the colonies."[119] Engels is not in any way claiming that the Irish are exempt from colonial abuse. But it is precisely because the Irish were already comprehended as a people, whether colonized or not, prior to the rise of Enlightenment racialization that they were easily understood as white.[120] The historical conditions of contact and collision, in the context of an Enlightenment modernity that was inseparable from an extractive imperialism along with the systemization of epistemological and aesthetic categories, matter both to the rise of "race" and to its transformation into the fundamental basis for chattel enslavement. By that time, as Godwyn's essay demonstrated, the Irish were already "white," to the degree to which that term held meaning.

This represents a transatlantic similarity rather than difference in the comparative racialization of Black and Irish persons. In *A Treatise on the Intellectual Character, and Civil and Political Condition of the Colored People of the U. States* (1837), the Black Boston minister Hosea Easton pointed out the importance of Irish whiteness in the structures of anti-Black racism as well as the fundamental differences between anti-Irish discrimination and Black chattel enslavement: "There is a prejudice in this country against the Irish, who are flocking here by thousands. Still there is nothing malignant in the nature and exercise of that prejudice, either national or personal. It grows out of the mere circumstance of their different manners and religion. The moment an Irishman adopts the maxims and prevailing religion of the country, he is no longer regarded an Irishman, other than by birth. It is to be remembered, also, that the Irish are not an injured, but a benefited party." In contrast, Easton affirms, "The injury sustained by the colored people, is both national and personal; indeed, it is national in a twofold sense. In the first place, they are lineally stolen from their native country, and detained for centuries, in a strange land, as hewers of wood and drawers of water. In this situation, their blood, habits, minds, and bodies, have undergone such a change, as to cause them to lose all legal or natural relations to their mother country."[121] For Easton, the Irish are a "benefited party"—despite prejudice, which he certainly doesn't deny—specifically because they are not "colored people."

In fact, by the nineteenth century—especially in the United States but also in some strains of Irish nationalism—to argue that the Irish were also "slaves" was not simply to run a thought experiment in good faith;

it was explicitly to take the side of the slavers against the abolitionists. In 1857, the *Arkansas State Gazette and Democrat* reported on a 1764 advertisement from the *Connecticut Gazette* for "a parcel of *Irish servants*, both men and women, *to be sold cheap*" and ran it under the snide headline "White Slavery in Connecticut": "So it seems that less than 100 years ago, men and women were brought from Ireland, and sold as slaves, in the State of Connecticut. And not 100 years before that time, Indians were sent from Connecticut, Rhode Island, &c., to the West Indies, and sold into slavery. Curious historical facts, these."[122] And in 1862, the slave trader, civic official, and proslavery activist Thomas Ryan placed a notice in the *Charleston Daily Courier,* festooned with harp, shamrocks, and the title of the nationalist ballad "Erin Go Bragh":

> THE UNDERSIGNED PROPOSES TO RAISE A Company of IRISH REBELS to enter Confederate service for the defence of South Carolina. The name of Rebel he prefers, because his ancestors have been so called for more than six hundred years. The fanatical Puritans have landed on our soil. Oliver Cromwell lives again in the person of Abraham Lincoln. Should they succeed in capturing Charleston the butcheries of Drogheda will be repeated in our streets. Come forward then, my countrymen, and unite with the Cavalier and Huguenot to expel them from our beloved State, and insure to ourselves and posterity peace and happiness for ages to come.[123]

The analogy that the Irish American Ryan draws between Lincoln and Cromwell—with particular reference to his actions in the aftermath of Drogheda—is telling, particularly given Cromwell's centrality in the mythology of Irish slavery. Even while he also highlights the slaughters at Drogheda (what he calls Cromwell's "butcheries"), the threat that Ryan proposes relies as well on a rhetorical stratagem through which the projected attack by Lincoln reenacts in the nineteenth century the putative seventeenth-century enslavement of the Irish by Cromwell. And it is certainly the case that Ryan's appeal to Irish Americans to "unite with the Cavalier and Huguenot" in support of the slave state of South Carolina against that Cromwellian Lincoln is predicated upon an alliance of whiteness. Thus does one myth of Irish slavery become a rhetorical grounding for an appeal to Irish whiteness in support of the regime of Black chattel slavery.[124]

As Ariela J. Gross relates, such evocations of putative Irish "slavery" practiced by the North could be used by the proslavery South as a "potent symbol in the political and moral war over slavery" by mocking what they represented as abolitionist hypocrisy. Gross observes drily, "The editors [of the *Arkansas State Gazette and Democrat*] replied to abolitionists' accusations by pointing their fingers at 'white slavery' in the North: the treatment of Irish indentured servants and Indians in the eighteenth century."[125] Indeed, however, even the putatively incriminating 1764 advertisement calls the Irish at issue "servants," not slaves. In contrast, Painter points out, the "process of turning 'servants' from Africa into racialized workers enslaved for life occurred in the 1660s to 1680s through a succession of Virginia laws that decreed that a child's status followed that of its mother and that baptism did not automatically confer emancipation. By the end of the seventeenth century, Africans had indeed been marked off by race in law as chattel to be bought, sold, traded, inherited and serve as collateral for business and debt services."[126] What happens from the late seventeenth century on is the bifurcation of race, a process that came to constitute Black persons as *racially* enslaved across generations and white persons—including Irish people transported into the British colonies in the New World—as servants; they might continue to be brutally treated and cheated, of course, but their servitude was for a term of years.

It is useful here to borrow Lynn Festa's striking terminology of "affective piracy." For Festa, this piracy arises in the work of white abolitionists; it is a type of theft through which "the sentimental mode's investment in affective and psychological interiority helped distinguish the particularity of the human from the interchangeability of the commodity, the self-possessed individual from the dispossessed slave."[127] In the claims of Irish slavery I have adduced, the piracy goes a step still further in that an abolitionist agenda itself becomes secondary, even dispensable; even such a sympathetic writer as Nicholson—like Byron, Wellesley, O'Byrne, and Moran—explicitly draws upon the image of the enslaved Black person *in order to* transfer that affective indignation to the white sufferer, at which point the situation of actual enslavement, while deplored, can be superseded *by* that white sufferer.[128] A signal example emerges in the Irish nationalist journal the *Nation*, for which Mitchel served as a writer and editor; as early as 1847, an editorial mobilized the metaphorical application of slavery to the situation of Ireland as an excuse to do nothing about the actual enslavement of Black people in the United States: "We have really so very urgent affairs at home—so much abolition of *white* slavery to effect if we can . . . that all our exertions will be needed in Ireland. Carolina planters never devoured our substance, nor drove away our sheep and oxen for a spoil. . . . Our enemies are nearer home than Carolina."[129] If this is not "solidarity based on color," in Ignatiev's terms, it is hard to know what is. The disavowal of the urgency of abolitionist activism here is predicated not only on distance ("home" as opposed to Carolina) and political salience ("Carolina planters never devoured our substance") but also, explicitly, on race, on the privileging of whiteness as the category that merits attention and care ("so much abolition of *white* slavery to effect if we can"), and the firm positioning of Irishness within that category.

In a now famous 1846 letter to William Lloyd Garrison, Frederick Douglass wrote from Ireland, where he had met O'Connell and lectured extensively, describing his wonder at the lack of racism he experienced there:

> Instead of the bright, blue sky of America, I am covered with the soft, grey fog of the Emerald Isle. I breathe, and lo! the chattel becomes a man. I gaze around in vain for one who will question my equal humanity, claim me as his slave, or offer me an insult. . . . I find no difficulty here in obtaining admission into any place of worship, instruction, or amusement, on equal terms with people as white as any I ever saw in the United States. I meet nothing to remind me of my complexion. I find myself regarded and treated at every turn with the kindness and deference paid to white people.[130]

The distinction between that description and Douglass's numerous accounts of Irish American racism frequently appears in claims that the Irish "became white" upon their arrival in the United States. But Douglass is not in any way proposing that race was not an operative concept in Ireland; after all, the Irish *in* Ireland are a people "as white as any I ever saw in the United States."

Throughout his long career, Frederick Douglass observed the interrelationships between the Irish (both in Ireland and in the United States), African Americans, and the politics and violence of white supremacy, considering that question deeply and from different perspectives. And the ruse of analogy was one that he would repeatedly confront—and consistently push back upon. Back in America, in 1850, Douglass would again insist upon the fundamental differences between Irish disadvantage and Black chattel enslavement: "It is often said, by the opponents of the Anti-Slavery cause, that the condition of the people of Ireland is more deplorable than that of the American slaves.... I must say that there is no analogy between the two cases. The Irishman is poor, but he is *not* a slave. He *may* be in rags, but he is *not* a slave. He is still the master of his own body."[131] Similarly, in an 1853 speech titled "A Nation in the Midst of a Nation," he analyzed the constitution of whiteness across ethnicity and class as that which was *not* Black (and therefore not enslaved), explicitly including the Irish:

> The Hungarian, the Italian, the Irishman, the Jew, and the Gentile, all find in this land a home, and when any of them, or all of them desire to speak, they find willing ears, warm hearts and open hands. For these people, the Americans, have principles of justice, maxims of mercy, sentiments of religion, and feelings of brotherhood in abundance. But for my poor people enslaved—blasted and ruined—it would appear, that America had neither justice, mercy nor religion. She has no scales in which to weigh our wrongs—she has no standard by which to measure our rights.[132]

What Douglass rightly observes here is that, despite national prejudice and the structures of political advantage and disadvantage, despite even violent histories of disenfranchisement and the horrors of the Famine, the person of Irish descent in the United States of the 1850s was *white*—and that whiteness brought with it a form of citizenship that structurally excluded Black people. Indeed, in 1863, he would single out Irish Americans—*as* whites—as a key obstacle to Black enfranchisement, that is, to affordances of citizenship: "I am told that the Irish element in this country is exceedingly strong, and that that element will never allow colored men to stand upon an equal political footing with white men.... Well, my friends, I admit that the Irish people are among our bitterest persecutors." In that same speech, Douglass detailed the long history of penal laws enacted against Irish Catholics in Ireland but noted pointedly that "religion, not color, was the apology for this oppression."[133] Chattel enslavement as a practice was established on the bodies of those perceived to be uniquely associated with it by the fact of their Blackness, as that Blackness was understood.[134]

Douglass's position was not a singular one. As early as 1787, Quobna Ottobah Cugoano deplored the suggestion that "the many hardships that the poor in Great-Britain and Ireland labour under . . . are worse than the West India slaves."[135] And Douglass's contemporary, the American Canadian abolitionist Samuel Ringgold Ward, in his 1855 *Autobiography of a Fugitive Negro*, similarly suggested that the distinction between the Irish and the English was contingent on historical and economic factors rather than the result of a fundamental racial difference. In contrast to Douglass, Ward did not find Ireland particularly inviting, but, like Douglass, he observed, "Of all Europeans, the Irish immigrant becomes, as a rule, the most ready dupe of the pro-slavery men. . . . The bitterest, most heartless, most malignant, enemy of the Negro, is the Irish immigrant."[136] Ward does, to be sure, indulge in some comparative ethnology of his own, drawing upon the rhetorics of a generalized and softened race science: "The wit, warmth, and enthusiasm—the capacity to imitate, to improve, and to endure—the cheerfulness, bravery, and love of religion—said to be peculiar to the Celt, are well-known natural characteristics of the Negro. They are in these points, when degraded and ignorant or when educated and refined, alike, in a most remarkable degree."[137] But he also proposes a cultural rather than biological etiology: "In America . . . , and in Canada, where corrupting influences are less common than in the United States, I have seen the material improvement of the Irish pauper elevate him above the depressions of mind and morals which were considered inseparable from his lot in Ireland."[138] When it comes down to the question of white supremacy in the United States, Ward finds that the Irish turn out to be no different from other immigrant whites of the British Isles: "Englishmen, Irishmen, and Scotchmen, generally become the bitterest of Negro-haters, within fifteen days of their naturalization—some not waiting so long."[139]

The English political economist John Stuart Mill likewise criticized the conflation of Irish hardship with the sort of racial difference that underwrote enslavement. By the composition of the "Occasional Discourse,"

Carlyle's racial rhetoric had become venomous enough that Mill wrote to the editors of *Fraser's Magazine for Town and Country* to object both to the article in general and to the posited analogy of Irish and Black persons in particular:

> For nearly two centuries had negroes, many thousands annually, been seized by force or treachery and carried off to the West Indies to be worked to death, literally to death; for it was the received maxim, the acknowledged dictate of good economy, to wear them out quickly and import more. In this fact every other possible cruelty, tyranny, and wanton oppression was by implication included.... I have yet to learn that anything more detestable than this has been done by human beings towards human beings in any part of the earth. It is a mockery to talk of comparing it with Ireland. And this went on, not, like Irish beggary, because England had not the skill to prevent it,—not merely by the sufferance, but by the laws of the English nation.[140]

In later chapters, I will have more to say about the way Mill's own form of liberalism was deployed across the Atlantic, but here I want to highlight what might be thought of as his appeal to *genre* as the structure that underlies categories of likeness and difference: enslaved people are not the same as Irish beggars; the Irish are not slaves. (Nor are they "negroes.") To Carlyle's specter of "a black Ireland," Mill insists that he has made a categorical error. For Mill, the category—the genre—that *does* unite the Irishman with the enslaved Black person is the category of the human; that is the only genre that matters.[141]

As messy and frequently incoherent as nineteenth-century understandings of race—like our own—could be, Cugoano and Douglass and Ward and Mill saw that they were not collapsible into generalizable forms of difference, that "county, religious, or national animosities," in Ignatiev's terms, simply did not have the salience of "solidarity based on color" on either side of the Atlantic. Douglass and Ward were an American and a Canadian visiting Ireland, and it might be objected that they brought with them notions of race that were foreign to this new context. Yet Freeman and Mitchel—an Englishman and Irishman in the United States, and with diametrically opposed racial politics to Douglass's and Ward's—base their own racism in a similar epistemological model: that whiteness existed as an operative category, and that Irishness was included within it, whatever disadvantages or characterological faults the Irish might bear.

The Irish and Irish Americans, of course, were not unique in claiming their whiteness through an alliance with the structures of white supremacy. The migration of Scottish people and Scottish literary tropes to the United States, for example, plays a similarly complex role, as Mark Twain wryly observed in his suggestion that "Sir Walter [Scott] had so large a hand in making Southern character, as it existed before the war, that he is in great measure responsible for the war."[142] But whereas Twain used Scott's influence in order to *diminish* the significance of slavery to the rise of the Confederacy and the Civil War, Ann Rigney has pointed out that the line from Scott to white supremacy is not particularly long: "The fiery cross that entered Ku Klux Klan practices through [D. W.] Griffith and [Thomas] Dixon can be traced directly back to *The Lady of the Lake* and seen as the most recent, and most obnoxious morphing of Scott's work."[143] It is telling of the complex entanglements of literature and race in the nineteenth century that it is in that very same poem, Scott's *The Lady of the Lake,* that the man called Frederick Augustus Washington Bailey at birth found the name under which he became famous: Douglass.[144]

But in part because the Irish risings and political activisms of the late eighteenth and early nineteenth centuries—along with their concomitant literary genres—were such an important recent touchstone; in part because the effects of the 1801 Union with Great Britain were still so raw and so startlingly available as a sort of geopolitical pun for the challenges of the United States' own Union; in part because the metaphor of slavery was both so ardently and so shamelessly attached to the Irish condition, the Irish example of the 1840s and 1850s is particularly significant in both its potential for interracial alliance and its failures to live up to that potential. Garrison, among others, made the pun—and its pitfalls—explicit: "As an abolitionist—as a friend of justice—as a man and a christian—I am for the repeal of the union between England and Ireland, because it is not founded in equity. . . . On the same ground, and for the same reason, I am for the repeal of the union between the North and the South—*alias,* between LIBERTY and SLAVERY—which is incomparably more unequal, more profligate, more intolerable, and more blighting, than that which ostensibly exists on the other side of the Atlantic." What he feared was a different "union": "The bargain obviously is . . . that the South shall go for Repeal, and the Irish, as a body, shall go for southern slavery!—Here is a 'union,' most unnatural and horrible!"[145] (John Mitchel would prove Garrison right: "I wished to repeal an enforced 'Union' of Ireland with England: and I wished to resist the enforcement of an Union between Virginia and New York," he declared in a letter to the pro-Confederate *New York Daily News* in June 1865. "Where is the inconsistency?")[146] The Irish *did* experience discrimination in both the United Kingdom and the United States, discrimination that was in various ways racialized, although not, I propose, to the extent that the nineteenth-century Irish were understood as nonwhite in any widespread way. Many brought that experience to a commitment to abolition; others, as Garrison predicted, did not. This book is the story of the stories they told—and the genres in which they framed those stories—about why that was.

2

The Gothic Palimpsest of Black and Irish Histories

From the distance spectres seemed to rise up.
—Harriet Jacobs, *Incidents in the Life of a Slave Girl* (1861)

"It has been suggested that romance is an evasion of history (and thus perhaps attractive to a people trying to evade the recent past)," Toni Morrison writes in *Playing in the Dark*. "But I am more persuaded by arguments that find in it the head-on encounter with very real, pressing historical forces and the contradictions inherent in them as they came to be experienced by writers." She highlights in particular "the strong affinity between the nineteenth-century American psyche and gothic romance."[1] By the 1840s, literary genres that had been central to the Irish nationalist imagination in the first decades of the nineteenth century indeed ran headlong into both "very real, pressing historical forces" and the attempt to "evade the recent past," especially in light of a half century of ruptures: the 1798 United Irishmen rebellion and the 1801 Union between Great Britain and Ireland; the succeeding uprisings, along with the rise of the unionist Orange Order; debates over Catholic enfranchisement; Feargus O'Connor's radical activism that spurred the Chartist movement; the Great Famine and its maelstrom of death, political instability, and emigration. Those confrontations with and evasions of the forces of history erupted as well when those genres were translated into the context of the United States and the monstrosity of its continuing chattel enslavement of Black people. In this and chapter 3, what I want to propose is that the encounter with history—or the evasion of that encounter—performed by these literary genres itself symptomatizes a failure in translation from one national context to another. In that, they come to manifest, in Morrison's words, "what racial ideology does to the mind, imagination, and behavior of masters."[2] Types of generic thinking, Morrison emphasizes, can subtend this racial ideology through the way that they shape thought. In this chapter, I trace the production of racial structures of similarity and difference in one of the central genres of early nineteenth-century Irish nationalist literature: the gothic romance, which—as Morrison astutely explains—appears to elude the racial violence of history but, inevitably, encounters its contradictions. From Matthew Gregory Lewis's "The Anaconda: An East-Indian Tale" (1808) to Edgar Allan Poe's "The Gold-Bug" (1843), I read the gothic as a paradigmatic instance of a genre that comes both to juxtapose the situations of Irish and Black experience and, too frequently, to fail to acknowledge the differences between those experiences. Irishness inflects these gothic tales' constructions of race, but it also serves as a sort of distraction, undermining any articulation of these radically distinct histories of racialization.

The political valences of the eighteenth- and nineteenth-century gothic are complex, self-contradictory, and contested.[3] "What is striking," Frances A. Chiu points out, "is how writers—conservative and progressive alike—magnified the image of the crumbling castle in their arguments on British government."[4] That ambidextrous political impact characterizes as well the relevance of the gothic to Irish contexts—radical, reactionary, liberal—from the eighteenth century forward. "Politically oppressed, underdeveloped in the far west and southwest, disrupted and distressed by famines, clearances, uprisings, and the depredations of the rural secret societies, devoutly Catholic in its majority population, and full of romantic scenery and prehistoric, not to say feudal, ruins," Julian Moynahan maintains, "nineteenth-century Ireland was an impressive candidate for Gothic treatment. The country was in fact sometimes seen as a sort of living Gothic, or agonized Gothic romance that had turned real."[5] The fact that Irish history, with its centuries of violence, appeared haunted is an important reason for the persistence of the gothic as a key literary form for nineteenth-century Irish writers, from Charles Robert Maturin's *Melmoth the Wanderer* (1820) and John Banim's *The Fetches* (1825), through Dion Boucicault's *The Vampire* (1852) and Sheridan Le Fanu's *In a Glass Darkly* (1872), to Oscar Wilde's *The Picture of Dorian Gray* (1890) and Bram Stoker's *Dracula* (1897).

That intertwining of history and genre frequently arose, Luke Gibbons shows, as a form of political reaction: "While the Jacobite ghost had been politically exorcized in the decades after Culloden, it assumed a new, cultural afterlife in the Irish and Scottish periphery, re-emerging in the national imaginaries of Ossian, Celticism, the historical novel, and, of course, the Gothic itself."[6] Likewise focusing on the dominant Irish Protestant production of gothic literature, Jarlath Killeen has diverged somewhat from that account by identifying the gothic as "broadly liberal" in its orientation, positing, "As this version of liberalism is articulated in an Irish context it reveals itself as both profoundly suspicious of Catholicism and yet simultaneously longing to reach out and embrace it in fraternal toleration, an ambiguity with enormous political implications for Irish society."[7] With its multiple valences of horror and fascination, the Anglo-Irish gothic came to be deployed in both anti-Catholic and more tolerant representations of Irish Catholicism.

Even that range, however, doesn't exhaust the gothic's relevance to Irish history and politics. Countering this focus on gothic representations of Ireland by Anglo-oriented writers, such critics as Seamus Deane, Richard Haslam, Christina Morin, and Niall Gillespie have highlighted Catholic and anticolonial manifestations of the eighteenth- and early nineteenth-century Irish gothic.[8] "Not just an allegorical expression of its Anglo-Irish writers' fear of the repressed past and its people (the Catholic majority)," Morin reveals, "the Irish literary gothic in this period proves a dynamic, cross-sectarian, and cross-cultural enterprise."[9] One significant manifestation of that, as Gillespie has compellingly related, is the rise of "Irish Jacobin gothic" beginning around 1796 as a response to the coercive state violence enacted in reaction to the rise of Irish republicanism: "In contrast to English gothic normatives, in Irish Jacobin gothic, the medieval terrorizers are those of an Anglican state (and its clergy who doubled as magistrates); the gothic landscape is located in the North and West, not in the Catholic South. State-sponsored Anglicanism, rather than Catholicism, is figured as villainous, superstitious, corrupt, irrational, and tyrannical.... Irish republican gothic was a de-imperializing gothic—it figured colonization as hell."[10] "Not solely associated with a besieged Anglican tradition," Claire Connolly writes, "Gothic modes pervade the [Irish] writing of the 1820s" against a "political backdrop that is already imagined in Gothic terms and which cannot be reduced to either Catholic resistance or Protestant fears of dispossession."[11] The gothic as a generic mode, that is, came not only to register imperial anxiety about the diabolical but fascinating superstitions of an intractably Catholic colonial people but also to give those people a way to name the monstrousness of the imperial system itself.

It also shapes descriptions of Irish hardship by outsiders, particularly during the Famine years of the mid-nineteenth century. For the American philanthropist Asenath Nicholson, visiting Ireland during the Great Famine, Irish poverty itself is, inescapably, gothic:

> Reader, if you have never seen a starving human being, *may you never!* In my childhood I had been frightened with the stories of ghosts, and had seen actual skeletons; but imagination had come short of the sight of this man. And here, to those who have never watched the progress of protracted hunger, it might be proper to say, that persons will live for months, and pass through different stages, and life will struggle on to maintain her lawful hold, if occasional scanty supplies are given, till the walking skeleton is reduced to a state of inanity. (*Annals*, 37; italics in original)

Another visitor of 1847, the radical journalist Alexander Somerville, also turned to gothic tropes to describe the horrors the Famine wreaked on the bodies of Irish people: "This man was tall; his children were tall for their age; all three looked like spectres with spades in their hands.... Their purpose was to dig for life, but they looked as if breaking ground for their own burial, and as if a very shallow grave would serve them, they were so thin."[12] Part of the affordance of the gothic in these reports, relying as they do on the uncanny alterity of what would come to be called the undead, is its suggestion that it is the only mode capable of describing the horrifically indescribable.

In that same year, John Mitchel, whose transformation from ardent Irish nationalist to virulent supporter of American racial slavery is the subject of this book's chapter 4, similarly represented his observations of the ravages of the Famine in figures both self-consciously "literary" and generically gothic:

> And we are here in the midst of one of those thousand Golgothas, that border our island with a ring of death from Cork harbour all round to Lough Foyle. . . . There is a horrible silence; grass grows before the doors; we fear to look into any door, though they are all open or off the hinges; for we fear to see yellow chapless skeletons grinning there; but our footfalls rouse two lean dogs, that run from us with doleful howling, and we know by the felon gleam in their wolfish eyes, how *they* have lived, after their masters died. We walk amidst the houses of the Dead, and out at the other side of the cluster, and there is not one where we dare to enter. We stop before the threshold of our host of two years ago, put our head, with eyes shut, inside the doorjamb, and say with shaking voice "God save all here!"—No answer—ghastly silence, and a mouldy stench, as from the mouth of burial-vaults. . . ; they shrunk and withered together, until their voices dwindled to a rueful gibbering, and they hardly knew one another's faces, but their horrid eyes scowled on each other with a cannibal glare. . . . Oh! Pity and Terror! what a tragedy is here,—deeper, darker than any *bloody* tragedy ever yet enacted under the sun, with all its dripping daggers and sceptered palls.[13]

There is, for Mitchel, no way to describe the devastations of the Famine without evoking the tropes of the gothic: the ruins, the "ring of death" and "mouldy stench," the burial vaults and grinning skeletons, the slide toward cannibalism, and more. Bryan P. McGovern has argued that this essay, rhetorically shrouded in the language of gothic horror, marks Mitchel's initiation into more radical forms of nationalist activism and rhetoric: "Mitchel would never forget the horror he witnessed on this trip. Thereafter, the transformation in him would be remarkable, as his eloquence became even more anti-British and more revolutionary. . . . The horrors made him realize that repeal was not the solution, and that the British would not grant the revocation of the Act of Union anytime soon. He concluded that an independent republic was the immediate solution."[14] In his headnote to this essay, reprinted as an appendix to his 1913 edition of Mitchel's *Jail Journal*, the founder of Sinn Féin (and future president of the revolutionary Irish Republic) Arthur Griffith similarly announced it "the most beautiful and terrible article that has ever come from the pen of an Irish journalist" and declared, "In it the John Mitchel of 1848 has his birth."[15] For Mitchel, this gothicized language of horror that is the only possible rhetorical vessel for the representation of such appalling deprivation opens the door to his explicitly militant Irish nationalism. The deployment of genre becomes a form of activism.

Along with—and at times because of—its role in the Irish colonial and anticolonial imagination, the gothic becomes central as well to the construction of race and racism in both the British Empire and the United States, at times operating by obscuring the boundaries of Black and Irish identities. Mark Hemenway underscores what he calls "the basic color-coded imagery of the Gothic psychology: 'enlightenment' as the clarity of science, 'blackness' as the irrationality of evil." "In actual fact," Hemenway explains, "this imagery is a racist component in Western thought, giving the Gothic a sociological burden even when there is no conscious intention of racial statement."[16] He thus presages Morrison in figuring this racialization as systemic rather than individual and in seeing generic literary expression as a key mode through which that systemic racialization is articulated and spread. Hemenway insists that racist intent is not necessary to the emergence of the gothic in depictions of race; in cases where there *was* such "intention of racial statement," the gothic provided an affectively powerful set of tropes for a complexly overlapping set of putatively dangerous political developments. In "The Grateful Negro" (1804), for example, the Irish writer Maria Edgeworth used her gothically inflected tale of a slave uprising in Jamaica to critique the prospect of immediate abolition; her benevolent Mr. Edwards (named for the Jamaican enslaver Bryan Edwards, whose 1793 *History of the West Indies* Edgeworth's character ventriloquizes), "wished that there was no such thing as slavery in the world; but he was convinced . . . that the sudden emancipation of the negroes would rather encrease than diminish their miseries. His benevolence therefore confined itself within the bounds of reason."[17] In contrast to the putatively rational enslaver, the diabolical "chief instigator of this intended rebellion"[18] is decked in the tropes of the literary gothic, a character dedicated to the practices both of Obeah and poison whom Edgeworth alternately calls a "sorceress," "hag," and "fiend." Edgeworth's vision of race was itself multivalent, as George Boulukos observes: she both promoted the Scottish author John Moore's "bizarre proto-gothic masterpiece," the antislavery *Zuluco,* and—with "The Grateful Negro"—helped to shape American conceptions of race, as "the key figure in the dissemination of 'the grateful slave'" trope in both the United Kingdom and the United States.[19] Joseph Rezek has pointed out that Edgeworth and the poet Thomas Moore were "undoubtedly the most popular Irish writers in the USA before the Civil War"; the literary circulation of the gothic across the Atlantic both popularizes Irish modes and mobilizes them to shape racial fantasies.[20]

In 1824, two decades after Edgeworth's "Grateful Negro," the British foreign secretary George Canning, in a speech to Parliament, similarly figured the threat of abolition in Britain's West Indian colonies in sensationally gothic terms. Beginning with the assertion, "In dealing with the negro, Sir, we must remember that we are dealing with a being possessing the form and strength of a man, but the intellect only of a child," Canning quickly explicates a racist vision of Black monstrosity by invoking Mary Shelley's creature:

> To turn him loose in the manhood of his physical strength, in the maturity of his physical passions, but in the infancy of his uninstructed reason, would be to raise up a creature resembling the splendid fiction of a recent romance; the hero of which constructs a human form, with all the corporeal capabilities of man, and with the thews and sinews of a giant; but being unable to impart to the work of his hands a perception of right and wrong, he finds too late that he has only created a more than mortal power of doing mischief, and himself recoils from the monster which he has made.

"Such," insisted Canning, "would be the effect of a sudden emancipation, before the negro was prepared for the enjoyment of well-regulated liberty."[21] Glossing this speech (with its fundamental misreading of Shelley's novel), H. L. Malchow has noted the political and racial versatility of the Frankensteinian bugbear: "This temptation to use the image of the Monster in the portrayal of 'uncivilized' and unwhite peoples abroad inevitably wandered into domestic politics.... If these were not Negro Monsters, they often suggested ethnic prejudice in associating the Creature with the Irish working man."[22] For the colonizer, Malchow emphasizes, the gothic could strategically conflate Irish radicalism with broader anxieties about racial and cultural alterity.

Robert Kiely, writing of the gothic novelist Matthew Gregory Lewis, characterized the gothic as a mode in which "excess of individual freedom thrives on the potential subjugation of everything but the self,"[23] and it is perhaps inevitable that that charged rhetoric of a freedom contingent upon subjugation crystallized around questions of race in the nineteenth-century American racial state. Marking that crystallization, Maisha L. Wester has shown that gothic writers in the early United States "mobilized the genre's tropes to mediate questions such as the legitimacy and prospects of American democracy, and the place of the racial Other within the new nation."[24] Wester's account establishes that one significant aspect of the gothic arose out of "notions that white and black relations would inevitably degrade, if not destroy, whites" and "fears of the racial Other as powerful, vengeful, and destructive," thus leading to "paranoia over maintaining distinct social boundaries."[25] In this case, the specific historical salience of the gothic exceeds its general racial "burden," in Hemenway's terms; as Teresa A. Goddu has argued, "the gothic's 'blackness' has strong historical connections to slavery: many male gothicists supported slavery, and the rise of the gothic novel in England (1790–1830) occurred during a period of increased debate over it."[26] An Englishman most famous for his gothic novel *The Monk* (1797), Lewis was himself an enslaver.

Those debates over slavery had their parallels in the arguments around Irish political aspiration, even if the conditions of Black and Irish oppression were far from equivalent. At times, the webs of association are tentative and suggestive, hiding in the seemingly accidental patterns of punning, verbal substitutions, and analogy rather than on the level of overt plot. What this chapter will explore is the ways in which Lewis and Poe, two authors from opposite sides of the Atlantic, deployed the generic force of the gothic to juxtapose Irishness and Blackness. Through that very juxtaposition, I argue, these tales of mystery depend upon notions of similarity but fail to articulate difference, ultimately subtending the constructions of racial ideology that Morrison located in the American development of gothic romance.

A set of interwoven representations of Irishness, slavery, and imperial violence, couched within the tropes of the gothic, arises in Lewis's tale of secret inheritance, colonial threat, and rhetorical misprision, "The Anaconda." In this story, Lewis cannily brings into proximity apparitional hints of Irish and Black alterity through the mediating image of South Asian coloniality, a rhetorical conjuring made possibly by his reliance on the gothic. When his *Journal of a West India Proprietor* was posthumously published in 1834, its title page insistently advertised his gothic authorship: "Author of 'The Monk,' 'The Castle Spectre,' 'Tales of Wonder,' &c." That title page further included a jingle from Lord Byron that suggestively linked the slave economy, fundamental to the narrative of the *Journal*, to Lewis's literary significance (which Byron did not rate overly highly): "I would give many a sugar cane, / Mat. Lewis were alive again!"[27] In an 1818 entry in the *Journal*, Lewis echoes Edgeworth (and Bryan Edwards) in a self-serving rhetorical performance of regretful resignation to slavery's inevitability, a resignation that permits him to appropriate the rhetoric of abolitionist sentiment while still figuring the material advantages of Black enslavement to white economic and political power as, sadly, necessary: "Every man of humanity must wish that slavery, even in its best and most mitigated form, had never found a legal sanction, and must regret that its system is now so incorporated with the welfare of Great Britain as well as of Jamaica, as to make its extirpation an absolute impossibility, without the certainty of producing worse mischiefs than the one which we annihilate."[28] Despite the deliberately impossible "wish" that chattel slavery had not become central to the global economy, he evokes an incipient version of scientific racism, arguing for a fundamental racial dichotomy between Black and white: "Naturalists and physicians, philosophers and philanthropists, may argue and decide as they please; but certainly, as far as mere observation admits of my judging, there does seem to be a very great difference between the brain of a black person and a white one. . . . Somehow or other, they never can manage to do anything *quite* as it should be done."[29] "The welfare . . . of Jamaica," for

Lewis, clearly does not extend to these enslaved people, nor does his understanding of "worse mischiefs" accommodate their lives or experiences.

"The Anaconda" opens with frame narrative: a debate around the origins of the wealth of an Englishman, Everard Brooke, recently returned from Ceylon (present-day Sri Lanka), which had been increasingly controlled by British interests since 1796. A Mrs. Milman, the aunt of Everard's fiancée, Jessy, has intuited from questioning his Ceylonese servant Mirza that he came into his wealth through the murder of his lover, a woman named Nancy O'Connor, who conspired with him to poison her rich husband or father (the aunt is unclear on the details) in order to obtain his wealth. Confronted with this accusation, Everard consents to tell his actual story, which he had hoped to keep confidential: he did not murder a woman named Nancy O'Connor (or Anne O'Connor, as his fiancée's aunt also gives the name) but, rather, killed an *anaconda* that was threatening the man for whom he worked as a secretary, an English plantation owner named Seafield. He was able to save Seafield long enough to become the heir to half his fortune and soon afterward, when Seafield's wife died, the entirety of it.

The generic transformation of the narrative from colonial adventure story, narrated by Everard, to what Julia M. Wright has called "Milman's gothic redaction"[30] occurs at the level of a verbal misunderstanding figured as a sort of linguistic joke, as the Ceylonese anaconda becomes "Anne O'Connor"; "an Irish family, I suppose," hypothesizes Mrs. Milman.[31] The line thereby drawn between Ireland and Ceylon indicates, in Wright's perceptive reading, both generic associations and racialized distinctions: "On Milman's malapropism—'Anaconda' altered to 'Anne O'Connor'—turns the tale. . . . Lewis's narrative thus draws clear, implicitly racial distinctions between colonial possessions: Ireland is the locus of sentimentality, and the East Indies are the locus of gothic terror; both Ireland and Ceylon are figured through the feminine, but, in the moral certainties of the gothic, one must be killed and the other must not."[32] Irish whiteness—figured in the vulnerability of the only-fantasized victim Anne O'Connor—produces by contrast the *non*whiteness of Ceylon, taking shape in the exotic, fascinating, seemingly preternatural, and deadly anaconda. And both emerge not only through Lewis's employment of the gothic but also through a comically failed "translation" that serves as a controlling metaphor for all of the other slippages of the tale, constructed as it is by a series of loose but misleading associations.

Ireland is not the only near-analogous colonial space that Lewis's tale brings into alignment with Ceylon through a set of allusive gestures. For while Everard's narrative is explicitly set in what Mrs. Milman calls "the East Indies" (5), the terms of its colonial alterity keep slipping toward the rhetoric of a different colonial space that Lewis had still more reason to be familiar with: the *West* Indies.[33] Underlying the tale's verbal games is a series of ambiguous terms that could similarly apply, sometimes with differences in connotation, to both Ceylon and Jamaica: the putatively murdered Anne O'Connor is "the daughter, or the wife of a rich planter" (11), a term that arose in the context of New World enslavement before migrating to Ireland and India;[34] Mirza is represented as speaking in a broadly racialized dialect ("you no say dat! Massa tell me no talk. . . . Massa grieve. . . . Massa angry" [22]);[35] while the Ceylonese characters are sometimes described as "servants" or "attendants," they are also frequently designated as "slaves" (e.g., 31, 69, 94, 95).[36] Freedom from enslavement is offered as an enticement (93) or reward (108) to Ceylonese characters, suggesting that their relationship to the British colonizers is not one of contractual employment. As Lisa Lowe has compellingly revealed, the racialization of colonial servitude provided the fantasy of freely contracted wage labor in the aftermath of abolition: "While antislavery ideas prevailed in Britain, indentured labor in the colonies could be represented as part of a system of free labor that appeared commensurate with ideas of free labor at home."[37] Britain's 1807 abolition of the Atlantic slave trade—but not colonial slavery—is an immediate context for the publication of "The Anaconda," with its confused racializations and designations of labor, just a year later.

The text's (or its narrators') understanding of Mirza's race itself seems to slip between categories. Mrs. Milman calls him a "little coffee-coloured barbarian" (9) as well as a "little copper-coloured hottentot" (21). She also, with similar racial nonchalance, deplores Everard's life "among tigers and alligators that swallow up poor dear little children at a mouthful, and great ugly black-a-moor monsters, who eat nothing but human flesh" (4). It is certainly the case that the narrative satirizes Mrs. Milman's geographical and anthropological ignorance, but it also uses the comic potential of that ignorance to highlight the rhetorical slippages of empire: from Ceylon to the Southern Africa of the Khoekhoen (the derogatively designated "hottentots"); from the geographical distribution of copper, including in northern Europe, to that of coffee, which by the late eighteenth century was largely centered in the slave states both of the New World and the East Indies;[38] from the "alligator," which usually names a crocodilian native to the Americas, to the "tiger," which could specifically name an Asian animal but also, suggestively, the jaguar of the Americas or the leopard of South Africa.[39]

This series of conflations makes of "The Anaconda" a nineteenth-century instance of what Ashley L. Cohen has identified as the late eighteenth-century "conceptual pairing of the two Indies" as an "Indies mentality,"[40] what she has elsewhere described as "a worldview in which the Atlantic and Indian Ocean regions form a single unit of analysis" through their "common name."[41] Lewis's tale enacts that conceptual proximity within the colonial imaginary through its reliance on the gothic, specifically *as* a literary mode that foregrounds both terror and a commitment to the encrypted, traumatic histories both of families and of nations.[42] In a telling linguistic development that Lewis likely could not have predicted—although his tale foreshadows it—the term "anaconda," while applied in the eighteenth century to Sri Lankan snakes, would in the nineteenth century come to name a South American boa.[43] Gothicized Ireland is somehow like Ceylon, which is somehow like both Southern Africa and Haiti or Brazil. The associations that Lewis both suggests and disavows are underwritten by a set of explicitly literary, even linguistic, forms of punning: as one notion of "the Indies" slides into another, so does an anaconda become "Anne O'Connor."

Even while it smudges some distinctions, though, Lewis's text subscribes to others. Building on Patrick Brantlinger's work on subgenres of the gothic, Wright has proposed that "the Anglo-Irish Gothic is arguably the earliest sustained expression of the imperial Gothic; written from the perspective of a settler class 'isolated from and threatened by the overwhelming majority of the unfranchised and confiscated Catholic native Irish,' it addresses the anxiety over proper lines of inheritance introduced in Horace Walpole's *The Castle of Otranto* (1764)."[44] But she adds an important distinction: "Brantlinger uses the term 'imperial gothic' to refer to a body of British fiction about distant spaces in relation to conquest; I use 'colonial gothic' here to refer to gothic literature written from and about the colonial space (whatever the author's position within that space). Unable to access the proprietorial simplicities which underpin English domestic gothic's concerns with proper lines of inheritance, Anglo-Irish gothic—and perhaps colonial gothic in general—is haunted by the violence which marks the origin of imperial property."[45] Wright's designation of the "colonial gothic" aptly names the cultural and political work that a narrative like "The Anaconda" performs, with all of the fascinations and anxieties that its phenomenological impact entails for the white colonist subject.

It also, I propose, applies with a similar political charge to what we might think of as the settler-colonial gothic of the United States. And, in particular, I want to turn here to Edgar Allan Poe's race-haunted short story "The Gold-Bug" as it brings the gothic—indeed, a specifically Anglo-Irish gothic—to bear on the understanding of race, slavery, and white supremacy in America. As I have observed in this book's introduction, it was Poe whom Oscar Wilde, on his tour of the United States, both compared to the Irish nationalist writer James Clarence Mangan and—in the context of Wilde's praise of Jefferson Davis—designated "the best poet of America." Himself of Ulster Protestant descent and the author of what Mary Burke has identified as "Scots-Irish Gothic,"[46] Poe stands as an important translator of gothic modes into the American context, even as he also contributes to the literature of racial caricature and white dominance in the setting of the southern United States.[47] And, I propose in this chapter, in "The Gold-Bug," Irishness both subtends and haunts Poe's gothic representation of race.

"The Gold-Bug" narrates the search for a buried treasure by William Legrand, "of an ancient Huguenot family," with the assistance of an encrypted message on old parchment and a mysterious scarab-like beetle, along with the narrator and "an old negro, called Jupiter, who had been manumitted before the reverses of the family, but who could be induced, neither by threats nor by promises, to abandon what he considered his right of attendance upon the footsteps of his young 'Massa Will.'"[48] "The Gold-Bug," it is true, is not explicitly in the mode of terror that characterizes such other Poe stories of the 1840s as "The Tell-Tale Heart," "The Black Cat," and "The Cask of Amontillado." Nevertheless, this tale of obsession, suspected madness, a literally buried past, and a human skull draws on gothic resonances and forms that had by the early decades of the nineteenth century become an important mode of literature of and about both Ireland and race.

Poe's biographer Terence Whalen notes that "The Gold-Bug" is one of only two, among Poe's more than sixty tales, to be set explicitly in the American South, and its racial politics have attracted considerable scholarly attention.[49] "Jupiter," writes Leonard Cassuto, "is a typical Sambo: a laughing and japing comic figure whose doglike devotion is matched only by his stupidity," and the tale itself offers a "beatific vision of slavery" that "enriches all involved."[50] Scott Peeples concurs, calling Jupiter "a minstrel-show sidekick whose main functions are to provide dialect humor and, through his stupidity, highlight Legrand's ingenuity."[51] Morrison, however, identifies a less stable racial representation. On the one hand, she emphasizes, "We can look to 'The Gold-Bug'. . . for the literary techniques of 'othering' so common to American literature: estranging language, metaphoric condensation, fetishizing strategies, the economy of stereotype, allegorical foreclosure." On the other hand, though, she reveals some oddly persistent countervailing instances, what she calls "unmanageable slips," most notably that "the black slave Jupiter is said to whip his master." She thus highlights the tale's complex, even contradictory, representation of the structures of power as well as its textual games.[52] Answering Morrison's call for a multivalent and nuanced analysis, Goddu has likewise advocated for "a more comprehensive and complex consideration of slavery and race in Poe's work" that would attend to his multiple sources and cultural discourses, including "the specific—and slippery—ways he deploys genre in his writings about race."[53] Jupiter's refusal to leave Legrand after his emancipation indeed echoes a generic racist fantasy, but it also hints at a counterintuitive form of resistance to genericism, manifesting in Jupiter's insistent individuality, his "right of attendance," his refusal of fungibility and replaceability.

Genre, as Goddu proposes, matters to the way "The Gold-Bug" contributes to the literature of nineteenth-century racialization. In a deconstructive analysis of Poe's tales, Leland S. Person has posited that "first-person psychological romance in the Gothic or sensational mode represented an ideal vehicle for representing and destabilizing the psychological constructs of white male racism."⁵⁴ "The Gold-Bug" certainly offers a number of such intradiegetic tropes for misdirection, encoding, and substitution. There is, for example, Legrand's sketch of the scarab on a piece of parchment that mysteriously becomes the image of a skull through the appearance of invisible ink after the accidental application of heat: "When I had completed the drawing," says Legrand, "I gave it to you [the narrator of the story], and observed you narrowly until you returned it. *You*, therefore, did not design the skull, and no one else was present to do it. Then it was not done by human agency. And nevertheless it was done" (25). The image that emerges—the skull—makes of the parchment a palimpsest, almost as though it completes the sketch that has been drawn inadvertently upon it: "You recollect," says Legrand, "that I became quite vexed at you for insisting that my drawing resembled a death's-head. When you first made this assertion I thought you were jesting; but afterwards I called to mind the peculiar spots on the back of the insect, and admitted to myself that your remark had some little foundation in fact" (22). The invisible ink, on the surface of the paper and yet unseen until manifested by heat, combines with the *visible* sketch to produce a hybrid of skull and beetle: text and subtext uncannily conjoin to produce the sign of the gothic within the tale of treasure hunting.

The relationship between the sketch of the beetle and the hidden drawing of the skull—a relationship that Legrand initially attributes to mere visual similarity—turns out to be spatial as well, as the beetle has been drawn exactly upon the (invisible) image of the skull: "My first idea, now, was mere surprise at the really remarkable similarity of outline—at the singular coincidence involved in the fact, that unknown to me, there should have been a skull upon the other side of the parchment, immediately beneath my figure of the *scarabæus,* and that this skull, not only in outline, but in size, should so closely resemble my drawing" (22–23). The skull is not the only image to emerge from the formerly invisible ink: there is also a rebus-like representation of a young goat—a kid—which by means of what Legrand calls "a kind of punning or hieroglyphical signature" (reminiscent of Lewis's punning association of the anaconda with "Anne O'Connor") refers to Captain Kidd, the pirate (26). And a further appearance of obscured text offers a field of numbers and symbols that Legrand translates as a simple substitution cypher to provide a message that *itself* must be read by means of various misdirections: "Bishop's hostel" in the parchment's instructions, for example, leads Legrand to "Bessop's Castle," which is "not a castle, nor a tavern, but a high rock" (33). Signifiers here seem always to deviate from their expected meaning, and yet they nonetheless signify. Following the decrypted message, Legrand finds the precise location at which he can drop the scarab through the eye of a skull to produce a plumb line that will indicate a point that then defines a line that leads to the buried treasure. He thereby juxtaposes in physical space the beetle and the skull that the textual space of the parchment had similarly overlain.[55] The tale thus doubles its own doubling: whereas, at the beginning of the story, Legrand's drawing accidentally refigures the unseen image of the skull as an illustrated beetle, at its climax the solution to the mystery requires the coordinated deployment of both skull and beetle in embodied relation.

That emphasis on substitutive doubling points simultaneously to the correlating effects of generic categories, to the brutal work of enslavement with its reduction of persons to fungible objects, and to the conflations of Irish and Black histories and experiences. Well might Legrand declare that "the singularity of this coincidence absolutely stupefied me for a time. This is the usual effect of such coincidences. The mind struggles to establish a connexion—a sequence of cause and effect—and, being unable to do so, suffers a species of temporary paralysis" (23). The tale, in fact, hinges on a double meaning of "coincidence," not only in its meaning as chance but also in its (related and older) suggestion of multiple things existing in the same place or time at once, that is, a correspondence or contiguity. For the story centers not only what we might think of as *accident* but also the vicissitudes of multiply nested *signification*: a palimpsest that reveals a rebus that indicates the presence of a cypher that, decrypted, produces a message that must be interpreted in order to determine a line in space that literally points to a treasure. This logic of signification and substitution might suggest a symbolic rebus through which racial categories as well slip into each other, one pointing to the other; that is, in fact, how Bridget T. Heneghan has read Poe's "The Devil in the Belfry" as evoking the race riots of 1830s Philadelphia by shuffling the signifiers of Blackness and of Irishness: "With his snuff-colored face and black suit of clothes, the devil remains indeterminately raced: he is dark like a clock hand, or like an African American slave, or like a lower-class worker.... Poe has him playing the Irish songs 'Judy O'Flannagan and Paddy O'Rafferty,' emphasizing the Irish folk music which comprised much of minstrelsy's songs and the Irish immigrant majority among minstrelsy audiences and actors."[56] Irishness and Blackness, in Heneghan's reading of Poe, seem themselves to exist in a sort of palimpsestic relation like the drawing of the scarab and the skull in "The Gold-Bug," each overwriting the other in a shimmering play of metonymic signification that flickers in and out of legibility.

Indeed, in a note to his 1856 rendering of "The Gold-Bug" into French, Charles Baudelaire strikes upon a telling cultural reference to ethnic substitution even in the midst of arguing for the *untranslatability* of Poe's racialized jargon in his representation of Jupiter's speech:

> La prononciation du mot *antennæ* fait commettre une méprise au nègre, qui croi qu'il est question d'étain: *Dey aint no tin in him.* Calembour intraduisible. Le nègre parlera toujours dans une espèce de patois anglais, que le patois nègre français n'imiterait pas mieux que le bas normand ou le breton ne traduirait l'irelandais.

> [The pronunciation of the word *antennae* makes the Black man commit a mistake, in that he believes that it is a question of *tin: Dey aint no tin in him.* Untranslatable pun. The Black man always speaks in a sort of English dialect, which the French Negro dialect would not imitate any better than the Lower Norman or the Breton would translate Irish.][57]

As Michael Malouf points out, Baudelaire's explanation of his translation of Jupiter's speech is curious: "It is not clear what he is referring to as '*le patois nègre français*' given [that] there was no literary equivalent at the time."[58] And Clayton Tyler McKee observes that Baudelaire's odd reference collapses the story's own double presentation—its coincidence— of cyphers on the level of narration as well as that of plot while, at the same time, reducing the complexity of Jupiter's representation to "comic relief": "What one sees in translation is a complete change of Jupiter's role. Jupiter is no longer a sociolect that requires decoding like the treasure map but is reduced to an ex-slave character that fulfills acts as asked by the two White-American characters and who, despite speaking standard French, cannot totally understand it or be understood. The idea of decoding exists exclusively in the riddles and treasure map."[59] In closing off one version of linguistic complexity, though, Baudelaire opens a different one, or perhaps makes it readable against the surface of the text, like the emerging skull drawn in invisible ink. For even in his choice to resolve the problem of the "untranslatable pun" by evoking a putative equivalency that does not exist (the imagined translation of the "patois anglais" into the fantasized "patois nègre français"), Baudelaire simultaneously introduces another form of translation: the hypothesized equivalency of Jupiter's sociolect with the ostensibly untranslatable "irelandais."

Baudelaire's abrupt introduction of Irishness—as language and, perhaps, as nationality—may not be as unmotivated as it appears. This logic of signification and substitution in fact works structurally in the tale as well, a result toward which Legrand himself has gestured: "This reflection," he says, "suggested some meaning—some relevancy—in the death's-head. I did not fail to observe, also, the *form* of the parchment" (24; italics in original). So what might we observe about the *form* of "The Gold-Bug"? The first text that appears, following the title of the story, is an epigraph:

> What ho! what ho! this fellow is dancing mad!
> He hath been bitten by the Tarantula.
>
> *All in the Wrong.* (1)

While Poe's use of chapter—or, in this case, individual short story—epigraphs is, by the mid-1840s, by no means unique, it is nonetheless telling, in that it functions as a sort of formal allusion back through the novels of Walter Scott to the popularizing of chapter epigraphs by the gothic novelists of the late eighteenth and early nineteenth centuries, most notably the sensationally popular English author Ann Radcliffe.[60] Of the twelve stories that appeared in Poe's 1845 first edition of the collected *Tales*, fully ten were introduced by chapter epigraphs. (The two exceptions are "The Black Cat" and "Mesmeric Revelation.") The institution of the epigraph, a brief extract from other literature, itself represents a form of transposition that, at the same time, functions as a system of signification, "invit[ing] readers to 'pause' and approach a chapter's narrative in relation to poetic texts and canonical themes that they already know—or implicitly should already know," in Edward Jacobs's characterization.[61] The epigraph points to another work to frame the meaning of the present text; by a reverse move, it places the present text into the literary tradition represented by the older work, appropriating its cultural capital. Poe's reliance on the epigraph functions both as a translation of the formal conventions of the European gothic into American literature and as a gesture toward the gothic's own generically anxious translocation of extracts from earlier literature to bolster its literary authority.[62]

Poe was in fact keeping his eye on Irish—and gothic—literature in the years prior to his publication of "The Gold-Bug." Burton R. Pollin, tracing the resonances in Poe's fiction of the poetry of the Irish nationalist Thomas Moore, muses on the fact that "the Irish writer lived on so strongly in the mind and reading of Poe."[63] By 1829, Thomas Ollive Mabbott reports, Poe had "become a disciple of Thomas Moore," and "the last book he read [before his death] was Moore's *Irish Melodies*."[64] Indeed, in an 1841 review of Charles Dickens's *The Old Curiosity Shop*, just two years prior to the periodical publication of "The Gold-Bug," Poe abruptly swerved from Dickens to a consideration of Moore, calling him "the most skilful literary artist of his day—perhaps of any day—a man who stands in the singular and really wonderful predicament of being undervalued on account of the profusion with which he has scattered about him his good things."[65] Poe turned his attention as well to the Irish gothic in particular. In his "Letter to B—," published as the preface to *Poems* in 1831, Poe joked about the Irish gothicist Maturin's 1820 *Melmoth the Wanderer*, specifically highlighting the novel's vexed relationship of form to content and the generic scale of that relationship: "I should no doubt be tempted to think of the devil in Melmoth, who labors indefatigably, through three octavo volumes, to accomplish the destruction of one or two souls, while any common devil would have demolished one or two thousand."[66] The fact that the Richmond-based *Southern Literary Messenger* republished excerpts from the "Letter," including this passage, in July 1836, when Poe was an editor of the magazine, suggests his interest in arguing for the relevance of this generic joke on the Irish gothic to the literary culture of the American South. It seems that Irish genres, for Poe, are themselves "scattering about [them their] good things," a detritus that he collects and refigures in his own writings.

An instantiation of that aggregative urge, Poe's epigraph to "The Gold-Bug" is excerpted neither from Shakespeare, as the bulk of Radcliffe's are, nor from a classical author, the typical source for the epigraphs to eighteenth-century moral fiction (a tradition that Poe picks up on with his epigraph from Seneca for "The Purloined Letter"). Instead, the epigraph states, it is borrowed from *All in the Wrong* (1761), by the Irish playwright Arthur Murphy, not quite a Shakespeare or a Seneca but still a European source transferred into Poe's insistently American setting. The content of the epigraph, though, is almost uncomfortably apposite, the tarantula's compulsive bite framing a story of obsession instigated by the tale's eponymous bug. As Legrand says of the scarab, "Upon my taking hold of it, it gave me a sharp bite, which caused me to let it drop" (23). Asked by the narrator whether he actually believes that "your master was really bitten by the beetle, and that the bite made him sick," Jupiter responds, "I do n't tink noffin about it—I nose it. What make him dream bout de goole so much, if taint cause he bit by de goole-bug?" (7). The bite, in Poe's tale as in his epigraphic quotation from Murphy, spreads madness.

Thus far, the epigraph's transfer into the story makes sense. But its *failures* to align—to translate—quickly add up. A scarab beetle is, of course, hardly anything like a tarantula, and a spider is not an insect. Even if both might be described as "bugs," the tarantula could not be mistaken for gold. Perhaps most significantly, the quotation is not, in fact, from *All in the Wrong*—a play in which the word "tarantula" does not appear—but is instead a paraphrase of a line from a different Murphy play, *No One's Enemy but His Own* (1764).[67] The authoritative and authorizing weight of the attributed epigraph collapses even before the tale begins. Perhaps the attribution should have warned us: "all in the wrong," indeed. Textual translocation here seems both to work and not to work, to name a truth and to tell a lie. It *almost* translates, but not quite. And it is, I would argue, significant not only that Arthur Murphy was an Irish playwright but that he began his (unsuccessful) career as an actor on the London stage by playing the role of Othello, in 1754, in Covent Garden.⁶⁸ In a symbolic transfiguration, the Irish-born white actor playing, in blackface, Shakespeare's Moor becomes for Poe the source for an Irish epigraph with which to open his tale of obsession and race in the American South. Or, rather, *not* the source, as both the attribution and the text have become transformed as though by a faulty translation.

The epigraph, that is, highlights its own *mistranslation* of Irish modes into the American context of race and enslavement. And the epistemological problem of the epigraph both frames and mirrors the interpretive problem of Jupiter's idiolect, about which Ambrose E. Gonzales wrote that Poe "put into the mouth of a Charleston Negro such vocables as might have been used by a black sailor on an English ship a hundred years ago, or on the minstrel stage, but were never current on the South Carolina coast."⁶⁹ As Liliane Weissberg puts it, "Jupiter's dialect designates him as different, but it does not ground its speaker in a specific geographic and cultural setting." But, Weissberg continues, "This may, however, be precisely the point. Poe not only turns an island into a wilderness but also erases all traces of an island population, although he finds a person who is knowledgeable enough to show the narrator a rock that would correspond to an 'obsolete word.'"⁷⁰ In an early version of her argument about the haunting presence of Blackness in canonical American literature, Morrison observed, "It could never have occurred to Edgar Allan Poe in 1848 that I, for example, might read 'The Gold-Bug' and watch his efforts to render my grandfather's speech to something as close to braying as possible, an effort so intense you can see the perspiration—and the stupidity—when Jupiter says, 'I knows,' and Mr. Poe spells the verb 'nose.'"⁷¹

In a tale in which the gothic plot of encryption and buried violence is troped by the emergence of the image of a skull, of all things—that is, a symbol that has to be read, in a pun that postdates Poe's narrative, as almost embarrassingly "on the nose"⁷²—Jupiter's malapropisms themselves become versions of the "Irish bull," what Brian Earls has characterized as "a comic contradiction between two of [a spoken utterance's] component parts of which the speaker is unaware but which is perceived by the person who has recorded the anecdote and by his readers."⁷³ And yet, like the utterances of the eponymous Mrs. Malaprop in *The Rivals* (1775), written by the Irish playwright and politician Richard Brinsley Sheridan, the Irish bull, in its very incoherence, expresses something. As Richard Lovell Edgeworth and Maria Edgeworth write in their 1802 *Essay on Irish Bulls*, the bull might be thought of as constituted by "a certain *laughable confusion of ideas*"; yet, from another perspective, "whether to call it a confusion of expression or of ideas, I can't tell."[74] That there might—somehow—be meaning in the Irish bull is suggested by the witticism, attributed to John Pentland Mahaffy, a Trinity College professor who taught Oscar Wilde, that "an Irish Bull . . . is always pregnant."[75] Like an Irish bull, like Jupiter's racialized dialect, and like the invisible ink that represents a buried meaning by being in fact on the very surface of the parchment, the suggestively Irish epigraph, misquoted and misattributed, both frames and fails to explain the American racial narrative that follows it. In the end, "The Gold-Bug" is a version of the gothic that is not quite gothic, including a castle that isn't a castle and a kid that isn't a kid, an allusion to Irishness that never quite gets clinched, a narrative of race that insists upon linguistic signs that don't reach the requirements of verisimilitude.

This satirical coyness is not, of course, the only way that the European gothic—and its potential radicalism in the context of early nineteenth-century Irish nationalism—could be translocated into an analysis of race and enslavement in the United States. Despite the entanglement of some aspects of the gothic with racist violence, Wester rightly shows that it could also be taken up by nineteenth-century Black Americans, including Frederick Douglass, Henry Walton Bibb, and Harriet Jacobs, and turned back on the institutions of white supremacy and chattel enslavement as a form of radical critique, a move that Teresa Goddu has dubbed "haunting back."[76] "Generations of black writers," Wester relates, "repeatedly return to this notion of slavery as a haunted and haunting institution, marking slavery as the inescapable, tumultuous past impeding their progress."[77] That mobilization of the gothic mode represents an active intervention, as both Wester and Goddu demonstrate: "By making the reader enter his narrative of slavery through the conventions of the gothic," Goddu writes, "Douglass discloses how the spectacle of slavery is mediated and structured generically. . . . However, in using gothic conventions, Douglass marks the differences as well as the similarities between gothic narrative and gothic history."[78] It matters, first and foremost, that Douglass and Jacobs tell their own stories not in the mode of romance but with the stark immediacy of autobiography, that which in fact happened. (The danger of slippage between those modes, as well as the bravery of publication, is underlined by Jacobs's own announcement, in her preface to the *Incidents*—representing her experiences under a fictional name—"Reader, be assured this narrative is no fiction" [5]; Lydia Maria Child similarly gestured, in her introduction to Jacobs's *Incidents,* to the challenge of generic ambiguity: "Those who know her will not be disposed to doubt her veracity, though some incidents in her story are more romantic than fiction.")[79] It is also significant that this literary mode, so frequently obsessed with the elaboration of contracts,[80] would be taken up to describe the experiences of those who, explicitly, were excluded from contractual agency. "The reader probably knows," Jacobs writes, "that no promise or writing given to a slave is legally binding; for, according to Southern laws, a slave, *being* property, can *hold* no property" (13).

What the mode of the gothic does is provide a set of literary tropes and affects through which the horrors of the real experience of enslavement can be articulated, albeit never fully. As Wester points out, the "horrific torments and 'escape'" that characterize the sensational terrors of the European gothic "are the norm in slavery."[81] In Douglass's *Narrative*, indeed, the figuration is explicit: "On the one hand," he writes, describing his thoughts before a planned escape, "there stood slavery, a stern reality, glaring frightfully upon us,—its robes already crimsoned with the blood of millions, and even now feasting itself greedily upon our own flesh. . . . Upon either side, we saw grim death, assuming the most horrid shapes" (85). Describing the horrors of the European gothic novel, Eve Kosofsky Sedgwick mused that "no nightmare is ever as terrifying as is waking up from even some innocuous dream *to find it true.*"[82] Douglass's experience is far from innocuous, but the theory holds; slavery is, in his account, a vampire, a monster, a cannibal, that is, a gothic nightmare come to life.[83]

The gestures toward and transformations of gothic conventions in the works of African American writers have become central to the critical understanding of the nineteenth-century narratives of enslavement and escape. Daneen Wardrop, for example, has catalogued the many tropes commonly associated with the gothic that appear in Jacobs's *Incidents:* "the family with a secret; the doubling or the *Doppelgänger* effect; the presence of a rapacious, imposing villain; graveyard scenes; uncanny occurrences including ghosts; the intrigues of letter exchanges; and panoply of spying activities, featuring windows, keys, latches, cracks that are whispered through, and trap-doors."[84] Wester makes the specific point that "Jacobs's description of the punishment and death of a slave in a cotton gin especially echoes gothic terrors over premature burial."[85] That horrific passage presages Jacobs's famous gothically inflected account of her own yearslong confinement, in her "loophole of retreat" (173), a term she takes from the eighteenth-century English poet William Cowper,[86] and which space she also calls a "dungeon" (192):

> To this hole I was conveyed as soon as I entered the house. The air was stifling; the darkness total. . . . The rats and mice ran over my bed; but I was weary, and I slept such sleep as the wretched may, when a tempest has passed over them. Morning came. I knew it only by the noises I heard; for in my small den day and night were all the same. I suffered for air even more than for light. . . . This continued darkness was oppressive. It seemed horrible to sit or lie in a cramped position day after day, without one gleam of light. (173–74)

In Jacobs's hands, that is, the gothic could be a form of protest, a naming of the horrors of enslavement.

Similarly, Douglass, early in his *Narrative,* evokes the gothic in his account of the whipping of Aunt Hester, an account that stresses the sexualized violence of enslavement while he also designates it "the blood-stained gate, the entrance to the hell of slavery," leaving the young Douglass "terrified and horror-stricken at the sight" of the "bloody transaction" (6–8). Goddu makes the case that Douglass's description "plays up but also resists its gothic effects. . . . It offers the reader the villain and the maiden but transposes their conventional associations: the black villain is white and the virginal, innocent maiden is a black slave. As the viewer of, rather than a participant in, this infernal scene, Douglass signifies against white narratives of gothic spectatorship. Framing the scene with his response to it, Douglass both plays to northern readers' sympathy and critiques their voyeurism."[87] Saidiya Hartman, declining to reproduce Douglass's description of the scene, likewise frames it in terms of gothic affect: "Only more obscene than the brutality unleashed at the whipping post is the demand that this suffering be materialized and evidenced by the display of the tortured body or endless recitations of the ghastly and the terrible."[88] In the hands of these writers, that is, the gothic could become the generic form that radical resistance takes, as it was for the early nineteenth-century Irish nationalists.

This is, perhaps needless to say, a different translocation of the gothic to the United States than is Poe's. That is, in Goddu's words, "The gothic might offer useful metaphors for depicting the historical event of slavery, but its narrative construction could also empty slavery of history by turning it into a gothic trope."[89] Even a writer like Harriet Beecher Stowe, in Goddu's keen analysis, "demonstrates how the gothic can resurrect or dematerialize history by turning it into a fiction; the gothic might allow the objects of terror to haunt back, but it also offers its viewer an avenue of escape."[90] That is a fair reading of Poe's treasure hunt, ultimately successful as it is for his white protagonist. Douglass and Jacobs refuse to offer that generic consolation. And, of course, while Poe figures the Black man as a sort of puzzle to be solved or tool to be used by the white subjects whose quest anchors the gothic tale, Jacobs and Douglass center Black agency, Black artistry, and the reality of Black lives in their generic transpositions. If Jacobs and Douglass bring the potentially radical energies of the gothic to the United States by transfiguring them, Poe enervates them by transforming them into a sort of parlor game.

While the particular significance of the gothic to Irish nationalist political activism—an activism that Douglass certainly considered deeply as he was publishing the *Narrative* and in the years immediately following—is less central to either of these texts than is the evocation of gothic modes more generally, Ireland and the Irish are in fact not totally absent from either. It is striking that, in the same chapter in which he recalls his admiration for Arthur O'Connor's speech in Parliament in support of Catholic enfranchisement, Douglass situates his self-emancipation from enslavement and his entry into abolitionist action in the context of a conversation with "two Irishmen":

> From this time I understood the words *abolition* and *abolitionist,* and always drew near when that word was spoken, expecting to hear something of importance to myself and fellow-slaves. The light broke in upon me by degrees. I went one day down on the wharf of Mr. Waters; and seeing two Irishmen unloading a scow of stone, I went, unasked, and helped them. When we had finished, one of them came to me and asked me if I were a slave. I told him I was. He asked, "Are ye a slave for life?" I told him that I was. The good Irishman seemed to be deeply affected by the statement. He said to the other that it was a pity so fine a little fellow as myself should be a slave for life. He said it was a shame to hold me. They both advised me to run away to the north; that I should find friends there, and that I should be free. I pretended not to be interested in what they said, and treated them as if I did not understand them; for I feared they might be treacherous. White men have been known to encourage slaves to escape, and then, to get the reward, catch them and return them to their masters. I was afraid that these seemingly good men might use me so; but I nevertheless remembered their advice, and from that time I resolved to run away.... Meanwhile I would learn to write. (42–43)

William Lloyd Garrison, in his preface to Douglass's *Narrative,* adduces Daniel O'Connell's Irish nationalism as part of his argument for African American fortitude and almost superhuman strength in the face of enslavement, an argument that takes on its own gothic tones: "It may, perhaps, be fairly questioned, whether any other portion of the population of the earth could have endured the privations, sufferings and horrors of slavery, without having become more degraded in the scale of humanity than the slaves of African descent. Nothing has been left undone to cripple their intellects, darken their minds, debase their moral nature, obliterate all traces of their relationship to mankind; and yet how wonderfully they have sustained the mighty load of a most frightful bondage, under which they have been groaning for centuries!" Moving from this to O'Connell—whom he designates "the distinguished advocate of universal emancipation, and the mightiest champion of prostrate but not conquered Ireland"—Garrison not only evokes both his persistent advocacy for abolition in the United States and his Irish political achievement; he also puts Douglass's text in conversation with the Irish quest for political enfranchisement and repeal of the Union.[91] But the Irish argument is not equivalent to the argument against human chattel enslavement, whatever well-meaning (and less well-meaning) writers might assert. Douglass's own ultimate disappointment in the racism of Irish Americans, in that failed translation of liberatory spirit in its translocation across the Atlantic, might stand as an instance of his astute caution about white treachery, in a situation less personally hazardous but of broad national significance in the years leading up to the American Civil War: "I was afraid that these seemingly good men might use me so."

In a similarly monitory move, Jacobs's description of her return to New York from England opens with the tropes of the gothic and concludes with an account of Irish American anti-Black racism put explicitly into the service of interethnic white solidarity:

> We had a tedious winter passage, and from the distance spectres seemed to rise up on the shores of the United States. It is a sad feeling to be afraid of one's native country. . . . Benny [the pseudonym the narrative gives her son] was not there to welcome me. He had been left at a good place to learn a trade, and for several months every thing worked well. He was liked by the master, and was a favorite with his fellow-apprentices; but one day they accidentally discovered a fact they had never before suspected—that he was colored! This at once transformed him into a different being. Some of the apprentices were Americans, others American-born Irish; and it was offensive to their dignity to have a "n[—]" among them, after they had been told he *was* a "n[—]." (279; italics in original)

Beginning with her description of her own country as a gothic land inhabited by spectres, Jacobs persistently evokes the rhetorics of migration and transformation as the keywords for the ruptures produced by American racism, including that of those "American-born Irish": that with the introduction of the chilling word of racial hatred, Benny is "transformed into a different being," that even Irish American otherness in relationship to the norms of United States citizenship (the fact that those "American-born

Irish" aren't *quite* the same as the "Americans") does nothing to obstruct their rush toward white supremacist bonding. As Jacobs insists, directly confronting the disingenuous suggestion that the experience of the enslaved Black person might be thought cognate with that of the Irish, whatever political and cultural disadvantages they might experience, "I would ten thousand times rather that my children should be the half-starved paupers of Ireland than to be the most pampered among the slaves of America" (49). It is a sentiment that echoes a similar claim that Jacobs had made earlier, in a letter to the white abolitionist Amy Kirby Post, with whom she had lived after her self-emancipation: "Far better to have been one of the starving poor of Ireland whose bones had to bleach on the highways than to have been a slave with the curse of slavery stamped upon yourself and Children."[92] Like Nicholson's, Jacobs's language suggests that Irish history might, indeed, be a gothic history replete with bleached bones, and the history of enslavement might as well; but Jacobs recognizes that that does not mean they are the same. Not all translocations of the tropes of the gothic into accounts of American race and slavery are adequate translations. If the comparative bloodlessness of Poe's linguistic games of gothic transposition demonstrates anything, it is that.

3

From Irish Bardicism to the White Nationalist Verse Epic

> Still Europe's saints, that mark the motes alone
> In other's eyes, yet never see their own,
> Grieve that the slave is never taught to write,
> And reads no better than the hireling white;
> Do their own plowmen no instruction lack,
> Have whiter clowns more knowledge than the black?
> Has the French peasant, or the German boor,
> Of learning's treasure any larger store;
> Have Ireland's millions, flying from the rule
> Of those who censure, ever known a school?
> —William J. Grayson, "The Hireling and the Slave" (1854)

IN 1854, THE FORMER United States representative from South Carolina William J. Grayson published a poem titled "The Hireling and the Slave." Generically, the poem exemplifies that eighteenth- and nineteenth-century oddity, the polemical tract in the form of an epic poem, around 1,500 lines of heroic couplets arguing for the superior situation of enslaved Black people in the American South to that of impoverished wage-earning whites in its North. Suggestive in form of Alexander Pope's satires, as well as some of Jonathan Swift's, it also specifically evokes Irish hardship and Irish labor, in both Ireland and the United States, as touchstones for its own racial politics of white superiority.

What I argue in this chapter is that "The Hireling and the Slave"—along with its companion poem "Chicora"—exemplifies the cynical manipulation of Irish American economic precarity by a proslavery writer precisely through an insistence upon Irish whiteness, forged into a rhetorical tool to split any potential Black and green coalition in the years leading up to the American Civil War. Grayson was not Irish, but his Charleston-based publisher, James Jefferson McCarter, was the son of an Irish immigrant; the publication of this group of poems is but one point among the range of ways in which Irish literary labor bolstered the dissemination of white supremacist ideas in the midcentury United States.[1] Indeed, Grayson's poems themselves work through explicit invocation and transformation of Irish genres of poetic nationalism, particularly the bardic romance from Ossian to Thomas Moore. But rather than representing the voice of an anticolonial consciousness, Grayson unabashedly centers the voice of what he designates the "master race," using his verse to construct an explicitly ethno-nationalist bardicism as the generic form of a settler-colonial white supremacy. Irishness, in fact, serves as the very key to the work of white racial consolidation that Grayson's poems enact.

As literature, "The Hireling and the Slave" would hardly emerge from the mass of nineteenth-century polemics forced into verse, a fact which was observed within that century itself: the American academic William Peterfield Trent, then professor of English and history at the University of the South (and, soon thereafter, professor of English literature at Columbia University), in 1895 designated "The Hireling and the Slave" "a work which should be studied by all those who are interested in determining what is the greatest extent of aberration allowed to a sane and cultivated mind."[2] Nonetheless, the poem was successful enough that Grayson produced two new (somewhat changed and expanded) editions in 1856 and 1857.[3] The *Southern Literary Messenger*, which had published Edgar Allan Poe's "Letter to B—" in 1836, waxed eloquent on what it represented as the poem's merits:

> "The Hireling and the Slave" is a composition which will hold a permanent place in the country's literature and continue to call for the reader's admiration long after the truths it so gracefully embodies have been recognized by all the world, and this, because the work is no feeble imitation of English

models, but a genuine offshoot of the soil of the palmetto and the cotton plant. Though the form of the versification is old and familiar, the imagery and thought are original and glow with the light and warmth of the Carolina sun.[4]

For the *Literary Messenger*, the generic significance of "The Hireling and the Slave" is key to its regional relevance, as the journal twice juxtaposes those concepts in successive sentences: "no feeble imitation of English models, but a genuine offshoot of the soil of the palmetto and the cotton plant"; "Though the form of the versification is old and familiar, the imagery and thought are original and glow with the light and warmth of the Carolina sun." Genre here functions as the organizing field in which both formal similarity and national distinction can be articulated.

While it emphasizes the originality of Grayson's poem ("no feeble imitation"), the *Literary Messenger*'s panegyric itself echoes the tropes of Irish nationalist literary ambition. The Young Irelander Thomas Davis's 1846 review of Charles Gavan Duffy's nationalist anthology, *The Ballad Poetry of Ireland*, for instance, similarly aligned poetic accomplishment and emergent national identity: "In possessing the powers and elements of a glorious nationality, we owned the sources of a national poetry. In the combination and joint development of the latter, we find a pledge and a help to that of the former."[5] Davis himself—one of Oscar Wilde's "Irish Poets of 1848"—is a key figure in the nineteenth-century deployment of generic adaptation in the interest of nationalist aspiration, transforming Thomas Moore's lyrically nationalist ballads into a militant mode.[6] But Davis's vision of nationalist poetics was explicitly *anti*racial (at least, that is, within the context of a splintered whiteness), alluding to the language of midcentury race science only to dismantle it: "Such nationality as could stand against internal faction and foreign intrigue, such nationality, as would make the Irish hearth happy and the Irish name illustrious, is becoming understood. It must contain and represent the races of Ireland. It must not be Celtic, it must not be Saxon—it must be Irish."[7] For Grayson as for the *Southern Literary Messenger*, however, the nationalist argument is *explicitly* predicated on racial division and white racial dominance; as even Grayson's title suggests, his is a national poetics of dichotomy and separation, of what he figures as the biological determinants that eternally divide "the hireling" from "the slave" along racial lines. Such are "the truths" that the *Literary Messenger* eagerly anticipates being "recognized by all the world" while they also "hold a permanent place in the country's literature." Whereas the Irish nationalist newspaper the *Nation*—founded in 1842 by Duffy and Davis, along with John Blake Dillon—used the masthead phrase "racy of the soil" to evoke its imagined relationship between the land and national identity,[8] the "genuine offshoot of the soil" for Grayson's poem is the violent enforcement of race itself.

The *Literary Messenger*'s encomium to Grayson's celebration of the American system of Black chattel enslavement both gestures toward and deflects a certain anxiety about this sort of protonationalist literary regionalism: the suspicion that it might *simply* be copying its generic antecedents. And, indeed, one of the signal characteristics of "The Hireling and the Slave" is its utter banality. Despite the *Literary Messenger*'s effusions to the contrary, the poem is not in any way original but literally and figuratively generic, in both its forthright racism and its form. At the same time, that is why Grayson's text is an exemplary one for this study tracing the transformation of literary forms of Irish nationalism into those of white supremacy: he provides a paradigmatic instance of the practice and for that reason, if for no other, is worth paying attention to. Even his title is an echo, taken from the third verse of "The Star-Spangled Banner," by the enslaver and antiabolitionist lawyer Francis Scott Key: "No refuge could save the hireling and slave, / From the terror of flight, or the gloom of the grave."[9] While Key's poem would not become the national anthem of the United States for decades yet, it was increasingly anthologized in collections of American verse; Grayson's invocation of it as a sort of touchstone of literary nationalism places racial enslavement—in the "land of the free," no less—at the very heart of American identity.

The three short epigraphs with which Grayson frames his 1856 collection *The Hireling and the Slave, Chicora, and Other Poems* themselves tell a story that is both ideological and generic. The first comes from the gothic novelist and enslaver Matthew Gregory Lewis, extracted from his *Journal of a West India Proprietor*: "After all, Slavery in their case (the Jamaica slaves) is but another name for servitude."[10] The second, quoting Thomas Carlyle's *Latter-Day Pamphlets,* declares that "Irish whites have been long emancipated, and nobody asks them to work, or permits them to work, on condition of finding them potatoes."[11] In the 1856 collection, Grayson adds a third epigraph, taken from the British writer and botanist Amelia M. Murray's account of her travels, here specifically in the state of Georgia: "I never saw servants in any old English family more comfortable or more devoted; it is a relief to see any thing so patriarchal after the . . . Northern States. I would rather be a 'slave' here, than a grumbling, saucy 'help' there."[12] As Catherine Gallagher has observed, the sort of rhetoric that structures these extracts has deep roots in forms of British economic reform that pits white labor against Black enslavement: "Proslavery writers and other conservative critics of eighteenth-century society had used models of traditional paternalistic communities as norms from which to attack capitalist practices."[13] By surrounding Carlyle with Lewis and Murray, Grayson's epigraphs make clear how useful the Carlylean critique of industrialism could become for American racism.

The argument advanced by Grayson's juxtaposition of these particular quotations is not a particularly subtle one. For Lewis, surveying the human beings whom he himself enslaves, race-based chattel slavery is simply a sort of synonym for working-class employment "now that no more negroes can be forcibly carried away from Africa," as he explains in the *Journal.* In this account, in fact, the worst aspect of enslavement is not the enforced labor or the violation of human agency and integrity but the means of transportation, what he calls being "subjected to the horrors of the voyage"—"horrors" that he imagines himself able to comprehend as part of his own experience, albeit under completely different conditions. (Lewis would die of yellow fever in 1818 while returning from the visit to his Jamaican estates that provided the basis of the *Journal of a West India Proprietor.*) In fact, Lewis asserts immediately before the quotation that Grayson pulls for his epigraph that, "to be sure, I never saw people look more happy in my life; and I believe their condition to be much more comfortable than that of the labourers of Great Britain."[14] That is, of course, a particularly self-serving delusion for the enslaving Lewis, who nonetheless imagines himself to be a thoughtful man of conscience.

This insistence upon Black "comfort" with slavery, in putative contrast to the misery of white labor, is a sentiment that Murray, in the series of letters that Grayson would opportunistically ransack, echoes in her implausible insistence that she herself would prefer enslavement to working-class employment in the northern United States. Like Murray, Grayson turns enslavement into a fantasy of georgic rusticity in the grotesquely idyllic description, in "The Hireling and the Slave," of enslaved life in the American South:

> Calm in his peaceful home, the slave prepares
> His garden-spot, and plies his rustic cares;
> The comb and honey that his bees afford,
> The eggs in ample gourd compactly stored,
> The pig, the poultry, with a chapman's art,
> He sells or barters at the village mart,
> Or, at the master's mansion, never fails
> An ampler price to find and readier sales. (51)

As in Murray's letters, there is in Grayson's verse a sort of prelapsarian fantasy of benevolent enslavement. Harriet Jacobs would respond specifically to Murray's misrepresentations, noting, "I do not deny that the poor are oppressed in Europe. I am not disposed to paint their condition so rose-colored as the Hon. Miss Murray paints the condition of the slaves in the United States. A small portion of *my* experience would enable her to read her own pages with anointed eyes. If she were to lay aside her title, and, instead of visiting among the fashionable, become domesticated, as a poor governess, on some plantation in Louisiana or Alabama, she would see and hear things that would make her tell quite a different story" (*Incidents*, 277–78). Jacobs thus punctures Murray's analogy by pointing out that it is a delusion of artistic cliché (as evidenced by Jacobs's repeated references to painting). If Murray were to actually experience life among the American poor and enslaved, Jacobs suggests, she would realize the failure of her *generic* assumptions; she would, that is, "tell quite a different story."

Carlyle's presence in Grayson's roster of epigraphs offers a specific ethnic touchstone for the texts' fundamental racism: it is Irishness in particular that provides these writers an object for white sympathetic attachment that counters and distracts from the demand for the abolition of Black enslavement. For Carlyle, the distinction between white (Irish) and nonwhite precarity is explicit: his point is that Irish starvation arises *from* freedom, whereas Black enslavement means sustenance. In fact, the Charleston-based *Russell's Magazine* would in 1859 quote this same passage from Carlyle in its article on what it called "The Dual Form of Labour," likewise using it as putative evidence that, in ostensible contrast with Ireland, "No slave starves to death. Such an event is unknown. The hired man is never safe from starvation."[15] The Irish Famine itself here becomes a rhetorical prop in support of the continued brutalization of Black people in the United States.

Carlyle, though, is not unique among these three writers in juxtaposing Irish and Black labor; Murray does so as well. For Murray, Irishness can prop up the sentimentalized fantasy of what she figures as the affective pleasures of slavery, a rhetorical parallel that, in a bizarre set of analogies and metaphors, overwrites slavery's violence with the tropes of familial affection: "Belmont [in South Carolina] is a charming spot; it is (like the Southern ladies) not over dressed; it has the Ettewan on one side, and the forest on the other; slaves who are adopted children, and Irish labourers who have adopted a master and mistress."[16] It is true that Murray's syntax figures the "Irish labourers" as the agents of adoption and the "slaves" as the passive objects of that same process. Through the repetition of her terms, however, she suggestively conflates their situations as cognate forms of family-making; even the two usages of "adopted" appear identical, despite the fact that the verb appears in significantly different grammatical contexts. But while she unites Irish and Black work under the umbrella of familial patriarchy, she also definitively distinguishes between these forms of labor, drawing a stark racial line between them. The Irish are "labourers"; Black workers are "slaves" (and children).

In line with the proslavery tenor of his epigraphs, Grayson's argument, as he lays it out in the preface to the 1856 collection, is that slavery is a largely benevolent system set up for the mutual benefit of both the slaver and the enslaved person, offering advantages that the system of wage labor of the white working class cannot: "Slavery," Grayson intones, "does for the Negro what European schemers in vain attempt to do for the hireling. It secures work and subsistence for all" (ix). Cynically drawing on the rhetoric of contractual labor that slavery fundamentally violates, Grayson suggests a structure of mutual responsibility: "The slave is an apprentice for life, and owes his labor to his master; the master owes support, during life, to the slave" (vii). He concedes that there might be abuses but disingenuously contends that they are both rare and contrary to the system of enslavement itself: "All cruelty is an abuse; does not belong to the institution; is now punished, and may be in time prevented" (vii). Indeed, in a flourish of bad faith, he exclaims in "The Hireling and the Slave," "No ennui clouds, no coming cares annoy, / Nor wants nor sorrows check the Negro's joy" (53). At the same time, Grayson proposes in a note to the poem that it is only through enslavement that people of African descent have survived: "A barbarous people perishes always, if placed in contact with a stronger civilized race," he insists, "except when they occupy to each other the relation of master and slave" (164–65n38). To the objection that enslaved people in the American South are denied even the education necessary to read and write, Grayson offers the example—included in my own epigraph to this chapter—of the illiterate Irish (kept in ignorance, he suggests, precisely by the abolitionist British) in order to suggest that there is no injustice: "Have Ireland's millions, flying from the rule / Of those who censure, ever known a school?" (44).

In the volume's preface, Grayson turns to an economic analysis that represents itself as up-to-date in its Millite liberalism: slavery, he contends, "establishes more permanent, and, therefore, kinder relations between capital and labor. It removes what Stuart Mill calls 'the widening and imbittering feud between the class of labor and the class of capital.' It draws the relation closer between master and servant."[17] The poem, that is, rests on a set of motivating assumptions that might seem to contradict each other: slavery, Grayson argues, is *preferable* to wage labor, because—in a Millite sense—it represents a more stable system of employment; but slavery also must be enforced by noncontractual coercion, since nobody (Murray's assertion in her letters notwithstanding) would actually choose it. As Grayson puts it in the "Argument" to part 1 of "The Hireling and the Slave," "the state of the hireling and the slave [is] the same substantially—the condition hard labor, the reward subsistence," but "the hireling does not always obtain the reward" and is subject to "miseries, starvation, vices, brutality, subjection to military service, expulsion from his country" (19). Indeed, he exclaims in the poem, "How freely would the hungry list'ners give / A life-long labor thus secure to live!" (50). And, at the very beginning of the poem, in an account of the fate—due to the biblical Fall—of humankind to labor, he presents three types of laborer as equivalent: "Slave, hireling, help—the curse pursues him still" (21).

The poem thus echoes an argument that the Irish-born (and anticapitalist) US Representative Mike Walsh had made, putatively as a sort of joke, during debate over the Kansas-Nebraska bill in 1854: "To others who have been overflowing with sympathy for the southern slaves, I have to say, that the only difference between the negro slave of the South, and the white wages slave of the North, is, that the one has a master without asking for him, and the other has to beg for the privilege of becoming a slave."[18] The son of a rebel in the 1798 United Irishmen uprising,[19] Walsh adduces his Irishness both as the ostensible warrant for his authority on the question of slavery and on his distinction from it, rooted in his non-blackness: "What is the difference? I have never gone through the one state [being Black in the South]: I have never had a black skin, but I have gone through the other state [being poor in the North]." (The transcript of the debate in the *Congressional Globe* records that Walsh's remarks were met with "Great laughter.")[20] For Walsh, the "evil" of slavery can be minimized through a rhetorical gambit that reduces it to equivalency with white wage labor; with another turn of the screw, the affective appeal of Irish economic precarity can obscure the moral need to oppose slavery. The laughter that the *Congressional Globe* records is relevant: for Congress of the 1850s, it seems, Irish wit and Irish poverty were more emotionally legible than the continued suffering of actual Black people. The whiteness of Irishness—the very fact that Walsh was giving this speech in the American Congress—is central to that legibility.

Grayson similarly insists that the situations of Black enslavement and white working-class economic precarity are analogous. While "you must confess, it is said, that slavery is an evil," he responds with equanimity:

"True enough; in the same sense in which the hireling's hard labor is an evil" (x). But, significantly, there are no enslaved white persons in Grayson's vision of labor in the American South, a seemingly insuperable flaw in his ostensibly rational economic argument. Why *don't* the Irish hirelings "freely" make that choice that Grayson's model suggests that they would? The answer, for Grayson, is race. That is, he draws a hard line between white and Black persons, not only in terms of background and experience but also in the very constitution of their humanity. "Slavery," Grayson announces, as though there is simply no other alternative, "is the Negro system of labor" (vii). Whereas he acknowledges that, as a general rule, "I do not say that slavery is the best system of labor," he insists that "it is the best for the Negro in this country" (viii). "Notwithstanding its abuses and miseries," he pontificates, "the hireling system works beneficially with white laborers; and so also, notwithstanding hard masters, slavery, among a Christian people, is advantageous to the Negro" (vi). The doubled sentence both juxtaposes and distinguishes between the two situations: the "hireling system" (for white workers) has "abuses and miseries"; "slavery" might have "hard masters." Here, it seems, he cannot even bring himself to admit the possibility of "abuses and miseries" in the system of chattel enslavement; displacing that onto the institutions of wage labor, he implies that there are only some "hard masters" in the slave economy—at least "among a Christian people."

Notably, it is not the case that situations designated as "slavery" in Grayson's poem are universally beneficent; he is more than willing to use the concept metaphorically to deride what he, bringing to bear the jargon of his own political vocation, represents as the limitations or narrowmindedness of *white* party politics:

> Here [in nature] every flower that gems the forest sod
> May guide the heart from Nature to its God,
> And higher hopes and purer joys bestow
> Than the poor slaves of faction ever know,
> When demagogues have won, with brazen throat,
> The loudest cheer and most triumphant vote.

The result, in Grayson's dystopian political account, is a stew of corruption:

> The curse of patronage and frauds of state,
> The caucus juggler and his pliant tool,
> The slaves of party and its tyrant rule,
> The knavish arts that demagogues employ,
> Lies that supplant, and whispers that destroy. (65)

"Slaves of faction"; "slaves of party." Here—in a description of the folly of white persons—to be a *figurative* "slave" is anathema, a representative of the demagogic "knavish arts." That hint of white slavery—even metaphorical—is condemned. And yet, in this same poem, Grayson represents the *literal* enslavement of Black persons as a positive, in fact precisely the antidote (with its smug rhyme) of the knavishness that characterizes white political machinations: "The negro freeman, thrifty while a slave, / Loosed from restraint, becomes a drone or knave" (27). The difference that motivates this shift in Grayson's opinion of "slavery" is, solely and sufficiently, race. As David R. Roediger has argued of the deployment of "hireling" and "slave" rhetoric in the years prior to the Civil War, "The white hireling had the possibility of social mobility as the Black slave did not," and whereas "the comparison could lead to sweeping critiques of wage labor as 'white slavery,'" it "also could reassure wage workers that they belonged to the ranks of 'free white labor.'"[21]

While much of Grayson's argument hinges on the "hireling's" generic whiteness, Irishness matters to the racial work of the poem precisely because Grayson figures the Irish worker as a paradigmatic instance, perhaps *the* paradigmatic instance, of that "free white labor"—and in explicit opposition to the enslaved Black person of the American South. When, in the introduction to his verse collection, he has cause to weigh the comparative hardships of Black enslavement and white poverty, he turns to the Irish playwright and statesman Richard Brinsley Sheridan for a deflection of the moral stakes of the question: "Cruelty to the slave is equally against the law. It is equally condemned by public opinion; and as to the courts of law being open to the pauper hireling, we may remember the reply of Sheridan to a similar remark, Yes, and so are the London hotels: justice and a good dinner at a public house are equally within his reach" (vi). Grayson uses his appeal to Sheridan's Irish wit as a form of distraction from the fundamental distinction between white hireling and Black slave that he alludes to only by omission: the enslaved person has no access to the courts of law.

In his posthumously published autobiography, Grayson explicitly juxtaposes the enslaved African person with the Irish migrant, insisting that the experience of the former is no worse than that of the latter: "In a broad view of the transfer of the African to America it may be regarded not merely as an act of commercial enterprise or avarice but as an emigration of the Black to a new country. It was an emigration hardly more forced than that of the starving Irish peasantry and not attended perhaps with greater suffering."[22] ("Hardly" and "perhaps," in such a sentence, bear a tremendous amount of weight.) Likewise in "The Hireling and the Slave," Irishness, as a specific instantiation of immigrant whiteness, serves Grayson as a key example of what he presents as cognate situations merely necessitated by the differential economic systems of the North and South: "If the free German or Irish emigrant is wanted in the northern, the African slave is equally needed in the southern regions of America" (167n43), he asserts in a note. And in another: "The African emigrant is as much wanted in America as the Irish or German. Their labor belongs to different climates, and is equally required." In Grayson's account, the transatlantic slave trade appears as a neutral form of "emigration," even as a service: "As the Negro can not come, they have been brought" (159n18).

Beyond that monstrously racialized form of "separate spheres" economic analysis, though, Irishness figures in a complex way in Grayson's account, both as the exemplar of abjected hireling-ness and as a model of white alliance precisely through the assumption of anti-Black political activism. We can find that argument, for example, in Grayson's gothic vision of a suggestively Irish impoverishment:

> To gross excess and brutalizing strife,
> The drunken hireling dedicates his life:
> Starved else, by infamy's sad wages fed,
> There women prostitute themselves for bread,
> And mothers, rioting with savage glee,
> For murder'd infants spend the funeral fee;
> . . . .

> In crowded huts contagious ills prevail,
> Dull typhus lurks, and deadlier plagues assail,
> Gaunt Famine prowls around his pauper prey,
> And daily sweeps his ghastly hosts away;
> Unburied corses taint the summer air,
> And crime and outrage revel with despair. (25)

The references to starvation, of "unburied corses," of disease in "crowded huts" echo the gothic-inflected set pieces that by the early 1850s had become recognizable tropes of the representation of Famine-era Ireland.[23] And it presages the same work of Carlylean juxtaposition that *Russell's Magazine* would perform in its 1859 article suggesting that slavery is a moral good in contrast to Irish starvation. But lest the particular allusion to Ireland be nevertheless overlooked, Grayson provides a contextual endnote to this passage: "During the famine in Ireland dead bodies were found lying about in the fields and in deserted houses, and despair put an end to all moral restraints" (157n10). It is a sort of naturalist pornography of Irish poverty.

What Grayson does in "The Hireling and the Slave" is take up those tropes of Irish impoverishment and put them in the service of an explicitly white supremacist argument. In contrast to the "starving pauper," Irish by implication, Grayson posits a "happier slave": "Safe from harassing doubts and annual fears, / He dreads no famine in unfruitful years" (50). That aligns with the argument of his preface, in which he quotes John Joseph Hughes, the first archbishop of the Catholic Archdiocese of New York and founder of Fordham University, as an authority on what enslaved Black people actually want: "Archbishop Hughes, in his late visit to Cuba, asked the Africans if they wished to return to their native country; the answer was always *no*. If the African is happier here than in his own country, can we say that, for him, the establishment of slavery is an evil?" (x). The Irish-born Hughes here appears as the figure for moral probity itself, for the very reason that he was equivocal on the question of abolition and argued that the condition of northern workers was often worse than that of enslaved people. By the 1850s, Kevin Kenny writes, Hughes had situated himself "among the most outspoken defenders of slavery."[24] It is support of slavery here that, from Grayson's perspective, manifests the whiteness of Irish Catholicism, as it is British abolitionism ("those who censure") that he cannily equates with political oppression of Ireland (the "rule" from which "Ireland's millions" are fleeing).

In fact, "The Hireling and the Slave" puts the white wage-laborer into juxtaposition with the enslaved Black person with precisely the same rhetoric that Carlyle (in his own mockery of Irish impoverishment) had used to discriminate between the Irish and British: aptitude for work. Reiterating his epigraphic extract from the *Latter-Day Pamphlets* in a note, Grayson invokes Carlyle's juxtaposition of putative Black and Irish laziness: "West-Indian Blacks are emancipated, and it appears refuse to work: Irish Whites have long been entirely emancipated, and nobody asks them to work, or on condition of finding them potatoes (which, of course, is indispensable), permits them to work."[25] What Grayson does is shift the line between what he represents as the categories of human beings amenable to labor and the categories who are not. For Grayson, the Black person is, seemingly essentially, "lazy and improvident" (vii). But in an odd acknowledgment, he further reports that "in hireling states there are thousands of idlers, trampers, poachers, smugglers, drunkards, and thieves," and he relates with satisfaction that the South has solved that problem by making of the enslaver himself "a Commissioner of the Poor on every plantation, to provide food, clothing, medicine, houses, for his people. He is a police-officer to prevent idleness, drunkenness, theft, or disorder" (ix). This is, of course, a précis of the stereotypes of Irish dissipation that Carlyle, among others, had emphasized. Yet the fact of *white* criminality and idleness in the "hireling states" never seems to suggest to Grayson that the system of chattel slavery should therefore be extended to those white workers.

For Carlyle of the *Latter-Day Pamphlets,* the Irish and the Black person are similarly (although, in Carlyle, never equally) animalistic: "In the progress of Emancipation, are we to look for a time when all the Horses also are to be emancipated, and brought to the supply-and-demand principle?"[26] But for Grayson, the Irish person is clearly on one side of the boundary—the white side—and the enslaved Black person on the other. Grayson's poem, that is, is not in any way about individuals but, rather, about broad categories—even genres—of humanity, some of which he represents as not even quite human. It is a work that brings to the United States the rhetoric, arising in Great Britain in the earlier part of the nineteenth century, of the "master race"; almost at the end of the poem, Grayson gestures to what he figures as the divine will underwriting the kidnapping and enslavement of Black people by whites:

> For these great ends hath Heaven's supreme command
> Brought the black savage from his native land,
> Trains for each purpose his barbarian mind,
> By slavery tamed, enlightened, and refined;
> Instructs him, from a master-race, to draw
> Wise modes of polity and forms of law,
> Imbues his soul with faith, his heart with love,
> Shapes all his life by dictates from above. (74)

As verse it is near doggerel; as theology and anthropology it is monstrous. It brings Carlylean rhetoric and European racial science into the New World, realigning their focus to smudge out the multiple distinctions and hierarchies of the various "races" of Knoxian polygenism to distinguish solely and inflexibly between Black and white, the "black savage" and the "master-race."

The review of "The Hireling and the Slave" in the *Southern Literary Messenger* registers the degree to which Grayson's poem is, even on the basis of its form, a work of literary translation, of the relocation of European genres into the United States. Grayson himself was keenly conscious of his generic choices, particularly in terms of the differential affordances of novel and verse for the purposes of racist polemic. As Thomas D. Jarrett relates, "it is significant that of the pro-slavery novels written between 1850 and 1860, no fewer than sixteen of the known [in 1951] twenty-six were written between 1852 and 1854. Almost all of them were admittedly attempts to answer Mrs. Stowe's *Uncle Tom's Cabin* in the same *genre* that she had utilized to attack Southern slavery."[27] Grayson situates his verse polemic as a deliberate generic shift, reminiscing in his autobiography that the turn to poetry itself registered a key strategy: "The question of negro Slavery in the United States had been discussed for many years. It had assumed all garbs except the garb of verse. I thought the subject possessed aspects both of argument and description which admitted a poetical dress."[28] Form matters to Grayson; he proposes, at least in retrospect, that part of the significance of his proslavery poem lay precisely in the fact that it *was* a poem rather than a novel or political tract or drama or autobiography.

Where the *Literary Messenger* and Grayson himself saw a literary rebirth, though, I want to highlight the ways the moral force of those generic predecessors fails, indeed gets twisted into something like its opposite. Most strikingly, Grayson's assertion that "the question of negro Slavery" had not taken "the garb of verse" by the 1850s is shockingly, ostentatiously wrong, made possible only by the explicit erasure of Black poets of the eighteenth and nineteenth centuries. As Samantha Pinto has pointed out, Phillis Wheatley "stands as the first black celebrity in the modern construction of blackness as a question about the relationship between race, rights, and the human"; her 1773 *Poems on Various Subjects* initiates, in Pinto's account, "a way of rethinking black women's infamy and its relation to fantasies of black freedom."[29] And Spencer Jackson frames Wheatley's innovations specifically in terms of her transfigurations of the generic forms of political thought, arguing that her verse rewrites Popean republicanism and, in doing so, "shatters the narrow, mystifying and racist idea of freedom advocated by America's Founders."[30] Poetry *as* poetry, as a set of formal choices that could echo, revise, speak back to generic antecedents had, notwithstanding Grayson's self-puffery, been part of the literary "question" of enslavement in the Americas for a long time.

Beyond Wheatley's signal accomplishments, poetry has a consequential history of significance to Black life and abolitionist politics. Douglas A. Jones Jr. has located "the advent of black literacy and eventually literature in British North America" in "slaves' and their descendants' refusal to dissociate or hierarchize the oral and the literary," producing verse that "contributed to (and archives) a critical discourse regarding shouting that slaves and free African Americans had to negotiate in their efforts to build autonomous, theologically robust socioreligious communities."[31] Frederick Douglass's *North Star*, Teresa A. Goddu notes, "regularly included prose and poetry that took the North Star as its subject," including James M. Whitfield's "The North Star" in 1849.[32] White abolitionists as well turned to poetry as a form of antislavery activism, as Goddu also relates, notably in the media campaigns by the American Anti-Slavery Society during the 1830s that included an "array of pictorial print" and "graphic items," including poetry and music and extracts from Scripture.[33]

The *Literary Messenger* ignores all of that. In fact, it also ignores the activist charge of the early nineteenth-century Irish literature that haunts Grayson's verse. For "The Hireling and the Slave" not only alludes to the condition of impoverished Famine-era Irish in its imagery; it also evokes, generically and structurally, the literary modes of Irish political resistance and nationalist activism, most frequently the polemical poem and the national romance. In fact, Grayson's insistence in his autobiography on the experiential equivalency of the transport of enslaved Africans to the United States and that of the Famine-era Irish ("It was an emigration hardly more forced than that of the starving Irish peasantry") appears immediately—and in the same paragraph—after his account of the decision to present his proslavery argument in verse, as though the two questions are for him somehow importantly linked.

Along with—and shaping the representation of—the subject matter of the poem, literary genre is one of the ways that Grayson establishes that interconnection. We might, for example, see in his poetry an affiliation with the eighteenth-century modes of national poetics, particularly in Ireland and Scotland, that came to be identified as bardicism, a transfiguration of the kind of imaginative poetic literature that the Irish literary historian Standish James O'Grady in 1880 called "the stumbling-block ... [and] also the glory, of early Irish history."[34] Katie Trumpener has described the nineteenth-century rise and diffusion of bardic nationalism as it moves "across periods, genres, and finally national borders," "reconceive[s] national history and literary history under the sign of the bard," and "binds the nation together across time and across social divides; it reanimates a national landscape made desolate first by conquest and then by modernization."[35] Bardicism, in Trumpener's account, created a national identity in nineteenth-century Scotland and Ireland precisely by a generic reanimation, a transposition of Gaelic oral traditions into a new historical context—much as the *Literary Messenger* would claim of Grayson's own verse.

A key instance of this movement of bardic nationalist modes across geographical, national, and racial boundaries arises in the particular influence of Moore's poetry. The so-called "Bard of Erin" and lyricist for the self-described "National Music" of Ireland in his widely popular *Irish Melodies,* published in successive volumes from 1808 to 1834, Moore has often been read as offering a domesticated and palatable Irishness, appealing to English sensibilities. Moore himself, though, emphasized the nationalist significance of the verses: "We have too long neglected the only talent for which our English neighbours ever deigned to allow us any credit. Our National Music has never been properly collected; and, while the composers of the Continent have enriched their Operas and Sonatas with Melodies borrowed from Ireland,—very often without even the honesty of acknowledgment,—we have left these treasures, in a great degree, unclaimed and fugitive."[36] For Moore, the fugitivity of Irish music mirrors the fugitivity of the Irish nation itself, dominated by the English but available for reclamation. That goal was not merely aspirational, as Jeffery Vail has shown, underscoring "the real power his works had in the context of his times to positively influence attitudes toward Ireland, the Irish, and Irish Catholicism."[37]

Despite its specifically Irish relevance, though, that bardic nationalism was powerfully mobile, as Moore's own allusion to national "borrowing" makes clear. In his account of the transimperial dissemination of Romantic tropes and lyrical forms, Manu Samriti Chander has noted the influence of Moore's verse in widely separated locations and historical moments: the European Indian poet Henry Derozio, for instance, gives his 1827 *Poems* an epigraph derived from Moore's "Dear Harp of my Country" before he transforms the context of Moore's Irish nationalism to his own; and the Guianese poet Egbert Martin similarly invoked Moore in an 1884 essay on originality and poetic influence.[38] Moore himself traveled, bringing with him both his Irish nationalism and his antislavery convictions. On the basis of his visits to the United States in 1803 and 1804, Moore satirized the hypocrisy of American slavery in the context of the United States' self-congratulatory language of freedom, the "whips and charters, manacles and rights, / Of slaving blacks and democratic whites": "To think that man, thou just and gentle God! / Should stand before thee, with a tyrant's rod / O'er creatures like himself, with soul from thee, / Yet dare to boast of perfect liberty."[39] Jane Moore, in fact, has proposed that it was his transatlantic experiences, mostly those in Canada but also in the enslaving United States, that *made* Moore an Irish writer, that he became "the Bard of Erin" by first being "Transatlantic Tom."[40]

Regardless of Moore's own politics, his poetic influence came to accommodate multiple, even opposed, ideologies. Notwithstanding his abolitionism, the power of Moore's nationalist verse could, when translated into the context of the United States, be harnessed to the aesthetics of racial hierarchy and the racist mockery of minstrelsy. Charles Hamm points out that the songwriter of American racialized nostalgia Stephen Foster was "of Irish extraction" and "grew up in a family conscious of its heritage, in an emotional and cultural environment shaped in part by the poems, songs, and sentiments of Thomas Moore," whose verse lies behind such songs as "Old Folks at Home," commissioned for the blackface troupe Christy's Minstrels in 1851.[41] And while Grayson certainly draws upon the resonances of "a national landscape made desolate first by conquest and then by modernization," as Trumpener has it, he reverses the political charge of that form of bardic nationalism by making it the poetry of an explicitly racist settler colonialism rather than that of an anticolonial patriotism.

Still more striking, perhaps, are the hints in Grayson's verse of generic allusion to the Ossianic models that, after the Scotsman James Macpherson's forgeries of the eighteenth century, had become a significant (although controversial) facet of Irish nationalist literary context.[42] In a footnote to her 1806 novel *The Wild Irish Girl*, for example, the Protestant nationalist Sydney Owenson rhapsodized that "the genius of the Ossianic style still prevails over the wild effusions of the modern and unlettered bards of Ireland."[43] Moore, while a student at Trinity College, published an "Extract for a Poem in Imitation of Ossian," in which he placed Ossian firmly in an Irish nationalist tradition: "O! children of Erin! you're robb'd: why not rouse from your slumber of Death? Oh! why not assert her lov'd cause, and strike off her chains and your own, and hail her to freedom and peace? Oh! that OSSIAN now flourished, and here; he would tell us the deeds of our Sires, and swell up our souls to be brave! for his Harp flow'd a torrent around, and incitement enforced as the stream; but silence now reigns o'er its ruins!"[44] When Moore was designated the "Bard of Erin," as he commonly was in the nineteenth century, it was repeating an appellation that Macpherson had used for his Ossianic minstrel Carril.[45]

It is by now easy to forget that Oscar Wilde's first name—given to him in 1854, the same year as the initial publication of "The Hireling and the Slave"—explicitly echoes that of the son of Oisín, as his second given name likewise evokes Fionn mac Cumhaill, the hero of the cycle and the namesake of Fenianism. "He is to be called Oscar Fingal Wilde," his ardently nationalist mother wrote to a friend shortly after his birth. "Is not that grand, misty, and Ossianic?"[46] In his 1882 American lecture "Irish Poets and Poetry of the Nineteenth Century," Wilde himself would position Macpherson's Ossian in relation to a simultaneously national and generic revolution:

> The influence of Celtic poetry was not merely the primary basis of Irish politics, the keystone of Irish liberty, for to it—to the Celtic imagination—we owe nearly all the great beauties of modern literature—we owe to it, to begin with, the spirit of modern romance, we owe to it the feeling for style in literature, rhyme (which is the basis of modern poetry) being a Celtic invention; to it we owe the sentiment of modern thought, and to it those chords of penetrating passion and melancholy which swept over Europe with the publication of Macpherson's Ossian and whose echo still lingers in the work of every poet of our day.[47]

From Moore to Wilde, the bardic tradition, exemplified in the Ossian poems, was crucial to the formulation of a specifically anticolonial Irish nationalism.

Grayson makes the allusion to Ossian explicit in the introduction to "Chicora," the poem paired with "The Hireling and the Slave" in his 1856 collection. Named for the legendary Indigenous kingdom (itself described by Spanish slavers) in the land that had, by the nineteenth century, become South Carolina, "Chicora" relates what Grayson figures as the fall of the great Native civilizations in the face of European colonization. Even the starkly evocative name of Grayson's poem hints at Macpherson's titles:

"Comala," "Fingal," "Oithona," "Temora." Macpherson's original Ossianic "translations" were in prose, but his retroconstructions of the putatively "original" Scottish Gaelic sources, published posthumously in 1807, were in verse, as were many later nineteenth-century English "translations" of his Ossian.[48] And as is the case in those retroactive verse reconstructions, Grayson presents his racial epic in *Chicora* in incantatory octosyllables.[49] By invoking Ossian—and by replicating the form of Macpherson's factitious "originals"—Grayson places his poem in the tradition of what Joep Leerssen has described as an "enormous 'boom' of national epics suddenly hitting the European literary scene" in the wake of Macpherson's forgeries; more particularly, it emerges as one of the "new-written epics originat[ing] in nations experiencing an existential crisis."[50] He suggestively juxtaposes, that is, the racial crisis of the United States in the 1850s with Ossian's Celtic world, as he juxtaposes—and cynically contrasts—Irish precarity with Black enslavement in "The Hireling and the Slave."

Ossian appears in Grayson's introduction in a passage that, although ostensibly about literary appropriation, uncannily tropes the colonialist pillaging that "Chicora" itself both narrates and aestheticizes. There, Grayson acknowledges that some of the material he drew upon had also been used by other poets (notably Henry Wadsworth Longfellow, whose *Song of Hiawatha,* while similarly in tetrameter, falls into insistent trochees, a meter distant from Grayson's iambs). He excuses what he claims is an inadvertent plagiarism through reference to the example of Macpherson's Ossian, presented here as a model for distinguishing between the differentiated intellectual property statuses appropriate to thematic content and generic form: "I have introduced to the reader two of their legends from Schoolcraft. One of them has been used by Professor Longfellow and by Mr. [Bayard] Taylor. I did not know it until I had written, or I would not have ventured into the same field. The property, however, is the Indian's, if, indeed, the legends, like M'Pherson's Ossian, be not rather the chattels of the compiler than of the nominal owner" (80–81). The set of allusions here is complex, overlaying the language of national dispossession with that of generic appropriation. Grayson's suggestion is that the Indigenous "legends" themselves might perhaps rightly belong to "the Indian" rather than to Longfellow and Taylor; they are thus, he suggests, cognate with the Ossian stories, in that those are rightly an aspect of Celtic literary heritage despite the fact that they arrive in Macpherson's forgeries. That apparently, according to the logic of the introduction, absolves Grayson of the charge of plagiarism. Yet the invocation of "property" here registers a key rhetorical sleight of hand, since the implication of the passage is that it is acceptable for Grayson to confiscate the literary "property" of "the Indian" (the "nominal owner") as it would not be for him to plagiarize the white "compilers" he names. Grayson's assumption that Indigenous ownership of their own historical and literary heritage is ceded by the Native American to the white poet offers a startling echo of the narrative plot of "Chicora" itself; focusing in particular on the Yuchi (whom Grayson calls the Uchee), the poem represents them as heroically resisting a duplicitous invasion and enslavement by the Spanish before their (putative) descendants are displaced by Anglo settler colonialism. The narrative arc of Grayson's own Ossianic poem thus describes what it figures as the inevitable ceding of Indigenous land to the white invaders; so too does its introduction make the "Indian" simply the background for the exchange of poetic materials among white authors.

In a parallel translation and appropriation of Indigenous literary production into white "compilation," it is telling in this context that Grayson names simply "Schoolcraft" as one of his sources; apparently referring to the ethnologist and US Indian agent Henry Schoolcraft, Grayson's invocation of the name here designates only by insinuation Schoolcraft's wife, Jane Johnston Schoolcraft, herself of Ojibwe and Irish descent, and the author of and source for a number of the poems and narratives that Henry Schoolcraft published. As Margaret Noori has pointed out, "It is ironic that we have Henry Schoolcraft both to blame for suppressing, plagiarizing, and heavily editing Jane's work and to thank for the texts that survived to this day."[51] Grayson gives no suggestion of her Ojibwe name, Obahbahmwawageezhagoquay, nor does he really evoke her at all except perhaps as a ghostly presence behind her white husband. That is, in Grayson's framing of his verse epic of the dispossession of Indigenous Americans and what he represents as their cultural disappearance, she herself (like the Yuchi figures he represents) has vanished rhetorically into the broad and undifferentiated designation of "the Indian."

Indianness, it emerges, is instrumental to Grayson's conception of race, juxtaposed at various points with Blackness and Irishness. But it is fundamental to the racial logic of these poems that Indians enter representation as a sort of ghostly presence, invoked to heighten the racial stakes of his bardic nationalism but always displaced into the past. Alluding alternately—but always spectrally—to both Blackness and Irishness, Grayson's Indians ultimately function through absence, an absence which consolidates his racial epistemology of the present, reducing multiplicity to dichotomy and, in that reduction, highlighting Irish whiteness.

Grayson's figuration of Indigeneity occurs through a series of allusions, a mapping of racial and generic rhymes and dissonances. On the one hand, what jumps off the page of Grayson's description of literary ownership and appropriation, of course, is the word "chattels," for the implicit argument of the poem is that the American Indian—*unlike* the enslaved African of the partner poem—is *not* "chattel," is not enslaved. "Though the Indian exists liminally in relation to the Settler," Frank B. Wilderson III has argued, "he or she remains ontologically possible. That is to say, the 'Savage,' unlike the Slave, is half-alive."[52] On the other, that Indian can be mourned precisely *because* he can be figured as lost, defeated as the Celtic heroes of the Ossianic cycle have been defeated. As Moore wrote in his "Extract for a Poem in Imitation of Ossian," "his Harp flow'd a torrent around, and incitement enforced as the stream; but silence now reigns o'er its ruins!" Matthew Arnold would, in 1867, write of the Celtic warriors of the Ossianic poems in similar terms: "They went forth to the war . . . *but they always fell.*" And Grayson:

> The time is come
> When the Great Spirit's hand no more
> Shall keep from harm the Indian's home
> And country as he kept of yore.
> A people comes, of hardier frame,
> Sedate and calm, but stern and bold,
>
> . . . .
>
> These seize the land, the woods, the fields,
> With grasping hand, unsated heart,

> And onward step, that never yields,
> Nor stops, nor rests, while left a part
> Of all the hapless Indian race
> Has ever held. (142)

In drawing this trajectory, Grayson conflates different peoples into a single "Indian" heritage; in order to make the teleological history of the poem work, he has to suggest—as he does in his introduction—that the Yuchi "were, perhaps, a kindred tribe of the great Yemassee nation, who held it [the South Carolina coast] when the English colonists arrived, a hundred and fifty years afterward" (81). They are, in Grayson's vision of historical progress, all "the hapless Indian race."

That vision is an instance of what Patrick Brantlinger has designated the "proleptic elegy, sentimentally or mournfully expressing, even in its most humane versions, the confidence of self-fulfilling prophecy, according to which new, white colonies and nations arise as savagery and wilderness recede." And, as Brantlinger proposes, "Proleptic elegy is thus simultaneously funereal and epic's corollary—like epic, a nation-founding genre."[53] It constructs a space for the safe aestheticization of a nonwhite people without any threat to white dominance, a phenomenon that Hosea Easton identified as early as the 1830s: "There exists a prejudice against the Indians, but it is almost entirely national [rather than personal], and for the very reason that the injury they have sustained is essentially national. The jealous eye of this nation is fixed upon them as a nation, and has ever exercised the rigor of its prejudice towards them, in proportion as they attempted to recover their rightful possessions; or, in other words, just in proportion as the physical powers of the Indians, have dwindled to inefficiency, prejudice against them has become lax and passive. It revives only as they show signs of national life."[54] What Easton astutely observes is that anti-Black and anti-Indigenous forms of racism function differentially insofar as the Indian can be understood as standing for an (overcome) obstacle to white settler nationalism rather than a person enslaved into the service of that white nationalism; the Indian here is figured as part of national narrative rather than a living individual. That is, in Gerald Vizenor's terms, "The simulation of the *indian* is the absence of the native, and that absence is a presence of the *other*, the eternal scapegoat, but not a native past."55

This nation-making mode of proleptic elegy does not, for Brantlinger, depend upon the actual absence of the performatively mourned race but, rather, on its "lack of a lack or, in other words, on a wished-for lack that is instead an all-too-real obstacle to identification."56 In fact, Brantlinger's model itself simultaneously diagnoses and symptomatizes a phenomenon characteristic of much critical theory in which, as Jodi A. Byrd has shown, "Indians are typically spectral, implied and felt, but remain as lamentable casualties of national progress who haunt the United States on the cusp of empire and are destined to disappear with the frontier itself."57 "Indians," Byrd writes, "are lamentable, but not grievable.... The lamentable is pitiable, but not remediable. It is past and regrettable."58 "Such a portrayal of Indigenous temporal stasis or absence," Mark Rifkin emphasizes, "erases extant forms of occupancy, governance, and opposition to settler encroachments. Moreover, it generates a prism through which any evidence of such survival will be interpreted as either vestigial (and thus on the way to imminent extinction) or hopelessly contaminated (as having lost—or quickly losing—the qualities understood as defining something, someone, or some space as properly 'Indian' in the first place)."59 There were, of course, Indigenous persons living in the United States—and in South Carolina—in the 1850s, as there are today; the way that this form of proleptic elegy works is that the *fantasized* absence of the "primitive race" must be ostentatiously mourned as lost precisely in order to imagine the nation as now inevitably white.

Brantlinger observes that the literary and cultural mode of racial elegy could function, as early as the sixteenth century, to constitute and contain Irish otherness as well, specifically in rhetorical relation to Indigenous Americans. By the time of the Famine, though, a significant distinction arose in the understanding of the Irish, in that they manifested "two characteristics not shared by Native Americans: overpopulation and starvation."60 Those might, at least in some ways, seem to be at odds with each other, insofar as the latter might solve the former, but the Great Famine, as Brantlinger observes, brought those tropes together. The London *Times* in 1849, for example, described Famine-ravaged Ireland as a promising site for a kind of early disaster capitalism precisely because the Irish—so populous that Swift, in *A Modest Proposal* (1729), could satirically suggest making their "prodigious number of Children" a source of "most delicious, nourishing, and wholesome Food, whether *Stewed, Roasted, Baked,* or *Boyled*"[61]—had seemingly vanished, a phenomenon that, in the *Times*' analysis, called for the importation of a new and more economically successful "race." Wrote the *Times,* "We see Ireland depopulated, her villages razed to the ground, her landlords bankrupt,—in a word, we see the hideous chasm prepared for the foundations of a future prosperity." Where, it asks "is the new race of tenants" who will, through "capital," move Ireland from "destruction" to "construction"?[62]

By 1854, the tropes of proleptic elegy appear in full force in a *Times* account of the "extinct" Irish Celt, even as the description explicitly overlays the Irish and the American situations:

> According to the authority of the *Galway Packet,* the Celtic race is fast disappearing even in its western stronghold. The editor has just completed a tour through Jar Connaught and Joyce's country, and for miles, he says, the traveller could not see a human habitation—all was utter desolation; not a trace of farm cultivation, and in lieu of houses nothing remained but heaps of stones and unroofed gables.... "Naked urchins and filthy-looking women, forcibly reminding the traveller of Indian s[—]s, emerge from the cloud of smoke which fills the wretched dwellings, and stare wildly at the traveller. The lithe and athletic mountaineers of Connemara are nowhere to be seen. The race is extinct."[63]

The allusion to the "Indian" here brings the description of the "extinct" "Celtic race" into alignment with a set of racialized rhetorical formulae that by the middle of the nineteenth century were immediately recognizable in their application to the Indigenous peoples of the Americas. In 1848, Carlyle had similarly proposed an analogy between the (prospective) fate of the Irish and the (retrospective) fate of the American Indian, also using the rhetoric of racial extinction:

> Ireland, at this moment and for a good while back, has been admitted and is practically invited to become British.... The Cherokees, Sioux, and Chactaws, had a like invitation given them, in the new Continents two centuries ago.

"Can you, will you, O noble Chactaws, looking through superficial entanglements, estrangements, irritating temptations, into the heart of the matter, join with us in this heavy job of work we Yankee Englanders have got to do here? Will you learn to plough the ground, to do carpentry, and live peaceably in obedience to those above you. If so, you shall be of us, we say, and the gods say. If not—"!—Alas! the answer was in the negative; the Chactaws would not, could not; and accordingly the Chactaws . . . are extinct.[64]

The "invitation" that Carlyle describes is for a kind of racial surrender, a capitulation to the "heavy job of work" that white settler colonialism ("we Yankee Englanders") requires, not *as* white workers but "in obedience to those above you." His claim is that in rejecting that "invitation," the "Chactaws" signed the warrant of their extinction; the same bargain is now offered to the Irish, reeling from famine, who are now "practically invited to become British." A historical irony shadows his words: the Choctaw people were not only not "extinct"; brutally displaced to present-day Oklahoma, they had just the previous year collectively sent a donation to County Cork to support the starving Irish.[65]

Grayson's invocation of Ossian alludes to what was by the mid-nineteenth century a central trope of the application of proleptic elegy to Ireland, a subgenre of what Leerssen has dubbed "Ossianic liminality," "the combination of a marginal, out-of-the-way setting of ambiguous ontological status with an experience of emotional turmoil and uncanny poetic inspiration." While not exclusive to "Celtic" literature, Leerssen proposes, it is particularly characteristic of it: "Celtic local colour has remained Ossianic, shadowy, and ontological borderland where mundane reality takes a back seat and wistful meditation, emotion or imagination gains the upper hand."[66] That wistfully elegiac mode is grounded not only in imagination but also in loss. As Matthew Campbell notes, "such epics remember Ilion rather than Ithaca, battle and eventual defeat rather than quest and homecoming."[67] It is the mode of Matthew Arnold's account of the doomed "Celt," once great but now fallen: "As in material civilisation he has been ineffectual, so has the Celt been ineffectual in politics. This colossal, impetuous, adventurous wanderer, the Titan of the early world, who in primitive times fills so large a place on earth's scene, dwindles and dwindles as history goes on, and at last is shrunk to what we now see him."[68] Like Arnold's Celt, Grayson's suggestively Ossianic "Indian race" is defeated through its inability to adapt to a more efficient (even "grasping") modernity; and similarly like Arnold's Celt, Grayson's Indian has, for that reason, dwindled over historical time: "The Indian character" Grayson declares at the beginning of his introduction to "Chicora," "is not generally interesting. He is a mere barbarian, as we now see him, drunken, stupid, filthy, and degraded." He continues, gesturing toward an irrecoverable time prior to loss: "It was not always so. When the first colonists arrived from England in North America, they found the Indians brave, high-spirited, generous, and hospitable" (79). For Grayson, the Indian once was "brave, high-spirited, generous, and hospitable"; for Arnold, the Celt once was "colossal, impetuous, adventurous." Proleptic elegy does indeed serve as a literary hinge between representations of the Irish and those of the American Indian.

This rhetorical proximity between forms of Irish and Indigenous loss, though, is not so much a question of construing the Irish as nonwhite as an imaginative transfer of generic modes from one set of national and historical circumstances to another. That nineteenth-century Irish people and their advocates often drew upon, in a form of affective theft, the imagery of nonwhite suffering to describe Irish hardship suggests how central Irish whiteness actually was to the deployment of these images. It is part of the process by which, in Mary L. Mullen's keen analysis, "Irish origin stories and analogies contribute to the construction of an Irish settler identity that depends as much upon the manner in which Irish people claim to share history with Indigenous peoples as on the way in which they differentiate themselves from them."[69] For instance, the infamous prediction that "in a few years more a Celtic Irishman will be as rare in Connemara as is the Red Indian on the shores of Manhattan" seems to be apocryphal, despite the fact that it is still frequently attributed to the London *Times* of the late 1840s. As John Simpson excavates the history of the quote in its move from polemic to "fact," its earliest version apparently emerges in the *Nation* in 1856, in a paraphrase of the *kind* of argument journals like the *Times* made: "Her organs of opinion rejoiced that the Irish were ceasing to exist in Ireland, and congratulated themselves that the Celt would be soon as rare here as the Red Indian is in

New England."[70] In an 1863 speech, the Irish nationalist Alexander Martin Sullivan—who edited the *Nation* starting in the mid-1850s, when the first instance of the claim appeared there—gave a different version of the trope, although still not presenting it as a direct quotation: "It was not British policy that nine millions of Celts should live in Ireland...; they sent across the channel the cynical sneer—the malignant scoffing of men without hearts, exulting in the hope that in a few years more a Catholic Irishman would be as rare in Ireland as a Delaware Indian on the banks of the Hudson."[71] By 1867, though, in *The Story of Ireland*, Sullivan had settled on the now canonical formulation that continues to circulate in scholarly works, started putting quotation marks around the sentiment, and attributed it directly to the *Times*: "Now at last this turbulent, disaffected, untameable race would be cleared out. 'In a short time,' said the *Times*, '*a Catholic Celt will be as rare in Ireland as a Red Indian on the shores of Manhattan.*'"[72] The entire history of the "quotation" is, I would suggest, an example both of the rhetorical translation of one situation to another *and* of the (mis)translation of myth into "fact" that then puts the image of denigrated nonwhite bodies into the service of (white) Irish grievance.[73] The putative disappearance of the Indian is taken as the backdrop against which Irish precarity can be deplored.

That notion of white grievance is central to Grayson's project as well. For while the Ossianic mode in nineteenth-century Ireland can construct a nationalist narrative on the basis of the *failure* to become a state, Grayson—in his own apocalyptic poem given the title of a legendary civilization—ultimately displaces that failure onto nonwhite bodies, onto Indigenous Americans whom his poem can sacrifice precisely in order that racial whiteness can emerge both coherent and supreme. In Campbell's account of the persistence of Ossianic liminality, "From the mid- to late nineteenth century, Celtic revival writers recolonised, as it were, these liminal locations."[74] For Grayson, that "recolonization" is forthrightly, even brutally literal. In his introduction to "Chicora," he states explicitly that the defeat of the Spanish invaders by the Indigenous American civilization at Chicora joins "the graver beauties of Justice . . . to the meretricious charms of Success. The combination of the two may enable us"—that is, the descendants not of the Spanish explorers and slavers under Lucas Vázquez de Ayllón in the early sixteenth century but of the British settler-colonists of later South Carolina—"to sympathize with the poor Indian" explicitly because "the defeated assailants were not our own people or kindred" (81).

Precisely through their erasure, in fact, American Indians play an important role in the historiography of white dominance performed by "The Hireling and the Slave." There, Grayson figures the putative disappearance of the Native American as a monitory presaging of Black erasure in the *absence* of slavery. Indeed, his representation of Indian dispossession—what he calls "the lost Eden of the Cherokee" (67)—is marked by a sentimentality of imagery and rhetorical structure that both aligns it with and distinguishes it from his more consistently disparaging racial accounts of African "savagery":

> To other griefs that changeful life supplies,
> Griefs of a race, awakened Memory flies,
> And backward as she turns her thoughtful view,
> The vanished Indian seems to live anew;
> Low voices whisper round from stream and bay,
> The mournful tale of nations passed away;
> And names, like spirits of the buried race,
> Of plaintive sweetness, tell their dwelling-place.
> . . . .
> Like their wild woods before the Saxon's sway,
> The native nations wither and decay. (66–68)

Grayson depicts this loss—one he performatively mourns without bringing himself to call it genocide—as the inevitable endpoint of any interracial encounter that doesn't include the enslavement of one race to another:

> Such, too, the fate the Negro must deplore,
> If slavery guard his subject race no more,
> If by weak friends or vicious counsels led
> To change his blessings for the hireling's bread.
> . . . .
> Hard the long toil the hireling bread to gain,
> Slight is his power life's battle to maintain;

> And war's swift sword, or peace, with slow decay,
> Must, like the Indian, sweep his race away. (68–69)

That *both* Black enslavement and the violent displacements of Indigenous communities were enabled by the same white settler racism that Grayson celebrates is of little interest to the poem. (It is telling that the coiner of the term "manifest destiny," in 1845, was the Irish American journalist John Louis O'Sullivan, of Irish Jacobite nationalist descent, who later supported the Confederacy and the continuation of race-based chattel slavery.)[75] Instead, for Grayson, the putative fate of the Indian serves as a warning of the consequences of *abolishing* chattel enslavement; his elegy for the "lost Eden of the Cherokee" emerges from Grayson's appalling encomium to the regime of slavery as itself a prelapsarian community of the common good. Drawing on the rhetoric of bardic nationalism, Grayson constructs his romance of American white supremacy.

As Toni Morrison has observed of the romance of America, what she identifies as the "problematics of wielding absolute power over the lives of others" is "called forth and played against and within a natural and mental landscape conceived of as a 'raw, half-savage world.'" That is certainly how it works in Grayson's poem, along with the racial consolidation that Morrison similarly notes: "Why is it seen as raw and savage? Because it is peopled by a nonwhite indigenous population? Perhaps. But certainly because there is ready to hand a bound and unfree, rebellious but serviceable, black population against which . . . all white men are enabled to measure these privileging and privileged differences."[76] In "The Hireling and the Slave," Grayson in fact stages the replacement of the Native American with the enslaved Black person that Byrd critiques, in a passage that the *Southern Literary Messenger* specifically highlighted for being "as remarkable for its beauty as its fidelity":[77]

> Where once the Indian's keen, unerring aim,
> With shafts of reed transfixed the forest game,
> Where painted warriors late in ambush stood,
> And midnight war-whoops shook the trembling wood
> The Negro wins, with well-directed toil,
> Its various treasures from the virgin soil. (31–32)

By his putative disappearance, Grayson's Indian leaves a void to be filled by enslaved labor: "The Negro ... with well-directed toil" implicitly echoing Carlyle's vision of the path the "Chactaw" did *not* take, to "join with us in this heavy job of work we Yankee Englanders have got to do here ..., and live peaceably in obedience to those above you." Grayson's white supremacist settler colonialism completes Carlyle's.

The collision in Grayson's poem of Black and Indigenous representation enacts a conceptual contraction in the wake of which a white and enslaving settler colonialism emerges as the putatively only possible future. In another critique (specifically of Lisa Lowe's *Intimacies of Four Continents* but also of more general import), Byrd theorizes the conceptual juxtaposition of Black and Native representation within much scholarship of race and labor: "The native peoples of the Americas are collapsed into slavery; their only role within the disavowed intimacies of racialization is either one equivalent to that of African slaves or their ability to die so imported labor can make use of their lands."[78] Or, as Eve Tuck and K. Wayne Yang put it, "though race is a social construct, Indigenous peoples and chattel slaves, particularly slaves from the continent of Africa, were/are racialized differently in ways that support/ed the logics and aims of settler colonialism (the erasure of the Indigenous person and the capture and containment of the slave)."[79] That seems to me, though, also what Grayson himself is doing in "Chicora." Even though he *does* represent Yuchi resistance in the face of Spanish colonial invasion, for his own vision of progress to occur, that agency must be displaced to a time triply "before": before "the great Yemassee nation" which itself rises only to be felled by "the Saxon's sway" that then accedes to the slaveholding United States in which Grayson's own South Carolina exists.

For Grayson, the sentimental representation of the "lost" Indian facilitates the "collapse" (to borrow Byrd's term) of racial difference into two consolidated categories: with the fantasized loss of the American Indian and the construction of a broadly understood whiteness that includes the Celt, all that remains in Grayson's vision of the United States is white and Black, set in balanced and precise contradistinction, schematically figured in his binary title itself: the "hireling" and the "slave." And he bolsters that dichotomous racialism in his turn to the word "Caucasian," which he takes directly from European race scientists: "In tropic climes," he insists, the Black man, "unguided by Caucasian skill, / Unurged to labor by a master will," must inevitably fall into "savage indolence" and "native sloth" (69–70). Here, the allusion to Johann Friedrich Blumenbach's schema of human "varieties" through the opposition of the "Negro" to the "Caucasian" allows Grayson to reconsolidate the multifarious ethnic types that later ethnologists like Robert Knox had painstakingly delineated (the French and the Irish and the "Caledonian" Celt all distinct from the "Saxon," for example). And he fully invests the term with the moral force of not only categorical difference but also racial hierarchy.

Matthew Frye Jacobson suggests that, in the 1850s, "the category 'Caucasian' was known in scientific discourse . . . but was still rare in popular discourse."[80] To the extent that this lexical history is true—as I have noted in chapter 1 of this book, Stephen A. Douglas was using that terminology in Senate debate at least by 1853—it only underscores the work of white racial consolidation that Grayson's rather unscientific poem performs. In contrast to the elaborate set of gradations in Knox's schema, in Grayson's poem Irishness is clearly white. And that whiteness is fundamental to the way he both appropriates and repurposes Irish nationalist literary modes. For Thomas Moore, in his Trinity College-era "Extract," Ossian is the poetic means by which the "children of Erin"—Ireland itself—can "strike off her chains and your own"; for Grayson, channeling both Ossian and Moore but translating them into the United States, that poetic form couches the argument to *keep* Black people enchained.

Morrison further reminds us that "there is no romance free of what Herman Melville called 'the power of blackness,' especially not in a country in which there was a resident population, already black, upon which the imagination could play; through which historical, moral, metaphysical, and social fears, problems, and dichotomies could be articulated."[81] The genres of Irish bardicism, in the wake of the Famine, provide for Grayson a romance of white precarity that both displaces Black pain and opens the way for a dualistic consolidation of race that naturalizes that pain as inevitable, even salutary. In Grayson's romance, with all of its Ossianic echoes, the Indian emerges as a haunting presence in a racial system that is collapsed into dichotomy, an instance of what Goddu has identified as "the ways that the institutionalization of slavery enabled and depended upon the dispossession of Native Americans."[82] For Grayson, sympathy can occur not only because the Spaniards are not "our own people or kindred" (although they, too, are racially aligned) but also—as is made clear in "The Hireling and the Slave"—because the Indian, while not white, is also not *Black,* is not, that is, in the word he uses for *generic* and literary ownership, "chattel."

"Chicora" can function in a sort of poetic diptych with "The Hireling and the Slave," precisely because one is the predicate for the other; with the noble but "hapless Indian race" putatively vanished in the face of European settler colonialism, and Spanishness—like Irishness—condensed into what he identifies as the coming of "the Saxon" (86), Grayson's South Carolina emerges as Black and white. He knows on what side of the line the Irish are.

4

Irish American Whiteness in *The Garies and Their Friends*

> The continual stream of Southern fugitives and rural freedmen into the city, the intense race antipathy of the Irish and others, together with intensified prejudice of whites who did not approve of agitation against slavery—all this served to check the development of the Negro, to increase crime and pauperism, and at one period resulted in riot, violence, and bloodshed, which drove many Negroes from the city.
>
> —W. E. B. Du Bois, *The Philadelphia Negro: A Social Study* (1899)

IN HIS 1853 SPEECH "A Nation in the Midst of a Nation," Frederick Douglass astutely observed that Irish immigrants to the United States escaped the persecution of British colonial rule through an implicit tactical alliance with the forces of white supremacy. It was, Douglass proposed, a devil's bargain by which Irish Americans paid for the privileges of whiteness through the assumption of racial violence of precisely the sort that Douglass, in 1846, had characterized as absent from Ireland itself. The Irish in the United States, he maintained, were a people duped into trading the possibility of a coalition of sympathy for the lie of whiteness, produced by and through racism, a lie that Douglass saw as damaging not only to Black people but also, ultimately, to Irish Americans themselves, once they discovered, too late, the deception: "The Irish people, warm hearted, generous, and sympathizing with the oppressed everywhere when they stand on their own green island, are instantly taught on arriving in this Christian country to hate and despise the colored people. They are taught to believe that we eat the bread which of right belongs to them. The cruel lie is told the Irish that our adversity is essential to their prosperity. Sir, the Irish American will find out his mistake one day.... But for the present we are sufferers."[1] Speaking in New York, he made the brutal bargain clear, figuring American Irishness as a kind of useful idiot of white supremacy.

Douglass, it is important to recognize, is not suggesting that the Irish "became white" upon their migration to the United States but, rather, that their whiteness comes to be expressed differently. The Irish in Ireland were "white," Douglass had already claimed; the difference was that Irish Americans mobilized their whiteness to enforce Black dispossession: "They are taught to believe that we eat the bread which of right belongs to them... that our adversity is essential to their prosperity." That analysis of racial theft and racist violence in the service of the Irish American alliance with white supremacy in the antebellum United States finds literary form in a significant subplot of Frank J. Webb's 1857 *The Garies and Their Friends,* published four years after Douglass's New York speech. Implicitly echoing Douglass's insights in that speech, a key element of *The Garies'* account of the racist violence perpetrated by northern legal (and extralegal) institutions, beyond the brute facts of enslavement, takes the form of the novel's plot of racial terrorism and economic dispossession. What Webb highlights is the performance of whiteness as racial violence, and the particular role of Irishness in that performance. Like Douglass, Webb recognizes that it is not really that the Irish only became white upon migration to the United States. Instead, he represents all racial categories as contingent, what we would call socially constructed. But he also recognizes that the structure of whiteness, constructed though it might be, can accommodate Irishness in a way that it will not accommodate people of African descent. Webb's novel presages Toni Morrison's understanding that "immigrant populations (and much immigrant literature) understood their 'Americanness' as an opposition to the resident black population."[2] And it presages as well Frantz Fanon's insight about the constitution of Blackness under the regime of white racism, that "not only must the black man be black; he must be black in relation to the white man."[3] Irishness for Webb is sufficiently amenable to white supremacy to act as the enforcer of that Fanonian imposition of Blackness as radical and abjected alterity. The consequences of Irish whiteness that limns the work of such authors as Edgar Allan Poe and William Grayson (and John Mitchel, Dion Boucicault, and Margaret Mitchell, who are the subjects of my later chapters) are laid out in stark relief by Webb's keen novelistic analysis. *The Garies*, that is, stands as an important instance of literary witness to the corporeal and economic terrorism of Irish whiteness, seen here not from the perspective of Irish migrants or Irish Americans but from that of a Black middle class which suffers the violent consequences of that alliance with American white supremacy by a new group.

The second published novel known to be written by a Black American writer, *The Garies and Their Friends* translates the realist novel of reform to the world of mid-nineteenth-century Black life in the United States, both South and North. Set most likely in the 1830s or 1840s,[4] it traces the interwoven lives of two families, the Garies and the Ellises. The Garies, who begin the novel near Savannah, consist of Clarence Garie, a white plantation owner (and slaveholder); his wife, Emily, a Black woman who is by law enslaved by him but who functions as the female head of the household; and their two children, also named Clarence (sometimes called Clary) and Emily (called Em). The Ellises are a free Black working-class family, what Webb calls "a highly respectable and industrious coloured family" (56), living in Philadelphia but also originally from Savannah, and comprising Charles and Ellen Ellis, a carpenter and seamstress, and their three children: Esther, Caroline (called Caddy), and Charlie. In the early chapters of the novel, the Garie family moves to Philadelphia at the urging of Mrs. Garie, who realizes the risk to herself and her children if they stay in Georgia. Arriving in Philadelphia, the Garies establish their household next to the malevolently racist Stevens family, headed by the attorney George Stevens and his wife, Jule. Although the Stevenses initially perceive the Garie children as white and welcome them as playmates for their own children, once they meet the more visibly Black Mrs. Garie, that changes. Mr. Stevens's increasing acts of white supremacist violence ultimately culminate in his hiring of an Irish-led mob to drive the Garies out, in the murder of the Garie parents,[5] and in his attempted seizure of the children's inheritance through the piracy and concealment of Mr. Garie's will and the revelation of his own blood relation to Mr. Garie.

Published in London by George Routledge in a "Cheap Series" edition (followed by a more expensive, clothbound version),[6] *The Garies and Their Friends* attracted significant attention by British reviewers from a range of political perspectives, including notices in the *Athenæum*, *Daily News*, *Standard*, *Observer*, *Literary Gazette*, and *Morning Post*. The only contemporary review to appear in an American publication was a republication of the *Daily News* account in *Frederick Douglass' Paper*.[7] A persistent concern of the reviews was how to think about Black accomplishment, both artistic and political, an issue somewhat oddly provoked by Harriet Beecher Stowe in her preface to the novel in which she situates its value in terms of whether liberal models of political and social progress could apply to Black persons: "The book which now appears before the public may be of interest in relation to a question which the late agitation on the subject of slavery has raised in many thoughtful minds; viz.—Are the race at present held as slaves capable of freedom, self-government, and progress?"[8] The *Daily News* took the opportunity to point out that the question itself, whatever its putative salience in Stowe's white communities, was absurd in its ahistoricity:

> As to the question which Mrs. Stowe . . . says it elucidates, it is one which we have never thought of asking. Our intercourse with the East has enriched our language with one delightfully expressive monosyllable, and that we shall apply to the interrogatory—are the negroes capable of freedom, self-government, and progress? To affect a doubt upon this matter is simply "bosh." Who ever heard of a dominant race that would admit of the presence of the governing faculty in those whom they oppressed? And our cousins on the other side of the Atlantic are only following out the old rule of might against right, in gravely asserting, as one of their excuses for slavery, that their slaves are radically unfit for freedom. The ethnologists have long since scattered such nonsense to the winds.[9]

Similarly, in response to Stowe's assertion, quoted in another preface to the novel (this one by the British abolitionist Henry Peter, Lord Brougham), that the book "shows what I long have wanted to show; what the *free people of colour do attain,* and what they can do in spite of all social obstacles,"[10] the *Observer* drily remarked, "We really think it is superfluous to give fresh instances of what great things 'people of colour' can do."[11] For the *Daily News* and the *Observer,* that is, the question posed by these white abolitionists was itself a racist absurdity; it did not take "many thoughtful minds" to mull the question of Black accomplishment, and the novel itself assumes that accomplishment as simply a fact of life.

In contrast, the *Athenæum*'s review spun the liberal narrative of social progress, sparked by Stowe's preface, into a legend of white superiority permeating Black attainments through racial admixture: "The question intended to be at once raised and answered by this work—whether slaves are capable of self-government—is not fairly stated. There is no doubt that the mixture of race gives to the original slave stock capabilities for civilization and moral qualities of self-control which render them capable of achieving freedom and undertaking all its responsibilities, which in their original state they were *not*."[12] Thus, for the *Athenæum,* does a twisted version of political liberalism become the basis of a racial retrenchment, an excuse for political passivity in the face of the moral atrocities of American slavery (as well as the ongoing racism that Webb portrays as occurring toward free Black citizens) on the assumption that history will eventually progress on its own. "When the majority are capable of being free," opines the *Athenæum,* "they will no more remain slaves than the Britons, whose 'Britannia rules the waves'; but *till then* all the amiable intentions in the world will not make them free or give them the souls of freemen."[13] Slavery, in the *Athenæum*'s racial imagination, is not a cause of Black disadvantage but the effect of it.

The *Athenæum*'s rhetorical move from American slavery to British imperialism, as troped by James Thomson's "Rule, Britannia" (1740), is a telling one, for it functions in two different registers. Most clearly, it constructs historical temporality as overlapping but uneven progress, marking the advancement of British culture against the backdrop of the putative stasis of Black America by aligning both in the same axis of national development. This is only a particularly cynical version of the imperialist vision of historical advance that Uday Singh Mehta has identified as "the problematic of progress," fundamental to but unacknowledged in Millite liberalism:

"The normative valuations that liberals make, that is of those who are deemed to be 'backward' and those who are not, are expressed as historical facts that can be redressed only through the instrument of political intervention and in the register of future time"[14] For the *Athenæum*, the very model of political progress is the consolidation of Britishness itself in the eighteenth century, the articulation, as Linda Colley has described it, of a national identity grounded in an imperial and economically liberal Protestantism[15] but also of a national identity forged under the aegis of *whiteness*. Thomson's own Scottishness can slip unmarked beneath the level of conscious articulation, since—in the *Athenæum*'s vision—the coalition of British whiteness has trumped the kind of proto-ethnic nationalism that the poem itself aims, at least in part, to render moot. Written in the wake of the 1707 Acts of Union between England and Scotland that legislatively created the kingdom of Great Britain, Thomson's text insists that "*Britons* never, never, never shall be slaves" precisely because they *are* "Britons" (and no longer Scotsmen or Englishmen); that racial consolidation at the expense of ethnic and cultural difference is what powers imperial conquest, as suggested by the insistent rhymed couplets linking the assertion that Britons "never shall be slaves" with the imperative that "Britannia rule the waves." And that progress into colonial dominance, aligned as it is with the liberal narrative grounding national significance in political self-determination ("thou shalt flourish, shalt flourish *great and free*" [italics added]) can only be enacted through the ghostly figure of Black enslavement; while *Britons* "never shall be slaves," Thomson's ode to innate British liberty, composed in 1740, emerges against the backdrop both of the British slave trade and the reality of enslaved persons in England and Scotland themselves, appearing as it does more than three decades before Lord Mansfield's *Somerset* decision in 1772, let alone the abolition of the slave trade in the next century.

One of the oddities of the reviews—instigated, to be sure, by Stowe's framing question—lies in their persistent assumption that slavery is the principal theme of Webb's novel; the *Observer*, for example, opens its review by calling it a "pretty and exceedingly interesting story about slavery in republican America."[16] Yet *The Garies*, despite what the reviewers repeatedly assert, is not first and foremost a novel about slavery. It is, instead, an account of free, although threatened, Black persons and families, both in the South and in the North (primarily in Philadelphia, although with some plot elements set in other northern states). In fact, the words "slave" and "slaves" appear only twenty-seven times in the entire novel, almost all in the early sections that take place in Georgia or in the mouths of some of the most repugnant characters (plus five more times in Stowe's two-page preface); "slavery" appears but four times (and twice in Stowe's preface). Those numbers suggest that all of these reviews, to some extent or other, miss the point of the novel, what the *Athenæum* misreads as "the question intended to be at once raised and answered."[17]

Webb does not in any way discount the horrors of slavery; the novel's settings range from the slave state of Georgia to the putatively "free" state of Pennsylvania, and it was published in the aftermath of the Fugitive Slave Act, which rendered self-emancipated Black people even in states like Pennsylvania subject to kidnapping and forced return to enslavement in the South. (Harriet Jacobs would write, in 1861, "I was, in fact, a slave in New York, as subject to slave laws as I had been in a Slave State. Strange incongruity in a State called free!" [*Incidents*, 290].) But Webb relocates his literary and political attention away from slavery in particular to what Douglass would call "the color line," which he figures as emerging out of but fundamentally distinct from Black enslavement. That is, he presages Christina Sharpe's account of "living in the wake" as "living the history and present of terror, from slavery to the present, as the ground of our everyday Black existence."[18] As Douglass writes in "The Color Line" (1881), "Slavery is indeed gone, but its shadow still lingers over the country and poisons more or less the moral atmosphere of all sections of the republic." In his account of the free Black American, "He has ceased to be the slave of an individual, but has in some sense become the slave of society."[19] By highlighting the atrocities of white supremacist enforcement of the color line—rooted in and intertwined with but not reducible to slavery—Webb similarly points both to the continuation of racism across both geography and time, beyond the specific details of southern slavery, and to the ideological construction of race, enforced by violence.[20]

He does so by taking up and transforming the tropes of the sentimental-realist novel that serves as a generic antecedent for his text. That term "realism," as I'm using it here, requires some explanation. The attachment of the designation to artistic mimesis only arises in the 1850s, just prior to the publication of *The Garies*,[21] and—as Elaine Freedgood has pointed out—critics did not generally think of it as being relevant to the Victorian novel until more than a century after that.[22] In placing *The Garies* in a realist tradition, I am drawing upon the broader and looser—but still particularly mid-Victorian—concept of literary realism that George Levine has described, in which "the primary conventions . . . are its deflation of ambition and passion, its antiheroism, its tendency to see all people and things within large containing social organizations and, hence, its apparently digressive preoccupation with surfaces, things, particularities, social manners."[23] This form of realism represents, Levine proposes, an "effort to make the ordinary significant."[24] In conjunction with that effort, Rae Greiner proposes, the particular realism of the nineteenth-century novel is a fundamentally "*sympathetic* realism," emerging from "forms designed to enact sympathetic habits of mind in readers: structures of consciousness shaped according to sympathetic protocols," including metonymy, free indirect discourse, and realist characterization.[25] Webb's novel certainly manifests those forms and techniques of realism, although in translocating its setting, Webb realigns the ethnic and classed stereotypes that underlie the kind of social caricature that midcentury British and Irish novelists were presenting with the structures of American racial prejudice.[26]

For a number of the novel's white, British reviewers, the issue of *The Garies'* literary merit frequently falls narrowly into the question of adherence not only to the general aspiration to verisimilitude we associate with literary realism but also to particular generic models. It is perhaps not surprising, given Stowe's preface, that her own work becomes for these readers the benchmark of specifically sentimental success within the ambit of mid-Victorian sympathetic realism, sometimes placed against the backdrop of English generic touchstones. For the *Literary Gazette*, maintaining a distinction between artistic quality and what it figures as race-based ethnology, "the dramatic power displayed in the story is not so vivid or intense as that of 'Uncle Tom,' and the delineation of character is not so subtle. But it is truer in all essential particulars to the instincts of African blood, and the habits of the mixed African race."[27] Nonetheless, for this critic, even sociological realism falters under the pressure of generic imitation: "Sometimes, indeed, [Webb's Black characters] are coarse and rude enough, but when occasion serves they can be as 'elegant' and sentimental as any of the exquisite ladies or powdered beaux of the old Sir Charles Grandison school."[28] (Not least of the transatlantic ironies suffusing the critical reception of this novel is the phenomenon of British reviewers tutting over what they insist is Webb's inaccurate representation of Black Americans.) The *Literary Gazette* is willing to accept the ethnological "truth"—the verisimilitude—of Webb's representation of free Black persons in the United States precisely up to the point that their values and behaviors, putatively under the spell of generic sentimentality, stop being "course and rude enough." And the supposed mimicry by the novel's free Black characters of elite whites here becomes a synecdoche for Webb's own ostensible mimicry of Stowe's (or, in this case, Samuel Richardson's) literary style.

The realist novel, as a genre, might not seem to have the immediate centrality to the Irish nationalist literary tradition as the gothic or the epic poem that I have described in earlier chapters of this book. And contemporary reviews tended in general to position *The Garies and Their Friends* in conversation with English antecedents—including Richardson (as in the *Literary Gazette*), Charles Dickens, and William Makepeace Thackeray—in addition to Stowe. Yet it is important to recognize, as Mary L. Mullen has recently demonstrated, the often overlooked mutual construction of British and Irish modes of realism, the fact that, in Mullen's words, "we cannot understand British realism without considering Irish realism" and that "nineteenth-century Irish realism is exemplary rather than anomalous."[29] In Mullen's analysis, to the extent that Irish realist novels can lay bare the foundational assumptions of British realism itself, it is through a set of stances vis-à-vis both the state and the conventions of genre. Irish novels, Mullen proposes, both bear "a more uneasy relationship with the institutional power of the state" and trouble the boundaries between literary realism and the ethnographic.[30] James Chandler has similarly located in the Irish writer Maria Edgeworth the roots of what he identifies as nineteenth-century "ethnographic realism": "It was in Edgeworth's posture as a scientific realist about such matters, not least her commitment to an analogical relation between moral and natural evidence, that she left her mark, by way of Austen and Scott, on nineteenth-century fiction."[31] An Irish approach to realism, in Chandler's account, thereby inaugurates the history of the nineteenth-century British novel as a genre through its influence on both English and Scottish adaptors; realism, that is, enters the English novel as an import *from* the Irish novel. Nonetheless, as Mullen argues, the relationships—and the distinctions—between the "ethnographic" and the "realist" impose specific ideological and national burdens on the Irish novel in particular: "Literary critics have used 'ethnography' to separate realistic nineteenth-century Irish writing with a cultural focus from the literary genre of realism."[32] That is, in fact, the same policing of the borders of the literary that undergirds the contemporary criticism of Webb's novel. And it helps to explain the significance of Irishness in *The Garies*, both in terms of subject matter and in terms of the related interrogation of generic boundaries that Webb presents. Irishness, I propose, provides for Webb a key trope for the problematics of raced identity and racial violence in the midcentury United States specifically through the slippery interaction between the realist and the ethnographic.

That slipperiness emerges in Webb's incisive querying of race itself, as it persists across both individual and historical time frames. Racial identity in *The Garies* is remarkably mutable and performative, even while the corporeal and generational effects of racial violence remain all too brutally real. Thus, on the one hand, Webb mocks the notion that race is "natural" or always legible; Mr. Garie, for example, laughs at the fantasies of racial detection expressed by a person like Mr. Priestly, a sort of armchair Knoxian who "prides himself on being able to detect evidences of the least drop of African blood in any one; and makes long speeches about the natural antipathy of the Anglo-Saxon to anything with a drop of negro blood in its veins" (45). On the other hand, he insists that the fictionality of race as an ontological category by no means obviates the murderous effects of white racism or its power to make the experience of that fiction real. "One thing I must tell you," Mr. Ellis warns the light-skinned Mr. Winston about life in the putatively free North, "if you should settle down here, you'll have to be either one thing or other—white or coloured" (79). Race itself might not be ontologically real in Webb's novel, but its consequences absolutely are.

The question of racial legibility arises almost immediately in the novel, in the description of young Clarence Garie, who becomes the principal focus of the text's sentimental narration: "The critically learned in such matters, knowing his parentage, might have imagined they could detect the evidence of his mother's race, by the slightly mezzotinto expression of his eyes, and the rather African fullness of his lips; but the casual observer would have passed him by without dreaming that a drop of negro blood coursed through his veins" (44). While both of the younger Garies are frequently interpreted as white by their white acquaintances, their relationship to race diverges starkly as the novel continues. Whereas Em maintains her affiliation with her family and her community, ultimately marrying Charlie Ellis, Clary largely disavows his background in order to enter a white world, experiencing both the advantages and the ultimately fatal costs of such "passing for white" (79).[33] The later chapters of the novel, describing events after the murder of their parents, focus on Clary's attempt to marry a white woman, Anne Bates, and live as a white man: echoing Mr. Ellis's warning much earlier in the text, Clary insists to Ada Bell, a sympathetic white woman, that "I can't be white and coloured at the same time; the two don't mingle, and I must consequently be one or the other" (311). The illusion that it is his choice to make, however, is ultimately shattered, this time by Stevens's similarly villainous son (also named George), who informs Anne's father that her fiancé is Black. Falling deeper and deeper into despair, Clary dies just as Anne is about to enter his room to speak with him one last time.

Webb's description of Clary's death and its aftermath can stand for the multiple responses that Webb's novel offers to its generic antecedents, its translation of the modes of sympathetic realism to a project of greater political urgency. His account of Anne's death and Clary's burial, the final episodes of the novel before a brief coda, is drenched in sentimental affect:

> They gently bore her away. That dull, cold look came back again upon her face, and left it never more in life. She walked about mournfully for a few years, pressing her hand upon her heart; and then passed away to join her lover, where distinctions in race or colour are unknown, and where the prejudices of earth cannot mar their happiness.

> Our tale is now soon finished. They buried Clarence beside his parents; coloured people followed him to his last home, and wept over his grave. Of all the many whites that he had known, Aunt Ada and Mr. Balch were the only ones that mingled their tears with those who listened to the solemn words of Father Banks, "Ashes to ashes, dust to dust."
>
> We, too, Clarence, cast a tear upon thy tomb—poor victim of prejudice to thy colour! and deem thee better off resting upon thy cold pillow of earth, than battling with that malignant sentiment that persecuted thee, and has crushed energy, hope, and life from many stronger hearts. (366–67)

As an example of ostentatiously affective sentiment, this is not quite the death of Dickens's Little Nell, but it similarly concentrates the literary markers of intense feeling: the mournful lingering and the prospect of reuniting in a heaven, where the biases of earthly existence are no more; the mingling of tears over the grave; the crushing power of "malignant sentiment."

This sort of scene did not escape the attention of the novel's first reviewers. The *Daily News,* in the review that *Frederick Douglass' Paper* would reprint, asserted that Webb "has evidently been a careful reader of Dickens and Thackeray, his book being full of reminiscences of both, and as imitators generally are most faithful in copying defects, he sometimes runs the sentimentality of the former to death."[34] And from an opposing political position, the *Morning Post* complained that "'Uncle Tom' has already painfully awakened English sympathies on behalf of the slave race in America, and more appeals to our feelings on precisely the same model may not unlikely prove tiresome and have an opposite effect to that intended."[35] This sentimentality, as both reviews suggest, is in fact an aspect of the Victorian realist tradition, as George Levine has proposed.[36] But Webb insists that the affordances of sentimentality within the context of the realist novel can (and must) encounter and accommodate a new source of narrative obstacles: the violence of identitarian assignation within the context of the American racial state, exemplified even by the casual epistemological violence enacted by the *Morning Post*'s reference to "the slave race." Across the Atlantic, such novelistic sentimentality had certainly pervaded the affective portrayals of "victims of prejudice," but

Clarence is specifically a sacrifice to the power of white supremacy and the demand for an essentialized racial identity that marks its American particularity.[37]

One of the most complex representations in the novel of both the instability of race and the injury that, notwithstanding that instability, attaches to Black bodies arrives in an ostensibly comic scene in which Stevens disguises himself in secondhand clothing in order to surveil his henchmen's racist terrorism against the Garies. The disguise backfires, though, as Stevens finds *himself* the victim of racist buffoonery, just at the point that he is leaving an Irish tavern. As he is inadvertently dressed, in his secondhand garb, as "a member of a notorious fire company" (197), he is attacked by adherents of a different company. Further, however, the mode of the attacks draws specifically on the tropes of racist performance and racial terrorism:

> His cries now became so loud as to render it necessary to gag him, which was done by one of the party in the most thorough and expeditious manner. They then dragged him into a wheelwright's shop near by, where they obtained some tar, with which they coated his face completely.
>
> "Oh! don't he look like a n[—]!" said one of the party, when they had finished embellishing their victim.
>
> "Rub some on his hands, and then let him go," suggested another. "When he gets home I guess he'll surprise his mammy: I don't believe his own dog will know him!". . .
>
> He was, indeed, a pitiable object to look upon. The hat he had so recently purchased, bad as it was when it came into his possession, was now infinitely less presentable. In the severe trials it had undergone, in company with its unfortunate owner, it had lost its tip and half the brim. The countenance beneath it would, however, have absorbed the gazer's whole attention. His lips were swelled to a size that would have been regarded as large even on the face of a Congo negro, and one eye was puffed out to an alarming extent; whilst the coating of tar he had received rendered him such an object as the reader can but faintly picture to himself. (199–200)

The passage concentrates some of the most explicitly racist imagery of the novel: the skin blackened with tar that rhetorically transforms Stevens into an "object," the swollen lips "that would have been regarded as large even on the face of a Congo negro," the racist expletives, the term "mammy" (a word that otherwise occurs in this novel only in a brief retrospective narrative of Mr. Winston's enslaved boyhood [50]), the mocking grandeur of the language of "embellishing." Despite the carnival atmosphere and the explicitly performative rhetoric of Stevens's costumed appearance as a kind of tramp figure, Webb's point is clear: blackface minstrelsy is itself a virulent form of racist violence.

And yet there is yet another twist in this piece of racial burlesque: having been transformed by working-class white rioters into a racist parody of Blackness, Stevens is then—again violently—transformed by a group of more upper-class white rioters into a performative whiteness. Having collapsed "upon the steps of a mansion" (200), he is accosted by *another* "party of young men, evidently in an advanced state of intoxication," but this time including some of his own acquaintances, who fail to recognize him. One of these drunken men takes up "a piece of chip" and "engage[s] in streaking the face of Mr. Stevens with lime," announcing, "I'm making a white man of him, I'm going to make him a glorious fellow-citizen, and have him run for Congress" (201). I want to mark this scene—as have a number of critics before me—as a key instance of Webb's figuration of whiteness as itself founded upon racial violence, here troped as blackface minstrelsy, and the way that violence subsumes white ethnicity into white supremacy. Analyzing a later period of American assimilation, Matthew Frye Jacobson has argued of Al Jolson's performance in *The Jazz Singer* (1927) that blackface renders Jewishness white, that "Jewishness as race is effaced only by the whiteness created by the blackface routine," and that "ultimately . . . the burnt cork serves not only to change the race of the Jew, but also to eradicate race from *Judaism*."[38] And in a compelling reading of this carnivalesque violence in *The Garies*, Robert Nowatzki makes a similar point: "Throughout this scene, Webb signifies on the practice of blacking up, an act that allowed white males to parody black but also to 'act black' and paradoxically to bolster their sense of whiteness by projecting their wildness onto blacks."[39] In Webb's doubled racial minstrelsy, I want to suggest, he marks a still more complex cultural transformation. For unlike both the free Black families of Philadelphia *and* the Irish immigrant, George Stevens seems for most of the novel curiously exempt from the imperative of racialized identity; unlike (some of) Webb's Black and Irish characters, for instance, he doesn't speak in the broad caricatures of stage ethnicity. Beyond its general Anglo orientation, his name is a kind of blank slate.[40] But through the doubled assaults, first with blackface and then with whiteface, Webb reverses the process that Jacobson identifies in *The Jazz Singer,* producing whiteness itself *as* racially inscribed, in Nowatzki's astute account, "as if his whiteness were painted on rather than natural."[41]

In this way, Webb's text exemplifies the complexities of antebellum minstrelsy that Eric Lott, in *Love and Theft: Blackface Minstrelsy and the American Working Class,* has described. Lott contends that "the range of responses to the minstrel show ... points to an instability or contradiction in the form itself," a form which, as "the most popular American entertainment form in the antebellum decades," emerges as "a principal site of struggle in and over the culture of black people" and "a ground of American racial negotiation and contradiction."[42] As a striking instance, he points to an 1842 description of blackface in the *Dial* by the antislavery and women's rights advocate Margaret Fuller, in which she asserts that "'Jump Jim Crow' is a dance native to this country, and one which we plead guilty to seeing with pleasure, not on the stage, where we have not seen it, but as danced by children of an ebon hue in the street."[43] By this conflation of the dancing of actual Black children in the street with that of blackface performers on the stage, Fuller's reminiscence, in Lott's account, includes "the assumption that the only music and dance which are *not* false coin are those found in blackface minstrelsy."[44]

As Lott acknowledges, what he identifies as a "struggle in and over the culture of black people" "took place largely among antebellum whites,"[45] and one contemporary observer who *did* notice how damaging those assessments were was Frederick Douglass, who in 1848 described blackface performers as "the filthy scum of white society, who have stolen from us a complexion denied to them by nature, in which to make money, and pander to the corrupt taste of their white fellow-citizens."[46] Far from Fuller's sentimentalized account, that is, Douglass realizes the economic grounding of the racial theft (highlighted in the title of Lott's book) that blackface represents. Reinforcing Douglass's critique, Matthew D. Morrison similarly points out that blackface minstrelsy was a tool in the construction and affirmation of a whiteness predicated on inherently violent appropriation: "The impact of minstrelsy ... was fundamental to the way particular civic and quotidian performances of a nonblack 'self' became culturally aligned with whiteness, as ethnic whites also felt free to perform the *limits* of self as citizen through blackface on and off the minstrel stage."[47] And, in Saidiya Hartman's trenchant analysis, "The seeming transgression of the color line and the identification forged with the blackface mask through aversion and/or desire ultimately served only to reinforce relations of mastery and servitude."[48] To read blackface as a suggestive dismantling of racist structures of identity through a sort of performative deconstruction is to ignore its essential violence *within* the racial history that spawned it.

Webb, I suggest, perfectly understands that, particularly since his representation of blackface lays bare its occasionally implicit but ever-present violence by moving the scene of racial performance from the stage to the streets and refusing the misdirection of aestheticized sentimentalism that characterizes Fuller's reminiscences of dancing Black children. He simultaneously foregrounds and complicates the rhetoric of the natural that pervades *both* Douglass's critique and Fuller's praise. For Douglass, blackface performance enacts the theft by whites of "a complexion denied to them by nature," while Fuller reads "Jump Jim Crow"—both in the streets and on the stage, it seems—as authentically "native to this country." What Webb does, in contrast, is highlight the *unnaturalness* of racial performance, either of Blackness or of whiteness. But, like Douglass, he remains alert to the economic violence underlying that performance of race in the interest of the consolidation of both whiteness and white power. By drawing on the rhetoric of contemporary debate over the possibility of Black citizenship, Webb here spins out a doubled travesty of racial violence that nonetheless argues a consistent point: *both* the forced assumption of blackface and the assault on a now ostensibly Black body in order to impose upon it a parodic whiteface are enacted by white mobs— and white mobs of two distinct classes.

Webb's account of that violence, though, is more ethnically specific than the general critique of the white brutality underwriting blackface performance it might appear to be. Irishness in particular is central to the way racial travesty functions, both in *The Garies* and in the history of mid-nineteenth-century minstrelsy more broadly. As Morrison observes, "Blackface performance emerged in the 1820s with white men (mostly Irish and/or working class) donning blackface and performing popular tunes according to stereotypical notions of black dialect and movement."[49] "Those who 'blacked up' and those who witnessed minstrel shows" in antebellum America "were often working-class *Irish* men," writes Lott; "the very instrumentation of minstrel bands followed this pattern: the banjo and jawbone were black, while the fiddle, bones, and tambourine ... were Irish."[50] The music to "Zip Coon," Morrison demonstrates, "is related to two Irish hornpipes, 'The Glasgow Hornpipe' and 'The Post Office.'"[51] I noted in chapter 3 the transmission of Thomas Moore's *Irish Melodies* into the minstrelsy of "Old Folks at Home" by the Irish-descended Stephen Foster. Irish artistic modes are the very ground out of which American blackface grows.

It is, I want to argue, no accident that Webb's nightmare minstrelsy occurs immediately after Stevens's departure from a pub "crowded with half-drunken men, the majority of whom were Irishmen, armed with bludgeons of all sizes and shapes," complete with an owner whose exclamations take such forms as "By the howly St. Patherick" (196). In the context of midcentury Philadelphia, when Stevens initiates his first identitarian masquerade in the garb of "a notorious fire company," what Webb means is that he disguises himself as an Irishman.[52] Beyond the novel's reliance on the caricature of the stage Irishman, however, Irishness becomes significant to Webb's argument in that it serves as a test case for whiteness's accommodation of ethnic variety precisely through racist violence. Whereas the *Athenæum,* in its review of the novel, would invoke the text of "Rule, Britannia" as its shibboleth dividing what it sees as the differentiated rights to freedom respectively of Britons and persons of African descent, what *The Garies and Their Friends* does is put pressure on Thomson's vision of (implicitly white) Britishness by introducing the complicating term of Irishness. It asks how Irishness, with its antagonistic relationship to Britishness in the mid-eighteenth century, became the enforcer of the racial color line a century later.

The answer for Webb is the inclusion of Irishness in an interethnic alliance of whiteness. In *The Garies,* the central figure in the performance of mob violence against Black people, although not its ultimate source, is the Irish immigrant McCloskey, who becomes one of Stevens's clients after participating in a violent brawl that left another person dead and who, through that connection, ends up as Stevens's most brutal enactor of white racial terrorism. Despite its apparent chaos, that terrorism, in Webb's account, performs a specific and deliberate function: the transfer of Black wealth to white hands. For Webb as for Douglass, the intergenerational transition of slavery into the color line is deeply intertwined with the predations of white capital. The novel narrates the processes through which capital ownership conjoins with racist violence not only to reduce Black persons to objects (enslaved people being designated, in one of the text's most biting instances of ironic metaphor, as "slippery property" [76]) but also to consolidate wealth into white control by disinheriting property-owning free Black families.

As Stevens reveals to one of his allies, he has a plan "for getting into our hands a large proportion of property in one of the lower districts, at a very low figure" (181). That plan is founded on a cynical yet shrewd understanding of the interrelationship between deliberately instigated race riots, the precarity of Black personal safety and institutional protection, and the movement of property from Black ownership to white: "You are probably aware," confides Stevens,

> that a large amount of property in the lower part of the city is owned by n[—]s; and if we can create a mob and direct it against them, they will be glad to leave that quarter, and remove further up into the city for security and protection. Once get the mob thoroughly aroused, and have the leaders under our control, and we may direct its energies against any parties we desire; and we can render the district so unsafe, that property will be greatly lessened in value—the houses will rent poorly and many proprietors will be happy to sell at very reduced prices. (181)

That is, in fact, the economic plot that Stevens dons his disguise in order to witness. It is in part through that plot, alongside the literally murderous violence of the northern racists, that Webb depicts the structural violence of systematic and intergenerational disinheritance that builds upon the crushing effects of that very murder. It is an argument that presages that of Ta-Nehisi Coates, who has compellingly catalogued the waves of property transfer, both legalized and extralegal, from Black people to white, both during and beyond the years of official slavery, "land . . . taken through means ranging from legal chicanery to terrorism."[53] From McCloskey's rampaging assault to Stevens's theft of the will, Webb's novel explores both ends of that range.

Nor is it an accident that the man Stevens taps to enact the racial terrorism that will shift the Garies' property to his own control is the Irish McCloskey. Indeed, Stevens's racist minstrelsy, along with its violent conclusion, finds a sort of analogue in Webb's ethnic stereotyping of McCloskey, along with his compatriots, as a figure of stock Irishness. In addition to his ostentatious brogue, he is, for one thing, almost always drunk. McCloskey is not alone in this role of Irishman as racial enforcer; in a scene of humiliating segregation on a northern train journey, the conductor relies upon "one or two of the Irish brake-men to assist him . . . in enforcing his orders" of Black-white racial segregation (135). But McCloskey takes to the role most effectively, exhibiting a mercenary motive that offers a tawdrier version of Stevens's own economic ambitions; in the stage-Irish accent that Webb gives him, McCloskey relates the mayhem he and his compatriots (including the stereotypically named "Mikey Dolan" and other Irishmen) have caused: "Haven't we bin raising the very divil every night for the last week—running a near chance of being kilt all the time—and all for nothing! It's gettin' tiresome; one don't like to be fighting nagurs all the time for the mere fun of the thing—it don't pay, for divil a cent have I got for all my trouble; and ye said ye would pay well, ye remember" (189). McCloskey's almost hackneyed Irishness is precisely what, for Webb, makes him a quintessential—although economically disadvantaged—white.

When McCloskey's gang breaks into the Garie house, the violence descends into rampant looting and drunkenness, both inspired and managed by McCloskey:

> Rushing forward over his [Mr. Garie's] lifeless form, the villains hastened upstairs in search of Mrs. Garie. They ran shouting through the house, stealing everything valuable that they could lay their hands upon, and wantonly

destroying the furniture; they would have fired the house, but were prevented by McCloskey, who acted as leader of the gang.

For two long hours they ransacked the house, breaking all they could not carry off, drinking the wine in Mr. Garie's cellar, and shouting and screaming like so many fiends. (228–29)

Webb's description echoes the Irish statesman Edmund Burke's late eighteenth-century account of the horrors of the French Revolution: "The royal captives who followed in the train were slowly moved along, amidst the horrid yells, and shrilling screams, and frantic dances, and infamous contumelies, and all the unutterable abominations of the furies of hell."[54] In this violence, as Webb represents it—performed in the domestic space of the home itself, enacted in the interest of white economic gain, and culminating in the deaths of both Garie parents—lies what Coates has identified as the "the for-profit destruction of the most important asset available to any people, the family."[55] Douglass's figuration of blackface minstrelsy as theft is mirrored in Webb's representation of Stevens's multiplied and enforced racial performance as cognate with the staged performance of Irish mob violence as the means by which Black property is transferred extralegally to white hands.

Webb's literary representation of that transfer was written and published in the aftermath of the Lombard Street Riot of 1842, an event that marked Philadelphia in particular as an epicenter of specifically Irish violence against Black persons and the culmination of a series of anti-Black and antiabolitionist actions.[56] In 1899, W. E. B. Du Bois would describe the five years of white mob terrorism in mid-nineteenth-century Philadelphia culminating in that riot:

> In 1838 two murders were committed by Negroes—one of whom was acknowledged to be a lunatic. At the burial of this one's victim, rioting again began, the mob assembling on Passyunk avenue and Fifth street and marching up Fifth. The same scenes were re-enacted but finally the mob was broken up. Later the same year, on the dedication of Pennsylvania Hall, which was designed to be a centre of anti-slavery agitation, the mob, encouraged by the refusal of the mayor to furnish adequate police protection, burned the hall to the ground and the next night burned the Shelter for Colored

> Orphans at Thirteenth and Callowhill streets, and damaged Bethel Church, on Sixth street.
>
> The last riot of this series took place in 1842 when a mob devastated the district between Fifth and Eighth streets, near Lombard street, assaulted and beat Negroes and looted their homes, burned down a Negro hall and a church.[57]

Although in this passage Du Bois merely identifies the assailants and looters as a "mob," elsewhere in his study of the racial history of Philadelphia he notes the particular centrality of Irish Americans to the mounting racial tensions of the early and mid-nineteenth century, referring not only to "the intense race antipathy of the Irish and others" but also to the fact that, by the middle of the century, "the city toughs were largely Irish and hereditary enemies of the blacks."[58] Of this riot, which started as an attack on a Black parade commemorating the emancipation of slavery in the West Indies, Noel Ignatiev writes that it, "more than any other Philadelphia riot of the period, was a distinctively Irish affair."[59]

Du Bois's observation that the extralegal mob terrorism was tacitly condoned, even encouraged, by the structures of the legal system itself (exemplified by "the refusal of the mayor to furnish adequate police protection") finds an analogue in Webb's allusions to the developing practices of the Philadelphia police. McCloskey first enters the novel as he is brought to Stevens, acting as his attorney, by an "accommodating constable" (178), thus putting into motion the blackmail plot that will lead to the staged riots and, ultimately, the murder of Mr. and Mrs. Garie. While acknowledging that "it is often said that Britain created the police and the United States copied it," Jill Lepore has proposed a reversal of that transatlantic movement, seeing in the enforcement of the New World slave regimes the template for later British anti-Irish action in the nineteenth century; she points out that the London magistrate Patrick Colquhoun, who wrote "A Treatise on the Police of the Metropolis" in 1797, "spent his teens and early twenties in Colonial Virginia, had served as an agent for British cotton manufacturers, and owned shares in sugar plantations in Jamaica. He knew all about slave codes and slave patrols." As she relates, "nothing came of Colquhoun's ideas about policing until 1829, when Home Secretary Robert Peel—in the wake of a great deal of labor unrest, and after years of suppressing Catholic rebellions in Ireland, in his capacity as Irish Secretary—persuaded Parliament to establish the Metropolitan Police, a force of some three thousand men, headed by two civilian justices (later called "commissioners"), and organized like an army."[60] In Lepore's account, it is not so much because the eighteenth-century Irish were understood as nonwhite (in relation to "white" Britons) that the systematic policing enacted upon them was transferred to "other" nonwhite communities but that the brutal policing developed to control nonwhite persons was then deployed to counter political and religious dissidence in Ireland.

Within the world of Webb's Philadelphia, the police function *simultaneously* to regulate Irish criminality ("Howly Mother," McCloskey exclaims in reply to Stevens's demand that he attack the Garies' house, "why, they would have the police and the sogers at our heels in less than no time" [192]) and as an adjunct to it: the constable who brings McCloskey to Stevens is named Egan, and he also speaks with an Irish brogue ("it's far down in the mouth he is, be jabers—the life a'most scared out of him" [178]). Webb's juxtaposition of the police with Irishness functions as a sort of synecdoche for the broader social structure in which the rise of a white working class—along with a criminality *within* the agencies of law enforcement that supports it—is predicated on racial violence. It presages Du Bois's insight that "the white group of laborers, while they received a low wage, were compensated in part by a sort of public and psychological wage.... The police were drawn from their ranks, and the courts, dependent upon their votes, treated them with such leniency as to encourage lawlessness."[61] The protean relationship of Irishness to the police in Webb's novel complicates but ultimately affirms its fundamental whiteness.[62] For Webb, that is, a key component of white supremacy is not only the maintenance of the color line in the interests of what Douglass would identify as the desire for "power and dominion" but, specifically, the economic and professional advantage accruing to whiteness—including for those groups, like the Irish, who could share in that advantage through anti-Black violence.[63]

This does not really mean that the Irish had to "become white" in Ignatiev's sense, though. In fact, for Douglass, that the Irish can represent the abjected term in a binary hierarchy demonstrates that intergroup hostility and discrimination is not, for any essential reason, necessarily *racial*:

> If it should be the same as that sometimes exhibited by the haughty and rich to the humble and poor..., the same as Christians have felt toward the Jews, the same as that which murders a Christian in Wallachia, calls him a "dog" in Constantinople, oppresses and persecutes a Jew in Berlin..., that scorns the Irishman in London, the same as Catholics once felt for Protestants, the same as that which insults, abuses, and kills the Chinaman on the Pacific slope—then may we well enough affirm that this prejudice really has nothing whatever to do with race or color, and that it has its motive and mainspring in some other source with which the mere facts of color and race have nothing to do.[64]

Webb would surely agree that the brutality of the color line is not something essential to human nature—his insistence upon Mr. Garie's professed love for his family, let alone the many other instances of sympathetic white characters throughout the novel, demonstrate as much. (In fact, in figuring Mrs. Garie's relationship to Mr. Garie as simultaneously that of loving wife and chattel property, he diverts attention away from the necessarily coercive nature of that sexual and familial structure under the aegis of slavery, a diversion that does undermine the novel's broader critique.)[65]

But for Webb, the Irish are not simply another persecuted group. It is their whiteness itself, in *The Garies and Their Friends,* that Irish Americans perform through racialized mob violence. They do not enter into a preexisting whiteness from outside it so much as they deploy their whiteness in the interest of the racial identity politics that is white supremacy. Webb's insight again presages Douglass's account of the role of Irishness in the brutal enforcement of the "color line": "Our Californian brothers, of Hibernian descent, hate the Chinaman, and kill him, and when asked why they do so, their answer is that a Chinaman is so industrious he will do all the work, and can live by wages upon which other people would starve. When the same people and others are asked why they hate the colored people, the answer is that they are indolent and wasteful, and cannot take care of themselves." And, further, "The trouble is that most men, and especially mean men, want to have something under them. The rich man would have the poor man, the white would have the black, the Irish would have the negro, and the negro must have a dog, if he can get nothing higher in the scale of intelligence to dominate."[66] For Douglass, as for Webb, Irish white supremacy finds both its motivation and its excuse in the appeal to economic as well as social advantage.

Despite McCloskey's brutality, he is not, in Webb's novel, the actual impresario of racial terrorism and dispossession; that role falls to George Stevens. At the end of the novel, McCloskey confesses on his deathbed the lies that have undergirded the narrative of violence and dispossession that *The Garies* has told:

> When they arrived at the hospital, they found him fast sinking—the livid colour of his face, the sunken glassy eyes, the white lips, and the blue tint that surrounded the eyes and mouth told at once the fearful story. Death had come. He was in full possession of his faculties, and told them all. How Stevens had saved him from the gallows—and how he agreed to murder Mr. Garie—of his failure when the time of action arrived, and how, in consequence, Stevens had committed the deed, and how he had paid him time after time to keep his secret.
>
> "In my trunk there," said he, in a dying whisper,—"in my trunk is the will. I found it that night amongst his papers. I kept it to get money out of his children with when old Stevens was gone. Here," continued he, handing his key from beneath the pillow, "open my trunk and get it." (356)

Novelistic sentimentalism once again permeates Webb's analysis of the structures of American race. For Webb, echoing Douglass, the Irish ravager is not the mastermind of white supremacy but, ultimately, its cat's-paw, performing his whiteness by enacting racial terrorism in the interest of the dominant Anglo class. That does not in any way excuse McCloskey's violence, his racism, his murderous bloodlust, or his greed; it simply makes it more vulgar.

This backdrop of class affiliation and economic struggle—fundamental to mid-nineteenth-century literary realism—both provides the setting for and complicates the drama of Irish racial violence that Webb narrates, for race and class intersect with each other in complex ways throughout the novel. For instance, whereas Webb often presents his Black families largely, in the words of the *Literary Gazette*'s reviewer, "as 'elegant' and sentimental as any of the exquisite ladies or powdered beaux of the old Sir Charles Grandison school," their economic class varies widely. Bernard W. Bell, in his study of the Black American novel, has noted that while Mr. Garie himself is a wealthy southern gentleman (and, it must be remembered, an enslaver), the Ellises are both "dark-skinned" and "lower middle-class"; in Bell's analysis, "The author-narrator's sympathies are clearly with the strivings of black morticians, realtors, and doctors ... who also figure in the narrative."[67] Their personal gentility, though, does not exempt them from the threat of interracial, class-based hostility that arises from friction with the growing numbers of working-class Irish immigrants in 1830s and 1840s.

That hostility, along with its tragic climax, is not the only narrative that *The Garies* tells, however. And here, genre matters as well. By centering Clary's arc, I have followed the lead of Webb's affect-laden final chapter. But, in fact, that is neither where that chapter begins, nor where it ends; both its first and last paragraphs focus not on Clary but on the perseverance of Black family life across generations and despite racist terrorism. The chapter opens with the recovery of the Garies' property; it closes—in its brief epilogue—with a prospect of generations unfolding into the future: "Charles and Emily took a voyage to Europe for the health of the latter, and returned after a two years' tour to settle permanently in his native city [Philadelphia]. They were unremitting in their attention to father and mother Ellis, who lived to good old age, surrounded by their children and grandchildren" (368). Emily here is Clary's light-skinned sister, the one who chose to root her life in Philadelphia's Black community, to marry Charlie Ellis, to disavow the ruses of whiteness that entrap her brother. Far from the fixation of British reviewers on slavery to the exclusion of the actual subject of the novel, Webb's vision of realism, the verisimilitude of Black life in nineteenth-century America, is thus capacious enough to accommodate not only suffering but also accomplishment and care and success, not only the cliché of the tragic mulatto but also the building of family and community through work and love. Those, Webb insists, are also real. And as the Irish McCloskey was the agent of the racist terrorism that threatened to dispossess the Garie children, so, too, is McCloskey, through his deathbed confession, the agent of the restoration that secures the foundation of that survival, that provides, in Webb's restrained description, a "comfortable support" (358).

The complexities of class, along with gender,[68] underlie the text's repeated use of the term "gentleman," which (together with its plural) occurs nearly one hundred times in the novel, far more than any of the variants of "slave," despite the reviewers' fixation on that term. It appears, in the first chapter of the novel, in opposition to Blackness, in the prejudiced opinions of a New York businessman and advocate for the forced relocation, under the guise of philanthropic charity, of free Black Americans to Africa; this is the same Mr. Priestly who prides himself on his ability to detect any hint of Black heritage in even the lightest-skinned of people. As he is described by Mr. Garie, "He says, the existence of a 'gentleman' with African blood in his veins, is a moral and physical impossibility, and that by no exertion can anything be made of that description of people" (46). In Webb's usage, though, the classed and raced connotations of the "gentleman" are far more unstable than this sort of instinctually racist set of categorical oppositions would suggest. In the course of the novel the term describes both white and Black men: the white plantation owner Mr. Garie and the Black superintendent of his plantation, the working-class Black son Charlie Ellis and the white minister, a white engraver and a liveried servant, a beggar boy and a white attorney, an upwardly mobile Black Philadelphia property owner and the bigoted Mr. Priestly himself, ministers, teachers, philanthropists, waiters. The two specific characters to whom the label most frequently attaches are the sophisticated, emancipated Mr. Winston and the brutally murderous white supremacist Mr. Stevens. While a number of the appearances of the designation "gentleman," in the words both of specific characters and of the narrator, are clearly ironic (frequently so in the descriptions of the vicious Stevens, for different reasons from that of the irony attaching to the term in descriptions of explicitly working- and lower-class figures), its persistence across racial and classed contexts is an important aspect of Webb's account of social capital and its complex relationship to race.

That is to say that Webb's use of the term "gentleman" aligns with Toni Morrison's analysis of that same term as an index of the eighteenth- and nineteenth-century consolidation of abjected ethnicities into whiteness.

In *Playing in the Dark*, Morrison quotes at length from Bernard Bailyn's account of the Scottish "*littérateur* and scientist" William Dunbar,[69] another white man from Britain's Celtic fringe who found himself in Philadelphia (and, thereafter, in Mississippi) more than three-quarters of a century before Webb's portrayal of the Irish immigrant McCloskey. As Morrison points out, Bailyn's description of Dunbar serves as an index of a broader social process, "a succinct portrait of the process by which the American as new, white, and male was constituted."[70] And, significantly, that constitutive process uses the rhetoric of class to constitute the European ethnic as white gentleman: "Whatever his social status in London, in the New World he is a gentleman. More gentle, more man. The site of his transformation is within rawness: he is backgrounded by savagery."[71] Webb's project is similar, although with a key distinction: to a significant extent, Webb proposes a particular kind of gentlemanly "class"—as in elegance and social sophistication—that supersedes racial and economic hierarchies. Anna Engle has observed that "by describing African Americans in terms conventionally limited to Euro-Americans, Webb startles the reader into recognizing that these class-based words ... have been conflated with whiteness. He also asserts that they are perfectly legitimate words with which to describe African Americans."[72] For Webb, the Irishman is white, but the gentleman isn't necessarily so.

In contrast, Webb's novel uses the term "savage"—the term to which Morrison so aptly turns in her description of the racial violence that accompanies the constitution of whiteness—only twice; both instances describe the actions of Mr. Stevens, the racist instigator of horrific violence (184, 185), and both occur in the same chapter in which he describes his plan to foster racist—and Irish-executed—mob violence in order to drive down the prices of Black-owned property (although it is not in that precise context that the term appears). The displacement is, perhaps, significant: for Webb, savagery is relocated from the language of imperial conquest to that of the monster at home, as "gentlemanliness," its opposite, is a function less of finances or family than of a kind of sentimentalized affect. As the *Literary Gazette*'s review notes, many of Webb's Black and white characters have it, although certainly not all.

I want, though, to build upon Engle's insight in terms of the specific way that the lexicon of "gentlemanliness" not only disrupts any notion of a stable relationship between class, affect, and race but also narrates a *particular* history of whiteness. For one of the few major characters of the novel who is *never* designated a "gentleman," even ironically, is McCloskey, a detail which points to the complicated role of Irishness both in Webb's suggestive dismantling of the social hierarchies of white supremacy and in the new hierarchy of "class" that his novel of reform constructs in its place. For McCloskey himself represents for Webb a key figure of transformation, enacted on the level of the historical sociology that Morrison would identify. The historical process here occurs against the backdrop of and, in an important way, in the reverse direction of the blackface farce of Stevens's inadvertent minstrelsy act: as Webb, through Stevens's multiple colorings, renders whiteness racial, he also—through McCloskey's arc—demonstrates the way in which ethnic Irishness enacts its own whiteness through both symbolic and actual violence against Black bodies, a violence that accompanies the Irish thug's attempt to render class less salient and race more.

Bell writes that, in Webb's vision of "the virulence of Northern race prejudice," "prejudice and discrimination in jobs, education, housing, public transportation, the media, and public officials culminate in terrorism by Irish immigrants and members of the white working class."[73] This is certainly true. But it is also the case that *The Garies and Their Friends* narrates the Irish American claim to working-class whiteness precisely through anti-Black mob violence. This is not really a story of how the Irish moved from nonwhiteness to whiteness but rather a testimony that they were already included within the epistemological category of whiteness from the perspective of those upon whose bodies was wreaked the brutality of that inclusion. "The history of racial capitalism," Walter Johnson reminds us, "is the history of wages as well as whips, of factories as well as plantations, of whiteness as well as blackness, of 'freedom' as well as slavery."[74] By moving the realist novel into the world of Black America—and by figuring that world in terms of the precarity of free Black families alongside the threat of chattel enslavement—Webb demonstrates that history. It is true that the real villain of the novel is the ostensibly more clearly and consistently "white" Stevens, whom Bell designates "the bigoted mastermind of the terrorism."[75] But neither that, nor the fact that it is McCloskey who, through his sentimentalized confession, saves the next generation of Garies from the penury that his own murderous violence has permitted, erases the sociohistorical significance of his role *as* the dupe of white supremacy; insisting upon its whiteness, Irishness, for Webb, stakes its claim as the brawn enforcing the color line at the orders of the Anglo brain.

5

John Mitchel and the Polemic of White Grievance

> Mitchel's influence comes mainly, though not altogether, from style, that also a form of power, an energy of life. It is curious that Mitchel's long martyred life, supported by style, has had less force than that of a man who died at thirty, was never in the hulks, did not write very well, and achieved no change of the law.
> —William Butler Yeats, *The Death of Synge* (1928)

THE IRISH NATIONALIST John Mitchel, as William Butler Yeats suggested, was an activist of words. It was through his militant, impassioned, inspiring, and often vicious language that he so vigorously opposed British control in Ireland that in 1848 he was convicted of "treason felony"—a crime invented largely to respond to his seditious rhetoric—and sentenced to fourteen years transportation; he was taken first to Ireland Island in Bermuda, then to the coast of the Cape Colony (now South Africa), and finally to the penal colony in Van Diemen's Land (now Tasmania), from which he escaped to the United States in 1853. Yeats was not alone in representing Mitchel's influence as a question of rhetorical style, in both writing and speech, and in considering the relationship between that style and his nationalist activism. Praising the *Jail Journal*, Mitchel's 1854 narrative of his transportation and escape, Arthur Griffith—the nationalist founder of Sinn Féin—announced in 1913 that "in the political literature of Ireland it has no peer outside Swift. In the literature of the prison it has no equal."[1] John Eglinton (the pen name of William Kirkpatrick Magee) found in Mitchel's work a "hearty directness of statement ... which had hardly been heard in Ireland since the days of Dean Swift," and he called the *Jail Journal* "a book so successful in giving expression to the instincts and antipathies of Irish nationality, that, in face of it, any further talk of the inefficiency of the English language in Ireland is somewhat audacious."[2] Mitchel's ardently nationalist speech from the dock upon his conviction has frequently been recognized as a classic of the genre: the nationalist Sullivan brothers included it in their 1867 collection of speeches by convicted Irish nationalists since the 1798 Rising, in fact concluding the entire volume with Mitchel's prophecy that "the passionate aspiration for Irish Nationality will outlive the British Empire."[3] What the Sullivans suggest by this arrangement—and, indeed, by their entire anthology—is that political polemic lies at the heart of nineteenth-century Irish nationalist activism.

In Yeats's account, the reference to style as "a form of power" resonates in multiple directions, shifting between the page and the state. Style, in Mitchel, is a "form" in multiple senses, both a *genre* of power and an *instantiation* of power, an efficacious expression and a rhetorical mode that is in itself the enactment of power. That interplay of the literary and the political is common in accounts of Mitchel's language, especially in readings of the *Jail Journal* and *The Last Conquest of Ireland (Perhaps)* (1858–59), and particularly in terms of their significance to Irish literary history. Situating his work as an exemplar of "the *aesthetic* form taken by Irish nationalist thinking," for instance, David Lloyd emphasizes the relationship Mitchel enacts between literary and historiographic genres and the constitution of nationalist identity. As Lloyd astutely observes, the *Jail Journal* represents a sort of battle between categories of *books,* in which Mitchel's own "form of nationalist writing is posed against the writings of the Empire, which are seen as symptomatic of the hidden disintegration of its constitution. . . . The very process of composing the *Jail Journal* thus becomes Mitchel's riposte to imperial power."[4] For Mitchel, Lloyd proposes, "the individual's positing of his identity as a *continuity* repeats the form that the nationalist gives the history of the nation, which he believes to be the source and guarantor of his own identity."[5] As Lloyd's account suggests, the term "form" shows up frequently, and tellingly, in analyses of Mitchel's language; it is by deploying and challenging various generic forms that Mitchel's rhetoric achieves its effect.

Even Oscar Wilde's 1882 inclusion of Mitchel among the great Irish poets of the nineteenth century, which I describe in this book's introduction, involves a rhetorical legerdemain, a generic alchemy. Although Mitchel edited and wrote introductions for collections of poems by James Clarence Mangan and Thomas Davis (the alternative to Mitchel that Yeats describes in the passage that serves as my epigraph to this chapter) and printed poems by others in newspapers that he ran, he is not himself primarily remembered as a poet, nor was he in the nineteenth century. (Malcolm Brown relates drily that "back in the 1840s it had been noted that as soon as any important poet like . . . Mangan was assigned to the staff of the old *Nation* or to John Mitchel's *United Irishman*, poetic inventiveness vanished.")[6] Wilde himself seems uninterested in making a case for whatever forgotten Mitchel poems there might have been. Instead, Mitchel enters Wilde's category of "Irish poets and poetry" through his *political* action, his central role among "these men of forty eight" (that is, those associated with the abortive Young Irelander Rebellion in 1848, which Mitchel had spearheaded); Wilde recalls that "I was indeed trained by my mother to love and reverence them as a Catholic child is the saints of the calendar."[7] Mitchel's appearance in a lecture dedicated to and titled "Irish Poets and Poetry" enacts its own generic transfiguration, even canonization, framing his nationalist polemic as itself a form of poetry, a manifestation of sacralized style.

Once he arrived in the United States, while continuing to rally fellow expatriates to Irish nationalist causes, Mitchel expanded the scope of his polemic to include enthusiastic support for the slave regimes of the American South and, eventually, the Confederacy. Indeed, he has the dubious distinction of shocking both Frederick Douglass and Harriet Jacobs, among others, with his forthright advocacy for race-based chattel slavery. Douglass—who had in 1848 presaged Wilde in declaring that Ireland's "cause is already sanctified by the martyrdom of Mitchell"[8]—was taken aback by Mitchel's quick alignment with the enslavers of the United States once he arrived in that country: "One of the first utterances of John

Mitchell on reaching this country, from his exile and bondage," Douglass recalled with incredulity, "was a wish for a 'slave plantation, well stocked with slaves.'"[9] Harriet Jacobs, describing her precarity in New York after the passage of the 1850 Fugitive Slave Act, similarly evoked Mitchel as an exemplar of the power of the racial state to do violence to Black lives while providing a literal platform for white-supremacist advocacy by politically disadvantaged Europeans: "John Mitchell was free to proclaim in the City Hall his desire for 'a plantation well stocked with slaves;' but there I sat, an oppressed American not daring to show my face. God forgive the black and bitter thoughts I indulged on that Sabbath day!" (*Incidents*, 298). From nationalist saint, he has—through the racism of his rhetoric—become a form of sacrilege. Years later, Jacobs continues to register her shock at the moral and political dissonance that Mitchel presented upon his arrival in New York in 1853, and, indeed, he provides one of the starkest case studies of the translation of the genres of Irish nationalist activism into explicit white nationalism. Once he emerged as a prophet of Irish *America*, the powerful rhetorical force of Mitchel's Irish writings come to support a thoroughly racist program of anti-Black activism rooted directly and explicitly in his insistence upon Irish nationalism as white grievance.

It is relevant that both Douglass and Jacobs encounter Mitchel through his words, as a rhetorician simultaneously of Irish freedom and of Black oppression, for it is through his polemic that Mitchel constructs and propagates his argument for Irish whiteness as racial supremacy. In fact, Mitchel ultimately grounds his case for Irish liberty precisely upon the denial of that liberty to others, arguing that Irish freedom is a fundamentally *racial* right, that Irishmen deserve it exactly because they are white. Part of the reason for Douglass's surprise at Mitchel's expressed desire to join the ranks of American enslavers lay in the seeming incompatibility between Mitchel's anticolonial rhetoric in Ireland and his virulent support for racial oppression and white violence in the United States. And yet, I argue, that apparent incongruity—that failure to apply his arguments for freedom in the Irish context to the American system of race-based enslavement—is fundamental to his racial politics. That failure is grounded in his insistence upon Irish whiteness, and the racial violence that is central to his conception of what that whiteness entails. Douglass's and Jacobs's shock erupts from the fact that the inarguably powerful liberatory genres of Irish political aspiration could so quickly become the medium for racial domination.

In his preface to the *Jail Journal,* Griffith refuses to condemn Mitchel's express racism, instead valorizing it as itself a form of Irish nationalism: "The right of the Irish to political independence never was, is not, and never can be dependent upon the admission of equal right in all other peoples.... He who holds Ireland a nation and all means lawful to restore her the full and free exercise of national liberties thereby no more commits himself to the theory that black equals white ... than he commits himself to the belief that sunshine is extractable from cucumbers."[10] Griffith laments that "even [Mitchel's] views on negro-slavery have been deprecatingly excused, as if excuse were needed for an Irish Nationalist declining to hold the negro his peer in right," and contends that "the liberty he fought for in Ireland, he wrote, was just the sort of liberty the slave-holding Corcyræans asserted against Corinth, the liberty the slave-holding Corinthians fought for against Rome, and the slave-holding Americans wrung from England. To 'What was your principle,' he replied in a memorable sentence—'My principle was simply that Irishmen were fitted for a higher destiny and sphere.'"[11] The comparative is telling: for Mitchel—and Griffith—the Irish deserved a "higher destiny and sphere" than they currently had, but both suggest as well that the Irish also deserve a "higher destiny and sphere" *than Black persons,* despite the claims of those who, in Griffith's contemptuous words, "pretended that human equality existed."[12] Precisely by disavowing any relationship between the conditions of American enslavement and the quest for Irish nationhood, Griffith centers race; the sort of citizenship that Mitchel envisions, and that Griffith elaborates, is explicitly underwritten by its whiteness.

At the date of his arrival in the United States, Mitchel was one of the most famous Irish nationalists in the world. By the early 1840s, he had taken the initial steps toward a radical form of nationalism by organizing a banquet for Daniel O'Connell and meeting Charles Gavan Duffy, one of the founders of the nationalist paper the *Nation.* In 1843, he joined O'Connell's

Repeal Association, a political organization dedicated to the reversal of the 1801 Union of Great Britain and Ireland. Unlike O'Connell, with whom he ultimately broke politically, he argued for the necessity of an armed response to British rule. In an 1848 debate among the members of the Irish Confederacy, for example, Mitchel asked, "must the force of opinion always be legal?—always be peaceful? . . . I hold that there is no opinion in Ireland worth a farthing which is not illegal. I hold that armed opinion is a thousand times stronger than unarmed."[13] In the *Jail Journal*, he similarly asserts, "We must openly glorify Arms, until young Irishmen burn to handle them, and try their temper;—and this we must do in defiance of 'Law'" (60). Particularly in *The Last Conquest*, written in the United States in 1858–59, Mitchel would famously advance the claim that the Famine was intentionally exacerbated by the British government as an act of genocide: "I had watched the progress of the Famine-policy of the Government," Mitchel writes, "and could see nothing in it but a machinery, deliberately devised and skilfully worked, for the entire subjugation of the island,—the slaughter of a portion of its people, and the pauperization of the rest" (157). Declaring at the end of the treatise that, by 1849, "The Conquest was now consummated," Mitchel contended, "When I say that the whole code of poor laws was a *failure*, I must qualify that expression. . . . They were a failure for their professed purpose—that of relieving the famine; but were a complete success for their real purpose—that of uprooting the people from the land, and casting them forth to perish" (210–11; italics in original). He (misleadingly but polemically effectively) quotes the London *Times* crowing, "Now, for the first time these six hundred years . . . England has Ireland at her mercy, and can deal with her as she pleases."[14] Calling the disaster "an artificial famine," he declares that "the Almighty, indeed, sent the potato blight, but the English created the famine" (219). In the face of that sort of colonial evil, an armed insurgency is, for Mitchel, not only justifiable but necessary.

Mitchel also explicitly aligned his militant version of Irish nationalism with white entitlements. In *The Last Conquest,* for example, he figures the Famine as a specifically *racial* offense: "Can the American mind picture a race of white men reduced to this condition? White men! Yes, of the highest and purest blood and breed of men" (117). In fact, among the Irish accomplishments that he lists that makes their destitution so appalling is that they, too, were enslavers, although of other white people, "sea-roving Macnamaras and O'Malleys, whose ships brought from Spain wine and horses,—from England fair-haired, white-armed Saxon slaves" (117). That it is the Celts enslaving the Saxons is, in Mitchel's polemic, the perfect riposte to Knoxian anti-Irish anthropology. For Mitchel, it is not so far a leap from that to the assertion that the violent enslavement of Black people in the United States of the 1850s is not tangential to the argument for Irish political emancipation but its very predicate.

A possibly surprising source underlies the generic and rhetorical representation of Mitchel's Irish nationalism as well as (perhaps less surprising) his anti-Black racism: Thomas Carlyle, whom the Irish cultural historian R. F. Foster has dubbed "the unrecognized founding-father of Irish national rhetoric"[15] and on whom—seemingly counterintuitively—Mitchel had modeled his early politics and his historical vision. In an 1838 letter, Mitchel praised Carlyle's volumes on the French Revolution: "It is the profoundest book, and the most eloquent and fascinating history, that English literature ever produced. The only thing that comes near it in *importance* (not in philosophy, nor in wisdom, nor in fancy, nor in liberality, nor in magnificence of language—what a long parenthesis) is the 'Decline and Fall.' Such men as Carlyle are the salt of the earth."[16] While Carlylean modes held a particular attraction for Mitchel, he was not unique among the Young Irelanders in finding in Carlyle a significant model for both rhetorical style and generic form, as Foster has pointed out: "The continuous connection of past and present, the eternal spirit of the nation, the notion of heroic destiny, the effort to saturate oneself in the atmosphere of history until the curtain of the past could lift and allow through an illuminating beam, the idea of History itself, in true Romantic style, as a progressive regression—all these Carlylean themes can be tracked through the ballads and historical reconstructions which the *Nation* pioneered from 1843."[17] Despite Carlyle's derogatory descriptions of the Irish, Mitchel and the other Young Irelanders could find in him an amenable version of history—in part, perhaps, because "the eternal spirit of the nation" and "the notion of heroic destiny" could be appropriated by Irish nationalist polemic as the language of their own *racial* progress.

Carlyle's influence was not merely formal: Mitchel likely picked up the mode of what Foster dubs "Carlylean stylistic tricks"[18] precisely because they so effectively couched the content of his own argument. One (also counterintuitive) instance of that occurs in Carlyle's often sneering accounts of Irish laziness, a characterization that Carlyle's fellow Scot Robert Knox offered as well in *The Races of Men*, published a year after the "Occasional Discourse." Of "the Celtic race" Knox declares, "in the ordinary affairs of life, they despise order, economy, cleanliness; of to-morrow they take no thought; regular labour—unremitting, steady, uniform, productive labour—they hold in absolute horror and contempt" (214). ("Beggars, beggars," Carlyle scoffs in his posthumously published *Reminiscences of My Irish Journey in 1849;* "only industry *really* followed by the Irish people.")[19] Alluding to this representation of Irish laziness by denying it, Mitchel insists, "The people of Ireland are not *idle*. They anxiously sought opportunities of exertion on fields where their landlords could not sweep off all their earnings" (*Last Conquest,* 70; italics in original). As Patrick Maume has observed, "Like his master Carlyle, Mitchel saw liberty as sustained by self-directed labour . . . and willingness to fight for one's rights."[20] The difference is that for Carlyle the Irish are not willing to fight; for Mitchel they are. That's the point of his chivalric representation of those enslaving "searoving Macnamaras and O'Malleys." Despite seeming to be an inauspicious source for the grounding of an Irish nationalist politics, Carlyle's theory of history and his representations of Ireland at the time of the Famine became an important model for someone like Mitchel precisely in Carlyle's alignment of nationalist value with the will to fight.[21]

For Carlyle, derision for Irish laziness runs parallel with his taunts of Black laziness. In contrast, what Mitchel does in taking up Carlyle's rhetoric for his purposes is separate the two, displacing upon nonwhite people the Carlylean accusation of laziness, now explicitly racialized across the color line. The inhabitants of Pape'ete, in Tahiti, are, Mitchel claims in the *Jail Journal,* "a tall, well-made, graceful and lazy race," "too lazy to climb mountains, and see no object in it" (352). "These slaves in Brazil are fat and merry," he asserts while en route from Bermuda to South Africa, "obviously not overworked nor underfed, and it is a pleasure to see the lazy rogues lolling in their boats, sucking a piece of green sugar-cane, and grinning and jabbering together" (170). In these descriptions, the denigrations of nonwhite people redound to the assumed superiority of the writer—as Carlyle's denigrations of the Irish do as well, of course. That is to say that Mitchel's opposition to Carlyle's claim of Irish laziness, even while taking on his broader political philosophy, aims to redeem Carlylean rhetoric for a white supremacist Irishness.[22]

In contrast to O'Connell, Mitchel—along with a number of other Young Irelanders[23]—tended to insist that any suggestion of an alliance between Irish and Black politics of liberation was spurious; he mocks the Irish abolitionist James Haughton, for example, as a person "desperately excited about *negro slavery*" who "even seemed to have associated together in his mind (by some logical process which I have not learned) the cause of 'Abolition' with the cause of Irish independence" (*Last Conquest*, 80; italics in original). And he similarly disparages O'Connell's abolitionist speeches of the 1840s: "He poured forth his fiery floods of eloquence in denunciation, not of the British Government, but of *American Slavery*, with which he had nothing on earth to do" (*Last Conquest*, 61). For Mitchel, in contrast to O'Connell and Haughton, the key analogy underwriting the relationship between his Irish and his American politics was between the slaveholding South and Ireland, with the American North and Britain cast as tyrannical industrial powers, dominating and humiliating agricultural nations. Writing in late 1857 to the Irish Catholic priest John Kenyon (who was himself aligned with the Young Ireland movement, opposed O'Connell, and refused to condemn slavery),[24] Mitchel figured the debate over American slavery as a clash of civilizations, grounded in a conflict between binarily opposed economic systems that mirrored those of the British Isles:

> The South is trying one form of civilization, and with signal success; England has tried another (I should say *the* other), and is going shortly to ruin. I want to promote the success of the one and the ruin of the other. Consider this one point alone—the danger, weakness, and unsoundness of England arise in great measure from her vast manufactures. . . . Let her be furnished just these few years to come with more and cheaper cotton—crammed, surfeited, choked with cotton, and she will soon lose entirely what is even now so much impaired, the military spirit, without which a nation cannot live.[25]

Here, Mitchel transforms Carlyle's disparagement of the Irish who would not fight into an attack on *England,* figured as a nation in danger of losing the essential "military spirit" and opposed by a pair of conceptually aligned rising nations: Ireland and the American South. He represents his full-throated advocacy for the enslavement of Black people and their violent subjugation within the American system of cotton production as in itself a blow against British political dominance and, by extension, for Ireland.

In his journal, Mitchel describes the establishment of the Knoxville-based *Southern Citizen,* in which *The Last Conquest* first appeared, as an explicitly rhetorical act in the simultaneous service of twinned political aims: an economy grounded in race-based enslavement and the promotion of the idea that the slave-based American South should be understood analogically with Ireland. On the one hand, he asserts that the goal is "exhorting and encouraging the southern people, by means of 'commercial conventions' and otherwise, to take measures for the promotion and vindication of their own industrial system, as the best, wholesomest, and most conservative in the world." On the other, he adds, "But all this while I was thinking of Ireland and contending for the South as the Ireland of this continent."[26] In a letter to his friend Mary Thompson, who had remonstrated against his support of slavery—understandably finding it "hard to reconcile [his] sentiments" in favor both of Irish emancipation and Black enslavement—he declared that "when any of your taunting friends asks you again, 'What do you think of Ireland's emancipator now? Would you like an Irish republic with an accompaniment of slave plantations'—answer quite simply, 'Yes.' At least, I would so answer."[27] For Mitchel, advocacy for continued Black enslavement and for Irish national autonomy are often the very same project.

Writing again to Thompson after his founding of the *Southern Citizen* in the fall of 1857, Mitchel described the aims of the newspaper as grounded explicitly in advocacy for the race-based chattel slave system of the American South:

> The South and the North are two nations, and cannot, as I believe, go on long together.... I prefer the South in every sense. I do really believe its state of society to be more sound, more just, than that of the North; and

whatever measures the South calls for and truly needs to secure and establish itself, I advocate. Mind, I deny that any nation can ever *need* to do that which is unjust, any more than an individual can. Well, then, I consider negro slavery the best state of existence for the negro, and the best for his master; and if negro slavery in itself be good, then the taking of negroes out of their brutal slavery in Africa and promoting them to a humane and reasonable slavery here is also good.[28]

Mitchel's proposition that the American South is "the Ireland of this continent" has simultaneously economic and racial ramifications. It is not that Mitchel argues that slavery in general is salutary; like William Grayson—and many others—Mitchel is not above drawing on the power of a *metaphorical* slavery as the badge of ethnic derogation even while he would come to promote, as an actual good, literal enslavement on the basis of race. In the *Jail Journal,* for example, he describes "the incessant efforts of the British Government to break down all individual self-respect amongst Irishmen . . . and so turn a whole nation into servile beggars" (90), but he quickly makes his political argument still more rhetorically pointed: "Better a transported felon than a quiet slave" (91). Off the coast of the Cape Colony, he similarly castigates the "colonists of British descent" who support the British government's policies as "the small party of moderate slaves" (208). Like a number of white proponents of Irish national advance, Mitchel deplored what he identified as the "slavery" of Ireland in relationship to English colonial dominance; it is specifically Black enslavement that he advocates as "humane and reasonable."

Mitchel's rhetorical equivalencies across the Atlantic continue in *The Last Conquest,* which moves swiftly to overlay the Irish situation with that of the American South. Ireland, Mitchel says (somewhat inaccurately), is "precisely half the size of the State of Georgia" (8). And the suggestive analogy becomes increasingly sharp as the tract continues. Mitchel maintains that the replacement of the Irish crops lost to the Famine blight by the importation of foreign corn "would have required an appropriation of twenty millions sterling," precisely the amount, he goes on, that the British government paid in compensation to West Indian enslavers to reimburse them for the costs of emancipation within the empire, what Mitchel calls "turning West Indian negroes wild" (103). That is, Britain was willing, in Mitchel's description, to borrow "twenty millions sterling to give away to their slave-holding colonists for a mischievous whim" (94) but unwilling to spend the same amount on its white colonial subjects in Ireland. The putative equality of the monetary expense exposes, in Mitchel's account, what he figures as the unnatural inequalities of the British colonial regime, which not only discriminates between castes of white subjects but also prioritizes the freedom of Black slaves over the lives of white Irish. He thereby sets the abolition of race-based slavery as the counter to and, indeed, diametric opposite of Irish national well-being; for Mitchel, both sit in the same set of scales, both competing for the same twenty million pounds sterling, but only one can win. That Britain chose to emancipate its Black slaves rather than feed its white Irish is, in Mitchel's analysis, the very mark of its violation of the laws of racial logic and nature.[29]

The *Jail Journal*, framed at times as a sort of adventure-escape memoir and frequently less forthrightly polemical than *The Last Conquest*, offers a more meandering narrative path toward this point, working its way into a racial theory that both juxtaposes Irish and Black claims to dignity and political rights and, ultimately, displaces the latter by the former. In fact, as Peter D. O'Neill has proposed, the *Jail Journal* itself represents a form of generic theft, the appropriation of the tropes of the slave narrative in the interest of "Mitchel's commitment to the cause of Irish whiteness."[30] It seems astonishing, given where he would end up, that while off the coast of Brazil, Mitchel briefly entertains approval of slave revolts, in part because they indicate a Carlylean will to fight: "A few months have passed by since there was a bloody insurrection of the slaves in this Pernambuco," he writes. "In the other two great cities of Rio and Bahia, also, there have been formidable insurrections of late. I see no great harm in this: the moment the black and brown people are able, they will have a clear right to exchange positions with the Portuguese race" (175). In a line added in a later edition, he went still further: "That is to say if the Portuguese have now any right to hold the others in slavery at all."[31] That repeated word—"insurrection"—suggests that, at this point, Mitchel imagines that there might be a kind of *global* anticolonial rebellion; he uses the same word for the armed risings that he advocates in Ireland: "The *United Irishman* was at that time admitted to be making great progress in stimulating the just disaffection of the people to the point of insurrection" (22); "An insurrection, indeed, has been too long deferred" (92). At one point, witnessing actually enslaved persons rather than merely imagining slavery as a concept, he expresses some queasiness about the brutality of the chattel system, even as he quickly forecloses it by abstracting them into economic material, owned objects: "I surveyed them long and earnestly, for before this day I never saw a slave in his slavery. . . . I do not pretend that I altogether like the sight of these slaves. If I were a rich man I would prefer to have my wealth in any other kind of commodity or investment" (170–71).

While confined off the coast of Africa, Mitchel broaches the possibility of a multiracial nationalism, united against the imperial power of Britain. When he first considers the possibility of a postcolonial South African national consciousness spurred by opposition to the transportation of British felons to that country, it is as a multiethnic but generally white confederacy: "One result of the present movement seems likely to be a true *national spirit*" that might "have power to make an accidental aggregation of settlers become a national brotherhood instinct with the vital fire of liberty, and can transform the sons of English and of Dutch fathers into a self-dependent, high-spirited, nation of South Africans. So be it! There will be one free nation the more" (208–9). A few days later, he expands his vision to imagine, although only tentatively and incompletely, a broader South African anticolonial coalition across racial differences, at least at some point in the future: "The whole Cape population, white, black, and brown, scattered over a vast territory, is under 200,000,—and they are not able to reproduce the grand drama of Boston, Saratoga, and Yorktown, just yet. And their cause is *more* righteous—the outrage sought to be put upon them a thousand times more grievous. But justice and right do not always prevail in this world, nor often" (213; italics in original). Here, at least momentarily, he imagines a multiracial form of justice. And he does so in relation to a different part of the history of the United States from his own antebellum period that typically preoccupied him: the American Revolution, to which he gestures with the names of solely northern rebellious cities. There's a hint here of an alternative understanding of the role that race might play in anticolonial action, but only a hint.

More frequently, Mitchel discriminates on the basis of race between what he figures as different forms of enslavement. When, off the coast of Brazil, he claims that, for the first time, he saw "a slave in his slavery," he moves swiftly both to distinguish the men he sees from the Irish and to suggest that the Irish may in fact be *worse* treated: "I mean a merchantable slave, a slave of real money-value, whom a prudent man will, in the way of business, pay for and feed afterwards" (*Jail Journal*, 170; italics in original). The distinction here quickly falls into the recognizable trope by which the politically disadvantaged Irishman under British rule becomes the paradigmatic slave: "The poor slaves I have been accustomed to see are not only of no value, but their owners will go to heavy expense to get rid of them—not imported slaves, but surplus slaves for export—slaves with a glorious Constitution, slaves with a *Palladium*—a Habeas Corpus to be suspended, and a Trial by Jury whereby they may have the comfort of being rooted out of house and home, transported and hanged at the pleasure of the 'upper classes.'" "Is it better, then, to be the slave of a merciful master and a just man, or to be serf to an Irish land-appropriator?" he asks, clinching both the association and the contrast between the condition of the enslaved Black person and that of the Irish serf. "God knoweth," he concludes (170). It is possible, as Anthony R. Hale has proposed, that the question is a real one for Mitchel: "By making the comparison at all, he is opening the door to the notion that there is a potential equivalency of human dignity, that both oppressed peoples might be members of the same family of humankind. The bright, distinct line between Black slaves who deserve slavery and 'white slaves' whose punishment is unjustified, blurs momentarily in the flash of a rhetorical question."[32] If so, Mitchel doesn't seem to have stayed in that state of openness to racial equality for long.

Bryan P. McGovern has suggested that it was Mitchel's encounter with the American context that inspired his move toward a more essentialized notion of race.[33] And it is true that, for Mitchel, race was at times a flexible concept, particularly when it came to the racialization of Irishness. It is not strictly the case, however, that Mitchel's racial vision "becomes white" only upon arrival in the United States. Even as a writer for the *Nation*, Mitchel made his racial positions clear. Its cofounder, Charles Gavan

Duffy, who hired Mitchel as editor, wrote later that "Mitchel tried my patience sorely by defending negro slavery, and denouncing the emancipation of the Jews"; in Duffy's account, this is what led to Mitchel's resignation from the journal.³⁴ When Mitchel, or other Young Irelander writers of the *Nation*, appropriated the Knoxian language of the "Celt" as what Joep Leerssen has designated a form of "ethnic essentialism," it could be mobilized *as* a form of white supremacy (as in the example of early twentieth-century Gaelic League anti-Semitism that Leerssen relates).³⁵

This racialization of rights and the insistence that the Irish, *as* whites, fall on one side and that Black people—whether enslaved or free—on the other emerges in Mitchel's writings through his rhetoric of the "citizen." The grounding of citizenship in whiteness per se, and not on the basis of free or enslaved status, is one that the United States, as Mitchel's adopted home after his escape from Van Diemen's Land, increasingly emphasized. The 1790 Naturalization Act restricted the access to naturalized citizenship to "free white person[s]"³⁶ (including those from Ireland), but the work of racializing citizenship in general intensified in the nineteenth century; as the century proceeded, Evelyn Nakano Glenn relates, "The articulation of new and more derogatory definitions of dependence as moral and psychological in nature drew tighter and more explicit race-gender boundaries around citizenship."³⁷ As the Trinity College (later Duke University) historian John Spencer Bassett would write in 1899, looking back at the history of Black citizenship in North Carolina in the years before the Civil War, "it was as late as 1844 that the [North Carolina] Supreme Court undertook to fix the status of free negroes. It then declared that 'free persons of color in this State are not to be considered as citizens in the largest sense of the term.'"³⁸ While there was some ambiguity in the early years of the Republic, by the middle of the nineteenth century, when Mitchel arrived in the United States and began his career as a forthright advocate for white dominance and Black enslavement, "citizen" had become a fundamentally racial term. That was, of course, the infamous finding of United States Supreme Court Chief Justice Roger B. Taney, in his 1857 opinion in *Dred Scott v. Sandford*, that Black people ("whether emancipated or not")³⁹ "are not included, and were not intended to be included, under the word 'citizens' in the Constitution, and can therefore claim none of the rights and privileges which that instrument provides for and secures to citizens of the United States."[40] Mitchel began writing *The Last Conquest,* published in the *Southern Citizen,* the following year.

Nineteenth-century Black writers responded to that increasingly explicit racial restriction of citizenship, both rhetorical and legal. In 1837, Hosea Easton vividly figured the violations of Black enslavement in relationship to citizenship, pointing out that enslaved persons, kidnapped from one country and brought in bondage to another, suffer a double loss:

> They sustain the great injury of losing their country, their birthright, and are made aliens and illegitimates. Again, they sustain a national injury by being adopted subjects and citizens, and then be denied their citizenship, and the benefits derivable therefrom—accounted as aliens and outcasts, hence, are identified as belonging to no country—denied birthright in one, and had it stolen from them in another. . . . In this light of the subject, they belong to no people, race, or nation; subjects of no government—citizens of no country—scattered surplus remnants of two races, and of different nations—severed into individuality—rendered a mass of broken fragments, thrown to and fro, by the boisterous passions of this and other ungodly nations.[41]

And Frederick Douglass, in an 1854 speech, explicitly framed the question of citizenship in terms not only of enslaved or free status but also of race itself:

> [The] constitution knows no man by the color of his skin. The men who made it were too noble for any such limitation of humanity and human rights. The word white is a modern term in the legislation of this country. It was never used in the better days of the Republic, but has sprung up within the period of our national degeneracy.
>
> I claim to be an American citizen. The constitution knows but two classes: Firstly, citizens, and secondly, aliens. I am not an alien; and I am, therefore, a citizen.[42]

The 1790 Naturalization Act did, in fact, use "white" as a key designation, but Douglass's observation that "the word white is a modern term in the legislation of this country" offers a keen index of the degree to which, by the middle of the nineteenth century, American citizenship in general was becoming, monstrously, a specifically racial category.[43]

The contemporary press recognized—and highlighted—the fact that Irish Americans in particular might have a vested interest in this increasing insistence upon the grounding of citizenship in racial whiteness. The pro-Republican *Chicago Press and Tribune*, for example, in its account of the first Lincoln-Douglas debate in 1858 (at which, its subhead trumpeted, "The Dred Scott Champion" was "Pulverized") represented the appeal of Stephen Douglas's racialism as substantially limited to the Irish; "enthusiasm" for "the pro-slavery champion," it reported, "was almost wholly confined to the Irish Catholics."[44] This is the debate at which Douglas proclaimed, "I believe that this government was made on the white basis. . . . I believe it was made by white men for the benefit of white men and their posterity forever, and I am in favor of confining the citizenship to white men—men of European birth and European descent, instead of conferring it upon Negroes and Indians, and other inferior races."[45] Opening its account of Douglas's first speech, the *Press and Tribune* described him moving to "the front of the platform, amid the cheers of the Hibernians, who had fought their way to the front."[46] The suggestion here is that the Irish—the "Hibernians"—cheer because they understand the restriction of citizenship to white men to be advantageous to them *as* whites.

For Mitchel as well, citizenship becomes the explicitly racial shibboleth of Irish national rights, as he—like Stephen Douglas—aligns it with whiteness in order to include the Irish and, explicitly, exclude Black people, whether enslaved or free. It is not an accident that the word "citizen" appears so prominently in Mitchel's American publishing ventures: the *Irish Citizen*, the *Southern Citizen*, and (simply) the *Citizen*, as he constructs a notion of Irish nationalist citizenship within the context of the United States. The titles both allude to that of the *Nation*, the Young Irelander publication he had left behind, and sharpen the juxtaposition of Mitchel's nationalism with the political structures of the racial state. Of his ambitions for the New York–based *Citizen* during the mid-1850s, he wrote (in the later *Irish Citizen*) that "one purpose was to advocate and maintain the full rights of Irish adopted citizens to all the privileges and powers which purport to be conferred upon them by the Act of Naturalisation," particularly given the rise of anti-Irish and anti-Catholic Know-Nothingism, what he calls "this new and violent outbreak of Native-Americanism."

And "to make clear and plain to naturalized Irishmen themselves *what their rights are* as American citizens, and what they may lawfully and conscientiously do in the direction of liberating their native country from British dominion."[47] The Naturalization Act to which Mitchel refers specifically limited naturalized citizenship to "free white person[s]"; Mitchel asserts the right of the Irish to that designation. At the same time, along with—and as part of—their Irish nationalism, his "Citizen" papers were explicitly in support of Black enslavement.

At the beginning of the *Jail Journal,* Mitchel transmutes the metaphorical usage of the term "slavery" into a fundamental political category precisely through its exclusion from the ambit of the political as such. There, he argues that citizenship and slavery were in fact the polar terms in relationship to which Irish subjects must be defined: of Irish Catholics, he claims that they were "deliberately, ostentatiously debarred from executing the common civic office of jurors in any case of public concernment—that is to say, that they are not citizens in their own land—that is to say, that they are *slaves*—for there is no middle term" (29; italics in original). Here, citizenship is not explicitly racialized, although the implicit argument contrasts Irish whiteness, which *should* have the rights of citizenship, to enslaved Blackness, which for Mitchel does not. For Mitchel's Irish, citizenship is something that can be lost or gained. Indeed, he similarly figures all Irish persons as symbolically convicted felons, deprived of political existence itself: "My moorings are cut. I am a banished man. And this is no mere *relegatio,* like Ovid's at Tomi; it is utter *exsilium,*—interdiction of fire and water—the loss of citizenship, if citizenship I had. . . ; there are no citizens in Ireland,—there is no citizenship, no law; I cannot lose what I never had; for no Irishman has any rights at present" (38). But much later in the narrative, having boarded the *Julia Ann* in Tahiti for the final sea voyage to California, Mitchel declares both that the various personae of his disguises have finally joined in his rightful character ("Here, then, Mr. Blake, Mr. Macnamara, Mr. Wright, and Mr. Warren, have all become once more plain John Mitchel" [357]) and that that newly reconstituted person emerges under the name of the citizen: "The passengers and crew are all Americans; and already I feel almost a citizen" (357).

In collapsing his Irishness into a form of Americanism, Mitchel claims his citizenship as a racial category, rejecting the status as "slave," which he also comes to figure as racial. In his letter to Kenyon, Mitchel makes clear that his vocal advocacy for the American slave system—indeed for restarting the global slave trade in order to support it—is grounded in a theory of fundamental racial difference:

> I . . . zealously maintain the cause of slavery, and try to make the people here proud and fond of it as a national institution, and advocate its extension by re-opening the trade in negroes. You say, in this letter of yours, "Actively to promote the system for its own sake would be something monstrous." Why? I cannot so much as conceive any reason for this judgment. Actively I promote it, for its own sake, and shall promote it. It is good in itself, good in its relations with other countries, good every way. . . . I bethink me that I do not perfectly know the position held just now by the Catholic Church with respect to the *enslavement* of men. Whatever that may be, however, it has no application to negro slaves bought on the coast of Africa. To enslave *them* is impossible, or to set them free either; they are born and bred slaves.[48]

In this manifesto, slavery—the oppositional term to Mitchel's notion of citizenship—is not conditional or even a question of law; it is fundamentally biological and racial. The "negro" here does not even fall into the category of "men."

That advocacy of race-based slavery shapes the generic choice to present *The Last Conquest* in the form of a series of letters to Alexander Stephens. It was Stephens who would, in 1861, declare that the fundamental basis of the Confederacy was white supremacy: "Its foundations are laid, its cornerstone rests upon the great truth, that the negro is not equal to the white man. That slavery—subordination to the superior race—is his natural and moral condition. . . . Many governments have been founded upon the principle of the enslavement of certain classes but the classes thus enslaved were of the same race [in] violation of the laws of nature. Our system commits no such violation of nature's laws."[49] While Stephens had not yet delivered this "Cornerstone Speech" when Mitchel addressed *The Last Conquest* to him, that sentiment of Providentially mandated *white* political equality—and the concomitant relocating of the line of supposedly naturally ordained hierarchies of political domination away from class and nation and onto race—is one that rhymes with the rhetorics of race and nation that Mitchel used in his series of letters. What he knew of Stephens's race politics is surely one of the reasons that Mitchel named him as the addressee of those letters.

"Is the American mind able to conceive it possible," Mitchel asks rhetorically in *The Last Conquest*, "that noble lords and gentlemen, the landlords and legislators of an ancient and noble people, should deliberately conspire to slay one out of every four—men, women, and little children—to strip the remainder barer than they were—to uproot them from the soil where their mothers bore them—to force them to flee to all the ends of the earth—to destroy that Tenant-Right of Ulster where it was, and to cut off all hope and chance of it where it was not?" "No," he answers—without any hint of even ironic awareness—"I can hardly suppose that an American is able to grasp the idea; his education has not fitted him for it" (70). That Mitchel's description of the uprooting and dividing of Irish families, the forced migration and the reduction of humanity to what Giorgio Agamben has identified as the condition of "bare life"[50] (presaged even by Mitchel's "remainder," stripped "barer than they were") could so clearly apply as well—indeed, far more appositely—to the enslaved persons of African descent laboring in the American South is an argument that Mitchel does not, indeed *cannot*, entertain. Writing about Agamben's representation of "bare life," Alexander G. Weheliye points out that "the fact that the Middle Passage, plantation slavery, Jim Crow, and so on, are not included in most conceptualizations of this category . . . only highlights just how routine the brutalization of black flesh continues to be in the world of Man."[51] Certainly for Mitchel, at least by this point, the designation of the race line as absolute—as the division between that which is worthy of human attention and that which is not—acts to abolish the salience of the lines of class and nation and religion that were central to Carlyle's representation of the Irish as fundamentally lazy. In the system of interlocking analogies that Mitchel's letters to Stephens construct, the unnatural act—as it would be for Stephens in his "Cornerstone Speech"—is to discriminate *within* a race on the basis of class or caste or nation. It is impossible, in Mitchel's account, for "an American" to grasp the idea of the wholesale uprooting and dehumanization of a people because for Mitchel to be "an American" (as to be "Irish") is necessarily to be white.

Terry Eagleton has posited that, in another alignment with Carlyle, it was "Mitchel's hostility to industrial capitalism" that "helps to explain (if not excuse) his enthusiasm for the slavery of the southern American states, which he obtusely misinterprets as a form of *gemeinshaftlich* bonding between masters and servants in contrast to the heartless cash-nexus of industrial capitalism."[52] This is, I agree, largely true, as Mitchel himself makes repeatedly clear his adherence to a model of historical change that is fundamentally economic in its structure and metaphors. In the *Jail Journal*, for example, he advocates for forcing Britain into increasingly undemocratic actions vis-à-vis Ireland, precisely because that will "strip British Whiggery bare of his treacherous, conciliatory, liberal lambs-wool, and show him gnashing his teeth like a ravening beast (for no brute is so ferocious as your frightened capitalist)" (59). "Commerce," he declares later in the *Journal*, is the "obscenest of earth-spirits, once named Mammon, and thought to be a devil" (289).

The economic basis of Mitchel's historiography provides support for Sara Maurer's observation that "Mitchel's scrutiny of the famine mirrors a Marxist analysis of the worker estranged from the product he has made, no longer able to recognize the rights he has to it."[53] That vision of alienated (Irish) labor emerges, for instance, in *The Last Conquest* when Mitchel declares of the victims of the Famine, "They died of hunger in the midst of abundance, which their own hands created" (219). And, quoting Carlyle, he reviles English economic practices that, in his account, impoverished the Irish: "The ultimate idea of English civilization being that 'the sole *nexus* between man and man is cash payment,'—and the 'Union' having finally determined the course and current of that payment, out of Ireland into England,—it had come to pass that the chiefs were exchanged for landlords, and the clansmen had sunk into able-bodied paupers" (117).[54] Eagleton is more reluctant than Maurer to read Mitchel's politics as specifically Marxist, correctly noting that Mitchel's antiliberalism straddles reactionary as well as revolutionary positions: "His Anglophobia, as with a good deal of

Irish nationalism, was in some ways less an abhorrence of the English than a hatred of modernity as such, a Carlylean contempt for commerce, manufacture and the 'cant' of progress and benevolence which sits as easily on the right as on the left. It led Mitchel himself in both directions at once: towards an autocratic anti-liberalism, as well as to a belief that the poor must not be abandoned to the mercy of the rich."[55] It is true that despite the relevance of anticapitalism to his nationalist thought, Mitchel would argue in an 1848 review, aptly titled "Poetic Politics" (thus neatly conjoining literature with ideology), that "communism, in its most limited extent, can exist only in the destruction of private liberty—among nations, it presumes an infringement on the national independence, without which there can be no personal freedom, or social order."[56] In that same review, though, he simultaneously attacks the "reign of capital" and proposes what David Lloyd has called a "utopic dream of a pre-capitalist rural society of independent yeoman farmers" not that far, after all, from Marx's own vision.[57]

That anticapitalist stance might have prompted Mitchel to align his radical politics with the struggles for Black emancipation and enfranchisement in the New World. The slave regime of the American South, as scholars including Caitlin Rosenthal and Daina Ramey Berry have detailed, involved a highly structured managerial system of classifying, accounting, and calculating forms of capital that "was central to the emergence of the economic system that now goes by that name" of capitalism;[58] "slaveholders," Rosenthal points out, "built large and complex organizations, conducted productivity analysis akin to scientific management, and developed an array of ways to value and compare human capital," even including the calculation of depreciation and mortgage collateral.[59] And Berry has constructed a vivid and detailed analysis of the economics of enslaved human beings in the nineteenth century, from prebirth through life to posthumous commodification.[60]

That combination of brutality, modern bureaucracy, and sanctimonious pieties about the good it was all accomplishing might, if he had less investment in aligning Irishness with whiteness in particular, have attracted Mitchel's satiric scorn. After all, as Bonnie Martin notes, particularly in terms of the reliance on commodified human beings for mortgage collateral, "Rather than putting the South and North on a sliding scale that is preset to rank the North as the model of complex nineteenth-century capitalism and the South as an inferior replica, it may be more useful to think of northerners and southerners as performing various social and economic experiments in capitalism."[61] But—although he would include mortgages among the forms of British extractive capitalism that violated Irish nationalist integrity[62]—that didn't become Mitchel's argument. Carlyle's work itself, of course, could provide Mitchel with a model not only for an anticapitalist rhetoric but also for the entwinement of that anticapitalism with a fundamentally racist social vision: Carlyle's "objectionable language (revealing of equally objectionable presumptions) regarding people of African descent," David Theo Goldberg writes, "was expressed against the background of a critique of the conditions of the working classes in Britain. Carlyle's negrophobia accordingly was tied up with a critical account of laissez-faire capitalist political economy prevailing at the time."[63] The same is true of Mitchel's racism.

I question, however, Eagleton's contention that Mitchel's support for the slave economy of the Confederacy was grounded in an actual "misinterpretation," a conceptual confusion through which enslavement is understood as "a form of *gemeinshaftlich* bonding between masters and servants." Yes, Mitchel occasionally makes that kind of claim (notably in his letter to Thompson); so did William Grayson in "The Hireling and the Slave," as I have observed in chapter 3 of this book. But to *believe* it as an authentic statement of Mitchel's overall representation of American slavery is to be taken in by a rather transparently cynical rhetorical ploy. Eagleton's vision of a sort of misplaced *Gemeinshaftlichkeit* is predicated upon Mitchel understanding Black people as in fact human persons, comprehended as individuals within the ambit of affective relation; Mitchel repeatedly denies that, implicitly and explicitly. His sneering assertion in his letter to Kenyon that the issue of "the *enslavement* of men . . . has no application to negro slaves" is one example. In another instance, while considering "the actual traffic of slaves from Africa" in the *Jail Journal*, he starts with the almost passing note that "it was always sad enough to think of"; those thoughts, of course, are those of the white spectator to Black suffering—the lived experience of being kidnapped, enslaved, and transported to the New World on slave ships makes no appearance—but even that gesture toward a kind of human emotional connection quickly vanishes in a polemical attack on abolitionism:

> But Sir [Thomas] Fowell Buxton (this I believe is the name of him) and his humane accomplices in the British Parliament have aggravated the horrors of it four-fold. For in order to procure the requisite supply now, in spite of the pirate cruisers of humanity, four times the number of slaves have to be shipped.... When slavers are chased by a humanity pirate, and in danger of being taken they simply pitch all the negroes into the sea, together with the loose planks that make the slave deck, and then lie to and invite the British officer on board. He finds no slaves, and by the terms of the treaties must let the ship go free. Then the captain proceeds along the coast of Africa again to get another cargo. But this is not the only loss the shippers have to count upon. (175–76)

Once Mitchel's thoughts move toward the political, enslaved Black people are no longer the object of white sympathy but rhetorically become objects: "another cargo," potentially a "loss." That there *is* a "requisite supply" makes clear that these human beings are, for Mitchel, a form of stock material, items, provisions, tools. Blame for the "horrors" of the Middle Passage land not on the enslavers—whom Mitchel figures as passively subject to irresistible economic laws—but on abolitionist legislators.

For Mitchel, to think economically and historically—the modes in which his writing most closely approaches both Marx and Carlyle—is to think structurally, analogically, systematically, rather than personally and individually. That form of thought subtends his rhetorical alignment of Ireland with the American South—and, therefore, the slave economy of the South with Irish resistance to English capitalism. In his letter to Kenyon, analogizing his nationalist activism in Ireland with his vigorous support for slavery in the United States, he expressly figures the latter as the climax of the former:

> In Ireland I sought to rouse up national pride to such a point that we could "dismember the empire," which would have ruined the whole affair, and sent the enemy (that is, the British system) a naked beggar on the world. Ireland, just then, was suffering the worst by that system; would have gained the most by its overthrow. I was Irish, and intensely Irish, so my

business then was clear and plain. But now I meet that evil power here also; he is everywhere, and nowhere more active and mischievous than in these United States. I perceive in the institutions, and of late in the tendencies, proclivities, aspirations (these are vile, vague words) of the southern states, a special hostility of the British system; not hostility arising from the accident of England being active in suppressing, and loud in denouncing slavery, but hostility founded on essential differences in the two types of human society.[64]

That it might be enslaved Black people who, in the United States, are now "suffering the worst by that system" falls utterly outside of Mitchel's analysis here for the precise reason that he *is* thinking of systems, as he understands them, rather than people. He can only imagine "the two types of human society" once he, seemingly counterintuitively, stops thinking of the human at all. It would fall to a far more sensitive writer—and more incisive thinker—like Harriet Jacobs, in *Incidents in the Life of a Slave Girl*, published just a few years after Mitchel's founding of the *Southern Citizen*, to note the horrific damage of this mode of systematically figuring Black persons as things to be calculated economically, at the cost of any sense of their individual humanity: "These God-breathing machines are no more, in the sight of their masters, than the cotton they plant, or the horses they tend" (16).

In fact, the public letter that Jacobs, like Douglass, quotes—the one in which Mitchel asserts, "We, for our part, wish we had a good plantation well-stocked with healthy Negroes in Alabama"—explicitly disavows any inclusion of Black persons into the ambit of human affective consideration: condemning Haughton's abolitionism, Mitchel figures it as a grotesquely misdirected sympathy:

> Mr. Haughton has written at least one thousand letters, all to this precise effect: and especially six or seven years ago, while the doomed white slaves of his own country were in the very crisis of their own agony, we well remember that this worthy gentleman was seized with a paroxysm of violent sympathy with the *fat negroes* of America. He was in the midst of the most hideous and ignominious slavery that ever deformed the world. 'Slave-drivers' were living in Eccles street, around his very gates; slaves were crowding the poor-house gaols, within sight of him, dying like dogs, surplus slaves that they were, in

the charnel-garrets of the Liberty. *Slaves,* we say, with no more rights, social or political, than Alabama negroes—the difference being that an Alabama negro is of value to his master. . . . [T]he poor creatures labored under two fatal disqualifications for the sympathy of *so benevolent* a man—*they were white, and they were at his own door.* His heart was in Africa; *his tenderness was all dark in its complexion,* telescopic in its view.[65]

Mitchel here performs a characteristic series of structural analogies, a progression of abstractions that allow one term in his equations to replace another: the Irish have "no more rights, social or political, than Alabama negroes"; "slave-drivers" are "living in Eccles street" in Dublin. At the same time that he accuses Haughton of a "telescopic" analysis, that is, he enacts his own set of schematic equivalencies. The differences that he concedes fall into two categories: the economic (unlike the Irishman, the "Alabama negro is of value to his master") and racial ("*they were white*"). And it is that very whiteness that, in Mitchel's analysis, renders the Irishman a fit object of sympathy: the "doomed white slaves of his own country . . . in the very crisis of their own agony" as opposed to the "fat negroes of America." It is whiteness—and, specifically, *Irish* whiteness—that undergirds Mitchel's support for American slavery, that allows him to construct a series of conceptual analogies that refuse the alignment of the Irishman with the enslaved American (as O'Connell had done) in favor of the alignment, through the construction of a transethnic whiteness, of the Irishman with the enslaver. In this letter that was first published in the *Citizen,* Mitchel insists that citizenship—and Irish citizenship in particular—is predicated on whiteness.

In his own generalizing logic, offered in an 1861 article on the British cotton trade written for the *New York Tribune* (founded by the liberal Horace Greeley), Marx himself would both align the situation of the Irish with that of enslaved Black people in the United States in terms of their relation to English industrial capitalism and hedge on that alignment:

English modern industry, in general, relied upon two pivots equally monstrous. The one was the *potato* as the only means of feeding Ireland and a great part of the English working class. This pivot was swept away by the potato disease and the subsequent Irish catastrophe. A larger basis for the reproduction and maintenance of the toiling millions had then to be adopted. The second pivot of English industry was the slave-grown cotton of the United States.... As long as the English cotton manufactures depended on slave-grown cotton, it could be truthfully asserted that they rested on a twofold slavery, the indirect slavery of the white man in England and the direct slavery of the black men on the other side of the Atlantic.[66]

Writing about this passage, Ashley L. Cohen insists that "Marx does not ignore or gloss over the singularity of African slavery in the Americas, and nor should we."[67] It is true that he suggests that, "in general," these two "pivots" are "equally monstrous," and "the white man in England" (suggestively Irish and/or working class) is neatly juxtaposed in his formulation, rhetorically and schematically, with "the black men on the other side of the Atlantic." Yet, as Cohen emphasizes, he nonetheless distinguishes between "direct slavery" and "indirect slavery" in a way that opens the possibility of distinguishing *between* forms of oppression, of refusing the ruses of analogy. And, of course, unlike Mitchel, he represents the Irish sufferer, as the object of potential political action, in relation to the enslaved Black man rather than to the enslaver.

"Nothing highlighted freedom—if it did not in fact create it," Tori Morrison writes, "like slavery," a relationship that she astutely diagnoses as the "parasitical nature of white freedom."[68] And in making that point, she states what was in fact known to the enslavers of the nineteenth century, that the identity politics of white solidarity is necessarily built upon violence against Black people. In an 1858 speech before the Mississippi Legislature, Jefferson Davis relied on a pseudo-Marxian economic model strikingly similar to Mitchel's (and to Grayson's):

> You all know that by interest, if not by higher motive, slave labor bears to capital as kind a relation as can exist between them anywhere; that it removes from us all that controversy between the laborer and the capitalist, which has filled Europe with starving millions and made their poorhouses an onerous charge. You too know, that among us, white men have an equality resulting from a presence of the lower caste, which cannot exist where white men fill the position here occupied by the servile race. The mechanic who comes among us, employing the less intellectual labor of the African, takes the position which only a master-workman occupies where all the

mechanics are white, and therefore it is that our mechanics hold their position of absolute equality among us.[69]

"America begins in black plunder and white democracy," Ta-Nehisi Coates has pointed out, "two features that are not contradictory but complementary."[70] For Mitchel, it seems that that was self-evidently true, even while he saw it as a boon rather than a crime. In a note to the *Jail Journal,* Mitchel reports happily on the postemigration life of the *Nation* poet (and cofounder, in 1848, of the *Irish Tribune,* the short-lived successor to Mitchel's *United Irishman*) Richard D'Alton Williams: "He is still alive, and in Alabama; though I fear he has not a very valuable plantation there. The best in the South is not too good for him" (136n). The prize for revolutionary Irish nationalism in Mitchel's fantasy of success is life as an enslaver. Like Davis, Mitchel bases the civil privileges of whiteness upon Black enslavement.

The triumphant assertion of Irish whiteness as the resolution of what we might see as the racial plot of Mitchel's narratives arrives as well near the close of *The Last Conquest,* where Mitchel figures himself as finally taking on—and defeating—the Carlylean bugbear:

> A plan was promulgated by Sir Robert Peel for a new "Plantation of Ireland"—that is, for replacing the Irish with good Anglo-Saxons; and this idea was warmly advocated by no less a person than Thomas Carlyle. *Væ victis!* was the word. "Ireland," said Carlyle, "is a starved rat that crosses the path of an elephant: what is the elephant to do?—*squelch* it, by heaven! squelch it!" From this time commenced that most virulent vilification of the Celtic Irish, in all the journals, books, and periodicals of the "sister island," which has been so faithfully reproduced (like all other British cant) in America, and which gave such venom to the Know-Nothing agitation. Then, more than ever, English writers were diligent in pointing out and illustrating the difference of "race" between Celt and Saxon; which proved to their own satisfaction that the former were born to be ruled by the latter. (207)

So far, that seems like an attack on Knoxian polygenesis and its appeal to a writer like Carlyle, as Mitchel brings his scathing wit to the idea of a "difference in 'race' between Celt and Saxon." But then Mitchel adds a twist:

> A peculiar feature in this species of literature, is, that the most zealous apostles and preachers of it have been themselves Celts of the Celts: Carlyle himself, for example, a Scotchman of Dumfriesshire, and with a name that convicts him of kindred with the Celtic people of Cumbria; and still more manifestly Macaulay, who was, by his father's side, at least, of the MacAmhlaidhs of the Highlands; but who wrote of the whole Celtic family—pandering to the ignorant pride of the English—with a real venom and affected contempt, which one might explain upon the theory that early in his life some Celt had crossed him in love, or pulled his nose, or done both the one and the other,—but which I am inclined to account for on a more commercial principle: he wrote his books *for* Anglo-Saxons and for those who ignorantly believe they are Anglo-Saxons. (207–8; italics in original)

Carlyle is no longer the "salt of the earth" as he was for the Mitchel of 1838. Instead, Mitchel takes on Carlylean racial historiography ("what is the elephant to do?") and turns it sideways. Using the language of the "plantation" that subtends his alignment of Ireland with the enslaving American South, he lays waste to the race theory that motivates Carlyle's distinction between "Celt" and "Saxon" by pointing out the hypocrisy of that racial vision: both Carlyle and Macaulay are, by that logic, Celts. (He might have included Robert Knox as well, although Knox regarded himself—as a Lowland Scot—to be Saxon.)[71] Containing this usage of the term "race" within disparaging quotation marks, Mitchel—with his characteristically "commercial" analysis—shrinks the system of racial discrimination *within* whiteness to a marketing ploy, a ruse of capitalism. He thus places himself within the same circle of racial identity as Carlyle himself. That move, however, is possible only because Mitchel has now figured that circle as naming *whiteness,* a category expansive enough to include the Saxon and the Celt, the Englishman and the Scot and the Irishman. But—as his play on the term "plantation" suggests—not the Black American.

Jean Paul Sartre, in "Black Orpheus," would meditate on what he saw as the interpolations of race and class as well as their structural and experiential distinctions: "The notion of race does not mix with the notion of class: the former is concrete and particular; the latter, universal and abstract; one belongs to what [Karl] Jaspers calls comprehension, and the other to intellection; the first is the product of a psycho-biological syncretism, and the other is a methodic construction starting with experience."[72] Sartre's analysis is manifestly wrong, so seduced by the elegance of its own abstractions that it becomes itself a painful form of racism, a theft of Black experience as the basis of an authentic epistemology. Frantz Fanon certainly thought so: "When I read this page, I felt they had robbed me of my last chance. I told my friends: 'The generation of young black poets has just been dealt a fatal blow.' We had appealed to a friend of the colored peoples, and this friend had found nothing better to do than demonstrate the relativity of their action. . . . Consciousness committed to experience knows nothing, has to know nothing, of the essence and determination of its being."[73] But precisely in Sartre's abstractions, his erasure of Black experience, he might perhaps provide a useful key to Mitchel's own failure. For with his analogies, his schematic understanding of history, his sneering disparagements of "laziness," Mitchel translates Carlylean polemic from its grounding in anti-Irishness first to the realm of Irish nationalism and then to the context of American white supremacy and anti-Black brutality. Proposing a structural alignment of the slaveholding South with politically disenfranchised Ireland, what he explicitly and brutally effaces is any account of Black experience, any acknowledgment of Black suffering or Black aspiration or Black accomplishment. Mitchel does, indeed, construct a form of progress novel that emerges even in his nonfiction polemics, articulating a historiography of revolution that culminates in a version of global citizenship that travels from Ireland, via the coast of Bermuda, Pernambuco, Cape Town, and Van Diemen's Land, to New York and Washington and Nashville, as fundamentally and essentially white and that includes Irishness in that vision of whiteness.

6

Performing Sympathy in *The Octoroon*

> The drama, therefore, has two parts: The action which causes suffering, and the persons who suffer. But persons differ by their natures, and suffer differently both in manner and degree according to their natures; this self-distinction defines the *character* of each.
>
> —Dion Boucicault, "The Art of Dramatic Composition" (1878)

BOTH DION BOUCICAULT AND his plays were well traveled. Born in Dublin as Dionysius Lardner Boursiquot, likely in 1820,[1] he was in London at the University College School by 1833 and acting at the Theatre Royal in Brighton in the summer of 1838.[2] "Between 1840 and 1880," Marjorie Howes proposes, he was "arguably the most famous and influential man of the theater in the Anglophone Atlantic world," and his "most popular plays were circum-Atlantic hits."[3] After the 1841 success of *London Assurance* at Covent Garden, his biographer Robert Hogan relates, "In 1842, five plays by Boucicault appeared in London; in 1843, there were three more plays; in 1844, there were seven; in 1845, there were two; in 1846, there were five."[4] He arrived in New York in September 1853, in Boston in 1854, in New Orleans in 1855, and in the District of Columbia to open the Washington Theatre in 1858. After that theater failed, he co-managed the Winter Garden Theatre back in New York. Although he returned to London in 1860, he continued to live in New York for extended periods from 1872 until his death in 1890, having become an American citizen in 1873.[5]

A fact of Boucicault's professional life, migration was central as well to his artistic vision. Howes points out that Boucicault's melodramas explore the relationships between places, local and distant, as a key driver of plot, inspired by what she identifies as the mid-nineteenth-century "changing reality" of geographic mobility and the "various infrastructures and exchanges that link the local" to the distant.[6] The plays themselves undergo a series of literary transfers and translocations, to the extent that the same characters and plots could appear in multiple dramas under different geographic names. It is often said that Boucicault wrote more than 150 plays, but a precise count is complicated by the fact that several recycle material to a significant or even total degree.[7] As Hogan observes, "*The Poor of New York, The Streets of New York, The Poor of Liverpool, The Streets of London, The Streets of Dublin, The Streets of Philadelphia*, and *The Money Panic of '57* are all the same play. . . . [H]e merely changed the title and the locale according to wherever he played it. It was extremely successful."[8] As this practice suggests, Boucicault saw this 1857 play, among others, as transportable to various settings while the titles themselves insist upon the relevance of a particular location (Dublin or New York or London or Liverpool or Philadelphia). And even before that whirlwind of resettings, the play itself—again, like many of Boucicault's plays—is in fact an adaptation of an earlier play, *Les pauvres de Paris* (1856), by Édouard Brisebarre and Eugène Nus.[9]

It might seem that a play like *The Octoroon; or, Life in Louisiana* (1859), inspired by Boucicault's time in New Orleans and first performed at the Winter Garden in New York,[10] would not be amenable to such dramaturgical relocation, firmly rooted as it appears to be in the practices and ideologies of the slave states of the American South. Joseph Roach, however, compellingly reads the play's Louisiana setting as a more generalizable "frontier," "a historic zone of circum-Atlantic encounter, for which the play soothingly—in careful increments of blood—substitutes binary oppositions based on variations of the theme of manifest destiny."[11] And Howes has proposed that Boucicault's "most intense and sustained engagement with Atlantic history appears in the generic conventions of his works, rather than in his topical references to issues such as American slavery or Irish politics that have so interested recent scholars."[12] What I will argue in this chapter, though, is that—as Howes's article itself makes amply clear—these are not truly separable concepts in Boucicault's work, that the development and adaptation of generic convention are the means by which he constructs his vision of American slavery, Irish politics, and the analogies he draws between them. And, further, that the failure of those generic conventions, here the affordances of melodrama, to comprehend the *differences* between Irish politics and American slavery is part of what leads to the failure of *The Octoroon* in particular to adequately represent the moral atrocity that chattel enslavement embodied. The imaginative analogies that undergird that alignment manifest in Boucicault's play as a series of tropes for dislocation and identification across difference, both within *The Octoroon* itself and across its performance history: translation, generic transposition, doublings of casting across plays, and—perhaps most importantly—the deployment of dramatic sympathy itself.

For Boucicault, the principal expressive mode for the representations of both Irishness and American enslavement is melodrama, what Linda Williams identifies as "the cultural force that, beginning in the nineteenth century, supplied story materials about race, gender, and class already organized into visually compelling forms of pathos and action."[13] Written almost precisely contemporaneously with John Mitchel's *Last Conquest, The Octoroon*, originally in five acts and then in rewritten versions of four or three, takes place in Louisiana, on a slave-worked plantation called Terrebonne; the deceased owner of the plantation—a Judge Peyton—has left the estate divided and mortgaged, half owned by his widow and half by the villainous former overseer, Jacob M'Closky. Judge Peyton's nephew George has recently returned from France, where he has been educated, and he finds himself romantically desired by the white heiress Dora Sunnyside but attracted to Zoe, the "octoroon" of the title who is the daughter of his uncle and an enslaved woman. Zoe, in fact, attracts the romantic attention not only of George but also of M'Closky and of the new overseer of the plantation, the dilettantish Yankee Salem Scudder. With her one-eighth of Black blood, Zoe is forbidden by Louisiana law from marrying a white man, although she has been (ostensibly) freed by the late Judge Peyton and otherwise seems to function largely as a member of the family. Whereas George proposes to Zoe that they might go to the North, where they could wed, Mrs. Peyton urges him to marry Dora in order to shore up the family's finances. Instead, crushed by debts, the Peytons are forced to sell Terrebonne and all of its holdings, including its human chattels. The twist occurs when M'Closky discovers that Zoe was emancipated while the estate was already mortgaged; under these conditions Judge Peyton had no legal right to diminish the value of the property, and—by law—Zoe is in fact still enslaved. The intertwined climaxes of the racial and romantic plots occur at a heartrending auction at which not only the physical property of the estate but also the enslaved persons are sold to the highest bidder; M'Closky outbids the rest to buy Zoe with the intention of forcing her into sexual servitude. That plan unravels when it is revealed that M'Closky knew that a letter had just arrived from England paying the first installment of a debt that had been owed to Judge Peyton and thereby obviating the need for any sale of the estate. In order to conceal that letter from the Peytons, M'Closky has stolen it from the mailbag; in the process of doing so, he murdered a young Black boy named Paul who had been sitting on the bag, a murder for which he framed the Native American Wahnotee. Miraculously, the moment of murder was accidentally caught in a photograph produced by one of Scudder's technological toys, a camera that Paul and Wahnotee had been playing with. Once that photographic evidence comes to light, M'Closky's guilt is clear, the letter from England is revealed, and the sale is cancelled. In the American version, however, Zoe has already despaired of her loss of freedom and taken poison, dying in George's arms.

Despite what appears to be its topical and geographic specificity, *The Octoroon*—which Daphne A. Brooks fittingly designates "Boucicault's traveling melodrama of sensation and dystopian reform"[14]—emerges from a series of generic adaptations and national transpositions. First and foremost, it develops characters and plot elements from a series of largely abolitionist works, in different genres, by white American authors of the 1840s and 1850s: Lydia Maria Child's short story "The Quadroons" and Henry Wadsworth Longfellow's poem "The Quadroon Girl," both from 1842, and the Irish-born Thomas Mayne Reid's 1856 novel *The Quadroon: Or A Lover's Adventures in Louisiana*, likely the proximate source for Boucicault's framing of his plot. More broadly, as Brooks has compellingly shown, the melodrama of Boucicault's play emerges out of a set of mutually constructive generic influences, growing from the "interstices of minstrel shows, pantomime, melodrama, and spectacular theatre."[15] At the same time, Boucicault would, in the following year, seemingly rewrite a set of central characters and events of *The Octoroon* as an *Irish* melodrama, *The Colleen Bawn* (1860), which was simultaneously an adaptation of the Limerick-born Gerald Griffin's 1829 novel *The Collegians*.[16] That history fills out the context of Roach's attention to the play's variations on a theme; through Boucicault's practices of adaptation and translocation, plays that were themselves reworkings of distinct source materials became versions of each other.

Perhaps counterintuitively, Boucicault's own relocation to the United States apparently refocused his attention on Ireland. While his Regency-inspired 1842 comedy *The Irish Heiress* featured a number of Anglo-Irish characters, it was set in London. His first play actually set *in* Ireland was *Andy Blake*, staged in Boston in the year after his arrival in the United States. Indeed, as Scott Boltwood has pointed out, "very few Irish authors had less direct experience in Ireland" than Boucicault did;[17] nonetheless, Boltwood also notes, during the second half of his career, particularly from the early 1860s forward (that is, after he had relocated to America), Boucicault became engaged in "an assertive Irish nationalism that expresses itself in his life as well as his drama." It was then that he became "a public apologist for Irish rebels, raising funds for transported exiles, [and] petitioning for the release of jailed Fenians."[18] Back in the 1850s, even *The Colleen Bawn*—sometimes identified as the first of his truly "Irish" plays[19]—offers merely, in Hogan's account, "a hint of realism here and there, of a true picture of Irish life; but largely Boucicault ... left out the poverty and the squalor and the hatred and the injustice."[20] If a similar charge can be leveled at *The Octoroon*, we might see in that fact a suggestive conjunction between Boucicault's initially tentative approaches to Irish nationalist politics and his ambivalence about the abolition of American slavery.

In fact, Irish and American generic tropes keep colliding in these two plays. In an echo of Frank J. Webb's brutish Irish American race-riot instigator McCloskey in *The Garies and Their Friends*, *The Octoroon*'s rapacious Yankee overseer sports the name M'Closky,[21] and he echoes the villainous overseers of the estates of absentee landlords in Irish nationalist romances; the mortgage melodrama of the play, steeped in rhetorics of dispossession and bad-faith dealing, had been the background as well of *The Irish Heiress*. (The *New York Times*, in a column arguing—bizarrely—against any specific political salience of *The Octoroon*, opined, "The only irreclaimable rascal in the piece, indeed, is a Yankee by origin, and by name a child of Green Erin.")[22] *The Colleen Bawn* similarly features a grasping and sexually threatening estate agent, the prospect of the loss of mortgaged property unless the son of the widowed owner marries a rich heiress he does not love, and the suggestion (here false) of suicide by its lower-caste female romantic lead. Agnes Robertson, who played Zoe in the first production of *The Octoroon,* played that romantic lead, Eily O'Connor, in the first production of *The Colleen Bawn;* whereas Zoe is part Black, Eily is "a peasant girl—a vulgar, barefooted beggar."[23] Boucicault himself, who originated the role of *The Octoroon*'s Indian Wahnotee played *The Colleen Bawn*'s Irish "outlaw," Myles na Coppaleen, suggesting that they were for him two comparable instantiations of the stage ethnicities that were his specialty. Whereas *The Octoroon* is set in the United States during the politically fraught 1850s, in the years leading up to the dissolution of the Union and the Civil War, *The Colleen Bawn* is set in Ireland, in the politically fraught 1790s, in the years leading up to the 1798 rebellion and, in response, the Act of Union through which the United Kingdom itself was formally established. The written stage dialect of the enslaved Black characters of Terrebonne slips—sometimes uncannily—into the stage Irish brogue of the peasant classes of Killarney.[24] In December 1861, London's Adelphi Theatre staged *The Octoroon* as a double bill with *The Colleen Bawn*.[25] In a version of Howes's observation that Boucicault's plots "depend largely upon events and forces in far-off locales," Ireland itself, as a setting for his plays, seems to come into focus for Boucicault from the vantage of America.

As Boltwood proposes, *The Colleen Bawn* itself *also* hinges on what it presents as racial difference, although in the context of the British "race science" of Celtic character rather than in that of American racial enslavement. *The Colleen Bawn*, Boltwood argues, brings Victorian racial ethnology to the stage by putting it into juxtaposition with structures of political power: "Whereas Boucicault's portrayal of the play's peasants resonates with the prejudicial stereotypes of [Robert] Knox and [Goldwin] Smith, the work focuses on the ambivalent relationship of the Irish to the Anglo-Irish Ascendancy that ruled them. Although this aristocracy claimed a cultural and racial identification with England's Saxon population that justified their separation from and superiority to the Irish Celt, they similarly asserted the existence of a special relationship to their subjects which necessitated their role as political surrogates for English authority."[26] That is, I think, true. It is further relevant, as Shaun Richards relates, that with *The Colleen Bawn* and, later, *The Shaughraun* and *Arrah-na-Pogue*, "The Irish titles of the plays, on which Boucicault insisted, suggest the exotic otherness of Ireland that was being purveyed on the international theatrical market."[27] And it is also the case that, within Boucicault's model of aligning the American situation with the Irish, both Zoe and Eily are, as Boltwood suggests, "differentiated from their English counterparts only by the cultural markers more directly associated with class than race."[28] But the very fact that Boucicault believed he could make that alignment, that he can figure Zoe's plight as one of class rather than race, is telling. That this play moves toward an emotional climax in which its romantic lead is put upon the block to be *auctioned* with the other property of the distressed Peyton plantation while still glancing at the Irish situation only demonstrates the extent to which Boucicault is unable to register the important differences between Zoe and Eily, and between the development of British "race science" of Celticness in the mid-nineteenth century and the experiences of enslaved African Americans. In an important sense, I want to propose, the attraction for Boucicault of what Frank B. Wilderson III has called "the ruse of analogy" arises from his emphasis on the emotional pull of individual characters of melodrama at the expense of an understanding of the broader historical forces that shape the possibilities for those characters.

Tactical performance, including that of the nineteenth-century theater, could, of course work against the hierarchicized categories of racial identity that underwrote the American white ethnostate. Gay Gibson Cima, for instance, has detailed the multifarious ways that Black and white women, in the four decades leading up to the Civil War, mobilized the power of performance and of sympathy, in its nineteenth-century meaning, toward abolitionist activism: "Transforming their homes, churches, and civic halls into stages, they adapted everyday performances—after-dinner conversations, neighborly visits, social events, and religious traditions—toward anti-slavery goals. They recited poems, transposed them into hymns, and sang them within family circles and at monthly 'concerts' for the slave. They staged activist dialogues and plays, read essays aloud, gave speeches, and used silence productively onstage."[29] She notes, pointedly, that in 1859, "as Dion Boucicault's blockbuster hit *The Octoroon* toured the United States, the Crafts [William and Ellen] opened their London home to Sarah Parker Remond, who was traveling in Great Britain for a lecture tour. Henry, Lord Brougham (1778–1868), an aging abolitionist and 'the most illustrious man in England,' visited Remond at the Crafts' home, conversing with her for an hour."[30] This is the same Lord Brougham who, two years earlier, wrote the preface to Webb's *The Garies and Their Friends*.

In contrast to that abolitionist mobilization of feeling, Boucicault's play registers a fundamental ambivalence about how directly to represent and criticize the institution of slavery as opposed to playing on the melodramatic possibilities of a nearly white woman who finds herself enslaved. And that ambivalence is reflected in the conflicting readings that emerged in the series of reviews and responses following the initial performances. The New York–based (and antiabolitionist) sportsmen's magazine *Spirit of the Times* called the play "a gross libel upon the social relations of the South" and asserted with shocked indignation that "in the first act, three white men, two of independent fortune, and one with character enough to be an overseer on a large estate, seriously propose to 'marry a n[—].' This is Bourcicault's idea of Southern institutions, and this idea is the English and the [abolitionist] Wendall Phillips [sic] idea, to endeavor, by false sympathy, to break down caste, and elevate the negro to the same level with the whites."[31] The *New York Herald*—edited by the then pro-southern and proslavery James Gordon Bennett—declared that *The Octoroon* "will carry with it the abolition aroma" and that "it is certainly disgraceful that the people of this metropolis ... cannot even go to the theatre without having the almighty n[—] thrust under their noses. Abolition doctrines on or off the stage should receive the severest denunciation from every citizen who has the good of the republic at heart."[32] In contrast, Horace Greeley's abolitionist *New York Daily Tribune* criticized the play for, in the end, exhibiting a "placatory tendency to the slave-owner."[33] In his 1889 autobiography, Joseph Jefferson, who played Salem Scudder in the original production, acknowledged that the play itself worked against a coherent politics, in part through a divergence of "feeling" from "action": "There were various opinions as to which way the play leaned—whether it was Northern or Southern in its sympathy. The truth of the matter is, it was non-committal. The dialogue and characters of the play made one feel for the South, but the action proclaimed against slavery, and called loudly for its abolition." In Jefferson's account, that ambivalence functioned most clearly on the level of spectatorial affect: "When *Zoe*, the loving octoroon, is offered to the highest bidder, and a warm-hearted Southern girl offers all her fortune to buy *Zoe* and release her from the threatened bondage awaiting her, the audience cheered for the South; but when again the action revealed that she could be bartered for, and was bought and sold, they cheered for the North as plainly as though they had said, 'Down with slavery.' This reveals at once," he concludes, "how the power of dramatic action overwhelms the comparative impotency of the dialogue."[34] Jefferson's reminiscence, that is, represents vicarious feeling both as manipulable and as stronger than any particular political or ethical position. Through that affective manipulation, he suggests, *The Octoroon* manages to position itself as being both for and against chattel enslavement.

Boucicault himself seems to have coveted that kind of interpretive ambiguity, along with the attention and financial windfall that could emerge from it. In a letter printed in the *New Orleans Picayune* in 1860, he noted that the play "has been attacked by the Press here—some alleging that it is a rank pro-Slavery drama, others that it is an Abolition play in disguise, and others that it is neither. As for my political persuasion, I am a Democrat, and a Southern Democrat, but do not mix myself up with politics in any way"; beside this letter he included another, startlingly requesting that the governor of Louisiana—of all people—accept the play's dedication.[35] In an 1861 letter to the London *Times*, following the play's British opening, Boucicault made the spurious claim that, in general, the experience of slavery was not as terrible, at least in its corporeal violences, as an English audience might assume: "A long residence in the Southern States of America had convinced me that the delineations in *Uncle Tom's Cabin* of the condition of the slaves, their lives, and feelings were not faithful. I found the slaves, as a race, a happy, gentle, kindly-treated population, and the restraints upon their liberty so slight as to be rarely perceptible.... [T]he slaves are in general warmly attached to their masters and to their homes, and this condition of things I have faithfully depicted."[36] Situating his play in opposition to Harriet Beecher Stowe's *Uncle Tom's Cabin*, a dramatization of which had appeared at the Adelphi in 1852, Boucicault duplicitously insists here upon the general benignity of the American slave system, whatever the melodramatic agonies of individual characters; in this erasure of slavery's violences, he almost could be the pro-enslavement poet and politician William Grayson.

This sort of claim has led critics like Sarah Meer to interpret Boucicault's claims, in other venues, that *The Octoroon* was forthrightly antislavery as strategic rather than trustworthy, particularly his insistence in the British press that Zoe's death was necessary to drive home the abolitionist argument. Instead, Meer suggests, it was Boucicault's keen sense of the business-generating uses of controversy rather than any authentic politics that motivated both his public statements about the play and his decision to rewrite its ending, after it had opened in London, with the marriage of Zoe and George: "The controversy," Meer points out, "was publicity; rewriting the play gave its run a new lease of life, renewing interest and drawing in seasonal audiences."[37] Meer's interpretation is supported by a lengthy contemporary account in the *New York Times* of Boucicault's lawsuit against the Winter Garden Theatre, as he attempted to stop the production after he and Robertson had broken their contracts to act in it; in that article, the *Times* reported that the Winter Garden manager, William Stuart, asserted in his deposition that Boucicault "had frequently asked deponent, during the performance of said 'Octoroon,' to use his influence with certain newspapers to attack said piece as an *Abolition piece*, and thus draw public attention to it."[38] The *accusation* of abolitionism is, for Boucicault, itself a marketing gimmick. He was willing to claim antiabolitionism in the South and abolitionism in the North and in Britain, in both cases using the represented bodies of enslaved Black characters—as well as his audience's affective responses to those representations—as material for his ceaseless publicity mill.

Despite his canny focus on the bottom line, Boucicault's play, as Jefferson recollected, *does* work toward its effect through the elicitation of feeling—of the audience if not necessarily the playwright. What I want to suggest here is that, for Boucicault, the moral evil of slavery can only be understood in a very local sense, an understanding both produced and delimited by the term that arises repeatedly in relation to *The Octoroon*'s reception: sympathy. It is invoked by both the *Spirit of the Times* ("false sympathy") and Jefferson ("whether it was Northern or Southern in its sympathy"). The grounding of Boucicault's moral vision—to the degree that he has one—in his insistence upon his characters as affectively real emerges in what looks like an odd contradiction in his claims about slavery in his letter to the London *Times*. Whereas he asserts near the beginning of the letter that, in his view, the restraints that slavery placed upon the liberty of enslaved people were, in general, "so slight as to be rarely perceptible," by its conclusion, he is making what appears to be a very different claim. In support of his argument against changing the ending of the play for a British audience that was both more amenable to the representation of interracial marriage and more desirous of a satisfyingly happy ending, he insisted, "In the death of the Octoroon lies the moral and teaching of the whole work. Had this girl been saved, and the drama brought to a happy end, the horrors of her position, irremediable from the very nature of the institution of slavery, would subside into the condition of a temporary annoyance." Ultimately, he relented and rewrote the ending.

But what are these "horrors" of slavery to which he refers if, in his account, "the restraints upon their liberty" are virtually imperceptible? To a large extent, Boucicault is consistent only in his appeal to the popular sentiments of the various locations where his play was performed. But the discrepancy between this claim and the earlier one is also in part explained, I think, by his contention that the evils of slavery do not lie in a checklist of specific violences and violations—the "corporal punishment and physical torture" that he falsely asserts do *not* occur in Louisiana—but in what he calls "the very nature of the institution of slavery," beside which any "physical suffering appears as a vulgar detail."[39] He suggests here that it is the loss of human agency rather than physical mistreatment that manifests slavery's fundamental evil, a suggestion that—notwithstanding the bad faith of his argument—has some similarities to one that Harriet Jacobs, two years after the first production of *The Octoroon*, made about the injuries of her enslavement:

> I was never cruelly over-worked; I was never lacerated with the whip from head to foot; I was never so beaten and bruised that I could not turn from one side to the other; I never had my heel-strings cut to prevent my running away; I was never chained to a log and forced to drag it about, while I toiled in the fields from morning till night; I was never branded with hot iron, or torn by bloodhounds. On the contrary, I had always been kindly treated, and tenderly cared for, until I came into the hands of Dr. Flint. I had never wished for freedom till then. But though my life in slavery was comparatively devoid of hardships, God pity the woman who is compelled to lead such a life! (*Incidents*, 174)

For Jacobs, corporeal torture is neither exceptional nor necessary for enslavement to be, in and of itself, a brutal violation. Her account, in contrast to Boucicault's, does not depend on melodrama for its power. Forthrightly naming violences, both physical and psychical, inflicted upon people (again in contrast to Boucicault's more benign representation of the practices of slavery in Louisiana), her narrative of her life—even a life described here as comparatively "kind"—is still horrific.

Boucicault's rhetorical gesture toward the "nature" of slavery still only goes so far in explaining why Boucicault insists that Zoe must die, that her destroyed body must be displayed to his audience in a sort of pornography of pain. And there, I would argue, lies the essence of Boucicault's approach to slavery: that because he understands its violations as only wrong on the level of their emotional effect on particular human beings, his vision—in a radical difference from Jacobs's—is fundamentally circumscribed by *which* human beings he comprehends as worthy of that moral attention. In the case of *The Octoroon*, I propose, both the motivating generic demand and the obstacle to a clear-sighted politics lie in what might seem to be an innocuous and even generative convention:

the deployment of sympathy. As Xine Yao has theorized, sympathy's fundamental work of "apprehending affects, feelings, and emotions—and deeming them legitimate" is deeply intertwined with racial hierarchies and racist epistemologies of the human.[40] For Boucicault, melodramatic sympathy functions ostensibly as a bridge between Irish and Black affect even while it effaces the reality of Black experience.

Elaine Hadley has convincingly argued for the importance of eighteenth-century notions of sympathy to the development of what she calls the "melodramatic mode" of the nineteenth century.[41] And, indeed, in the opening chapter of *The Theory of Moral Sentiments* (1759), Adam Smith famously described the experience of sympathy as one which aligned the affective experience of a person with a sufferer while still rendering the sufferer's actual experience inaccessible: "As we have no immediate experience of what other men feel, we can form no idea of the manner in which they are affected, but by conceiving what we ourselves should feel in the like situation. Though our brother is upon the rack, as long as we are at our ease, our senses will never inform us of what he suffers.... It is the impressions of our own senses only, not those of his, which our imaginations copy."[42] In "The Art of Dramatic Composition" (1878), an essay he published in the *North American Review* three years before Frederick Douglass's essay "The Color Line" would appear in that same journal, Boucicault explicitly made Smithian sympathy the basis of effective drama. In that treatise, Boucicault argues that the "object" of drama "is to give pleasure by exciting in the mind of the spectator a sympathy for fellow-creatures suffering their fate."[43] He continues: "If such an imitation of human beings, suffering their fate, be well contrived and executed in all its parts, the spectator is led to feel a particular sympathy with the artificial joys or sorrows of which he is the witness. This condition of his mind is called the theatrical illusion. The craft of the drama is to produce it, and all its concerns conduce to, and depend upon, this attainment" (43–44). But, as generative as sympathy is in this account of dramatic composition, for Boucicault it presents conceptual obstacles as well, particularly since he, following Smith, suggests that the ambit of sympathetic identification is necessarily bounded: "There is a limit to sympathy," Boucicault theorizes, "and, if a variety of calamities happen to many persons, the spectator cannot feel simultaneously sympathy with them all" (44). Boucicault's sympathy, that is, is a function both of the capacity of the feeler but also, and importantly, of who and how many are to be felt for.[44]

Once this "limit" is established, the question of who falls inside and who outside the circle of sympathetic affect becomes critical. As Yao puts it, "one must be recognized *as* sympathetic to be deserving of sympathy from those with the agency to sympathize."[45] This is an issue that bedevils the entire notion of sympathy in Romantic and post-Romantic British and colonial thought, as Manu Samriti Chander has made clear. And the question of whether sympathy can attach to a group, to "many persons," in Boucicault's words, is a vexed one. Reading the poetry of the Australian economic radical and racist Henry Lawson, for instance, Chander points out that "for Lawson, as for [Percy Bysshe] Shelley, sympathy means not simply feeling with another but with 'many others'; it enables a collective unity that we see especially in his early republican and socialist poems."[46] On the one hand, that collective understanding of sympathy—what Rae Greiner has identified as "not the transfer of a single, embodied feeling but a generalized propensity to feel and think collectively with others"[47]— suggests the possibility of a politics. And indeed, Amit S. Rai has proposed that a version of sympathy understood as "a non-propriative identification with others" might even be understood under a different name: solidarity.[48] That understanding of a politically charged sympathy is implicit in the related term "sympathizer," which, according to the *Oxford English Dictionary*, first arises in the early nineteenth century. The political usage of the term in fact became key to the rhetoric of the antiabolitionist attack on *The Octoroon*: locating the real-world effect of Boucicault's play in its appeal to spectatorial affect, the proslavery *New York Herald* argued, "In the case of the play of 'Uncle Tom's Cabin,' every man could see from the outset the drift of the piece. But in this drama the object is carefully concealed, and the spectator is drawn on by degrees, without perceiving it, till at the end he finds himself a sympathizer with John Brown."[49] Here, in the view of the *Herald*, sympathy for abolition is a seductive ruse surreptitiously produced by the emotions a play produces, even if the audience member is steeled in advance against its explicit ideological gist.

On the other hand, though, that expansive sense of sympathetic collectivity—even in the *Herald*'s rather hysterical assertion that "to kindle the flames of sedition and treason is the object of such plays as 'The Octoroon'"[50]—inevitably requires, as Chander demonstrates, a bounded vision of who merits inclusion in that fellowship: "By shaping Romanticism according to a different hemispheric perspective," Chander observes, "Lawson exposes the central paradox of British sympathy—namely, its reliance on antipathy. To imagine 'the pains and pleasures of his species,' Lawson must rhetorically exclude those with whom he cannot sympathize from that species."[51] In Rai's terms, even while sympathy is "a principle of sociality and cohesion," it also requires an "abjected other, as the constitutive exclusion that would cohere its own fantasy of identity."[52]

For Boucicault, the Romantic notion of a collective sympathy of the crowd or species is not actually possible, in that it brings the viewer into the ambit of history rather than personal connection and thus represents a different order of experience. He makes that point by distinguishing between what he identifies as sympathy and what he calls "interest": "Interest," he insists, "is concerned about events, sympathy about persons" ("Dramatic Composition," 47). This distinction presages the conceptual difference that Nel Noddings, in her account of ethical care, has articulated between "caring about" and "caring for."[53] And it also corroborates Talia Schaffer's argument that, by the middle of the nineteenth century, sympathy has lost whatever activist charge it might have earlier had (in the abolitionist movements that Cima describes, for example); diverging from what Schaffer calls "an ethics of care—an action-based, performative set of deeds," it has collapsed into "specular passivity."[54] Explicitly directed toward the immobilized experience of the playgoer, Boucicault's model of sympathy suggests a limit to the extrapolation of human feeling at the point that it runs into what he calls "events" or what we might think of as the historical conditions that demand a broader *political* action than the theatrical "pleasure" produced by contemplating "fellow-creatures suffering their fate."

Smith, again, theorizes precisely this kind of political quietism as the result of sympathy's inability to function at larger scales, even in the face of disaster:

> Let us suppose that the great empire of China, with all its myriads of inhabitants, was suddenly swallowed up by an earthquake, and let us consider how a man of humanity in Europe, who had no sort of connection with that part of the world, would be affected upon receiving intelligence of this dreadful calamity. He would, I imagine, first of all, express very strongly his sorrow for the misfortune of that unhappy people, he would make many melancholy reflections upon the precariousness of human life, and the vanity of all the labours of man, which could thus be annihilated in a moment.... And when all this fine philosophy was over, when all these humane sentiments had been once fairly expressed, he would pursue his business or his pleasure, take his repose or his diversion with the same ease and tranquillity, as if no such accident had happened.[55]

For Smith, sympathy cannot be scaled to this degree. And for Boucicault, following Smith, that is precisely the sort of "event" that can solicit "interest" but not "sympathy." Further, Smith's example, inadvertently or not, highlights another challenge to sympathetic identification: "China" here stands not only for geographical distance but also for a racialized alterity. While the (presumably) white European is the subject of potential feeling here (he is, after all, "a man of humanity"), the imagined victims of the "dreadful calamity" are both nonwhite and multiple. Unlike Smith's singular European subject—who can "be affected," "express very strongly his sorrow," "make many melancholy reflections," express "humane sentiments," and ultimately "pursue his business or his pleasure, take his repose or his diversion"—they can only be conceived by that subject as a mass ("myriads of inhabitants," an "unhappy people") that can suffer an "accident" but that displays no individuation susceptible to sympathetic identification.

In fact, sympathy—and its limitations—could be, and was, explicitly deployed in the mid-nineteenth century in the interests of white dominance and the perpetuation of slavery, in part because it offered a sort of double-edged salience: while it might permit real or performative sorrow at the treatment of enslaved persons, it also provided a channel into which those feelings could be diverted, thus blunting the demand for actual rectification of injustice. Thus, in the American South, Grayson could mock sympathy as cheap sentiment, the province of weak-thinking northerners who were willing to impose economic damage on the slaveholding South but not upon themselves:

> Let them show their sympathy for the Negro, not by eloquent speeches, but more eloquent acts; not with sentiment, but with sovereigns. They can buy any number of Negroes and carry them where they please. . . . They feel profoundly for the Negro; let them feel to the amount of a million a year. This would be better than bringing Coolies from Asia and negroes from Africa by a system of very doubtful character. It would convince the world that their sympathy is an honest one, and not the offspring of vanity or arrogance. (*Hireling*, xii–xiii)

It is likewise relevant that Oscar Wilde would in 1882 declare to the *New Orleans Daily Picayune* that Jefferson Davis's "cause"—which Wilde juxtaposes with the Irish nationalist "struggle for autonomy"—"must necessarily arouse sympathy" in that both "causes" are white rebellions.[56]

In the North, the *Pilot*—the Catholic-oriented Boston newspaper owned and edited in the 1840s by the Irish-born Patrick Donahoe[57]—could make sympathy the justification for *inaction*. In an 1842 editorial opposing Daniel O'Connell's abolitionism, it opined, "So far as the utterance of sympathy for the bondman of the South is put forth in that address from Ireland, we honor them, as it evinces a broad and boundless philanthropy that embraces the whole human family, and stops not to enquire the color of the oppressed, in their denunciations of the oppressor." The ethical demands upon the *Pilot*'s sympathy, however, only stretch so far, as the editors themselves quickly reach their limits: "We agree with the abolitionists in the abstract question of Slavery, but have no sympathy with that fiery enthusiasm, which would bathe the whole South in blood, rather than the black should remain in nominal bondage."[58] Sympathy, for the *Pilot*, is fine as long as it stays in the realm of feeling, "a broad and boundless philanthropy that embraces the whole human family" but doesn't lead to antislavery action. (The County Cork–born New York congressman Mike Walsh, as I noted in chapter 3, similarly ridiculed those "who have been overflowing with sympathy for the southern slaves" during his speech in support of the 1854 Kansas-Nebraska Act, which repealed the Missouri Compromise and extended the regime of enslavement.)[59]

The *Pilot*'s resistance to a path from sympathy to rectification is not consistent, though. It is not clear what the editors mean by the "nominal bondage" of chattel slavery, but it *is* clear that they do not always deem the threat of civil unrest an insuperable obstacle. For while the *Pilot* exhibits its deep concern with the stability of the *American* Union, it explicitly urges action—whatever the consequences—for the repeal of the *British* Union (that is, the incorporation of Ireland into the United Kingdom). That the *Pilot* urges repeal of one "union" while simultaneously appealing to another as a self-evident good in order to marginalize support for the abolition of slavery represents the cynicism and bad faith throughout. The way that the editors navigate what would seem to be a fatal argument against their double editorializing is to directly juxtapose the experiences of enslaved Black people in the United States and disenfranchised Irishmen under the terms of "Union," and to declare that the enormity of the latter dwarfs that of the former, explicitly in terms of sympathy: "As individuals, their generous sympathies may be extended to the slave of the South. But a worse slavery in Ireland is imposed upon a noble and intelligent people, in a condition to appreciate and enjoy immediate emancipation, and they should therefore let no extraneous considerations divide their zeal for the triumph of freedom in their own oppressed county." For the *Pilot*, repeatedly, sympathy for enslaved Black people is personal and individual, specifically *opposed* to the sort of direct political action that it—at the same time—urges in the case of the Irish cause of the Union's repeal. Within this conceptual framework, Black persons in the South are held in merely "nominal bondage," whereas the Irish suffer "a worse slavery," in part because the editorial represents those Irish as "a noble and intelligent people." The former might receive sympathy, but the latter require "zeal for the triumph of freedom."

At some point in the future, the *Pilot* concedes, it might be necessary to oppose slavery: "When the period shall have arrived in which American sympathisers for the slave, take this lofty character in their prosecution of his claims [that Daniel O'Connell does for Repeal], the man who withholds from them his sympathy, is false to the institutions of his country, and unworthy the blessings of a free government. But until it assumes this grand moral aspect, we believe the flattering of demagogues, or the professions of hypocrites, will fail to enlist the Irish in the cause of Negro Emancipation." Again, the rhetoric of political enfranchisement gets twisted up in that of abolition: opposing precipitate action toward "Negro Emancipation," the editorial nonetheless argues for "immediate emancipation" in Ireland. The confusion of the future perfect verb construction ("When the period shall have arrived") merely stands in for the infinitely delayed prospect of "American sympathisers for the slave" actually meriting the sort of direct and present activism that the editorial demands for Ireland; sympathy here excuses quietism in the face of moral horror as an individual feeling whose time has simply not—and may never—come.[60]

For Grayson, sympathy for enslaved Black people is hypocrisy; for the *Pilot*, sanctimoniously gesturing to putatively more pressing moral and political obligations, it replaces the need for any present action whatsoever to abolish chattel enslavement. For both, though, it is the affective province of *whiteness;* neither pays any attention to what enslaved Black people themselves might feel. While Grayson's specific proposal is monstrous (and deliberately ineffective, as the purchase and emancipation of enslaved people by white abolitionists would only enrich the southern slavers with funds to purchase still more human beings for chattel labor), he gets at an actual moral failure at the heart of sympathetic identification; sympathy becomes a way of being white in the United States without having any responsibility for antislavery or antiracist action.

The fundamental whiteness of sympathetic identification in both Grayson's work and the *Pilot*'s editorial—arising as they do from very different regional constituencies—underlines as well the racialist underpinnings of the very concept of sympathy in the nineteenth century. Saidiya Hartman, reading what she identifies as "the difficulty and slipperiness of empathy," brilliantly diagnoses the issue:

> Can the white witness of the spectacle of suffering affirm the materiality of black sentience only by feeling for himself? Does this not only exacerbate the idea that black sentience is inconceivable and unimaginable but, in the very ease of possessing the abased and enslaved body, ultimately elide an understanding and acknowledgement of the slave's pain? Beyond evidence of slavery's crime, what does this exposure of the suffering body of the bondsman yield? Does this not reinforce the "thingly" quality of the

captive by reducing the body to evidence in the very effort to establish the humanity of the enslaved? Does it not reproduce the hyperembodiness of the powerless?[61]

What Hartman clearly demonstrates is that an ethic of affect that substitutes the experience of the feeler for the felt-for—as Adam Smith insists sympathy inevitably must do—is itself a form of violence that uncannily mirrors the process of imagining other persons as things that buttresses the practice of enslavement itself. It runs alongside what Lynn Festa identifies as the "affective piracy" manifested, for example in Josiah Wedgwood's famous medallion "Am I not a man and a brother?" in a phenomenon she calls "a trope of redundant personification," "bestow[ing] the attributes of the person—a voice, consciousness, a soul—upon the figure of the slave to recreate the humanity of someone who is already human."[62] Victorian applications of Smithian sympathy, as Audrey Jaffe theorizes, function as a kind of mirror, using the suffering other as a prosthesis for the comfortable self: "The sufferer," she writes, "is effectively replaced by the spectator's image of him or herself."[63] In the *Pilot*'s editorial view, the spectator to the brutalities of Black enslavement—most specifically in this case the Irish and Catholic spectator—seems to be unquestionably white.

The substitution of the spectator's feelings for those of the sufferer that Jaffe identifies is also, I propose, what Boucicault enacts with the figure of Zoe through his melodramatic production of her humanity as a form of whiteness, performed for an audience that he can only imagine as white. Tellingly, the play's account of the monstrousness of slavery is largely grounded in its shocking application to Zoe, and—in particular—to her as, specifically, an "octoroon," that is, a person of one-eighth African heritage. Many of Boucicault's sources among abolitionist literature focus on—and take their titles from—characters identified as "quadroons." Boucicault's title, in contrast, emphasizes a smaller relative proportion of Zoe's African ancestry, a fact which lies behind the performance, in the original production, by the Scottish Robertson, Boucicault's wife. As Jennifer DeVere Brody posits, "Although 'tawny' stage makeup was manufactured in the 1800s, it is unlikely that Robertson would have 'blacked up' for her performances."[64] Published illustrations of the play, as staged in both New York and London, depicted Zoe as markedly white, her skin often even lighter than that of white characters around her, let alone the other Black personages. And yet, this is not, strictly, a melodrama of "passing." While it is true that George Peyton, returning from Paris, does not initially know that Zoe has Black ancestry nor that she was born into slavery, Zoe herself is never anything but forthright about her racial status.

Instead, what the play does is emphasize the proportion of Zoe's descent that is *not* descended from Africa and the visual markers of her *white* inheritance. Boltwood correctly notices that "unlike the play's other 'Yellows' and 'Blacks' who appear in black-face and speak a coarse English dialect, Zoe speaks an educated, standard English and appears as pale as any of the play's planters."[65] Or, as Hartman puts it of both *Uncle Tom's Cabin* and *The Octoroon*, on the same stage on which "the disparity between identity and appearance contributed to the hero's or heroine's affliction and his or her usually tragic end . . . , black characters bearing a striking resemblance to Zip Coon, Jim Crow, and Coal Black Rose, the bumbling, loyal, and childish Sambos and wenches of minstrel fare, provided the comic b(l)ackdrop of virtue's triumph."[66] That juxtaposition is, I would argue, precisely the point of *The Octoroon*'s facile racial politics. Boucicault's critique of Zoe's enslavement is, at its heart, predicated upon racial assumptions that mirror those underwriting the American slave regime. Under the Louisiana law that Boucicault's romantic plot putatively attacks, Zoe's enslavement is authorized by the fact that she is one-eighth Black (and born to an enslaved mother); as Zoe declares, "Of the blood that feeds my heart, one drop in eight is black—bright red as the rest may be, that one drop poisons all the blood."[67] For Boucicault, in contrast, that enslavement is fundamentally unnatural because she is seven-eighths white—or, oddly, that her blood, beyond the "one black drop," is seven-eighths *red*, and that "Those seven bright drops give me love like yours, hope like yours—ambition like yours" (that is, like white George Peyton's). In its muddled conception of race, Boucicault's play reflects the unsettled epistemologies that characterized midcentury racial legalities even as they converged on the brutal violations of Black bodies and minds. Walter Johnson has pointed to two competing "ways of thinking about race" in the United States of the 1850s: "South Carolina, Georgia, and Delaware assigned status on the basis of observation and reputation; other slaveholding states, including Louisiana, attempted to establish presumptions of freedom based upon fractions of 'black blood': halves, fourths, eighths, sixteenths, and so on down to one drop, which was the standard only in Arkansas during the antebellum period. The first standard emphasized appearance and performance; the second, more popular standard relied on a supposedly scientific estimation of an imagined blood quantum."[68] Boucicault's Zoe here uses the specific language of the latter—declaiming her Blackness—while drawing on the affective power of the former—performing her whiteness. As Brody argues, "In appearance, manner, and form, [Zoe] is not 'black.' . . . It is her belabored confession that 'delivers' her blackness."[69] The racial logic of *The Octoroon* insists that Zoe has to die because she is Black—and that the audience should sympathize with that death because she is white.

In his elicitation of dramatic sympathy, that is, Boucicault draws upon the midcentury trope of "white slavery." As Ariela J. Gross has pointed out, the trope functioned simultaneously albeit divergently in both abolitionist and antiabolitionist discourse, the former particularly in the North. While, as I have noted in chapter 1, proslavery polemicists could accuse the North of hypocrisy by evoking the specter of "Irish slaves," either in the historically recent past or (as in Grayson's argument) in an ongoing condition of "wage slavery," some abolitionists drew upon the suggestion of "white slavery" as a way of bringing home the horrors of slavery with (to a white readership) a heightened emotional charge. Race and gender frequently work in tandem in these cases, with the figure of the white woman positioned as both uniquely vulnerable and uniquely worthy of sympathetic identification. "They conjured the horror," Gross writes, "of the wrongful enslavement of pure white womanhood."[70] That is precisely how Boucicault structures Zoe's appeal to his audience, through an act simultaneously of racial exploitation and racial erasure. And the fact that it was the well-known Robertson who played Zoe in the original performances was a significant component of the racialized emotional impact of the auction scene, as Brooks argues: "For the audience, the chiasmic twist of witnessing Robertson feign (white) blackness and Zoe earnestly claiming (black) whiteness served as a climactic spectacle which would go unparalleled in the production."[71]

Boucicault's articulation of public racial and gendered categories through the (only) putatively personal and interiorized experience of sympathy underlines Kyla Schuller's insight that "sentimentalism, in the midst of its feminized ethic of emotional identification, operates as a fundamental mechanism of biopower."[72] And, as if explicitly prefiguring Patricia J. Williams's theorization of slavery as "a structure of denial—a denial of the generative independence of black people" through which "instead of black motherhood as the generative source for black people, master-cloaked white manhood became the generative source for black people,"[73] Boucicault's play makes clear that Zoe is "the natural daughter" of the (deceased) Judge Peyton, but it never names her enslaved mother; the widow Mrs. Peyton loves "this girl, that another woman would a hated . . . as if she'd been her own child" (26). The Irish Boucicault himself, as if mirroring this structure, becomes the impossibly parthenogenetic white authorial father of *The Octoroon*, as Judge Peyton appears as the parthenogenetic father of "the octoroon" within the play, displacing the generative power of such female or Black creators as Lydia Maria Child and Frank Webb, whose resonance lingers in the margins of the drama. Zoe's female Blackness itself appears, in this play, only under the structures of erasure that sympathy enacts. "The act of looking at a sympathetic object provokes a narrative in which that object is by definition—the term 'object' says it all—displaced into representation," Jaffe writes, pointing to "the tendency to ward off actual bodies in the sympathetic encounter."[74] Boucicault doesn't precisely erase Zoe's body; in fact, he emphasizes its suffering through the heightened spectacle of melodrama. But he does so, in Jaffe's terms, by displacing it into a form of representation that divests her of her Blackness.

The appeal to sympathetic feeling as a province of whiteness also emerges in a kind of mirror-image trope through which, as Lisa Merrill argues, "in a rhetorical allusion that effaced the enormity of the brutality of chattel slavery, [Boucicault] equated the degraded social position of *actors* to those of actual enslaved persons."[75] In an open letter to the abolitionist Henry Ward Beecher, who had criticized the theater as immoral, Boucicault insists that

> the social degradation, the wrongs borne with patience, and the slavery to prejudice endured by those whose state you assign even lower than that of the slave, are subjects as interesting to a Christian mind as that which has engaged your sympathy for many years. It is true the actor cannot, like the slave, show the letters on his wrist; he cannot exhibit the stripes on his back; and therefore his case is less succulent in the mouth of an orator; it is not so pictorial, so profitable. But wrong is wrong, and the physical well-being of a class is no plea that their wrongs should be set aside, leisurely regarded, or their injuries aggravated with impunity.[76]

Boucicault here invokes "sympathy" but pointedly redirects it from the tortured body of the enslaved person to the (presumably white) actor, presenting that metaphorical "slavery to prejudice endured by those whose state you assign even lower than that of the slave" as the proper object of sympathetic affect. Beecher, clearly recognizing the bad faith in Boucicault's appeal to sentiment, wryly responded that if the condition of the actor was really so dire, he would certainly be willing to advocate for abolishing the theater as well as the slave system:

> Our compassion is touched. We are the friends not of sections, of classes, of races, but of men. We are abolitionists. We would break every yoke, open every prison door, sunder every fetter. Show us a slave, and there we are willing to apply our doctrine, whether to a Circassian slave, a slave of the needle, of the plantation, or to those newly discovered slaves of the theatre. We take Mr. BORCICAULT at his word. We will treat those much abused persons whose cause he pleads as we would other slaves. . . . When the actor is abolished, ten thousand others will be emancipated with him.[77]

In suggesting that abolitionist sympathy be directed toward the actor, the putative victim of a "slavery of prejudice," Boucicault makes a claim for the suffering of that actor even in the absence of the embodied signs of torture that the enslaved person bears ("the letters on his wrist," "the stripes on his back"), suggesting that that absence makes the plight of the actor "less succulent in the mouth of an orator." His eye ever on the ledger book, Boucicault—himself, it must be remembered, an Irish actor—even seems to lament that those absences make the suffering of the stage *less* theatrical, less visually appealing to the structures through which sympathetic connection can be monetized, than that of actually enslaved people: "it is not so pictorial, so profitable."

Boucicault's inconsistency here, along with his persistent instinct toward moral misdirection, arises, I propose, not only from his financial obsessions but also from his apparent belief, likewise exhibited in the letter to Beecher, that the tactical deployment of melodramatic sympathy—in any instance—dissolves whatever ethical morass he has written himself into. Smith himself described a situation that so radically and violently violates the human expectations of justice that sympathy would almost necessarily cease to function: the appearance of "a man ... so absurdly constituted as to approve of cruelty and injustice as the highest virtues, and to disapprove of equity and humanity as the most pitiful vices." In that case, Smith suggests,

> surely if we saw any man shouting with admiration and applause at a barbarous and unmerited execution, which some insolent tyrant had ordered, we should not think we were guilty of any great absurdity in denominating this behaviour vicious and morally evil in the highest degree, though it expressed nothing but depraved moral faculties. . . . Our heart, I imagine, at the sight of such a spectator, would forget for a while its sympathy with the sufferer, and feel nothing but horror and detestation, at the thought of so execrable a wretch. We should abominate him even more than the tyrant who might be goaded on by the strong passions of jealousy, fear and resentment, and upon that account be more excusable. But the sentiments of the spectator would appear altogether without cause or motive, and therefore most perfectly and compleatly [sic] detestable.[78]

For Smith, the example of barbarism is of an "insolent tyrant"; that the widespread practice of chattel slavery while he was composing *The Theory of Moral Sentiments* is not the exemplary instance here is telling. And, almost precisely a hundred years later, that is the problem that Boucicault runs into as well in his representation of slavery in and with regard to *The Octoroon*. From his perspective, to maintain what Merrill aptly dubs "spectatorial sympathy,"[79] it is not enough that Zoe be written as a proper object of sympathy; the system of slavery must emerge as, at least in some key aspects, rationally motivated rather than simply monstrous. (Even M'Closky's villainy gets figured as the result of the "strong passions" of greed and lust.) If too much attention strays toward chattel enslavement itself as "most perfectly and compleatly detestable," sympathy, in the generic terms in which Boucicault understands it, fails.

That is nowhere more clear than in *The Octoroon*'s representation of its romantic plot between Zoe and George Peyton. In order to highlight M'Closky's sexual threat as uniquely odious, Boucicault figures George's competing romantic overtures to Zoe as authentic and consensual. Both the melodramatic malignity that the play ascribes to M'Closky and, in opposition to that monstrousness, the romanticization of George's erotic interest fundamentally and inevitably figure enslavement as something that it was not. Boucicault, that is, ignores the quotidian sexual violence within the context of enslavement that Hartman identifies: "The rape of black women existed as an unspoken but normative condition fully within the purview of everyday sexual practices." "This is evidenced in myriad ways," Hartman continues, "from the disregard for polite discourse and the evasion and indirection that euphemized rape as ravishment or sex as carnal knowledge to the utter omission and repression of the crime in slave statute and case law."[80] As Hartman's analysis would predict, Boucicault represents M'Closky, in the complaint to the London *Times* about the tepid response of British audiences to *The Octoroon*, in the horrifically euphemistic rhetoric of a rakish villain of melodrama: "When the Octoroon girl was purchased by the ruffianly overseer to become his paramour, her suicide to preserve her purity provoked no sympathy whatever."[81] The attempted rapist is a "ruffianly overseer"; his intended victim is a "paramour." What Boucicault complains about is that British viewers failed to feel "sympathy" when confronted with that representation. That they might instead experience "horror and detestation," as Smith proposed would arise in the face of "behaviour vicious and morally evil in the highest degree," does not enter his analysis, shaded as it is with the tropes of romance.[82]

But given the fundamental differences in George's and Zoe's legal and personal precarity, George's proposal of marriage is similarly violent, similarly exploitative, even if the play represents it as the solicitation of Zoe's freely given consent. Jacobs, in the chapter of *Incidents* titled "The Trials of Girlhood," demolishes the notion that sex between an enslaver and an enslaved person can be consensual: "He told me I was his property; that I must be subject to his will in all things. My soul revolted against the mean tyranny. But where could I turn for protection? No matter whether the slave girl be as black as ebony or as fair as her mistress. In either case, there is no shadow of law to protect her from insult, from violence, or even from death; all these are inflicted by fiends who bear the shape of men" (45). And in making that point, Jacobs explicitly disavows the kind of individualized structure of sympathy that characterizes Boucicault's representation of Zoe, instead arguing for a collective affect that moves not to aestheticized feeling but to action: "Reader, it is not to awaken sympathy for myself that I am telling you truthfully what I suffered in slavery. I do it to kindle a flame of compassion in your hearts for my sisters who are still in bondage, suffering as I once suffered" (47). Individual feeling is not enough, Jacobs points out; while the brutality continues, action is necessary.[83]

What Boucicault's play enacts by the framing of M'Closky's sexual threat as echoed but opposed by George Peyton's courtship is to milk the situation of enslavement by adding a sort of regional piquancy to what might, with some renaming and resetting of the plot, be an Irish play. If *The Poor of New York* could just as easily be *The Poor of Liverpool*, how much reworking of *The Octoroon* would be necessary for it to become something titled *The Girl of Limerick* or, indeed, *The Colleen Bawn?* Boucicault would, in his 1864 melodrama *Arrah-na-Pogue* (set in 1798, the year of a failed anti-British rebellion, and with a primary character whose name hints at Fenianism),[84] make romance both the allegory for and the solution to historical division.[85] In that play, the competing suitors stand in for Irish and Anglo-Irish modes of political and cultural authority; the romance plot of *The Octoroon* suggests that the structures of racial and ethnic difference in Louisiana—including M'Closky's Irish name itself—might function similarly.

It is true that, in the original American production of *The Octoroon*, Zoe dies, as Eily in *The Colleen Bawn* does not. Despite Boucicault's strongly stated objections, this changed in the London production. The *Illustrated London News*, in its plot summary of the revised Adelphi Theatre ending, reports that—in a still more complete alignment with *The Colleen Bawn*, which by that point was being performed along with *The Octoroon*—"The fair Octoroon is thus set at liberty; and the piece concludes with a declaration that in another land Zoe and Peyton will solemnise a lawful union, and live for the happiness of each other."[86] In fact, the *Examiner*, in an irony-laden review of the London version of *The Octoroon*, sent up the facile emotions sparked by the play, along with Boucicault's cynical monetization of ethics: "Mr Boucicault is a merciful man. He will not break the public heart. He has compassion on the tender sympathies he excites. His Octoroon poisons herself no more. She dies no more. She has done dying. She lives now against all the rule upon which her author insisted she ought to die. This is all very well for the future peace of the town, but what reparation can Mr Boucicault make to persons whose shillings he has taken, and whose hearts he has wrung by his previous cruel treatment of his Octoroon?"[87] In its facetious account, the review brilliantly skewers Boucicault's deployment of what Schaffer describes as sympathy's affect, that which "happens when we watch someone else's suffering passively, with a kind of melancholic self-congratulation."[88] "There are some," the *Examiner* reports, "who like the sensation of a death scene." It goes on to needle not only Boucicault's political ambivalence but also, suggestively, the tactical duplicity of Zoe's racial characterization: "Can he not compromise the matter by an alternate performance, the heroine dying one night and living happy ever after, another?"[89] This fantasy of a doubled ending, alternating between performances, aptly parodies Boucicault's dissimulations in proposing abolitionist and antiabolitionist intent, as it also parodies Zoe's shifting significances as white and Black.

Boucicault himself frames Zoe's death, in the American version, as the result of a series of mistakes and belated revelations rather than as an accusation against the broader brutalities of chattel enslavement; she takes poison before she learns too late that she is, in fact, emancipated, and in her final words she proposes that her death will solve the love triangle that the play has established: "When I am dead," she tells George, Dora "will not be jealous of your love for me, no laws will stand between us" (75). The melodramatic tragedy ultimately lies in a set of accidents that are specific to Zoe's situation and *not* in fact "irremediable from the very nature of the institution of slavery." That is, in opposition to the conditions of nineteenth-century American slavery and the white racial state, the play early on establishes Zoe's erotic agency vis-à-vis a white enslaver figured as a chivalric suitor precisely in order to deny her of it; it does so not through the horrors of real-life enslavement that Jacobs would narrate a few years later but through the pathos of melodramatic unluckiness. That other characters remain enslaved by the same Peytons we have been taught to admire as the heroes of the drama is rushed past, since the fundamental violence and dehumanization of the *structures* of slavery lie beyond the play's circle of sympathetic attention.

Boucicault provides an important juxtaposition and contrast to Mitchel, his contemporary and odd double across the trajectories of their American careers. In opposition to Mitchel's contempt for the norms and practices of political liberalism (what he mocks as "a 'liberal,' a 'progressive,' a 'conciliatory' British government" [*Jail Journal*, 147]), Boucicault offers a kind of gradualist and individual model of social progress through affect: insisting that its viewers care about Zoe—and about Paul, a "yellow boy," as the list of "Characters in the Play" describes him—*The Octoroon* seems to pride itself on that range of sympathetic inclusion without challenging the larger system of enslavement or of the racial hierarchies through which Zoe (and, indeed, Paul) are figured as particularly worthy of sympathetic attachment. In fact, the play—along with Boucicault's various contradictory apologias for it in the press—offers a signal example of what David Theo Goldberg, analyzing the exchanges between Thomas Carlyle and John Stuart Mill on the topics of race and colonialism, has identified as "liberalism's limits": "Liberalism's racially mediated meliorism and commitment to a moral progressivism . . . translates into an undying optimism that its racist history will be progressively overcome, giving way ultimately to a standard of nonracialism."[90] Given Boucicault's multiple equivocations, it is not clear that he aspired to look that far ahead, unlike Mill, who explicitly supported abolition. Instead, a sort of passive liberal tolerance permeates the affective modes of *The Octoroon*.

Those differences between Mitchel and Boucicault, I propose, are both reflected in and produced by the generic choices of these two Irish expatriates. Mitchel's mode is a kind of economic analysis that, by turning persons into numbers in his alignment of the amount of money spent by Britain on payment to West Indian slaveholders with the amount that could have saved millions of Irish lives during the Famine, completely erases enslaved people themselves except insofar as they are ledger lines in Britain's account books. For Boucicault, in contrast, the lived experiences of a single enslaved person are the focus of intense attention, to the exclusion of any engagement with the system as a whole. Mitchel's mode is schematic analysis, and his genre is the polemical tract; Boucicault's is affect, and his genre is melodrama.

In his 1881 autobiography, Frederick Douglass would lament that, with Daniel O'Connell's death, "the cause of the American slave, not less than the cause of his country, had met with a great loss." He elaborates: "All the more was this felt when I saw the kind of men who came to the front when the voice of O'Connell was no longer heard in Ireland. He was succeeded by the Duffys, Mitchells, Meagher, and others,—men who loved liberty for themselves and their country, but were utterly destitute of sympathy with the cause of liberty in countries other than their own."[91] Douglass is, I suggest, absolutely correct to highlight the specific issue of sympathy, a term that is echoed in the proslavery argument of the *Spirit of the Times* that Boucicault's play attempts to render Black and white persons equal by the application of "false sympathy." In his 1854 open letter to James Haughton, as I have noted in chapter 5 of this book, Mitchel himself represented Haughton's abolitionism as a sort of affective seizure, "a paroxysm of violent sympathy with the *fat negroes* of America."[92] For all of Mitchel's appeals to an emotional investment in the plight of the Famine's victims, he is not actually all that interested in sympathy; instead, his argument is about citizenship, and within his schema, Black persons are—collectively—not citizens, whereas the Irish—again, collectively—should be.

Boucicault, at the other end of the spectrum, seems unable to make the conceptual transition from the particular to the general, to bring his melodramatized grief at the violation of a character like Zoe to an attack on slavery overall as a *systemic* evil. That is, the *New York Herald* got it only half right in its antiabolitionist broadside against *The Octoroon*, asserting that "Bourcicault passes over all that is beautiful, beneficent and good in the relations between master and slave; singles out an exceptional feature, and exhibits that as the prevailing aspect of slavery. He takes an extreme case, and puts it forward as the general rule."[93] Boucicault's play does indeed focus intently on the particular—which he figures as the appropriate object of spectatorial sympathy—but he seems unwilling or unable to formulate a general rule that might be the basis of what he would later call "events," the possible foundation for political action grounded in "interest." "The *situation* of slavery," Brooks shows, "remains deeply fetishized, sensationalized, and unresolved."[94] Nineteenth-century sympathy—as scholars like Cima have demonstrated—need not be blinkered in this way. O'Connell, for one, as I have noted in my introduction, both gestured toward the understanding that sympathy was necessarily delimited while also insisting that those limitations might be overcome; in Douglass's account, O'Connell asserted, "My sympathy with distress is not confined within the narrow bounds of my own green island. No—it extends itself to every corner of the earth."[95] Wendell Phillips's introductory letter to Douglass's *Narrative* likewise picks up on the necessity of understanding both the details of individual injury and the systemic injustices that make it possible: "In reading your life, no one can say that we have unfairly picked out some rare specimens of cruelty. We know that the bitter drops, which even you have drained from the cup, are no incidental aggravations, no individual ills, but such as must mingle always and necessarily in the lot of every slave. They are the essential ingredients, not the occasional results, of the system."[96] Neither Boucicault nor Mitchel seems able to see both the ingredients and the system.

The divergence in political and literary approach to race-based chattel enslavement by these two Irish nationalists symptomatizes a crux at the heart of nineteenth-century liberal theory that Uday Singh Mehta has observed. For Mehta, Millite liberalism emerges from a fundamental contradiction, that its central "claim to distinction, namely articulating political and social norms of toleration and comity," stands in tension with the fact that it simultaneously "cannot avoid notions of superiority and inferiority, backward and progressive, and higher and lower."[97] In this analysis, nineteenth-century liberalism's explicit claims to broad-minded toleration are in fact *necessarily* underwritten by imperial conceptions of racial and national difference that provide the spectrum in which Britain's civilizational progress can be measured. As Mehta observes, "for both the Mills [James and John Stuart], civilizational achievement, which is paradigmatically the work of collectivities, is the necessary condition for the realization of the progressive purposes immanent in history, and hence of its continued progress."[98] While the isolation of the individual can distract from systemic injustice, schematic models—even progressive ones—can run roughshod over individual lives.

As his account in "The Art of Dramatic Composition" of what he figures as the necessary limits of sympathy (as *opposed* to "interest") would suggest, Boucicault's generic model seems unable to accommodate the clear naming of the systemic and collective violence of slavery, instead narrowing its vision to the melodramatic plight of the (worthy and virtually white) individual. He cares about Zoe's injury in part because he can imagine her (and predict that his paying audiences would imagine her) as both an individual subject and as not-quite-other; he fails to imagine slavery in general as injury because—as in Smith's example of an earthquake in China—it simultaneously is too huge and affects those who are more clearly racially other. "There exists," Elaine Scarry has written, "a *circular relation* between the infliction of pain and the problem of otherness. *The difficulty of imagining others is both the cause of, and the problem displayed by, the action of injuring.*"[99] She continues: "*The human capacity to injure other people is very great precisely because our capacity to imagine other people is very small.*"[100] In a signal instance of Scarry's "circular relation," the affective work of Boucicault's play depends largely upon a fundamental miscomprehension of slavery as, in general, noninjurious in order to produce Zoe's individual enslavement as an injury worth caring about. Despite his protestations, Boucicault cannot quite get to Marx's argument, in *Grundrisse* (1857–58), which he was drafting at almost precisely this same time, that "the most general abstractions arise only in the midst of the richest possible concrete development, where one thing appears common to many, to all. Then it ceases to be thinkable in a particular form alone."[101]

But a strain of liberalism does pervade Boucicault's politics of dramatized sympathy, a generic manifestation of a form of violence that Lisa Lowe situates at the heart of the construction of race: "While violence characterizes exclusion from the universality of the human, it also accompanies inclusion or assimilation into it.... *Race as a mark of colonial difference is an enduring remainder of the processes through which the human is universalized and freed by liberal forms, while the peoples who created the conditions of possibility for that freedom are assimilated or forgotten.*"[102] That is not only the political *effect* of *The Octoroon* but its very plot, as it is the buried plot as well of the quasi-novel of progress that constitutes Mitchel's nonfiction *Jail Journal*. In this, Mitchel and Boucicault might stand as exemplars of a divergence that Goldberg has traced, between what he calls, respectively, the "naturalist" and "historicist" accounts of race, the former progressing from Hobbes to Carlyle and the latter from Locke to Mill.[103] "Naturalist forms," in Goldberg's account, "tended to be more viscerally vicious and cruel, historicist ones more paternalistic"; the naturalist assumptions are "bald, bold, and direct concerning racist presumption and commitment" whereas the historicist ones are "ambiguous, ambivalent, indeed, hypocritical." And, as he argues, this racial "historicism" tended "to politeness, coded significance..., and tolerance as veils for continued invocation of racial power."[104] Boucicault's melodramatic ambivalence may strive for individual amelioration, but whatever broader attacks on the system he might contemplate he leaves for another day.

Strikingly, Boucicault's affective and social account, opposed to modes of abstracted systematization and driven by the financial benefits of playing on popular sentiment and public controversy, may find its roots in what Mehta has offered as a different and perhaps surprising source for Irish liberalism, Edmund Burke. In Burke, we might locate that opposition to abstraction and focus on individual, embodied sentiment, for example, in his *Reflections on the Revolution in France* (1790), in which he asserts, "I cannot stand forward, and give praise or blame to any thing which relates to human actions, and human concerns, on a simple view of the object, as it stands stripped of every relation, in all the nakedness and solitude of metaphysical abstraction. Circumstances (which with some gentlemen pass for nothing) give in reality to every political principle its distinguishing colour, and discriminating effect. The circumstances are what render every civil and political scheme beneficial or noxious to mankind."[105] Pointing to the way in which Burke balances the particular and the general, David Dwan writes, "It was through an appeal to circumstance that Burke attacked, first, a 'geometrical' or *a priori* approach to politics, second, an atomistic method—an inquiry that began with an account of the individual removed from his social and historical contexts—and third, a reductive positivism, one which derived its concept of proof and evidence from the natural sciences."[106] That dichotomy between the "atomistic" and the "geometrical" effectively names the division between Boucicault's melodramatic appeal to the individual character and Mitchel's putatively more radical analysis, what he (in the *Jail Journal*) calls his "root-and-branch Revolutionism" (252), blinkered by its own schematically political vehemence. Nineteenth-century Irish nationalism's divergence when it comes to the encounter with American slavery is, perhaps, rooted in its own self-division from the start. As this book has argued, it is riven by the different generic forms in which it could imagine its political capacities, as well as in its concomitant uncertainty about what kind of politics it should align itself with, that is, in its only fitful understanding of the moral as well as the instrumental significance of its literary intervention.

Coda

THE IRISH NATIONAL TALE AND CONFEDERATE NOSTALGIA

THE AMERICAN CIVIL WAR represents an inflection point, not a conclusion, within the ongoing relationship of Irish whiteness and its literary representations to the complicated and often painful history of American race. David T. Gleeson offers a telling historical example of a kind of generic translocation of the totemic names of Irish nationalist uprisings directly into the Confederate military, as "Irish heroes and themes dominated the specifically Irish ethnic units that served in the Confederate army. . . . Emmet [for Robert Emmet, the leader of the 1803 Rising] was the most popular name."[1] John Mitchel, who had left the United States for Paris, returned to Richmond to support the Confederacy as a journalist. All three of his sons fought for the South: James was wounded—he lost an arm—but survived; William was killed during Pickett's Charge at Gettysburg in 1863; the eldest, John, died at Fort Sumter in 1864.[2] Even as the war was ending, Mitchel continued to write in support of the Confederate cause, inviting prosecution in the United States for his vociferous rhetorical support of the white supremacist insurrection as he had in the United Kingdom for his advocacy of armed Irish resistance. Having taken on an editorship at the pro-southern *New York Daily News,* he was arrested in June 1865 for supporting the Confederacy and held without charge in Fort Monroe, in Virginia, adjacent to Jefferson Davis's cell.[3] The *New York Freeman's Journal and Catholic Register* protested against the arrest on the basis that it was a punishment not for Mitchel's actions but for his *words:* "He never was in the Confederate milita[r]y service. He never held civil office under the Confederacy.

He never, in America, was seized of property over $20,000.... He wrote in newspapers his *opinions*."⁴ Those opinions, despite some hedging after his arrest, supported both the Confederate states and the continuation of (indeed, increase in) Black enslavement.

In contrast, Mitchel's fellow Young Irelander (and fellow transportee) Thomas Francis Meagher—whom Frederick Douglass had included in his list of those Irishmen who "loved liberty for themselves and their country, but were utterly destitute of sympathy with the cause of liberty in countries other than their own"⁵—rose to the rank of brigadier general in the Union army, leading the Irish Union Brigade. (Some Confederate militia units named after Meagher altered their names in protest.)⁶ Archbishop John Hughes of New York—praised by William Grayson in his preface to *The Hireling and the Slave, Chicora, and Other Poems*—strongly supported the Union even while he continued to insist, as Kevin Kenny relates, "that Catholics would fight only for the preservation of the Union, that the abolitionists were dangerous and insane and that the slaves were in any case better off in the United States than they would have been in Africa."⁷ "In practice," Kieran Quinlan writes, "persons of Irish birth, like almost everyone else, ended up fighting for whatever region of the country they happened to live in. This meant that numerically more of them were in the Union army—often unwillingly, it appears—though, proportionate to their numbers in the South, there was a higher representation of the Irish in the Confederate ranks."⁸ Through the Civil War, that is, Irish Americans continued to serve as a key element of American racial and racist politics, although of course not the only one.

The frequent (although not universal) Irish alignment with anti-Black racism was not limited to the American South. Kenny underscores as well the Irish role in the July 1863 Draft Riots in New York: "For four days, mobs of Irish workers, with longshoremen at the vanguard, roamed the waterfront in search of black workers, beating, lynching and driving them out. The city's Colored Orphan Asylum was burned to the ground. Contemporaries estimated the number killed in the riots at between 1,200 and 1,500, most of them shot by police and troops called in from the recent battle of Gettysburg."⁹ And Peter D. O'Neill has demonstrated that the nineteenth-century Irish American alliance with white supremacy was not limited to the Civil War period, the eastern seaboard, or anti-Blackness in particular, relating that "in California in the 1870s and 1880s, the Irish led the often-violent anti-Chinese movement."[10] In fact, as David Brundage has emphasized, these anti-Chinese actions were not only Irish-led but at times also explicitly based on Irish nationalist tactics: it was the Belfast-born Fenian Frank Roney "who developed a plan in the early 1880s to adopt the tactic used in the [Irish] Land War in the city's anti-Chinese movement, the boycott of businesses employing Chinese labor."[11] (The term "boycott" itself, often naming in the nineteenth century a form of racist economic terrorism, derives from Irish nationalist activism: the Irish Land League's 1880 actions against the land agent Charles C. Boycott.)[12] As O'Neill concludes, "Examples of inspiring solidarity between the Irish and other ethnicities exist—the San Patricio Battalion is one—but examples like these are the exception rather than the rule."[13]

Literary forms would continue to both reflect and mediate the relationship between Irishness and the politics and rhetorics of American race in the decades following the 1850s, not least in the literature of the Civil War itself. The case of the Irish American Catholic priest Abram Ryan, for example, is instructive in this regard. Of Ryan, Gleeson writes, "His poems, such as 'The Conquered Banner' and 'The Sword of Robert E. Lee,' brought him fame throughout the South and made him the 'voice of the Lost Cause.'. . . Virulently opposed to any compromise with the Radicals, he believed that the 'fungus' of 'negro equality' would not 'survive' in the South. Although Ryan aimed the *Banner of the South* at southern readers, he also published it for Irish Catholics throughout the nation."[14] For Ryan, the mutual construction of Irish nationalism and Lost Cause advocacy emerges even in the patterns of his language and the structures of his poetry. In "The Conquered Banner" (1865), which he composed after hearing of General Lee's surrender, he wrote:

> Furl that Banner—furl it sadly;
> Once ten thousands hailed it gladly,
> And ten thousands wildly, madly,
> > Swore it should forever wave;

> Swore that foeman's sword should never
> Hearts like theirs entwined dissever,
> Till that flag should float forever
> 	O'er their freedom, or their grave!
> . . . .
> Furl that Banner! True, 'tis gory,
> Yet 'tis wreathed around with glory,
> And 'twill live in song and story,
> Though its folds are in the dust.[15]

In the strikingly similar "Erin's Flag," also published in 1865, the sword and the dust and the folds of the flag are still there, but the banner is Irish, and Ryan imagines it rising again:

> Unroll Erin's flag! fling its folds to the breeze!
> Let it float o'er the land, let it flash o'er the seas;
> Lift it out of the dust—let it wave as of yore,
> When its chiefs with their clans stood around it and swore
> That never!—no!—never, while God gave them life,
> And they had an arm and a sword for the strife,
> That never!—no!—never, that Banner should yield
> As long as the heart of a Celt was its shield;
> While the hand of a Celt had a weapon to wield,
> And his last drop of blood was unshed on the field.[16]

Even the blithe conventionality of Ryan's diction—the "banner" that has fallen "to the dust," the aspiration that it might once again "float" and "wave," the image of a populist collective "swearing" that they will "never" yield—bolsters the alignment that he draws between the cause of Irish nationalism and that of the enslaving Confederacy. Underlining the Celtic echoes in Ryan's Lost Cause aesthetics is the fact that he initially published both of these poems under the pseudonym "Moina," a name he took from James Macpherson's Ossian forgeries.[17]

As was often the case, postemancipation Black American writers both noted the alignments between Irish nationalism and white supremacy and strove to expose or disrupt them. In his reading of Frances Ellen

Watkins Harper, for example, Michael Stancliff has demonstrated that "after Reconstruction, Harper found in the Irish a versatile didactic tool with resonant heuristic force."[18] Frederick Douglass drew upon this versatile analogy as well. Speaking in Boston in 1869, in an address titled "Our Composite Nationality," Douglass offered a vision of a powerfully multiracial postwar United States that centered parallel contributions of Black and Irish Americans: "It is no disparagement to Americans of English descent to affirm that much of the wealth, leisure, culture, refinement and civilization of the country are due to the arm of the negro and the muscle of the Irishman. Without these, and the wealth created by their sturdy toil, English civilization had still lingered this side of the Alleghanies, and the wolf still be howling on their summits."[19] But he also tempered this praise of the Irish with a warning of the necessity of vigilance toward the threat that Irish American racism posed to that multiracial community in the form of the anti-Chinese activism in California: "Already have our Celtic brothers, never slow to execute the behests of popular prejudice against the weak and defenceless, recognized in the heads of these people, fit targets for their shil[l]alahs. Already, too, are their associations formed in avowed hostility to the Chinese."[20] With his sly rhetoric of the Celt and the shillelagh, Douglass evokes the so-called race science of the mid-nineteenth century that queried whether the exoticized Irish might in fact represent a different race than the Saxon. But he also remains clear-sighted about the relationship of race to the possibility of a truly *United* States: expanding the circle of racial belonging to Chinese immigrants rather than collapsing it to a white-Black dichotomy, he starts from the premise of Irish whiteness and the need to defend against the violence that that whiteness continued to enact.

Fourteen years later, in "This Decision Has Humbled the Nation," Douglass again considered the impoverishment of Ireland in relation to the situation of postemancipation Black Americans, now unprotected by the 1875 Civil Rights Act that the Supreme Court had overturned: "But in Ireland, persecution has at last reached a point where it reacts terribly upon her persecutors. England to-day is reaping the bitter consequences of her injustice and oppression. . . . Fellow-citizens! We want no black Ireland in America. We want no aggrieved class in America. Strong as we are without the negro, we are stronger with him than without him. The power and friendship of seven millions of people scattered all over the country, however humble, are not to be despised."[21] With his echoes of Thomas Carlyle's disparagement of the very idea of Black emancipation ("To have 'emancipated' the West Indies into a *Black Ireland;* 'free' indeed, but an Ireland, and black!"),[22] Douglass enacts his own generic transmutation, turning one of the most malignantly anti-Black (and anti-Irish) texts of the mid-nineteenth century into an appeal for racial justice. And while Carlyle used the racist bugbear of Blackness to tar the Irish with laziness, Douglass turns the analogy around, figuring Ireland—and Irish class-based hardship—as a model and a warning for the future of Black life and enterprise in the United States.

There were certainly many Irish and Irish Americans in the years following the Civil War who continued the conversations begun by such figures as Frederick Douglass and Daniel O'Connell by forging coalitions against colonial and racial violence. Amy E. Martin, for example, has written convincingly about the alliance of Irish Fenians with Black activists both during and after the 1865 Morant Bay Rebellion in Jamaica, which led to brutal suppression by the colonial governor Edward John Eyre, with both the *Nation* and the *Irishman* offering regular updates.[23] The *Nation*'s first mention of the rebellion, in early November 1865, was actually rather breezy, even dismissive, largely relying on the reporting of the *Times* and couched in terms of the question of whether Black people had suffered "grievances" serious enough to justify violence: "It is hardly conceivable that the negroes should have attempted such a movement without some external instigation. It is quite certain that they have no grievance whatever even to afford a colourable pretext for insurrection."[24] By late November, though, the *Nation* was turning the racialized language of savagery back at the English: "The military despatches ... prove that the dominant race has utterly lost sense and courage and self-command in the frenzy of fear which has fallen upon them. They prove that the ferocity, the thirst of blood, which we denounce in savages, can take possession, too, of English hearts, and that mercy and justice can be forgotten by English officers as thoroughly as by the Indian or the Cossack."[25] As Michael G. Malouf points out, the atrocities in Jamaica led the editors of the *Nation* to rhetorically reorient the categories provided by much of mid-nineteenth-century colonial racism; it is the English here who are the "savages" (although "the Indian" and "the Cossack" still are as well). Further, Malouf finds, the *Nation*'s writers "were also able to identify with the martyr of the rebellion, George Gordon, who is described in heroic terms similar to those used in other parts of the paper to describe contemporary Irish nationalist figures."[26] By then, the *Nation* was bestowing upon the Jamaican rebellion, among other terms, the honorable designation of "Rising." This alliance, Martin emphasizes, could become the basis of a global and truly multiracial anticolonialism: "Interestingly these writings connect British violence against the Morant Bay rebels with other instances of counter-insurgency and of the repression of anticolonial resistance.... Thus, Fenian newspapers develop a prose of counter-counter-insurgency, one that makes space for a critique of British violence as an indiscriminate, extreme practice of a kind of state terror rather than a systematic and necessary response to resistance."[27] And this coalition expanded beyond Morant Bay, Martin relates: "Fenian cells collected money for relief of the families of insurgents in Morant Bay, sent funds and arms to Zulu insurgents during the Anglo-Zulu war, and sent operatives to enlist on the side of the North in the Civil War not only to gather military training but also to fight slavery in the U.S."[28] Martin's scholarship demonstrates that, in some places, the politics of solidarity could breach the color line. And it is certainly true that many Irish nationalists brought to the Americas not only the literary modes that had influenced the fight for rights within the British context but also a commitment to multiracial anticolonial action.[29]

By the 1870s, the *Pilot*, the Boston paper that had earlier opposed O'Connell's abolitionism, began to argue—with specific reference to O'Connell—for a specifically *Irish* antiracism. Now under the editorship of John Boyle O'Reilly, the *Pilot* responded in 1877 to a Georgia-based reader condemning the paper's advocacy for "social equality between whites and blacks" by asserting: "There is nothing Irish about his principles.... We glory in the very things he hates—and the Irish people have ever gloried in them. 'God forbid,' said Daniel O'Connell, 'that I should ever receive for the cause of Ireland one shilling wrung from negro slavery!' And this has ever been the spirit of Ireland and her people at home and abroad."³⁰ A Fenian born in County Meath and convicted of treason in 1866 (and transported to Western Australia the following year), O'Reilly performs a certain rhetorical evasion when describing the motivations of those Irish and Irish Americans who fought for the Confederacy: "The brave men who fought in the Southern army never fought for slavery; they struggled for a righteous settlement of a question that they thought should have been constitutionally decided, having been constitutionally acknowledged." This would have been a surprise to Mitchel and his compatriots. Having claimed that "social equality between whites and blacks" has "ever been the spirit of Ireland and her people," the editorial needs to efface race completely from the context of the Civil War—and from the motivations of those Irish Americans who most certainly and forthrightly *did* fight "for slavery." But that erasure of race from the most telling of recent manifestations of Irish white supremacist thought facilitates the O'Connell-esque analogy that follows: "The colored man should stand on a perfect equality with the white man; and the Catholic cathedrals of America are as free to the negro as to the Irishman."³¹

Despite the assurance of O'Reilly's *Pilot*, race did continue to rupture Irish nationalism, serving, in Martin's words, "as a fracturing presence within Fenian politics."³² And the failures by Irish people themselves and by writers who invoked Irishness in order to say something about race and enslavement to align themselves fully with occasionally rhyming but by no means identical demands for justice, both before and after the end of state-sanctioned enslavement, demonstrates the extent to which their grounding is—and, indeed, had been—in whiteness. The Irish in Ireland continued, in this regard, along a somewhat different path than Irish Americans. Nevertheless, the affiliation of Irishness with whiteness was not limited to the United States. Despite Irish nationalist assertions of political sympathy across race and nation in the late nineteenth and twentieth centuries, Jonathan Schneer has noted that "the anti-imperialism of London's Irish nationalists was circumscribed by the same racism that characterized so many British-born anti-imperialists. For example, T. M. Healey, a leading member of the Irish Parliamentary Party, admired the Boers, who were resisting incorporation into the British empire because they rightly objected to the 'pleasure of having a n[—] as a magistrate probably, certainly as a policeman ruling over them.'"[33] The anticolonialism manifested by Healey is, explicitly, that of *white* grievance.

The colonial ramifications of that Irish whiteness are clear, especially as the century continues. Writing about the era of the Celtic Revival, for example, D. G. Boyce observes, "Some English might claim that the Irish were comparable to the Indians, needing the smack of firm government; but this was contradicted by the spectacle of Irishmen (Protestant and Catholic) spread throughout the empire busily ruling (and shooting) black and brown races."[34] As F. S. L. Lyons relates, in 1889 the antiseparatist Irish nationalist John Dillon—a protégé of Mitchel and the brother of Mitchel's early biographer William Dillon—"declared at Auckland that the Irish deserved self-government 'because we are white men,'" an appeal, Lyons remarks sardonically, "to an emotion deeply felt by many of his hearers, who, however sympathetic to Irish Home Rule, had no intention of applying that exhilarating doctrine to the people of Samoa."[35] It is true, as Schneer's account demonstrates, that no totalizing description is possible of the way that Irish nationalism came to understand and respond to the injuries enacted by the American racial state or its parallels around the world; distinctions of class, gender, religion, politics, and regional origins—as well as of personal and family history and even reading practices—certainly created the space for radically different responses. But as with Mitchel's own voyage around the world, the Irish nationalism of a figure like Dillon could become a global phenomenon without necessarily shedding its assumptions of specifically white rights.

In the introduction to this book, I considered the nineteenth-century translation of "Lost Cause" rhetoric from Irish nationalism to Confederate nostalgia grounded explicitly in white supremacy. As a conclusion, I want to briefly explore how that alignment of Lost Causes, from nationalist Ireland to the racist state of the antebellum South, enters the twentieth century (and beyond) by looking at another literary instance of retrospective nation-making: Margaret Mitchell's 1936 *Gone with the Wind*.[36] In its very first paragraph, Mitchell describes Scarlett O'Hara's appearance as "sharply blend[ing] the delicate features of her mother, a Coast aristocrat of French descent, and the heavy ones of her florid Irish father" (5), and the novel is filled with Irish names from O'Hara itself to the name of the family's slave-worked plantation: Tara is named after the Hill of Tara that is the legendary seat of the High Kings of Ireland.[37] "It is all but inconceivable to think of Scarlett as bearing any surname other than that with which she is born," James P. Cantrell contends, "not the Scottish Lowland or northern English Hamilton, nor the Highland or Irish Kennedy, nor the Hiberno-Norman Butler, and certainly not the English Wilkes."[38] Irishness, that is to say, is fundamental to the world of Mitchell's novel.

The first name of Scarlett's father—an immigrant from County Meath, where the Irish Tara stands—is Gerald, a name that aligns him with the fiercely nationalist and centuries-long resistance to British rule by the Hiberno-Norman Fitzgeralds, praised in the Young Irelander Thomas Davis's 1844 poem "The Geraldines."[39] It is also a name from Mitchell's own genealogy of Irish nationalism; as Quinlan relates, "in the 1820s, Mitchell's American Catholic line was revitalized by a Phillip Fitzgerald, whose family had fled Tipperary for France after the 1798 uprising."[40] *Gone with the Wind* places its Gerald into this Geraldine tradition through his rebellious past, presented as a sort of condensed version of Irish resistance and defeat from the seventeenth century on:

> Gerald had come to America from Ireland when he was twenty-one. He had come hastily, as many a better and worse Irishman before and since.... There was no Orangeman this side of hell worth a hundred pounds to the British government or to the devil himself; but if the government felt so strongly about the death of an English absentee landlord's rent agent, it was time for Gerald O'Hara to be leaving and leaving suddenly. True, he had called the rent agent "a bastard of an Orangeman," but that, according to Gerald's way of looking at it, did not give the man any right to insult him by whistling the opening bars of "The Boyne Water."
>
> The Battle of the Boyne had been fought more than a hundred years before, but, to the O'Haras and their neighbours, it might have been yesterday when their hopes and their dreams, as well as their lands and wealth, went off in the same cloud of dust that enveloped a frightened and fleeing Stuart prince, leaving William of Orange and his hated troops with their orange cockades to cut down the Irish adherents of the Stuarts. (44–45)

Gerald's history puts him at the center of a remarkable line of Irish grievances, from absentee landlordism to the Battle of the Boyne to the rise of the paramilitary Orange Order in the 1790s. Even before his migration to the United States, he has experienced a series of Irish Lost Causes.

The transmutation of Gerald's Irish nationalism into the cause of the American South emerges in a telling verbal conflation of historical political contexts: when he declares that "the South should show by arms that she cannot be insulted and that she is not leaving the Union by the Union's kindness but by her own strength" (108), Gerald implicitly echoes John Mitchel's appeal to an explicitly violent opposition to a different—but here suggestively parallel—"Union." In a 1937 letter to the Irish envoy Michael MacWhite, who had sent her an "inscribed copy of Mangan's poems" in admiration for *Gone with the Wind*, Mitchell herself suggested the significance of the Irish resonance of Gerald's name through a juxtaposition of the Irish with the (white) American South: "As it was once said in Ireland of the Fitzgeralds, 'they became more Irish than the Irish themselves,' so our Southern Irish became more Southern than the Southerners. When the trouble in the 'sixties began they went out with the Confederate troops and did great deeds for their new land."[41] Gerald brings with him from Ireland to the United States not only his hotheadedness and his fondness for whiskey but also the literary genres of Irish nationalism exemplified by Thomas Moore: "He knew no poetry save that of Moore and no music except the songs of Ireland that had come down through the years" (46). Father Abram Ryan himself shows up in Mitchell's novel, "the poet-priest of the Confederacy" who "never failed to call [on Melanie Wilkes] when passing through Atlanta" (753). "*Gone with the Wind*," as Quinlan finds, "is far more Irish—and far more Catholic in its references also—than has generally been acknowledged."[42]

Even beyond the novel's suggestive nomenclatures and historical backstories, Amy Clukey has argued for the broader significance of Irish literary representation to the settings and narrative structure of *Gone with the Wind*'s plantation romance; that literary genealogy mobilizes Irish modes as the materials for a Lost Cause mythology, combining "sentimental images of drunken Irishness with a planter mythology that posits the South as a gracious but doomed culture ground under the heels of industrial capitalism."⁴³ "Southern plantation culture," she contends, "is itself a continuation of Irish plantation culture, a continuity that *Gone with the Wind* registers, however ironically or incoherently."⁴⁴ Clukey convincingly traces Mitchell's generic antecedents to what she identifies as Ireland's "own version of plantation fiction in nineteenth-century big-house novels that centered on the social foibles and marriage plots of the [Anglo-Protestant] Ascendancy class," and she notes as well that, "uneducated but literate, soft-hearted but hotheaded, with a predilection for drink and ballads, Gerald is the stereotypical Irishman of popular nineteenth-century drama."⁴⁵

"One of the most obvious ways that Gerald upholds planter hegemony," Clukey observes, "is in his role as a slave owner." She continues: "As members of the lower classes, Irish Southerners rarely owned slaves. However, they were just as likely to support slavery as other whites in a region where both Catholic and Protestant Irish religious leaders usually buoyed the monied elite."⁴⁶ The economic claim is relevant, particularly in reference to the 1840s and 1850s, when many Irish migrants to the United States were fleeing famine—or, like Mitchel, criminal conviction for anti-British activism—and Irish enslavement of Black people in the American South might have been comparatively rare. (In *Gone with the Wind*, Scarlett repeatedly identifies the Slatterys, with their Irish surname, as "white trash," in part because they don't own enslaved people.)⁴⁷ But Irish slaveholding was not limited to the realm of fiction: controlling for overall property levels, one analysis of the 1860 census data has indicated that while all foreign-born whites across five southern cities (Baton Rouge, Columbia, Montgomery, Natchez, and Savannah) owned considerably fewer enslaved persons than did native southerners and native northerners living in the South, Irish immigrants—male and female—ranked second only to the British for per-person "slave use."⁴⁸

Gleeson relates that, "although the vast majority of Irish in the region did not own slaves, they did not object to slavery itself, and when they could afford it, had no compunction about purchasing slaves."⁴⁹ He details the conditions under which early nineteenth-century Irish immigrants who "were able to take advantage of the 'flush times,' along with those who inherited wealth from an American family, often became major slave owners," and he provides representative examples: Maunsel White (who "eventually owned hundreds of slaves"); Frederick Stanton (who "got into the cotton business, and eventually earned enough to own six plantations and 333 slaves, making him one of the richest planters in the South at his death in 1859"); the Scots-Irish James Adger (who "owned more than a dozen domestic 'servants' to cater to his new lifestyle among the Charleston elite").[50] The attorney John Kingsbury Elgee, Oscar Wilde's maternal uncle (brother to the nationalist poet Speranza), was a delegate to the Louisiana Secession Convention in 1861, representing rural Rapides Parish; at that date, he owned sixteen enslaved people.[51] Michèle Mendelssohn describes a vast expansion in Elgee's fortunes over a short number of years: "By 1860, his personal estate was valued at $405,000. It later grew to include three plantations, 9,600 acres, and 515 slaves. It was said to be worth almost a million dollars."[52]

Nor was it only the Protestant Irish in the United States who were enslavers, although they frequently had more financial resources with which to purchase human chattel. Gleeson reports that the Ryans of South Carolina (among them Thomas Ryan, who placed the 1862 notice comparing Lincoln to Cromwell that I discussed in chapter 1 of this book) "exploited Irish connections for their business, most notably when they went to Lancaster County to settle the estate and sell the more than one hundred slaves of established Irish Catholic planter William McKenna."[53] In 1838, Thomas F. Mulledy, then provincial superior of the Maryland Province of the Jesuits and former president of Georgetown College, sold approximately three hundred enslaved men, women, and children who were the property of the Maryland Jesuits, to Louisiana planters in order to resolve the college's debts.[54] Georgetown's president at the time, the Jesuit William McSherry, was previously the Maryland provincial, and he—like Mulledy—was of Irish descent. Eliza Clark, the mother of Patrick Healy (who became president of Georgetown in 1874), was enslaved by his father, Michael Healy; of this Irish immigrant (and naturalized United States citizen), James M. O'Toole writes, "By 1850 he owned forty-nine slaves, well above the local average of fourteen; of nearly five hundred slaveowners in Jones County [Georgia], he ranked eighteenth."[55] The last known smuggling of (more than a hundred) kidnapped African people into slavery in the United States was overseen by the Irish American Timothy Meaher (or Meagher or O'Meagher) in 1860; descended from Jacobite Catholic nationalists in Kilkenny, his family enslaved significant numbers of human chattel in Mobile, Alabama.[56]

That context, in which immigrant Irish and Irish American enslavers—including Catholics—were understood as normal, if not fully typical, is the background to *Gone with the Wind*'s depiction of Tara. The novel imagines an alternative reconstruction to that enacted by the United States in the years following the Civil War: the reconstruction of a lost Celtic Ireland *as* slave plantation. Seeing her father's reluctance to leave his Georgia estate—made possible only by enslaved labor—Scarlett recognizes that "there were too many Irish ancestors crowding behind Gerald's shoulders, men who had died on scant acres, fighting to the end rather than leave the homes where they had lived, ploughed, loved, begotten sons" (418). Making her own vow to maintain Tara, Scarlett explicitly frames it in the context of Irish nationalist resistance to British control: "There were the Scarletts who had fought with the Irish Volunteers for a free Ireland and been hanged for their pains, and the O'Haras who died at the Boyne, battling to the end for what was theirs" (428). "Tara" is not just any Irish geographical designation; written in the wake of the 1922 establishment of the Irish Free State, *Gone with the Wind* names the legend of pure Irish self-rule prior to English incursion that, while lost to Ireland itself, might be imaginatively rebuilt on the antebellum South's own mythological geography of the Lost Cause.

The "trouble in the 'sixties" that Mitchell evokes in her letter to MacWhite is, of course, the Civil War, and that "new land," in Mitchell's account, is not the United States as a whole but the Confederacy in particular, established on the basis of white supremacist violence. "With the deep hunger of an Irishman who has been a tenant on the lands his people once had owned and hunted," Mitchell writes of Gerald, "he wanted to see his own acres stretching green before his eyes. With a ruthless singleness of purpose, he desired his own house, his own plantation, his own horses, his own slaves. And here in this new country, . . . he intended to have them" (48). The novel's description of Gerald's ambition, that "the white walls of Tara should rise," and the process through which "in time the white house became a reality instead of a dream" (50) takes the white-painted exterior of the plantation estate as metonym for the inclusion of Irishness in white racial dominance. This narrative of personal and historical progression—from Ireland to Georgia and, suggestively, back to Tara—built upon the bodies and labor of enslaved Black people, reclaims the "Celt" as necessarily and essentially white.

Genre matters here. Clukey is correct to contextualize Mitchell's narrative within the traditions of the Big House novel and the sentimental stage Irishman. And to that literary catalogue, I want to name another genre of nineteenth-century Irish nationalist literature that becomes central to American white supremacist aesthetics: the national tale, which Ina Ferris has identified as "the most important literary form emerging out of the debate on Ireland."[57] In a retrospective account of the significance of her own 1806 novel, *The Wild Irish Girl*, Lady Morgan (born Sydney Owenson) emphasized her generic innovation within the context of the literature of nationalist resistance:

> At the moment the "Wild Irish Girl" appeared, it was dangerous to write on Ireland, hazardous to praise her, and difficult to find a publisher for an Irish tale which had a political tendency.
>
> For even, ballads sung in the streets of Dublin *had been* denounced by government spies, and hushed by Castle sbirri! because the old *Irish refrain* of *Eiren go Brach*, awakened the cheer of the ragged, starving audience....
>
> No work, however, of fictitious narrative, founded on national grievances, and borne out by historic fact, had yet appealed to the sympathies of the general reader, or found its way to the desultory studies of domestic life. "The Wild Irish Girl" took the initiative in an experiment since carried out to perfection by abler talents.[58]

Morgan gave *The Wild Irish Girl* the generically insistent and politically defiant subtitle "A National Tale."[59] Her catalogue of her novel's characteristics—a "fictitious narrative, founded on national grievances, and borne out by historic fact, . . . appeal[ing] to the sympathies of the general reader"—names the central accomplishments of the national tale, whether in Ireland or elsewhere. "The national tale," writes Murray Pittock, "was originally a distinctively Irish inflection of the novel, . . . an inflection of genre towards national conditions."[60] That national inflection takes particular forms. Referring to Morgan's own description, Ferris has delineated the generic attributes of the national tale: "As a romantic genre, the national tale is a genre of 'minor' nations, that is, of small European nations that stand in a certain relation of hostility to a larger and oppressive nation with whose fortunes their own are intertwined."[61] Importantly, Ferris emphasizes (as Morgan did before her) the centrality of political grievance to the national tale as a genre:

> The matter of grievance is crucial. To present Ireland as an anomaly... is to present it as a case for deliberation, and thus to move into the foreground the viewing/reading subject as the one who determines and judges. To present it as a grievance, however, is to write Ireland less as a problem to be resolved than as a claim that demands to be heard. It is thus to alter the narrative pragmatics of the case by directing attention to the one who presents the case rather than to the one who determines it.[62]

In Ferris's account, neither Leo Tolstoy's *War and Peace* nor Jane Austen's *Persuasion* is, despite their focuses on the nation, strictly a "national tale"; grievance is the key constitutive element, and it shapes both Morgan's *Wild Irish Girl* and Mitchell's return to that "wild Irish" figure in the context of the Confederacy in *Gone with the Wind*.

That the early nineteenth-century national tale would at points propose a near equivalence between the condition of the Irish under British rule and that of enslaved people of African descent is both dispiriting and unsurprising, given the political and cultural salience of debates over abolishing the slave trade in the years that witnessed the emergence of the genre. *The Wild Irish Girl,* the novel that Ferris—like Morgan herself—designates as the inauguration of the Irish national tale,[63] itself draws that analogy as part of its political argument. Near the beginning of the novel, its narrator, the Anglo-Irish Horatio, writes to a friend in London about the estate agent on his father's Connaught property: "I perceive," Horatio writes, "my father emulates the policy of the British Legislature, and delegates English ministers to govern his Irish domains."[64] And he aligns that political domination with the brutality of enslavement itself: "It is certain, that the diminutive body of our worthy steward, is the abode of the transmigrated soul of some *West Indian* planter."[65] The novel's initial 1806 publication placed it amid debates in Parliament and beyond over the proposed termination of the British slave trade, culminating in the Act for the Abolition of the Slave Trade the following year. Through the imagined transmigration of the soul from one type of plantation to another, Horatio (and Owenson through him) makes the argument for an Irish national awakening on the basis of its putative equivalency to the demand for the abolition of slavery in the British West Indies. In its nonchalant allusion to actual chattel enslavement the novel enacts a particularly pernicious form of what Lynn Festa calls "affective piracy," not here the ventriloquism of the voice of the enslaved subject by the white abolitionist but the theft of the political power of the demands of justice for enslaved Black people in the interests not of those enslaved people themselves but of the Irish nationalist cause. The "West Indian planter" is invoked for the image's capacity to shock white liberal sensibilities, but the beneficiary of that invocation is the (white) Irish laborer.

What Mitchell does in *Gone with the Wind*, written more than a century later, is a continuation of the nineteenth-century translation of Irish nationalist genres into the context of the racial regimes of the United States. But there is a difference: whereas Owenson had appropriated the imagery of Black suffering to bolster the case for Irish relief, Mitchell makes Irish nationalist resistance the analogy not of the enslaved person but of the enslaver, putatively oppressed by an abolitionist North. She mobilizes the political, aesthetic, and affective resonances of the national tale—now transferred from Ireland to the American South—and focuses them on the synecdochally significant "Big House" at Tara:[66] the hostility toward what the novel figures as the oppressive forces of a militarily superior but culturally inferior, hostile "nation"; the fostering of grievance in the interests of a national identity; the centering of the demand for attention rather than the adjudication of that demand. Mitchell's novel shapes the narrative of grievance into the particular form of the neo-Confederate Lost Cause, echoing Edward A. Pollard's nineteenth-century announcement of the maintenance of white dominance as the central aspect of that cause.

The normative whiteness of Irishness emerges even in Mitchell's orthographic (and ethnographic) conventions. While the novel might announce that Gerald bears "the brogue of County Meath still heavy on his tongue in spite of thirty-nine years in America" (31), it almost never represents his speech in anything other than normative English (peppered with the rare colloquialism); it is the Black characters whose racial alterity is marked by insistently "faulty" speech, a stereotyped dialect that suggests an inability to master the pronunciations and idioms that Mitchell presents as the norm.[67] It may be true, as Cantrell has suggested, that "to atone for her mistakes and prepare for her future, Mitchell's symbol of the South [his reading of Scarlett] must return to the roots of her Irish culture."[68] But Mitchell insists that that return to Irishness is, first and foremost, an assertion of whiteness within the context of American racial nationalism.

Gone with the Wind, it must be said, is not unironic about its own conceptual laundering of an Irish Lost Cause into its southern instantiation.[69] There is, for example, its satirical representation of the carpetbagging "ladies of the new aristocracy" who idolize what they imagine to be Scarlett's authentic southernness but "only knew that Scarlett's father had been a great slave-owner": "No one would have thought that red-haired Bridget Flaherty, who had a sun-defying white skin and a brogue that could be cut with a butter-knife, had stolen her father's hidden hoard to come to America to be chambermaid in a New York hotel" (895). Scarlett's own appearance as a version of Morgan's wild Irish girl is also frequently limned with irony; "A red-hot little Rebel," Rhett Butler calls her (194), and—at the close of the novel—she confronts her future "with the spirit of her people who would not know defeat, even when it stared them in the face" (1056). Scarlett's mingling of nursing and flirtation during her wartime work at the hospital ("a perfect happy hunting-ground" [224]) similarly echoes Glorvina's own nursing of Horatio after he breaks his arm, an act that instigates the romance plot of *The Wild Irish Girl*, but with some implicit narratorial eye-rolling in Mitchell's version.[70] Late in the novel, the narration's ironizing of the ideology that the novel itself was so effective in propagating becomes coruscating: "The Lost Cause was stronger, dearer now in their hearts than it had ever been at the height of its glory. It was a fetish now" (892).

This irony, though, never truly challenges the novel's racial assumptions or the role of Irishness in supporting them. At one point, for example, Scarlett encounters a Yankee woman from Maine who is looking for a nurse to care for her children; to Scarlett's suggestion that she "find a darky," the Maine woman declares, "Do you think I'd trust my babies to a black n[—]? . . . I want a good Irish girl." Scarlett's reply is haughty: "I'm afraid you'll find no Irish servants in Atlanta. . . . Personally, I've never seen a white servant and I shouldn't care to have one in my house." In that response, she underlines both Irish whiteness and its appropriation of Black work as service for white people (686). One of the stages of Scarlett's coming into her own self of identity and control—a move, in a sense, away from her French mother and toward her Irish father—is, in the novel's account, her domination of the young Black woman Prissy through the verbal violence of white supremacy: "'There,' she thought, 'I've said 'n[—]' and Mother wouldn't like that at all'" (408). It is language—specifically *racist* language—that functions as the threshold to a white supremacist Irishness.[71]

When it is framed in the language of chivalry rather than satire, the Lost Cause represents for Mitchell—as it did for John Mitchel—a crisis of white citizenship in which the inclusion of Irishness within that circle of citizenship is as necessary as the exclusion of Blackness from it:

> An ageless dignity, a timeless gallantry still clung about them and would cling until they died, but they would carry undying bitterness to their graves, a bitterness too deep for words. They were a soft-spoken, fierce, tired people who were defeated and would not know defeat, broken yet standing determinedly erect. They were crushed and helpless, citizens of conquered provinces. They were looking on the state they loved, seeing it trampled by the enemy, rascals making a mock of the law, their former slaves a menace, their men disfranchised, their women insulted. (621)

The "menace" of "their former slaves" lies, in the novel, not only in their freedom but also in their right to vote, in their assertion of their citizenship, which the novel's white characters experience as an erosion of their own enfranchisement. Describing the situation during Reconstruction, *Gone with the Wind* echoes John Mitchel's sneering assertion, in *The Last Conquest of Ireland (Perhaps),* that the British government, in abolishing slavery in the West Indies, was "turning West Indian negroes wild" (103): "Like monkeys or small children turned loose among treasured objects whose value is beyond their comprehension," Mitchell writes, "they ran wild" (668). For Scarlett, the restoration of "gentility"—a term that straddles the boundary of the chivalry rhetoric of the Lost Cause and the raced and classed rhetoric of the modern "gentleman" or "gentlewoman" (or, in the nineteenth century, the "gentlelady")—requires the reestablishment of a racial order in which Black people labor for the benefit of whites in the context of the Irish-named plantation: "Harsh contact with the red earth of Tara had stripped gentility from her and she knew she would never feel like a lady again until her table was weighted with silver and crystal and smoking with rich food, until her own horses and carriages stood in her stables, until black hands and not white took the cotton from Tara" (623). The Irish national narrative becomes a racial narrative of white privilege. It is not just that the dispute between "the agricultural South" and "the industrial North" (285) conceptually rhymes with nineteenth-century Irish nationalist rhetoric of Ireland vis-à-vis Britain, as in Mitchel's writing; it is also the case that the novel represents the fantasy of Irish recovery in the United States after Ireland's own centuries of lost causes as being predicated upon Black submission to white dominance. *Gone with the Wind* not only portrays nineteenth-century Irish America; it is a culmination of the tropes of white nationalism that nineteenth-century Irish America developed. Mitchell grows from the seed that Mitchel planted.

That seed and its growth and propagation on both sides of the Atlantic through the literary genres of Irish nationalism has been the subject of this book. "No pen can give an adequate description of the all-pervading corruption produced by slavery," wrote Harriet Jacobs (*Incidents*, 79), in a clear-eyed description of both the aspiration and the inevitable failure of literature to capture the experience of enslavement, which wrote its own stories upon the bodies and the lives of Black Americans in the nineteenth century and beyond. A number of the writers I have turned to here—Douglass, for example, and Jacobs herself—can see Irishness from the perspective of their own histories. Others, like Boucicault or Poe, gesture toward connections while foregrounding their own literary inventiveness, at times at the expense of the lived experience of others. Some, including Mitchel and Grayson, cynically draw upon Irish political, religious, and economic disadvantage in order to argue for the continuance of chattel slavery, as Mitchel would turn Irish rebellion into the inspiration for a nostalgic refiguration of racial terrorism as chivalric aesthetic. Webb, born free in Philadelphia, provides a sharp analysis of the grounding of Irish whiteness and the making of a white working class precisely in anti-Black violence. This constellation of texts, representing a significant strand of the history of the mid-nineteenth-century literary engagements between Irish nationalism and American race, should indicate, I hope, one key aspect of the long, complex, and painful relationship between Irishness and American racial violence that we must acknowledge before we can strive to dismantle that violence: that the distance between the literature of the Last Conquest and that of the Lost Cause is smaller than we might believe.

NOTES

Introduction

1. Quoted in Strode, *Jefferson Davis*, 459.
2. For an account of the visit, see Friedman, *Wilde in America*, 222–25; and Strode, *Jefferson Davis*, 459–61.
3. Friedman, *Wilde in America*, 223.
4. "Davis and Wilde," 2.
5. See Friedman, *Wilde in America*, 223–24.
6. "Oscar Wilde," 11.
7. "Oscar Wilde: Arrival of the Great Esthete," 8.
8. "Oscar Wilde: Arrival of the Great Esthete," 8.
9. See Ellmann, *Oscar Wilde*, 196; and the note by editors Holland and Hart-Davis in Wilde, *Complete Letters*, 159n1. For the billing of the lecture as "Irish Poets and Poetry of the Nineteenth Century," on the evidence of contemporary newspaper accounts, see Pepper, introduction to *Irish Poets and Poetry*, by Wilde, 14.
10. Wilde, *Irish Poets and Poetry*, 27.
11. Wilde, *Irish Poets and Poetry*, 28.
12. Wilde, *Irish Poets and Poetry*, 30.
13. Wilde, *Irish Poets and Poetry*, 31.
14. Mendelssohn, *Making Oscar Wilde*, 207.
15. Jerng, *Racial Worldmaking*, 11, 12.
16. Todorov, "Origin of Genres," 163.
17. See the accounts, for example, in Ellmann, *Oscar Wilde*, 167–72; McKenna, *Secret Life*, 31–33; Friedman, *Wilde in America*, 102–15; Mendelssohn, *Making Oscar Wilde*, 125–34; and Sturgis, *Oscar*, 215–17.
18. See Ellmann, *Oscar Wilde*, 197. Sturgis provides somewhat more context; see *Oscar*, 255–56. Recent important exceptions include Friedman's and Mendelssohn's books, which offer detailed analyses of the significance of the visit; and Quinlan, *Strange Kin*, 114–15.
19. "Oscar Wilde: Arrival of the Great Esthete," 8.
20. Wilde, *Complete Letters*, 175–76.

21. For an account of the "persistent cult of chivalry" that arose in the early nineteenth century, becoming the "chief legacy of Southern romanticism to the post-1865 history of the United States" (215), see Osterweis, *Romanticism and Nationalism*.
22. Pollard, *Lost Cause*, 50, 534, 699.
23. Pollard, *Lost Cause Regained*, 14; italics in original.
24. Winn, *Emancipation*, 57n. The *Oxford English Dictionary* lists this as the first instance of "white supremacy" in print.
25. Nini Rodgers relates that Blair "received £83,530-8-11 for his 1,598 slaves. He thus claimed for more slaves and received more money than any other slave holder in the British empire" (*Ireland, Slavery and Anti-Slavery*, 94). Because the British government's compensation at the time of abolition was calculated on the basis of estates, other enslavers received more in total than Blair, whose distinction lies in the highest payment for the claim of a single estate.
26. E. Burke, *Reflections*, 113.
27. Arnold, *On the Study of Celtic Literature*, 106–7; italics in original.
28. Watson, "Yeats, Macpherson and the Cult of Defeat," 222.
29. Mitchel, *Jail Journal* (1854), 9; italics in original. Unless otherwise noted, subsequent references to *Jail Journal* are cited parenthetically in the text as they appear in this edition.
30. Mitchel, *Last Conquest*, author's ed., 136; subsequent references to this edition are cited parenthetically in the text.
31. Mitchel, "Letter to the Protestant Farmers," 209; italics in original.
32. In contrast to Wilde, Mitchel would actually break with Davis—as he had with O'Connell—on the basis of what he characterized as Davis's too-chivalric refusal to support the tactics of total war in defense of the Confederacy and racial slavery (see J. Quinn, "Southern Citizen," 33).
33. I use the term here in the sense that David Theo Goldberg has established: "Racial states attempt . . . to regulate through the rule of race, to impose race upon a population so as to manage and control, divide and rule" (*Racial State*, 122).
34. Kinealy, *Black Abolitionists in Ireland*, 4; on Equiano's eight months in Ireland, see also 41–59.
35. See Orr, "Enlightened Ulster, Romantic Ulster," 163.
36. Rudy, "Beyond Universalisms," 93–94. See also Hansord, "Eliza Hamilton Dunlop's 'The Aboriginal Mother.'"
37. Chatterjee, Christoff, and Wong, "Undisciplining Victorian Studies."
38. Rodgers, *Ireland, Slavery and Anti-Slavery*, 273.
39. On O'Connell's abolitionist activism, see, for example, Rodgers, *Ireland, Slavery and Anti-Slavery*, 259–77; and Kinealy, *Daniel O'Connell and the Anti-Slavery Movement*.
40. Phillips, *Speeches, Lectures, and Letters*, 407.
41. David Brundage explains that, in fact, O'Connell "was one of the last to sign the document," but "abolitionists sought to highlight his support of the Irish Address, making it almost seem as though he was its author" (*Irish Nationalists in America*, 72–73). Brundage assigns primary authorship of the Address to the Black American activist Charles Lenox Remond and the Irish abolitionist Richard Davis Webb (72), whereas Christine Kinealy credits Webb and the Irishman James Haughton (*Black Abolitionists*

in Ireland, 93). The Address was brought by Remond from the 1840 World Anti-Slavery Convention in London, where it was conceived, to Ireland for signature gathering and then to Boston. For the history of the Address and its equivocal reception by Irish Americans, see Kinealy, *Black Abolitionists in Ireland*, 11–17.
42. O'Connell, *Daniel O'Connell upon American Slavery*, 40.
43. Quoted in *Daniel O'Connell upon American Slavery*, 41.
44. Wilderson, *Red, White & Black*, 37.
45. For biographical accounts of Douglass's travels in Ireland and his lifelong engagement with questions of Irish nationalism (including significant ambivalence at various points about O'Connell), see Chaffin, *Giant's Causeway*; and Kinealy, *Black Abolitionists in Ireland*, 106–34.
46. Douglass, "Letters," 170.
47. Blight, *Frederick Douglass*, 143.
48. Quoted in Douglass, "Letters," 170.
49. Ferreira, "Frederick Douglass in Ireland," 58.
50. Blight, *Frederick Douglass*, 153.
51. Douglass, *Life and Times*, 242.
52. Douglass, *Narrative*, 39–40; subsequent references to this edition are cited parenthetically in the text.
53. Bingham titles the extract "Part of Mr. O'Connor's Speech in the Irish House of Commons, in Favour of the Bill for Emancipating the Roman Catholics, 1795" (*Columbian Orator*, 243). On the significance of O'Connor's speech to Douglass, see Coughlan, "Frederick Douglass, Arthur O'Connor, and the *Columbian Orator*." As Coughlan points out, "The majority of Douglass's commentators have accepted the accreditation" to Sheridan (69), while Blight compounds the error by attributing the speech to Daniel O'Connell (*Frederick Douglass*, 44).
54. Blight, *Frederick Douglass*, 44.
55. Douglass, *Frederick Douglass Papers, Series One*, 2:520–21.
56. Douglass, *My Bondage and My Freedom*, 98.
57. "Frederick Douglass," *Limerick Reporter*, 11 November 1845; quoted in Kinealy, *Frederick Douglass and Ireland*, 1:231.
58. "Mr. Frederick Douglass's Address," *Banner of Ulster* (Belfast), 9 December 1845; quoted in Christine Kinealy, *Frederick Douglass and Ireland*, 1:244.
59. Roediger, *Wages of Whiteness*, 137.
60. Lootens, "Looking Beyond (and Before) Ancient Ballads," 274.
61. C. Levine, *Forms*, 14.
62. *Oxford English Dictionary* (online), s.v. "genre, n.," definition 1b.
63. Jerng, *Racial Worldmaking*, 10; italics in original. Compare Fredric Jameson's account of the novel as a generic type, "not so much an organic unity as a symbolic act that must reunite or harmonize heterogeneous narrative paradigms which have their own specific and contradictory ideological meaning" (*Political Unconscious*, 144).
64. Dimock, "Introduction," 1379. See also Nathan K. Hensley's account of formalization through which "Humans work both within and outside of these shaping protocols, rupturing old forms to create new ones. This dialectic of newness and convention is the structuring condition of all expression" (*Forms of Empire*, 14).

65. Goyal, *Runaway Genres*, 31.
66. Fielder, *Relative Races*, 8, 57. See also Jerng, *Racial Worldmaking*, esp. 16–19.
67. See, for example, Christina Morin's caution that it is not always possible—or analytically useful—to draw rigid distinctions between "national" and "gothic" Irish literature ("'Gothic' and 'National'?").
68. Rezek, "Racialization of Print," 419. On the "convergence of racial, civilizational, and proto-class terms" in the "discourses on language" from the late eighteenth into the early nineteenth centuries, see also Makdisi, *Making England Western*, 21–22.
69. Leerssen, *Remembrance and Imagination*, 94.
70. Taine, *History of English Literature*, 1:1, 10; italics in original.
71. See Evans, *Before Cultures*, 93–99.
72. Taine, *History of English Literature*, 1:10.
73. On the encounter with (primarily British) Victorian literature by African American writers of the late nineteenth and early twentieth centuries, see Hack, *Reaping Something New*. For an analysis of the transatlantic networks of influence in the other direction, again focusing on British literature, see Lee, *American Slave Narrative and the Victorian Novel*.
74. See C. Levine, "From Nation to Network."
75. Rezek, "Transatlantic Influences and Futures," 385.
76. Ferreira, "Frederick Douglass in Ireland," 58.
77. T. M. Foster, *Genre and White Supremacy*, 88. See also Spillers, "Moving on Down the Line," for an analysis of African American sermons as "a paradigmatic instance of reading as process, encounter, and potential transformation" (85).
78. As an additional twist to the colonial spiral of generic adaptations, beginning in the late eighteenth century, "the first model of mass education in Britain," as Makdisi points out, "was actually adapted from a method developed to teach orphan children in Madras and imported in order to teach 'the lower orders' or 'the inferior classes' at home" (*Making England Western*, 82). On the significance of Irishness and Irish literature to nineteenth-century institutional theory and its discontents, see Mullen, *Novel Institutions*.
79. Corfe, "'Erin go Bragh' in London."
80. Hankins, "What the Folk Printed," 532, 535.
81. T. M. Foster, *Genre and White Supremacy*, 3. Foster's book focuses on a somewhat later period, primarily from the 1860s through the 1890s, as popular genres (in particular, the campus novel, the women's magazine, the Civil War elegy, and the gospel sermon) "maintained racial belonging as the overarching criterion for white social organization in the wake of emancipation," while they also, "for African Americans, provided a method for affirming, energizing, and organizing radical collectivities" (3).
82. Lorimer, "Reconstructing Victorian Racial Discourse," 189.
83. Appiah, "Race," 276.
84. Gross, "Litigating Whiteness," 133.
85. Deane, *Short History of Irish Literature*, 73. On Young Ireland in relation both to O'Connell and to Fenianism, see, for example, Eagleton, *Scholars and Rebels*, 127–41; Dwan, *Great Community*, 23–75; and Brundage, *Irish Nationalists in America*, 79–94.
86. Dolan, *Irish Americans*, 74.

87. J. Quinn, "Exiled History," 163.
88. Delahanty, "Transatlantic Roots," 165. On O'Connell's abolitionism, see also Riach, "Daniel O'Connell and American Anti-Slavery." The population of Irish migrants to the United States, while always manifesting a range, also shifts during and after the Famine from, in Mary Burke's characterization, primarily "relatively comfortable or skilled Anglicans, non-conformists, and Catholics from Ireland's more Anglicized and urbanized eastern seaboard" to frequently "unskilled Catholics from predominantly agricultural and Irish-speaking or somewhat bilingual western seaboard regions" (*Race, Politics, and Irish America*, 2).
89. Rezek, "Racialization of Print," 436.
90. H. Jacobs, *Incidents*, 79; subsequent references to this edition are cited parenthetically in the text.
91. Defoe, *Roxana*, 323.

1. Nineteenth-Century Irishness and the Construction of Race

1. Mufti, "Hating Victorian Studies Properly," 392.
2. Curtis, *Apes and Angels*, 21.
3. Brantlinger, *Dark Vanishings*, 98.
4. de Nie, "'Medley Mob,'" 216.
5. Ignatiev, *How the Irish Became White*, 111.
6. Lloyd, "Black Irish, Irish Whiteness and Atlantic State Formation," 4.
7. O'Neill, *Famine Irish*, 5. On the designation of "free white persons" in the early Republic, see also Jacobson, *Whiteness of a Different Color*, 22–31.
8. See Sancho, *Letters*, 2:204.
9. A. E. Martin, "Victorian Ireland," 52.
10. Wilderson, *Red, White & Black*, 37.
11. See, for example, Jacobson, *Whiteness of a Different Color*, 95.
12. Heng, *Invention of Race*, 3.
13. Heng, *Empire of Magic*, 71; italics in original. See also K. F. Hall, "Reading What Isn't There." Compare Sylvia Wynter's account of the way in which a model of alterity grounded in religious difference was transformed into a model grounded in racial difference in "Unsettling the Coloniality of Being," esp. 291–303.
14. Lecourt, *Cultivating Belief*, 37.
15. Wheeler, *Complexion of Race*, 7.
16. Tucker, "Historicizing the Theorization of Race," 528. Arguing that "the powerful work of naturalizing representation performed by aesthetics is an indelible determinant of the modern racial regime," David Lloyd likewise situates the roots of that regime in eighteenth-century aesthetic theory (see *Under Representation*, 9). See also Chuh, *The Difference Aesthetics Makes*, esp. 17–21 and 42–50; and Hoffman, "Kant's Aesthetic Categories."
17. Painter, "How We Think about the Term 'Enslaved' Matters." On the eighteenth-century development of a "science of race," see also Painter, *History of White People*, 64–71.

18. Knox, *Races of Men*, 13–14; subsequent references to this edition are cited parenthetically in the text.
19. See Hoffman, "Kant's Aesthetic Categories," for an account of the tension between Immanuel Kant's seemingly contradictory notions of race as "physiological or biological fact" and as nonbiological "aesthetic form" (72), both articulated as essential.
20. Jacobson, *Whiteness of a Different Color*, 48.
21. Beddoe, *Races of Britain*, 5.
22. Beddoe, *Races of Britain*, 11.
23. Brantlinger, *Dark Vanishings*, 43.
24. Carlyle, "Occasional Discourse," 672; italics in original.
25. Carlyle, "Occasional Discourse," 672.
26. For one strong analysis of the relationship between Carlyle's view of West Indian slaves and the Famine-era Irish, see MacKenzie, "Thomas Carlyle's 'The Negro Question.'"
27. Carlyle, "Occasional Discourse," 678.
28. Carlyle, *Chartism*, 29–30.
29. Carlyle, "Repeal of the Union," 276; italics in original.
30. Curtis, *Apes and Angels*, 29.
31. "Missing Link," 165. The reference to "the Irish Yahoo" encodes its own sly literary allusion, since the term "yahoo" was coined by the Anglo-Irish satirist Jonathan Swift for the filthy and bestial humans of the fourth book of his 1726 *Gulliver's Travels* (see *Oxford English Dictionary* [online], s.v. "yahoo, n.," definition 1.
32. Curtis, *Apes and Angels*, 101.
33. Reginald Horsman provides an excellent overview of the crosscurrents and contradictions in "Origins of Racial Anglo-Saxonism."
34. Painter, *History of White People*, 79. On the rise of a science of whiteness, see also Jacobson, *Whiteness of a Different Color*, 31–38.
35. Blumenbach, *Anthropological Treatises*, 271 (from the 1795 third edition of the *Natural Variety of Mankind*). Except as indicated, subsequent quotations from *The Anthropological Treatises* will be cited parenthetically in the text as they appear in this edition.
36. John S. Michael has argued that an overreliance on the 1865 English translation by the forthrightly racist Thomas Bendyshe has led to a misunderstanding of the more egalitarian argument implicit in Blumenbach's original Latin (see "Nuance Lost in Translation"). Nonetheless, this was the primary means by which Blumenbach's ideas entered nineteenth-century Britain.
37. Walters, "The 'Sallow Mr. Freely,'" 435.
38. See Stocking, *Victorian Anthropology*, 64–69 and 182–83; and Lecourt, *Cultivating Belief*, 36–42, 50–58. While polygenism became more influential after 1800, David Theo Goldberg traces its roots back to the seventeenth century (see *Racist Culture*, 63–65).
39. Stocking, *Victorian Anthropology*, 67.
40. For the argument that polygenism, at least as articulated by Sir Richard Burton, could provide a more nuanced perspective, even "a surprising openness toward different ways of being," see Lecourt, *Cultivating Belief*, 34, 55–56.
41. Painter, *History of White People*, 201.

42. *Oxford English Dictionary* (online), s.v. "white, adj. (and adv.) and n.," definition I.5.a.
43. Vaughan, *Roots of American Racism*, 263n75.
44. Nott and Gliddon, *Types of Mankind*, 89; italics in original.
45. Horsman, "Origins of Racial Anglo-Saxonism," 405.
46. Stocking, *Victorian Anthropology*, 65.
47. Brantlinger, *Dark Vanishings*, 40.
48. Horsman, "Origins of Racial Anglo-Saxonism," 406.
49. Blumenbach, *Anthropological Treatises*, 188; Blumenbach, *De generis humani varietate nativa*, 65.
50. Blumenbach's reference is to Meiners's *Grundriß der Geschichte der Menschheit*, 2nd ed. (1793).
51. *Oxford English Dictionary* (online), s.v. "race, n.6," definitions I.1.d, I.1.b, I.1.c, I.1.a; see Tennyson, *Poems*, 1:132.
52. Broca, *On the Phenomena of Hybridity*, 12.
53. Broca, *On the Phenomena of Hybridity*, 10–12.
54. Stocking, *Victorian Anthropology*, 64.
55. Carpenter, *Zoology*, 1:151.
56. "Art. IX," 528. The tripart racial model—in contradistinction to Blumenbach's five-variety model—derives primarily from Georges Cuvier (see *The Animal Kingdom*, 96–103).
57. Nott and Gliddon, *Types of Mankind*, 52.
58. J. W. Jackson, "Race Question in Ireland," 58, 60, 59.
59. Arnold, *On the Study of Celtic Literature*, 90.
60. See, e.g., Brantlinger, *Dark Vanishings*, 40.
61. Arnold, *On the Study of Celtic Literature*, 22.
62. Lecourt reports that Arnold most directly encountered Prichardian monogenesis through the work of Max Müller (*Cultivating Belief*, 50, 68).
63. Prichard, *Researches*, 1:260. For Prichard's discussion of and dissention from the category of the "Caucasian," see 1:259–62; for reference to "the Indo-european race," see, e.g., 1:8. See also Lecourt, *Cultivating Belief*, 36–42.
64. Prichard, *Eastern Origin of the Celtic Nations*, 91, 8.
65. Lecourt, *Cultivating Belief*, 165, 72.
66. R. F. Foster, *Paddy and Mr Punch*, 192–93; subsequent references to this edition are cited parenthetically in the text. Curtis disputed Foster's critique in the 1997 revised edition of *Apes and Angels* (109–47).
67. On *Punch*'s broadly anti-Irish and anti-Catholic outlook, see Banta, *Barbaric Intercourse*, 65; and Gibbons, *Gaelic Gothic*, 46–47.
68. Allen, *Racial Oppression and Social Control*, 79.
69. Ignatiev, *How the Irish Became White*, 216.
70. *The British Lion and the Irish Monkey*, 147. The artist was the prolific anti-Irish caricaturist John Leech (see Jones and Shaw, "Artists and 'Suggestors,'" 8).
71. Curtis, *Apes and Angels*, 100; see also 34 and 130.
72. McGovern, *John Mitchel*, 120.
73. See A. E. Martin, *Alter-Nations*, 52–158; de Nie, "'Medley Mob.'"
74. J. Johnson, *Tour in Ireland*, 105, 146, 283, 144.

75. Goldberg, *Racial State*, 109.
76. Counterexamples do exist, especially in earlier periods; Kim F. Hall, for instance, describes one early seventeenth-century text (Sir Thomas Herbert's 1634 *Discription of the Persian Monarchy* [sic]), in which the racialization of the "savage inhabitants" of the Cape of Good Hope is at least partly grounded in a prior racialization of Irishness: "Their pronunciation is like the Irish: their customes not much unlike the rude ones, of antique times" (quoted in K. F. Hall, "'Troubling Doubles,'" 125).
77. Freeman, *Some Impressions*, 139.
78. See Douglass, "The Color Line." The *Oxford English Dictionary* traces the term to 1874, in the *Jackson (MS) Weekly Clarion*, which places it in quotation marks, suggesting it was already a recognizable locution. By using the term as his title, Douglass establishes it as central to post–Civil War American culture and polity, and it would become the key term of W. E. B. Du Bois's insight, in *The Souls of Black Folk*, that "the problem of the twentieth century is the problem of the color-line" (Du Bois, *Souls of Black Folk*, 3, 15).
79. Freeman, *Some Impressions*, 142–43.
80. Freeman, *Some Impressions*, 145–46.
81. Freeman, *Some Impressions*, 143. An oft-cited example of Irish-Black juxtaposition from the United States just a few years prior to Freeman's travels is an 1876 *Harper's Weekly* cover illustration by the abolitionist Republican Thomas Nast, which represented a giant scale in which are precisely balanced and facing each other an emancipated Black man from the southern United States and an apish Irish American from the North. Each figure in this Reconstruction-era caricature draws on racial stereotypes, and the image puts their faces almost into a form of mirroring. Nonetheless, it surely matters, in a detail that occasionally falls out of analyses of this image, that the pans of the scale are clearly labeled "Black" and "White"; the Irishman is a threat, Nast suggests, but it is *as* a white man that he is so (see Nast, *The Ignorant Vote—Honors Are Easy*).
82. Carlyle, "Repeal of the Union," 276.
83. Carlyle, *Latter-Day Pamphlets*, 46; italics in original.
84. Dickerson, *Dark Victorians*, 83–84.
85. Dickerson, *Dark Victorians*, 84.
86. Dickerson, *Dark Victorians*, 83, quoting Carlyle, *Latter-Day Pamphlets*, 32.
87. Lloyd, *Under Representation*, 82.
88. Gilley, "English Attitudes," 86. As Kim F. Hall points out, referring to Edmund Spenser's *A View of the Present State of Ireland* (1596), intermarriage between the English and Irish was not universally lauded in earlier periods: there, the specter of an "'unhealthy' mixture of Irish and English" comes to be troped as an "infection of foreign difference, a danger so perilous that intermarriage needs to be avoided at all costs" (*Things of Darkness*, 147). In terms of interracial marriages between white and Black people, Winter Jade Werner has offered compelling evidence of a shift in racial thinking from the late eighteenth century, when the London Missionary Society "celebrated marriages of missionaries to African women" as an instantiation of "universal kinship," to the 1820s, when those "mixed marriages were shunned" (*Missionary Cosmopolitanism*, 127, 130).
89. See J. W. Jackson, "Race Question in Ireland," 63. The term "eugenics" was pioneered by Francis Galton in his 1883 *Inquiries into Human Faculty and Its Development*, 24.

90. Kingsley, *Charles Kingsley*, 107.
91. Conrad, *Heart of Darkness*, 139.
92. Gilley, "English Attitudes," 86. Gilley's allusion to Kingsley's praise of Irish intermarriage refers to his novel *Yeast: A Problem* (1848).
93. Roediger, *Wages of Whiteness*, 141.
94. J. Davis, *Papers*, 2:389, 391. Certainly by 1892, in *Iola Leroy*, Frances E. W. Harper could represent a characteristic conversation about race in American in which the Irish were clearly and explicitly white; in that novel, when Dr. Latimer asks, "Why... should any place be assigned to the negro more than to the French, Irish, or German?," Dr. Latrobe, a southerner, responds cavalierly: "Oh, ... they are all Caucasians" and that, *as* Caucasians, "I think... that we belong to the highest race on earth and the negro to the lowest" (*Iola Leroy* 227).
95. Calhoun, *Speeches*, 505.
96. Cong. Globe, 32nd Cong., Appendix, 3d Sess., 275 (Douglas, 16 March 1853).
97. Cushing quoted in Fuess, *Life of Caleb Cushing*, 2:230–31; italics in original.
98. *Parliamentary Debates*, 22:643.
99. *Parliamentary Debates*, 22:626–27.
100. *Parliamentary Debates*, 22:393.
101. Quinlan, *Strange Kin*, 49. If nineteenth-century Irish people did not actually believe their own metaphor, that hasn't stopped some virulent credulity among such later defenders as Don Jordan and Michael Walsh, who quote Daniel Defoe describing indentured servants as "more properly called slaves," and then literalize the figure of speech: "Taking his cue, we should call a slave a slave" (*White Cargo*, 15).
102. Rezek, "Transatlantic Influences and Futures," 382–83. Christine Kinealy cautions that while "by the late eighteenth century there were dozens of black people in Ireland" and that "the majority were domestic servants who had been sold into service and received no wages, ... [i]t was, however, substantially different from the type of servitude that existed across the Atlantic" (Kinealy, *Daniel O'Connell and the Anti-Slavery Movement*, 16).
103. Edgeworth and Edgeworth, *Practical Education*, 1:211; italics in original.
104. O'Connell, *Select Speeches*, 1:408.
105. T. Moore, *Poetical Works*, 1:xv.
106. Cromwell, *Oliver Cromwell's Letters and Speeches*, ed. Carlyle, 2:60. On the siege of Drogheda and other seventeenth-century brutalities in Ireland, particularly in relationship to Irish racialization, see Nelson, *Irish Nationalists*, 18–23.
107. The linguistic conflation of penal servitude and chattel enslavement also stretches back to the seventeenth century and, in particular, to Locke's *Two Treatises on Government*. On the internal contradictions of Locke's account of slavery in relationship to the construction of race, see, for example, Bhabha, "Of Mimicry and Man," 126–27; Lepore, *These Truths*, 52–55; Goldberg, *Racial State*, 44–46; Nyquist, *Arbitrary Rule*, 326–61; and Armitage, *Foundations of Modern International Thought*, 90–113. John Donoghue has contended that Cromwellian and post-Cromwellian transportees were in fact designated as "chattel" but for a set number of years and that this "chattel term bondage" (which he considers a form of "slavery") is fundamentally distinct from "racial slavery" ("The Curse of Cromwell," 28).

108. O'Byrne, *Leixlip Castle*, 12.
109. Moran, *Historical Sketch*, 325.
110. Nicholson, *Annals*, 143; subsequent references to this edition are cited parenthetically in the text.
111. Hogan, McAtackney, and Reilly, "The Irish in the Anglo-Caribbean," 19. See also M. Burke, *Race, Politics, and Irish America*, 66–67.
112. Hannah-Jones, "Democracy," 12. On slavery as "social death," see Patterson, *Slavery and Social Death*; see also Smallwood, *Saltwater Slavery*, 60–61. Deirdre Cooper Owens has convincingly detailed both the similarities and, importantly, the differences between the encounters of immigrant Irish and enslaved Black women with the medical system of the mid-nineteenth-century United States (see *Medical Bondage*, 89–107).
113. Vaughan, *Roots of American Racism*, 168.
114. Godwyn, *The Negro's and Indians Advocate*, 36. On Godwyn's travels in the New World and abolitionist writing, see Vaughan, *Roots of American Racism*, 55–81.
115. Godwyn, *The Negro's and Indians Advocate*, 35–36; italics in original.
116. Godwyn, *The Negro's and Indians Advocate*, 83; italics in original.
117. Vaughan, *Roots of American Racism*, 57.
118. Vaughan, *Roots of American Racism*, 79.
119. Marx and Engels, *On Colonialism*, 316.
120. Using the evocative term "racecraft," Karen E. Fields and Barbara J. Fields propose that it was the context of a kind of historical blank slate that allowed the encounter of Africans with Europeans to culminate in the brutality of chattel enslavement of a sort to which other Europeans, even politically disadvantaged Europeans, were not subject: "Africans and Afro-West Indians," they posit, "had not taken part in the long history of negotiation and contest in which the English lower classes had worked out the relationship between themselves and their superiors. Therefore, the custom and law that embodied that history did not apply to them. . . . Africans and Afro-West Indians were thus available for perpetual slavery in a way that English servants were not" (*Racecraft*, 125). The same might be said of the "long history of negotiation and contest" between England and Ireland, and, in fact, Fields and Fields turn to the Irish as an exemplary instance of their argument that racism is not a response to essentialized racial difference but, rather, its origin: "No one dreams of analyzing the struggle of the English against the Irish as a problem in race relations" (117).
121. Easton, *Treatise*, 36. Compare Wilderson's identification of "White civil society's junior partners," including "people of color and White women who are targets of White supremacy and patriarchy, respectively, and, simultaneously, the agents and beneficiaries of anti-Blackness" (*Afropessimism*, 176, 94n).
122. "White Slavery in Connecticut," 2.
123. T. Ryan, "Erin Go Bragh," 2; italics in original.
124. On Thomas Ryan's centrality to the Charleston trade in enslaved Black people in the mid-1800s, see Yuhl, "Hidden in Plain Sight"; and Gleeson, *Green and the Gray*, 18.
125. Gross, "Litigating Whiteness," 128.
126. Painter, "How We Think about the Term 'Enslaved' Matters." See also Coates, *We Were Eight Years in Power*, 180–82.
127. Festa, *Sentimental Figures of Empire*, 2–3.

128. Catherine Gallagher has traced the deployment of the idea of "white slavery" in Britain from the eighteenth century into the nineteenth, for both proslavery and reformist writers (see *Industrial Reformation of English Fiction*, 3–35). On the importance of actual chattel enslavement to the metaphor of white slavery in the United States from the revolutionary period through the early and mid-nineteenth century, in both abolitionist and proslavery accounts, see Roediger, *Wages of Whiteness*, 27–36, 65–92.
129. "Answers to Correspondents," 280; italics in original.
130. Douglass, *My Bondage and My Freedom*, 371.
131. Douglass, *Frederick Douglass Papers, Series One*, 2:258; italics in original.
132. Douglass, *Frederick Douglass Papers, Series One*, 2:424–25.
133. Douglass, *Frederick Douglass Papers, Series One*, 3:581.
134. The qualifier is important, given the historical construction of race, even while that construction does not prevent the concept from having deep and damaging consequences, what Brigitte Fielder identifies "as complex, as mythos, and as entirely real in its import and impact on racialized bodies and relations of kinship and power" (*Relative Races*, 5). See also, among many others, hooks, "Essentialism and Experience"; West, *Race Matters*; S. Hall, "New Ethnicities"; and Schuller, *Biopolitics of Feeling*.
135. Cugoano, *Thoughts and Sentiments*, 17.
136. Ward, *Autobiography*, 382–83. On Ward's travels in Ireland, see Kinealy, *Black Abolitionists*, 201–25.
137. Ward, *Autobiography*, 383.
138. Ward, *Autobiography*, 376.
139. Ward, *Autobiography*, 39.
140. Mill, "The Negro Question," 26.
141. In 1868, Mill would offer a blueprint for a more effective and humane colonial control over Ireland: in order to render Ireland "a consenting party to her union with England," he proposes, it should be governed more like India: "India is now governed, if with a large share of the ordinary imperfections of rulers, yet with a full perception and recognition of its differences from England. What has been done for India has now to be done for Ireland" (*England and Ireland*, 22–23; italics in original). On Mill's ameliorative proposals as a counterinsurgent liberalism in the face of Fenian activism, see A. E. Martin, *Alter-Nations*, 87–103.
142. Twain, *Life on the Mississippi*, 420.
143. Rigney, *Afterlives of Walter Scott*, 124–25.
144. See Douglass, *Narrative*, 112.
145. Garrison, "Irish Address," 54.
146. Mitchel, letter to *New York Daily News*, 4.

2. The Gothic Palimpsest of Black and Irish Histories

1. T. Morrison, *Playing in the Dark*, 36.
2. T. Morrison, *Playing in the Dark*, 12.
3. For analysis of the gothic's complicated politics, see, among others, Townshend, *Gothic Antiquity*; F. Price, "The Politics of Fear"; Horrocks, "More Than a Gravestone";

Canuel, *Religion, Toleration, and British Writing*, esp. 55–85; Watt, *Contesting the Gothic*; and Temple, "Imagining Justice."
4. Chiu, "Faulty Towers," n.p.
5. Moynahan, *Anglo-Irish*, 111.
6. Gibbons, *Gaelic Gothic*, 19.
7. Killeen, *Emergence of Irish Gothic Fiction*, 50.
8. See, for example, Deane, *Strange Country*, 126; Haslam, "Irish Gothic"; Morin, *Gothic Novel in Ireland*; and Gillespie, "Irish Jacobin Gothic."
9. Morin, *Gothic Novel in Ireland*, 4.
10. Gillespie, "Irish Jacobin Gothic," 63.
11. Connolly, *Cultural History of the Irish Novel*, 170–71.
12. Somerville, *Letters from Ireland*, 152. See also David Lloyd's haunting account of the gothic language that permeates Famine memory and Famine literature in "The Indigent Sublime."
13. Mitchel, "June in the Famine Year," 295–96; italics in original.
14. McGovern, *John Mitchel*, 34–35.
15. Griffith, headnote to "The Famine Year," 421.
16. Hemenway, "Gothic Sociology," 106. Hemenway aligns this "burden" with Frantz Fanon's insight that "*In Europe, evil is symbolized by the black man*. . . . In Europe, the black man, whether physically or symbolically, represents the dark side of the personality" (*Black Skin, White Masks*, 165–66; italics in original).
17. Edgeworth, *Popular Tales*, 3:195.
18. Edgeworth, *Popular Tales*, 3:218.
19. Boulukos, *Grateful Slave*, 237.
20. Rezek, "Transatlantic Influences," 395. For an even earlier period, Robert Smart has proposed that "the Gothic roots of American literature were inherited from [the] early Irish settlers and not just cultivated indigenously" ("'Vital Blood,'" 50).
21. *Parliamentary Debates*, new series, 10:1103.
22. Malchow, *Gothic Images of Race*, 33–34.
23. Kiely, *Romantic Novel*, 115.
24. Wester, *African American Gothic*, 17–18. Mark Neocleous similarly observes the alliance between what he calls "Gothic fascism" and racialist thought in the nineteenth century, as "the question of *aristocratic* heritage became less and less of an index of national identity, being gradually usurped by a newer form of national identity increasingly dependent upon the category of race" ("Gothic Fascism," 140).
25. Wester, *African American Gothic*, 19.
26. Goddu, *Gothic America*, 73. See also DeLamotte, "White Terror, Black Dreams."
27. Lewis, *Journal*, title page.
28. Lewis, *Journal*, 402. Lewis goes so far as to assert that "certainly there can be no sort of occasion for continuing in the colonies the existence of *domestic slavery*, which neither contributes to the security of the colonies themselves, nor to the opulence of the mother-country, the revenue of which derived from colonial duties would suffer no defalcation whatever, even if neither whites nor blacks in the West Indies were suffered to employ slaves" (402–3; italics in original). There's a caveat, however, as

he quickly notes: "except in plantation labour," precisely the sort of white theft of enslaved labour upon which his *own* "security" and "revenue" depend.
29. Lewis, *Journal*, 392; italics in original.
30. Wright, *Ireland, India, and Nationalism*, 128.
31. Lewis, "Anaconda," 11; subsequent references to this edition are cited parenthetically in the text.
32. Wright, *Ireland, India, and Nationalism*, 136.
33. Lewis did not inherit his two Jamaican plantations until 1812, four years after the publication of "The Anaconda," but his family was deeply connected with the practices of West Indian enslavement throughout his life. For detailed accounts of Lewis's relationships to slavery, including his ambivalence toward it, see Mulvey-Roberts, *Dangerous Bodies*, 67–79; and Malenas, "Reform Ideology and Generic Structure."
34. The *Oxford English Dictionary* (online) observes that the term's meaning as "the owner or manager of a plantation or large estate" emerged "originally in the Caribbean and the southern United States," from 1619 on, with strong resonances of racially based enslaved labor, although it could sometimes be used more broadly (s.v. "planter, n.," definition I.3.a). Tellingly, the *OED* notes that "in Ireland," the term "planter" could also mean "an English or Scottish settler planted on forfeited lands in the 17th cent." (s.v. "planter, n." definition I.2.a). John Mitchel evokes it in this sense in his complaint that the 1849 Incumbered Estates Act "contemplated a sweeping confiscation and a new 'Plantation' of the island" (Mitchel, *Last Conquest*, 213). For a comparative analysis of what she calls "plantation modernity" across national boundaries (including the United States, Ireland, the Caribbean, and India), see Clukey, "Plantation Modernity," esp. 507–11 and 517–21.
35. The *Oxford English Dictionary* (online) lists as the first appearance in print of a variant of "massa" an eighteenth-century derogation of a young Black man's speech in a South Carolina newspaper (s.v. "massa, n.").
36. On the history of Sri Lankan slavery, see Wickramasinghe, "Abolition of Colonial and Pre-Colonial 'Slavery' from Ceylon."
37. Lowe, *Intimacies of Four Continents*, 45.
38. See Pendergrast, *Uncommon Grounds*, esp. 17–19.
39. See *Oxford English Dictionary* (online), s.v. "tiger, n.," definitions 1 and 2.
40. Cohen, *Global Indies*, 4.
41. Cohen, "Global Indies," 9.
42. I borrow the language of conceptual proximity from Harris, "Introduction," 2.
43. See *Oxford English Dictionary* (online), s.v. "anaconda, n."
44. Wright, "Lewis's 'Anaconda,'" 262.
45. Wright, *Ireland, India, and Nationalism*, 127.
46. M. Burke, *Race, Politics, and Irish America*, 5. On Poe's Irish ancestry, see M. Burke, *Race, Politics, and Irish America*, 25–29; and A. H. Quinn, *Edgar Allan Poe*, 13–19.
47. Poe, infamously, derided William Wadsworth Longfellow's 1842 *Poems on Slavery* as being "intended for the especial use of those negrophilic old ladies of the north, who form so large a part of Mr. Longfellow's friends" ("Longfellow's Poems," 131). For analysis of the authorship of the review—published anonymously and possibly

cowritten—see Whalen, *Edgar Allan Poe and the Masses*, 136–38. *Romancing the Shadow: Poe and Race* (ed. J. Gerald Kennedy and Liliane Weissberg) offers diverse accounts of Poe's relationship to race, from Whalen's claim that Poe manifests a reticently "average racism" ("Average Racism," 30) to Betsy Erkkila's observation that "a simultaneous identification with and revulsion against the figure of the slave, the specter of slave insurrection, fear of a reversal of the master-slave relation, and an apocalyptic vision of the domination of blacks appear to energize and propel Poe's aestheticization of whiteness" ("Poetics of Whiteness," 43).

48. Poe, "Gold-Bug," 1, 2; subsequent references to this edition are cited parenthetically in the text.
49. Whalen, *Edgar Allan Poe and the Masses*, 138.
50. Cassuto, *Inhuman Race*, 160.
51. Peeples, "Love and Theft in the Carolina Lowcountry," 39.
52. T. Morrison, *Playing in the Dark*, 58. Lori Leavell has similarly argued for a nuanced reading of Jupiter's characterization in the tale (see "Poe's Steadfast Servant").
53. Goddu, "Rethinking Race and Slavery in Poe Studies," 15.
54. Person, "Poe's Philosophy of Amalgamation," 207.
55. Poe's substitution cypher offers a more complex version of a trope for decoding that Lewis had similarly represented in "The Anaconda"; there, Everard communicates with the trapped Seafield by means of a simple set of sonic substitutions, using a hammer and reverberating board to strike "as many blows, as the alphabet required (that is, one to A—two to B—twenty-four to Z, &c.) till I had gone through it regularly" ("Anaconda," 64).
56. Heneghan, *Whitewashing America*, 73–74.
57. Baudelaire, *Histoires extraordinaires*, 128–29n.
58. Malouf, "The Poe Test," 44.
59. McKee, "Translation and Audience," 5.
60. Anne H. Stevens has located a few earlier examples of chapter epigraphs but argues, "If Radcliffe did not invent the device she at least helped to popularize it, particularly with her bestselling *Mysteries of Udolpho* (1794)" (*British Historical Fiction before Scott*, 106). See also O'Malley, "'It May Be Remembered,'" 503–4.
61. E. Jacobs, "Ann Radcliffe and Romantic Print Culture," 60.
62. See L. Price, *The Anthology and the Rise of the Novel*, 90–99; and E. Jacobs, "Ann Radcliffe and Romantic Print Culture," 57–63.
63. Pollin, "Light on 'Shadow' and Other Pieces by Poe," 171.
64. Mabbott, "Introduction to the Poems," xxvii–xxviii. For details of Moore's influence on Poe, see Mabbott, "Index," 615.
65. Poe, *Literary Theory and Criticism*, 36.
66. Poe, "Letter to B—," 501.
67. See editor Kevin J. Hayes's note in Poe, *The Annotated Poe*, 266n1. "Spirits!" says Murphy's character Careless, "with one foot in the grave, he dances about the world, as if he was bit by a tarantula" (A. Murphy, *No One's Enemy but His Own*, 16).
68. See "Life of Arthur Murphy," 255. Emily Hodgson Anderson relates that, in the eighteenth century, "many of the most successful Othellos and Oroonokos . . . were Irish

(Barry, Mossop, Dexter) or of Irish descent (Quin)" (*Shakespeare and the Legacy of Loss*, 50). In the nineteenth century, they were displaced as Othellos and Oroonokos by Ira Aldridge, the first major Black Shakespearean actor. On his British, Irish, and European performances as Othello—and in white makeup as white characters—see MacDonald, "Acting Black"; and Lindfors, "'Mislike Me Not for My Complexion.'"
69. Gonzales, *Black Border*, 12–13.
70. Weissberg, "Black, White, and Gold," 140.
71. T. Morrison, *Source of Self-Regard*, 175.
72. The *Oxford English Dictionary* (online) provides a date of 1883 for the emergence of the phrase in this context (s.v. "nose, n.," definition P3.h.b).
73. Earls, "Bulls, Blunders and Bloothers," 1.
74. Edgeworth and Edgeworth, *Essay on Irish Bulls*, 234, 297; italics in original. In both cases, the Edgeworths are quoting putatively representative speakers or characters on Irish bulls, so the import of these quotations cannot necessarily be directly attributed to their own analysis.
75. See R. Hogan, *Macmillan Dictionary of Irish Literature*, 430.
76. See Goddu, *Gothic America*, 131–52. Compare Henry Louis Gates Jr.'s designation of the slave narrative as a "countergenre" (*Figures in Black*, 81). See also Amit S. Rai's claim that "the Gothic provided a new language to represent the savagery of slavery" (*Rule of Sympathy*, 75).
77. Wester, *African American Gothic*, 42. Hemenway has similarly suggested that "slavery is an extreme form of gothic entrapment" ("Gothic Sociology," 113).
78. Goddu, *Gothic America*, 139.
79. Child, introduction to *Incidents in the Life of a Slave Girl*, 7.
80. See Nadler, "Equation of Consent and Coercion."
81. Wester, *African American Gothic*, 42.
82. Sedgwick, *Coherence of Gothic Conventions*, 13; italics in original.
83. J. Gerald Kennedy has pointed out that, "whether or not Poe and Douglass ever crossed paths," "for about two years (ca. April 1831–March 1833), [they] inhabited the same Baltimore neighborhood, only a few blocks from each other" ("'Trust No Man,'" 225).
84. Wardrop, "'What Tangled Skeins,'" 25.
85. Wester, *African American Gothic*, 41. On live burial as a foundational gothic convention, see, for example, Sedgwick, *Coherence of Gothic Conventions*, esp. 20–95.
86. See Cowper, *The Task*, book 4, line 88.
87. Goddu, *Gothic America*, 137.
88. Hartman, *Scenes of Subjection*, 4.
89. Goddu, *Gothic America*, 135. See also Laura Doyle's argument that "for the African-Atlantic writer, the literary gothic is both more real and more surreal than for the Anglo-Atlantic writer" (*Freedom's Empire*, 256).
90. Goddu, *Gothic America*, 144.
91. Garrison, preface to *Narrative of the Life of Frederick Douglass*, vii.
92. "Harriet Jacobs to Amy Kirby Post" (letter), between 27 December 1852 and 14 February 1853, in Jacobs, *Harriet Jacobs Family Papers*, 1:191.

3. From Irish Bardicism to the White Nationalist Verse Epic

1. See McCarter, *Memorial*, 114–17.
2. Trent, *William Gilmore Simms*, 175.
3. See Jarrett, "Literary Significance," 490.
4. "Editor's Table," 308.
5. T. Davis, "Ballad Poetry of Ireland," 223.
6. See Deane, *Short History*, 77.
7. T. Davis, "Ballad Poetry," 222.
8. See Duffy, *Young Ireland*, 80. The *Oxford English Dictionary* (online) traces the phrase, already in quotation marks in the *Nation*'s prospectus, to the Irish Roman Catholic MP Stephen Woulfe during an 1837 debate in the House of Commons (see "Municipal Corporations [Ireland]," 3).
9. Key, "Star-Spangled Banner," 233.
10. Grayson, *Hireling*, title page, quoting Lewis, *Journal*, 62. Except as otherwise indicated, subsequent quotations from Grayson's poems, along with his introduction and notes, will be cited parenthetically in the text by page number as they appear in this edition.
11. The epigraph is somewhat paraphrased from Carlyle, *Latter-Day Pamphlets*, 30.
12. Quoted, with some minor edits, from Murray, *Letters*, 218. Grayson uses asterisks instead of ellipsis points to indicate the omitted text.
13. Gallagher, *Industrial Reformation of English Fiction*, 18–19.
14. Lewis, *Journal*, 62.
15. "Dual Form of Labour," 4.
16. Murray, *Letters*, 205–6.
17. Grayson, *Hireling*, vii–viii, quoting John Stuart Mill, *Principles of Political Economy* (1848). On the development of the rhetoric of the white hireling's wage labor in relation to Black enslavement in the early nineteenth century, see Roediger, *Wages of Whiteness*, 44–47.
18. Cong. Globe, 33rd Cong., 1st Sess. (1854), 1232.
19. On Walsh's Irish roots and pro-(white) labor activism, see Wilentz, *Chants Democratic*, 326–35.
20. Cong. Globe, 33rd Cong., 1st Sess. (1854), 1232.
21. Roediger, *Wages of Whiteness*, 46–47.
22. Grayson, *Autobiography*, 29.
23. Compare, for example, Nicholson, *Annals*, 133, 243, and elsewhere.
24. Kenny, *American Irish*, 119. For a detailed account of Hughes's shift from abolitionism to strong support for slavery, see O'Neill, *Famine Irish*, 75–81.
25. Carlyle, *Latter-Day Pamphlets*, 30; somewhat misquoted in Grayson, *Hireling*, 155n2.
26. Carlyle, *Latter-Day Pamphlets*, 30. On the play of alignment and distinction in this passage, see Dickerson, *Dark Victorians*, 83–84.
27. Jarrett, "Literary Significance," 489; italics in original.
28. Grayson, *Autobiography*, 29.
29. Pinto, *Infamous Bodies*, 34, 33.
30. S. Jackson, "A Black Tory Abolitionist in Early America," 384.

31. D. A. Jones, "Slave Evangelicalism, Shouting, and the Beginning of African American Writing," 70, 80.
32. Goddu, *Selling Antislavery*, 275n32. See Whitfield, "The North Star," 4.
33. Goddu, *Selling Antislavery*, 141.
34. O'Grady, *History of Ireland*, 13.
35. Trumpener, *Bardic Nationalism*, 11, xii.
36. T. Moore, *Poetical Works*, 4:112–13.
37. Vail, "Thomas Moore," 1:312. Jim Shanahan relates that the outward-looking self-presentation of Moore's Irishness in fact caused some Young Irelanders to decry him as denationalized, including Charles Gavan Duffy, who nonetheless included him in his 1845 *Ballad Poetry of Ireland* (see "Imperial Minds," 143–50).
38. Chander, *Brown Romantics*, 28, 44–45.
39. T. Moore, *Poetical Works*, 2:291–92.
40. See J. Moore, "'Transatlantic Tom.'"
41. Hamm, *Yesterdays*, 215. See also Lott, *Love and Theft*, 98. Joseph Rezek has cautioned that, in the United States, Moore was "valued as much as a literary luminary as an Irish bard" and that when he died, he "was mourned generally, not nationally" ("Transatlantic Influences and Futures," 395).
42. Macpherson claimed that his "originals" were Scottish rather than Irish, although that distinction is a complicated one (see Ní Mhunghaile, "Ossian and the Gaelic World"; and Trumpener, *Bardic Nationalism*, 75). On the significance of Ossianic tropes to Irish literature, see also Leerssen, *Remembrance and Imagination*, 40–42; and O'Halloran, "Irish Re-Creations of the Gaelic Past."
43. Owenson, *Wild Irish Girl*, 110.
44. Quoted in "Moore," 389. On Moore's Ossianism, see also Larrissy, "Moore's Romantic Neoclassicism," 60–63.
45. See Macpherson, *Works of Ossian*, 2:56. In his 1818 *Lectures on the English Poets*, William Hazlitt was already calling Moore "the bard of Erin" (301). Along with Carril, Ossian himself could also be designated the "bard of Erin," as in John Hawkins Simpson's 1857 *Poems of Oisin, Bard of Erin*.
46. Quoted in Ellmann, *Oscar Wilde*, 17.
47. Wilde, *Irish Poets and Poetry*, 28.
48. See Macpherson, *Poems of Ossian, in the Original Gaelic*.
49. Nineteenth-century accounts of Macpherson's metrical practices in the Ossian poems include Archibald Clerk's "Dissertation on the Authenticity of the Poems," xlvi; and Patrick MacGregor's "Preliminary Dissertation," 59. Clerk's translation renders Macpherson's verse as (mostly, although inconsistently) iambic tetrameter stanzas of varying length and irregular patterns of rhyme, close to the form of Grayson's "Chicora."
50. Leerssen, "Ossian and the Rise of Literary Historicism," 119, 117.
51. Noori, "Bicultural before There Was a Word for It," 8.
52. Wilderson, *Red, White & Black*, 48.
53. Brantlinger, *Dark Vanishings*, 3.
54. Easton, *Treatise*, 36.
55. Vizenor, *Fugitive Poses*, 35; italics in original.

56. Brantlinger, *Dark Vanishings*, 4.
57. Byrd, *Transit of Empire*, xx.
58. Byrd, *Transit of Empire*, 38.
59. Rifkin, *Beyond Settler Time*, 5.
60. Brantlinger, *Dark Vanishings*, 94.
61. Swift, *Modest Proposal*, 3, 6; italics in original.
62. *Times* (London), 2 April 1849, 4.
63. "Ireland," *Times* (London), 14 March 1854, 11.
64. Carlyle, "Repeal of the Union," 276.
65. See the essays by Choctaw and Irish scholars in Howe and Kirwan, *Famine Pots: The Choctaw-Irish Gift Exchange, 1847–Present*.
66. Leerssen, "Ossianic Liminality," 9.
67. Campbell, *Irish Poetry under the Union*, 137.
68. Arnold, *On the Study of Celtic Literature*, 106.
69. Mullen, "How the Irish Became Settlers," 92.
70. "Anglo-Saxon Ideas," 665.
71. "State of the Country," 3.
72. A. M. Sullivan, *Story of Ireland*, 566; italics in original.
73. On the various appearances of the putative quotation in the nineteenth century, see John Simpson, "Vengeance and the Shores of Manhattan," n.p.; see also Mullen, "How the Irish Became Settlers," 90–91.
74. Campbell, *Irish Poetry under the Union*, 137.
75. See M. Burke, *Race, Politics, and Irish America*, 44.
76. T. Morrison, *Playing in the Dark*, 44–45.
77. "Editor's Table," 308.
78. Byrd, *Transit of Empire*, xxv.
79. Tuck and Yang, "Decolonization Is Not a Metaphor," 11–12.
80. Jacobson, *Whiteness of a Different Color*, 45.
81. T. Morrison, *Playing in the Dark*, 37; quoting Melville, "Hawthorne and His Mosses," 126.
82. Goddu, "Rethinking Race and Slavery in Poe Studies," 16.

4. Irish American Whiteness in *The Garies and Their Friends*

1. Douglass, *Papers, Series One*, 2:433.
2. T. Morrison, *Playing in the Dark*, 47.
3. Fanon, *Black Skin, White Masks*, 90.
4. See Howell and Walsh, introduction to *Garies*, 14.
5. Stevens shoots Mr. Garie at close range; Mrs. Garie, having fled the house, dies in childbirth, a death apparently caused by the shock of the invasion (see Webb, *Garies*, 226–31, 307; subsequent references to this edition are cited parenthetically in the text).
6. See Howell and Walsh, "A Note on the Text," 29.
7. See "*The Garies and Their Friends*" (review), *Frederick Douglass' Paper*.
8. Stowe, preface to *Garies*, by Webb, 41.
9. "The Garies and Their Friends" (review), *Daily News*, 2.

10. Stowe, quoted in Brougham, "From Lord Brougham," 39; italics in original.
11. "*The Garies and Their Friends*" (review), *Observer*, 7.
12. "*The Garies and Their Friends*" (review), *Athenæum*, 1320; italics in original. Frederick Douglass would diagnose this racialized separation of human qualities by different admixtures of blood in "The Color Line": "We are not, as a race, even permitted to appropriate the virtues and achievements of our individual representatives. . . . One drop of Teutonic blood is enough to account for all good and great qualities occasionally coupled with a colored skin; and on the other hand, one drop of negro blood, though in the veins of a man of Teutonic whiteness, is enough of which to predicate all offensive and ignoble qualities" ("The Color Line," 569).
13. "*The Garies and Their Friends*" (review), *Athenæum*, 1320; italics in original.
14. Mehta, *Liberalism and Empire*, 107.
15. See Colley, *Britons*.
16. "*The Garies and Their Friends*" (review), *Observer* (London), 7.
17. Robert S. Levine has suggested that *The Garies*' relative disinterest in slavery (and antislavery activism) is "a rather chilling blind spot in the text" (see "Disturbing Boundaries," 368–69).
18. Sharpe, *In the Wake*, 15.
19. Douglass, "The Color Line," 573, 568.
20. On the midcentury overlaps between antiabolitionism and "anti-amalgamationism" (which *is* central to Webb's plot, given the interracial marriage at the heart of the narrative), see Fielder, *Relative Races*, 59–72. For antiabolitionist and anti-amalgamationist riots in Philadelphia in the 1830s (and an anti-amalgamationist cartoon by Philadelphian Edward W. Clay that includes a portrait of Daniel O'Connell in its racist representation), see Lemire, "*Miscegenation*," 87–102.
21. The earliest example in the *Oxford Dictionary* (online) for the use of "realism" as "fidelity of representation" comes from John Ruskin's *Modern Painters*, in 1856 (s.v. "realism, n.," definition II.4.a). On the rise of literary, journalistic, and imagistic realism more broadly within the specific historical context of mid-nineteenth-century Britain, see Teukolsky, *Picture World*, 84–138.
22. See Freedgood, *Worlds Enough*, esp. 1–33. For Freedgood's analysis of the "aesthetic racism" (139) underwriting the critical privileging of the British and French "realist" novel, see 134–46.
23. G. Levine, *Realistic Imagination*, 15.
24. G. Levine, *Realistic Imagination*, 13.
25. Greiner, *Sympathetic Realism*, 15; italics added.
26. On *The Garies*' realism, in relation to sentimentalism and melodrama, see R. S. Levine, "Disturbing Boundaries," 351, 364–66.
27. "*The Garies and Their Friends*" (review), *Literary Gazette and Journal of Archæology, Science, and Art for the Year 1857*, 919.
28. "*The Garies and Their Friends*" (review), *Literary Gazette and Journal of Archæology, Science, and Art for the Year 1857*, 919.
29. Mullen, *Novel Institutions*, 6, 13. For Renée Fox, the relevance of realism to the nineteenth-century Irish novel lies in part in its "formal tools—among them, an overbearing omniscient narrator, a preoccupation with mundane material detail, a social

conscience, and an investment in the politics inhering in domestic relationships" ("Realism's Irish Forms," 562). On the historical pressures obscuring the realism of Irish novels, see also Ingelbien, "Realism, Allegory, Gothic." For a critique of the common critical assumption, beginning in the nineteenth century, that Irish literature had not achieved "high-Victorian realism" (2), see J. H. Murphy, *Irish Novelists and the Victorian Age*, 1–4.

30. Mullen, *Novel Institutions*, 37.
31. Chandler, "Edgeworth and Realism," 200.
32. Mullen, *Novel Institutions*, 71.
33. In his juxtaposed but explicitly divergent narrative arcs for Clary and Em, Webb both contributes to and complicates the melodramatic cliché of the "tragic mulatto." Observing the continuing effects of racist constructions in the antebellum North, P. Gabrielle Foreman has powerfully critiqued the critical focus on the "white mulatta" trope and demonstrated that nineteenth-century African American writers, often women, frequently disrupted it through what she calls "anti-passing" narratives (see "Who's Your Mama?"). By focusing his tragic plot of racial ambiguity on Clary, Webb also shifts away from what Brigitte Fielder has compellingly demonstrated as "the white woman as a definitive site for racial construction in nineteenth-century US popular and literary culture" (*Relative Races*, 15). In Webb's novel, it is the light-skinned *female* character who rejects "passing for white" and aligns herself with her Black community.
34. "The Garies and Their Friends" (review), *Daily News* (London), 2. On Webb's "various Dickensian tropes," see, for example, Hack, *Reaping Something New*, 37.
35. "The Garies and Their Friends" (review), *Morning Post*, 7.
36. George Levine situates Thackeray at the center of his study of "Mid-Victorian Realism" (see *Realistic Imagination*, 131–80). His account of "Dickensian melodrama" within the sphere of realism (13) is similarly an important context for Webb's own sentimentally realist project.
37. For Du Bois's refiguration of "the sentimental politics of life" to promote Black activism in the early twentieth century, see Schuller, *Biopolitics of Feeling*, 185–94.
38. Jacobson, *Whiteness of a Different Color*, 120–21; italics in original.
39. Nowatzki, "Blurring the Color Line," 50. Compare Roediger, *Wages of Whiteness*, 104.
40. In fact, the relationship between naming and identity is so loosely defined in the case of Mr. Stevens that in the 1857 edition of the novel the very first time he is mentioned (in the first sentence of chapter 12) he is called "Thomas"; by the next page, he is "George." See Webb, *Garies* (1857 edition), 93, 94.
41. Nowatzki, "Blurring the Color Line," 50.
42. Lott, *Love and Theft*, 15, 18, 30.
43. [Fuller], "Entertainments of the Past Winter," 52.
44. Lott, *Love and Theft*, 16. Compare Nowatzki, *Representing African Americans*, 10–11.
45. Lott, *Love and Theft*, 18.
46. Douglass, "Hutchinson Family," 2.
47. M. D. Morrison, "Race, Blacksound," 790.
48. Hartman, *Scenes of Subjection*, 29. See also Hartman's interrogation of Lott's claims for "the subversive effects of minstrelsy" (*Scenes of Subjection*, 212n53).

49. M. D. Morrison, "Race, Blacksound," 786.
50. Lott, *Love and Theft*, 36, 97; italics in original. As Lott points out, the roots of blackface minstrelsy were actually in "the industrializing North" rather than the plantation South—as Stevens's inadvertent racial performance occurs in Philadelphia, not Savannah—and "some cities in the South even bann[ed] it as the slavery controversy escalated in the 1850s" (*Love and Theft*, 39.)
51. M. D. Morrison, "Race, Blacksound," 814. The American-born actor and playwright Ira Aldridge enacted his own subversive reversal of Irish minstrelsy through his tours of Ireland, starting in 1829; Aldridge not only played Othello and other tragic and comic stage roles but also minstrel songs, including the popular "Possum up a Gum Tree," which, Riach asserts, "is one of these rare instances of a minstrel song which could be interpreted as being critical of slavery" (Riach, "Blacks and Blackface," 239); for descriptions of Aldridge's performances in Ireland, see Riach, "Blacks and Blackface," 238–40.
52. On the significance of race to the Philadelphia fire companies and the role of Irish Americans in them, see Ignatiev, *How the Irish Became White*, 166–68, 174–95.
53. Coates, *We Were Eight Years in Power*, 165.
54. E. Burke, *Reflections*, 106.
55. Coates, *We Were Eight Years in Power*, 184.
56. Nowatzki suggests that Webb's depiction of wild Irish violence might also be thought of as evoking the 1834 "Flying Horses Riot," "which was begun by a group of whites at a merry-go-round frequented by blacks and whites and escalated into a full-scale mob assault on African-Americans" (Nowatzki, "Blurring the Color Line," 46). On the role of Irish Philadelphians in particular in that 1834 riot, see Runcie, "'Hunting,'" 194–200. On the centrality of Irish rioters in the Philadelphia riots of the 1830s and 1840s more generally, see Ignatiev, *How the Irish Became White*, 144–63.
57. Du Bois, *Philadelphia Negro*, 17.
58. Du Bois, *Philadelphia Negro*, 6, 22.
59. Ignatiev, *How the Irish Became White*, 159.
60. Lepore, "Long Blue Line," 65–66.
61. Du Bois, *Black Reconstruction*, 700.
62. "The Irish cop," writes Ignatiev, "is more than a quaint symbol. His appearance on the city police marked a turning point in Philadelphia in the struggle of the Irish to gain the rights of white men" (*How the Irish Became White*, 189).
63. On the mid-nineteenth-century Irish American deployment of their whiteness in competition with free Blacks for jobs, see Roediger, *Wages of Whiteness*, 144–50.
64. Douglass, "The Color Line," 574.
65. See, e.g., R. S. Levine, "Disturbing Boundaries," 352–53.
66. Douglass, "The Color Line," 575, 576.
67. Bell, *Afro-American Novel*, 43.
68. Gender, in conjunction with class, certainly complicates Webb's racial narrative, not only in the divergent paths that Clary and Em take in terms of the relationship between racial affiliation and the marriage plot but also in terms of the ways misogynist tropes shape some of Webb's satirical portraits of women, including the generally positively portrayed Mrs. Garie.

69. T. Morrison, *Playing in the Dark*, 41; quoting Bernard Bailyn's *Voyagers to the West: A Passage in the Peopling of America on the Eve of the Revolution* (1986).
70. T. Morrison, *Playing in the Dark*, 43.
71. T. Morrison, *Playing in the Dark*, 44.
72. Engle, "Depictions of the Irish," 157.
73. Bell, *Afro-American Novel*, 43.
74. W. Johnson, "To Remake the World," 21–22.
75. Bell, *Afro-American Novel*, 43.

5. John Mitchel and the Polemic of White Grievance

1. Griffith, preface to *Jail Journal*, by Mitchel, xv–xvi.
2. Eglinton, *Bards and Saints*, 39, 40.
3. Sullivan and Sullivan, *Guilty or Not Guilty?*, 192.
4. Lloyd, *Nationalism and Minor Literature*, 54, 51–52.
5. Lloyd, *Nationalism and Minor Literature*, 51; italics in original.
6. Brown, "Fenianism and Irish Poetry," 246–47.
7. Wilde, *Irish Poets and Poetry*, 30.
8. Douglass, *Papers, Series One*, 2:139. This edition, based on the printing of the speech in *North Star*, on 4 August 1848, gives Mitchel's name as "Mitchell." As this was a common misspelling, I will not flag it each time in the text.
9. Douglass, *Life and Times*, 243. The quotation comes from an 1854 open letter from Mitchel to the Irish abolitionist James Haughton, published in Mitchel's New York–based *Citizen*. William Lloyd Garrison's *Liberator* republished Mitchel's letter on its front page, along with a series of responses ("John Mitchel vs. Daniel O'Connell," 1).
10. Griffith, preface to *Jail Journal*, by Mitchel, xiv–xv.
11. Griffith, preface to *Jail Journal*, by Mitchel, xiii–xiv, xii.
12. Griffith, preface to *Jail Journal*, by Mitchel, xii.
13. Quoted in Dillon, *Life of John Mitchel*, 1:195.
14. Quoted in Mitchel, *Last Conquest*, 210. Thomas Flanagan notes, "There is no need to caution the reader that Mitchel has wrenched the sentence from its context in *The Times*; by his own reckoning, perfidious Albion was unlikely to give such naked expression to its unholy glee. That sentence, stripped bare by Mitchel of its surrounding context of charity, concern and wish to ameliorate, expressed what was, for him, the root fact, the fact of power" ("Rebellion and Style," 28).
15. R. F. Foster, *Irish Story*, 11.
16. Quoted in Dillon, *Life of John Mitchel*, 1:37; italics in original.
17. R. F. Foster, *Words Alone*, 49.
18. R. F. Foster, *Words Alone*, 50.
19. Carlyle, *Reminiscences*, 223; italics in original.
20. Maume, introduction to *The Last Conquest*, by Mitchel, xvii.
21. On Carlyle's travels in Ireland, including a meeting with Mitchel and a series of arguments with Charles Gavan Duffy over the relationship of labor to Irish national aspirations, see Nally, *Human Encumbrances*, 175–201.

22. For an alternative reading of this passage's revision of Carlyle that finds in it a sort of redemptive identification with the enslaved Brazilians, see Nelson, *Irish Nationalists*, 109–10.
23. See McGovern, *John Mitchel*, 127–29.
24. In an 1847 letter to the *Nation* in response to a speech by Haughton, Kenyon wrote that he was "by no means prepared to admit" that slavery was wrong: "The Scriptures nowhere formally condemn this crime. The Church has never defined it to be such. Priests and Bishops maintain communion with slave-holders unblamed. They have themselves owned slaves. They may own some yet for anything I know to the contrary" (quoted in Fogarty, *Father John Kenyon*, 73). On the roles of Kenyon and Haughton in the debate over American slavery in the context of Irish and Irish American anti-abolitionism more generally, see Delahanty, "Transatlantic Roots," 170–73.
25. Quoted in Dillon, *Life of John Mitchel*, 2:106; italics in original.
26. Quoted in Dillon, *Life of John Mitchel*, 2:101.
27. Quoted in Dillon, *Life of John Mitchel*, 2:49.
28. Quoted in Dillon, *Life of John Mitchel*, 2:107; italics in original. By 1865, in the *Richmond Examiner*, Mitchel was publishing his qualms about whether even Robert E. Lee was "a 'good Southerner'" in that Mitchel wondered "whether he is thoroughly satisfied of the justice and beneficence of negro slavery" (Keneally, *The Great Shame*, 409; quoting *Richmond Examiner*, 16 February 1865).
29. Mitchel was not alone in figuring the monetary analogy as a form of racial betrayal; the London *Times* in 1852 quotes a County Cork priest (a "Roman Catholic clergyman of some note") exhorting his parishioners to "recollect 1847, when our Celtic millions perished of starvation. . . . English gold could be had to rescue the dark Indian from the lash of his taskmaster, but nothing could be granted to rescue the mere Irish from the agonies of starvation" ("Ireland," *Times* [London], 25 June 1852, 5).
30. O'Neill, "Memory and John Mitchel's Appropriation of the Slave Narrative," 333.
31. *Jail Journal* (1913 ed.), 159. The 1913 edition states, in a prefatory note, "Save for some half-dozen verbal changes subsequently made by Mitchel, this Edition is an exact reproduction of the 'Jail Journal' as it first appeared" (n.p.). This addition is one of those changes.
32. Hale, "Martyrs for Contending Causes," 208.
33. See McGovern, *John Mitchel*, 121.
34. Duffy, *Four Years of Irish History*, 500–501.
35. Leerssen, *Remembrance and Imagination*, 23–24.
36. *Public Statutes at Large of the United States of America*, 1:103.
37. Glenn, *Unequal Freedom*, 29. Glenn points out that, while customary practices varied from place to place, "Only at the end of the colonial period and in the early years of the republic did states begin to establish constitutional and legal bars against Native Americans, blacks, and women voting. . . . Perhaps more surprising is that North Carolina, Maryland, Kentucky, and Tennessee permitted propertied blacks to vote until the mid-1830s" (30).
38. Bassett, *Slavery in the State of North Carolina*, 37. The case was State v. Newsom. On the challenge that free Black persons born in the United States posed to nineteenth-century models of citizenship, see Kettner, *Development of American Citizenship*,

311–33. For an overview of the ways in which American citizenship depended upon notions of race and gender from the colonial era through Reconstruction, see Glenn, *Unequal Freedom*, 18–55.
39. Howard, *Reports of Cases*, 405.
40. Howard, *Reports of Cases*, 404.
41. Easton, *Treatise*, 36–37.
42. Douglass, *Papers, Series One*, 2:540. From 1849 to 1851, the American-born abolitionist Samuel Ringgold Ward, in a similarly important rhetorical move, edited the *Impartial Citizen*, designated by Christine Kinealy "Syracuse's first black newspaper, which he had helped to found" (Kinealy, *Black Abolitionists in Ireland*, 205). For Ward's own journey through Ireland and his account of it, see Kinealy, *Black Abolitionists in Ireland*, 201–25.
43. Edlie L. Wong provides a powerful account of one effect of the alignment of citizenship with whiteness in the difficulty that mid-nineteenth-century Black people, including free Black people, had in attaining passports for travel outside the United States (see Wong, *Neither Fugitive nor Free*, 240–62). On the Black State Conventions of the 1840s in New York and Pennsylvania, and the powerful arguments they made for Black citizenship and enfranchisement, see Spires, "Imagining a State of Fellow Citizens."
44. "Great Debate between Lincoln and Douglas at Ottawa," 1.
45. *Lincoln-Douglas Debates*, 54–55.
46. "Great Debate between Lincoln and Douglas at Ottawa," 1.
47. Quoted in Mitchel, *Jail Journal* (1913 ed.), 394; italics in original.
48. Quoted in Dillon, *Life of John Mitchel*, 2:106; italics in original.
49. Quoted in Hébert, *Cornerstone of the Confederacy*, 223–24.
50. See Agamben, *Homo Sacer*, esp. 166–80. For more on Mitchel's appropriation of what would come to be called "bare life" for Famine-era Irishness, see O'Neill, "Memory and John Mitchel's Appropriation of the Slave Narrative," 325–27.
51. Weheliye, *Habeas Viscus*, 38.
52. Eagleton, *Scholars and Rebels*, 138.
53. Maurer, *Dispossessed State*, 119.
54. The quotation is a paraphrase of a number of passages in Carlyle's *Chartism*, including "O reader, to what shifts is poor Society reduced, struggling to give still some account of herself, in epochs when Cash Payment has become the sole nexus of man to men!" (Carlyle, *Chartism*, 61; see also 58 and 66.) As Gallagher notes, "To many [nineteenth-century British] reformers, free labor was not only a myth but also a dangerous ideal, for it implied a society in which the classes were connected only through the 'cash nexus'" (Gallagher, *Industrial Reformation of English Fiction*, 122).
55. Eagleton, *Scholars and Rebels*, 138. For an analysis of Carlyle's influence on Friedrich Engels, see A. E. Martin, "Blood Transfusions."
56. Mitchel, "Poetic Politics," 186.
57. Lloyd, *Nationalism and Minor Literature*, 53.
58. Rosenthal, *Accounting for Slavery*, 3. See also Paul Gilroy's point that "a concern with the Atlantic as a cultural and political system has been forced on black historiography and intellectual history by the economic and historical matrix in which plantation slavery—'capitalism with its clothes off'—was one special moment" (*The Black Atlantic*, 15).
59. Rosenthal, *Accounting for Slavery*, 2. On the use of enslaved people as mortgage collateral, see also Baptist, *The Half Has Never Been Told*, 273–80.

60. See Berry, *Price for Their Pound of Flesh*.
61. B. Martin, "Neighbor-to-Neighbor Capitalism," 119.
62. See, for example, Mitchel, *Last Conquest*, 154.
63. Goldberg, *Racial State*, 60.
64. Quoted in Dillon, *Life of John Mitchel*, 2:105–6.
65. "John Mitchell vs. Daniel O'Connell," 1; italics in original.
66. Marx, *Dispatches*, 279–80.
67. Cohen, "Wage Slavery, Oriental Despotism, and Global Labor Management," 207.
68. T. Morrison, *Playing in the Dark*, 38, 57.
69. J. Davis, *Jefferson Davis, Constitutionalist*, 3:357.
70. Coates, *We Were Eight Years in Power*, 180.
71. See Nelson, *Irish Nationalists*, 37. Despite Mitchel's account of the name's history, Carlyle (another Lowland Scot) also claimed to be Saxon (see M. Burke, *Race, Politics, and Irish America*, 49).
72. Sartre, "Black Orpheus," 49.
73. Fanon, *Black Skin, White Masks*, 112–13.

6. Performing Sympathy in *The Octoroon*

1. See R. Hogan, *Dion Boucicault*, 13, and Fawkes, *Dion Boucicault*, 3–4. Boucicault himself used a number of different spellings of his name at various points in his career, as did contemporary accounts; I will not flag them each time they appear in the text.
2. R. Hogan, *Dion Boucicault*, 26.
3. Howes, "Melodramatic Conventions," 84.
4. R. Hogan, *Dion Boucicault*, 32.
5. See R. Hogan, *Dion Boucicault*, 38–45, and Fawkes, *Dion Boucicault*, 186–87.
6. Howes, "Melodramatic Conventions," 97–98.
7. Fawkes reports that Boucicault "wrote, adapted or doctored more than 200 plays," of which a "hundred or so . . . survive today" (*Dion Boucicault*, xv, xvii).
8. R. Hogan, *Dion Boucicault*, 66–67.
9. See Flynn, "Sites and Sights," 8.
10. See R. Hogan, *Dion Boucicault*, 40.
11. Roach, *Cities of the Dead*, 199.
12. Howes, "Melodramatic Conventions," 84.
13. L. Williams, *Playing the Race Card*, 23.
14. Brooks, *Bodies in Dissent*, 30.
15. Brooks, *Bodies in Dissent*, 29.
16. See Boltwood, "'Ineffaceable Curse,'" 394–95n2.
17. Boltwood, "Dion Boucicault," 461.
18. Boltwood, "Dion Boucicault," 467–68.
19. See Boltwood, "'Ineffaceable Curse,'" 383.
20. R. Hogan, *Dion Boucicault*, 87.
21. In a front-page advertisement for the opening night of *The Octoroon* that ran in the *New York Herald* on 5 December, the character's name is almost always spelled "McCloskey," although it once appears as "McClosky" (see "Amusements," 1).

22. "The Octoroon," *New York Times*, 15 December 1859, 4.
23. Boucicault, *Colleen Bawn*, 7.
24. See McFeely, *Dion Boucicault*, 14–21, and Mouton Kinyon, "'I'm Apparently Not Famous Anymore.'"
25. As Boltwood points out, *The Colleen Bawn* represents Boucicault's rewriting of *The Octoroon* as Irish, rather than the other way around: "Tellingly. . . , the first heroine is the mulatto freed-slave Zoe, while the second is the Irish peasant Eily O'Connor" ("'Ineffaceable Curse,'" 383).
26. Boltwood, "'Ineffaceable Curse,'" 388.
27. Richards, "Dion Boucicault," 282.
28. Boltwood, "'Ineffaceable Curse,'" 390.
29. Cima, *Performing Anti-Slavery*, 1.
30. Cima, *Performing Anti-Slavery*, 225; quoting from "Miss Sarah P. Remond," 150.
31. "'The Octoroon.' A Disgrace to the North, a Libel on the South," 529.
32. "Abolition on and off the Stage," 6. For Bennett's pro-southern sympathies in relation to the *Herald*'s attacks on *The Octoroon*, see Kaplan, "*The Octoroon*."
33. "The Five Act Drama—The Octoroon," 5.
34. J. Jefferson, *Autobiography*, 214–15.
35. Quoted in "The Octoroon Gone Home," 2.
36. Boucicault, "*The Octoroon*. To the Editor of the Times" (letter), 5.
37. Meer, "Boucicault's Misdirections," 84.
38. "Law Reports. The Octoroon War," 3; italics in original. Bluford Adams points out the *New York Evening Post* also suspected that the *Herald*'s antiabolitionist attacks on the play were part of the "publicity stunt masterminded by none other than Boucicault himself" (*E Pluribus Barnum*, 149, 220n86).
39. Boucicault, "*The Octoroon*. To the Editor of the Times" (letter), 5.
40. Yao, *Disaffected*, 13.
41. See Hadley, *Melodramatic Tactics*, 15–21. On the influence of Smith's concept of sympathy on Victorian literature, see also Greiner, *Sympathetic Realism*. On the Victorian divergences from Smithian sympathy, see Schaffer, *Communities of Care*, esp. 119–27.
42. Smith, *Theory of Moral Sentiments*, 2. There is, in fact, an Irish source for Smith's notion of sympathy, in that it responds to—and critiques—the argument for a sympathetic instinct proposed by his mentor at the University of Glasgow, the Ulster-born Francis Hutcheson; see *Short Introduction to Moral Philosophy*, 14. For Smith's critique of Hutcheson's argument that sympathy arises "without any consideration of our own Interests," see *Theory of Moral Sentiments*, 400–411.
43. Boucicault, "Art of Dramatic Composition," 41; subsequent references to this edition are noted parenthetically in the text.
44. On sympathy as a form of *resistance* to identification, see Greiner, *Sympathetic Realism*, 4–5.
45. Yao, *Disaffected*, 4; italics in original.
46. Chander, *Brown Romantics*, 69.
47. Greiner, *Sympathetic Realism*, 44.
48. Rai, *Rule of Sympathy*, 161.
49. "Anti-Slavery Theatres and Litterateurs," 6.

50. "Anti-Slavery Theatres and Litterateurs," 6.
51. Chander, *Brown Romantics*, 69; quoting Shelley, "Defence of Poetry," 17. Compare Bloom, *Against Empathy*, 33–34. Cima rightly cautions against conflating "nineteenth-century sympathy with empathy or the present-day idea of sympathy as 'being thus affected by the suffering or sorrow of another': for nineteenth-century practitioners," she points out, "pain was not necessarily a prerequisite" (*Performing Anti-Slavery*, 40). The shifting connotations of "sympathy"—especially in reaction to the introduction of the similar but distinct term "empathy"—can indeed lead to some confusion. According to the *Oxford English Dictionary* (online), the term "empathy" in the modern sense enters written English only in the early twentieth century (s.v. "empathy, n.," definitions 2.a. and 2.b.); as Bloom notes, his own usage of the term is in fact "in the sense of Adam Smith's *sympathy*—feeling what another feels" (*Against Empathy*, 70). That said, for both Smith and Boucicault, pain *could* be a powerful basis for sympathetic identification, as when Boucicault falls back upon the trope of "fellow-creatures suffering their fate" as the archetypical instance. On the relationship between "empathy" and Smithian sympathy, see also Yao, *Disaffected*, 210.
52. Rai, *Rule of Sympathy*, xix, 42.
53. See Noddings, *Caring*, 112–13.
54. Schaffer, *Communities of Care*, 118, 124. On the activist potential of sympathy as "the demand of the other for a certain justice" (xv), particularly in terms of abolitionism in the eighteenth and early nineteenth centuries, see Rai, *Rule of Sympathy*.
55. Smith, *Theory of Moral Sentiments*, 211–12. On the implications of Smith's thought experiment of a Chinese earthquake for concepts of sympathy and the afterlives of that thought experiment, see Hayot, *Hypothetical Mandarin*, esp. 3–35. On the racial underpinnings and ramifications of Smithian sympathy, see Yao, *Disaffected*, 12–15; and Rai, *Rule of Sympathy*, 54–57.
56. "Oscar Wilde," 11.
57. For a collection of short histories of the *Pilot* and its relevance to nineteenth-century Catholic and Irish communities in New England, see Vara-Dannen, appendix 1, 161–62.
58. "O'Connell and the Abolitionists," 46; all quotations from this article appearing here are from this page.
59. Cong. Globe, 33rd Cong., 1st Sess. (1854), 1232.
60. Mehta's analysis in *Liberalism and Empire* of "the problematic of progress" is again relevant here.
61. Hartman, *Scenes of Subjection*, 18, 19.
62. Festa, *Sentimental Figures*, 12. On this same image and other forms of antislavery consumption that deployed sympathy toward "the production of white identity through the purchase of black freedom" (93), see also Goddu, *Selling Antislavery*, 85–107.
63. Jaffe, *Scenes of Sympathy*, 2.
64. Brody, *Impossible Purities*, 52.
65. Boltwood, "'Ineffaceable Curse,'" 386.
66. Hartman, *Scenes of Subjection*, 28. On *The Octoroon*'s affiliations with nineteenth-century minstrelsy, see also Sonstegard, "Performing Remediation."
67. Boucicault, *Octoroon*, 43; subsequent references to this edition are noted parenthetically in the text.

68. W. Johnson, "The Slave Trader, the White Slave, and the Politics of Racial Determination," 21. Gross similarly notes that, "over the course of the antebellum period, law made the 'performance' of whiteness increasingly important to the determination of racial status. Doing the things a white man or woman did became the law's working definition of what it meant to be white" (Gross, "Litigating Whiteness," 112).
69. Brody, *Impossible Purities*, 50.
70. Gross, "Litigating Whiteness," 128. For an extensive analysis of a particular 1857 Louisiana case (that of Alexina Morrison) and its challenge to stable notions of race, see W. Johnson, "The Slave Trader, the White Slave, and the Politics of Racial Determination."
71. Brooks, *Bodies in Dissent*, 39.
72. Schuller, *Biopolitics*, 2; see also 55–67.
73. P. J. Williams, *Alchemy of Race and Rights*, 163.
74. Jaffe, *Scenes of Sympathy*, 7.
75. Merrill, "'May She Read Liberty in Your Eyes?,'" 135–36; italics in original.
76. "War about Theatres," 3.
77. "War about Theatres," 3.
78. Smith, *Theory of Moral Sentiments*, 403–4.
79. Merrill, "'May She Read Liberty in Your Eyes?,'" 133.
80. Hartman, *Scenes of Subjection*, 85.
81. Boucicault, "*The Octoroon*. To the Editor of the Times" (letter), 5.
82. On the significance of race to the "discourses of seduction" and the possibilities both of agency and sympathy—in this case in eighteenth-century Barbados—see Fuentes, *Dispossessed Lives*, esp. 80–86.
83. On Jacobs's disavowal of "sympathy" in its "cultural equation between true feeling and right action," see Yao, *Disaffected*, 3–4.
84. On Boucicault's use of the name Mac Coul as Beamish's family name, see Wright, *Representing the National Landscape*, 88–89.
85. See O'Malley, *Liffey and Lethe*, 127–33.
86. "The Theatres" (review), 597.
87. "A Drama with Variations," 788.
88. Schaffer, *Communities of Care*, 124.
89. "A Drama with Variations," 788.
90. Goldberg, *Racial State*, 70.
91. Douglass, *Life and Times*, 243.
92. "John Mitchell vs. Daniel O'Connell," 1; italics in original.
93. "Anti-Slavery Theatres and Litterateurs," 6.
94. Brooks, *Bodies in Dissent*, 46; italics added.
95. Quoted in Douglass, "Letters," 170.
96. Phillips, "Letter from Wendell Phillips, Esq.," xiv–xv.
97. Mehta, *Liberalism and Empire*, 20.
98. Mehta, *Liberalism and Empire*, 82.
99. Scarry, "Difficulty," 102; italics in original.
100. Scarry, "Difficulty," 103; italics in original.

101. Marx, *Grundrisse*, 104.
102. Lowe, *Intimacies of Four Continents*, 6–7.
103. See Goldberg, *Racial State*, 43. Goldberg also detects this "naturalist tradition" at work in the seventeenth-century English accounts of colonized Ireland (77).
104. Goldberg, *Racial State*, 79. Goldberg counts Marx among the historicists (45). While I have considered Mitchel in relation to Marx here, I find this alignment convincing; it is not historicism that Mitchel takes from Marx but, rather, an anti-industrialist revolutionism that turns all human interactions into economics, thereby opening the door to imagining nonwhite people as property, a racist politics that he adopts from Carlyle (one of Goldberg's "naturalists").
105. E. Burke, *Reflections*, 7–8; quoted in Mehta, *Liberalism and Empire*, 175. As early as the *Philosophical Enquiry*, the Irish Burke was figuring Blackness as a form of essential difference; in a section entitled "Darkness Terrible in Its Own Nature," he relates the story of a boy who, having been born blind, regains his sight: "Upon accidentally seeing a negro woman," Burke writes, "he was struck with great horror at the sight. The horror, in this case, can scarcely be supposed to arise from any association" (*Philosophical Enquiry*, 143). There is no question that Irishness would, in Burke's aesthetic theory, provoke that reaction.
106. Dwan, *Great Community*, 26.

Coda

1. Gleeson, *Green and the Gray*, 46.
2. See McGovern, *John Mitchel*, 179–80 and 184; see also Quinlan, *Strange Kin*, 83.
3. See McGovern, *John Mitchel*, 185.
4. "John Mitchel," *New York Freeman's Journal*, 4; italics in original.
5. Douglass, *Life and Times*, 243.
6. Quinlan, *Strange Kin*, 80. On Meagher's initial ambivalence about the institution of slavery and his understanding that he was fighting for the Union but not to end the practice of enslavement, followed by his transition to a full-throated abolitionism, see Egan, *Immortal Irishman*, 161–63, 171, 255–57.
7. Kenny, *American Irish*, 124.
8. Quinlan, *Strange Kin*, 80.
9. Kenny, *American Irish*, 126. Quinlan notes that while "the riots were bitterly xenophobic," "Irish policemen were prominent among those deployed to quell them" (*Strange Kin*, 81). On Irish whiteness as context for the riots, see Jacobson, *Whiteness of a Different Color*, 52–55; and Bernstein, *New York City Draft Riots*, 113–23.
10. O'Neill, *Famine Irish*, 50; for a detailed account of those Irish American anti-Chinese actions, see 184–208.
11. Brundage, *Irish Nationalists in America*, 122.
12. *Oxford English Dictionary* (online), s.v. "Boycott, v."
13. O'Neill, *Famine Irish*, 50. O'Neill relates that "the San Patricio, or Saint Patrick, Battalion was composed of Irish immigrants who deserted the Union Army to fight for the Mexicans during the Mexican-American War" (52n39).

14. Gleeson, *Irish in the South*, 182.
15. A. Ryan, *Father Ryan's Poems*, 150–51.
16. A. Ryan, *Father Ryan's Poems*, 76. On Ryan's poetry, see also Quinlan, *Strange Kin*, 103–14; and Gleeson, *Green and the Gray*, 208–10.
17. See Beagle and Giemza, *Poet of the Lost Cause*, 104–6, 120.
18. Stancliff, *Frances Ellen Watkins Harper*, 106. See also Engle, "Depictions of the Irish," 162–67.
19. Douglass, *Papers, Series One*, 4:256.
20. Douglass, *Papers, Series One*, 4:250.
21. Douglass, *Papers, Series One*, 5:117–18.
22. Carlyle, "Occasional Discourse," 672; italics in original.
23. See A. E. Martin, "Fenian Fever," 27–30.
24. "Insurrection in One of the British Dependencies," 173.
25. "Insurrection in Jamaica," 212.
26. Malouf, *Transatlantic Solidarities*, 34.
27. A. E. Martin, "Fenian Fever," 27.
28. A. E. Martin, "Fenian Fever," 22. On the *Nation*'s attention to the 1857 Indian Revolution as a model for international anticolonial activism, see also A. E. Martin, "Representing the 'Indian Revolution' of 1857."
29. In contrast, the antislavery journalist Samuel Ringgold Ward, who had found little to like in Ireland in the 1850s, condemned the Morant Bay Rebellion and justified its brutal suppression in *Reflections on the Gordon Rebellion* (1866), a pamphlet with a title evocative of that by the Irish statesman Edmund Burke, *Reflections on the Revolution in France* (1790). Addressing Ward's unexpected support for the violent response to the rebellion, Jeffrey R. Kerr-Ritchie has proposed that Ward understood the British Empire as grounded in freedoms that were elsewhere abrogated (see Kerr-Ritchie, "Samuel Ward and the Gordon Rebellion").
30. "Stop My Pilot!," 4.
31. "Stop My Pilot!," 4. On O'Reilly's approach to racial egalitarianism as a strategy for redefining Irish Americanism, see Onkey, *Blackness and Transatlantic Irish Identity*, 32–62.
32. A. E. Martin, "Fenian Fever," 22.
33. Schneer, "Anti-Imperial London," 176. The quotation is from a speech of December 1900. Schneer does list a few "honorable exceptions—for instance, the Irish Quaker Alfred Webb, upon whom the oppressed of every race, religion, and sex could always rely, and the [Social Democratic Federation] activist John Scurr, who lectured [United Irish League] branches on the need for solidarity with all victims of British domination" (176).
34. Boyce, "'Marginal Britons,'" 265. Kevin Kenny reports that "in the year 1857, when Ireland made up roughly 20 per cent of the UK population, 33 per cent of all [Indian Civil Service] recruits were Irish," and that, in that same year, "half of the [East India] Company's 14,000 soldiers, and perhaps 40 per cent of the 26,000 regular British troops in India, were Irish. Most were Catholics of low income" ("Irish in the Empire," 103, 104–5).
35. Lyons, *John Dillon*, 105. Lyons proposes, however, that Dillon "was not a 'racist,' but he was a realist" (105).

36. Mitchell's novel itself repeatedly and throughout the text turns to the explicit rhetoric of the Lost Cause. See, for example, Ashley Wilkes's mournful letter to Melanie from the front ("I wonder if they know they are fighting for a Cause that was lost the minute the first shot was fired, for our Cause is really our own way of living and that is gone already") and the description of Rhett Butler's enlisting on the Confederate side of the Civil War: "Why had he gone, stepping off into the dark, into the war, into a Cause that was lost, into a world that was mad?" (*Gone with the Wind*, 217, 399; subsequent references to this edition are noted parenthetically in the text).
37. In the middle of the nineteenth century, an artifact was discovered and quickly dubbed the "Tara Brooch," frequently reproduced as a symbol of medieval Irishness; Queen Victoria bought two copies. On the uncertainty surrounding the discovery of the brooch and its dissemination of a (replicable) form of Irish authenticity through the 1893 Chicago World's Columbian Exposition, see M. M. Williams, *Icons of Irishness*, 45–66, 80–81.
38. Cantrell, *Celtic Culture*, 198–99. On the Irish names of Mitchell's characters, often unremarked in the text itself, see also Quinlan, *Strange Kin*, 129.
39. See T. Davis, *Poems*, 89–94.
40. Quinlan, *Strange Kin*, 119. On Mitchell's Irish ancestry, see also M. Burke, *Race, Politics, and Irish America*, 105–6, 123–24. Burke points out that Mitchell herself "did not identify strongly as Irish Catholic, though claimed by that community" (*Race, Politics, and Irish America*, 32; see also 105).
41. Mitchell, *Margaret Mitchell's "Gone with the Wind" Letters*, 113–14. Mary Burke points out that Mitchell's allusion is to the saying that the "Old English" Fitzgeralds became "more Irish than the Irish themselves," particularly in terms of their anti-British nationalism (*Race, Politics, and Irish America*, 106).
42. Quinlan, *Strange Kin*, 129.
43. Clukey, "Plantation Modernity," 512.
44. Clukey, "Plantation Modernity," 507. On *Gone with the Wind* as a form of belated plantation romance, see Jerng, *Racial Worldmaking*, 71–88.
45. Clukey, "Plantation Modernity," 510, 512.
46. Clukey, "Plantation Modernity," 513. See also M. Burke, *Race, Politics, and Irish America*, 126–27.
47. Cantrell observes that the Slattery family name "derives from the Irish *slátra*, meaning 'strong,' which, if Mitchell had known any Gaelic, would have made her use of the name ironic" (*Celtic Culture*, 197).
48. Rousey, "Friends and Foes of Slavery," 376–79; Rousey acknowledges that small sample sizes might in some instances skew the data.
49. Gleeson, *Green and the Gray*, 10.
50. Gleeson, *Green and the Gray*, 17.
51. See Gleeson, *Green and the Gray*, 40.
52. Mendelssohn, *Making Oscar Wilde*, 203–4.
53. Gleeson, *Green and the Gray*, 18. As Thomas Ryan compared Lincoln to Cromwell, so does Mitchell's Scarlett compare Sherman's siege to "the siege at Drogheda when Cromwell had the Irish, and they didn't have anything to eat and Pa said they starved and died in the streets. . . . And when Cromwell took the town all the women were—."

To Rhett Butler's qualification that "Sherman isn't Cromwell," Scarlett declares, "No, but he's worse!" (*Gone with the Wind*, 314).
54. See Swarns, *The* 272. While the number 272 is commonly listed as the number of persons sold, as that was the number given on the 1838 Sale Agreement, further research has shown that the actual number was larger (see GU272 Memory Project, https://gu272.americanancestors.org/fate-and-legacy-gu272/).
55. O'Toole, *Passing for White* 12.
56. See Diouf, *Dreams*, 7–11.
57. Ferris, *Romantic National Tale*, 11.
58. Morgan, "Prefatory Address," xxv–xxvii; italics in original.
59. Despite Morgan's claims, other scholars have identified earlier Irish works as "national tales," even if they were not explicitly designated as such. Miranda J. Burgess, for instance, has called Regina Maria Roche's 1796 gothic-inflected *Children of the Abbey* "the earliest Irish national tale" ("Violent Translations," 40).
60. Pittock, "'My Country,'" 326.
61. Ferris, *Romantic National Tale*, 49.
62. Ferris, *Romantic National Tale*, 50.
63. Ferris, *Romantic National Tale*, 51.
64. Owenson, *Wild Irish Girl*, 31.
65. Owenson, *Wild Irish Girl*, 34. Maria Edgeworth, in her national tale *The Absentee* (1812), describes an absentee landlord with a similar language of equivalency between Irish hardship and Black enslavement: "He might as well be a West India planter, and we negroes, for any thing he knows to the contrary" (*Tales of Fashionable Life*, 6:125).
66. For the relationship between the "Big House" novel, the historical novel, and the national tale in Irish literature, see Norris, "The Big House."
67. The non-Black character whose language the novel most consistently represents in a sort of semi-mocking stage dialect is the Creole Rene Picard, who after the Civil War playfully imagines a new order in which Irish rather than Black people are enslaved: "You, my Tommy, you weel own ze Irish slaves instead of ze darky slaves. What change—what fun!" (617).
68. Cantrell, *Celtic Culture*, 204.
69. On the novel's ironizing of Scarlett, see also Quinlan, *Strange Kin*, 123.
70. Compare Owenson, *Wild Irish Girl*, 53–55, with Mitchell, *Gone with the Wind*, 164, 224.
71. Jerng points out that Frank Yerby's plantation romance *Foxes of Harrow* (1946) is a specifically *generic* response to *Gone with the Wind*'s racial worldmaking that exposes the "stereotypes and conventional racism of the plantation romance genre... by making clear the economic, social, and political infrastructure that they support and facilitate" (*Racial Worldmaking*, 96). Burke offers an important reading of Yerby as not only a Black American writer but also—in his own account—an *Irish* American one (see M. Burke, *Race, Politics, and Irish America*, 127–31).

BIBLIOGRAPHY

"Abolition on and off the Stage." *New York Herald*, 5 December 1859, 6.

Adams, Bluford. *E Pluribus Barnum: The Great Showman and the Making of U.S. Popular Culture*. Minneapolis: University of Minnesota Press, 1997.

Agamben, Giorgio. *Homo Sacer: Sovereign Power and Bare Life*. Translated by Daniel Heller-Roazen, Stanford, CA: Stanford University Press, 1998.

Allen, Theodore W. *Racial Oppression and Social Control*. Vol. 1 of *The Invention of the White Race*. 2nd ed. London: Verso, 2012.

"Amusements." *New York Herald*, 5 December 1859, 1.

Anderson, Emily Hodgson. *Shakespeare and the Legacy of Loss*. Ann Arbor: University of Michigan Press, 2018.

"Anglo-Saxon Ideas." *Nation* (Dublin), 14 June 1856, 665.

"Answers to Correspondents." *Nation* (Dublin), 6 February 1847, 280.

"Anti-Slavery Theatres and Litterateurs." *New York Herald*, 9 December 1859, 6.

Appiah, Kwame Anthony. "Race." In *Critical Terms for Literary Study*, edited by Frank Lentricchia and Thomas McLaughlin, 2nd ed., 274–87. Chicago: University of Chicago Press, 1995.

Armitage, David. *Foundations of Modern International Thought*. Cambridge: Cambridge: Cambridge University Press, 2013.

Arnold, Matthew. *On the Study of Celtic Literature*. London: Smith, Elder, 1867.

"Art. IX." *North British Review* 11, no. 22 (August 1849): 528–68.

Banta, Martha. *Barbaric Intercourse: Caricature and the Culture of Conduct, 1841–1936*. Chicago: University of Chicago Press, 2003.

Baptist, Edward E. *The Half Has Never Been Told: Slavery and the Making of American Capitalism*. New York: Basic, 2014.

Bassett, John Spencer. *Slavery in the State of North Carolina*. Baltimore, MD: Johns Hopkins Press, 1899.

Baudelaire, Charles. *Histoires extraordinaires par Edgar Poe*. Vol. 5 of *Baudelaire's Complete Works*. Paris: Michel Lévy Frères, 1869.

Beagle, Donald Robert, and Bryan Albin Giemza. *Poet of the Lost Cause: A Life of Father Ryan*. Knoxville: University of Tennessee Press, 2008.

Beddoe, John. *The Races of Britain: A Contribution to the Anthropology of Western Europe.* Bristol, UK: J. W. Arrowsmith; London: Trübner, 1885.

Bell, Bernard W. *The Afro-American Novel and Its Tradition.* Amherst: University of Massachusetts Press, 1987.

Bernstein, Iver. *The New York City Draft Riots: Their Significance for American Society and Politics in the Age of the Civil War.* Oxford: Oxford University Press, 1990.

Berry, Daina Ramey. *The Price for Their Pound of Flesh: The Value of the Enslaved, from Womb to Grave, in the Building of a Nation.* Boston: Beacon, 2017.

Bhabha, Homi. "Of Mimicry and Man: The Ambivalence of Colonial Discourse." *October* 28 (Spring 1984): 125–33.

Bingham, Caleb, ed. *The Columbian Orator: Containing a Variety of Original and Selected Pieces; Together with Rules; Calculated to Improve Youth and Others in the Ornamental and Useful Art of Eloquence.* Boston: Manning & Loring, 1797.

Blight, David W. *Frederick Douglass: Prophet of Freedom.* New York: Simon & Schuster, 2018.

Bloom, Paul. *Against Empathy: The Case for Rational Compassion.* New York: HarperCollins, 2016.

Blumenbach, Johann Friedrich. *The Anthropological Treatises of Johann Friedrich Blumenbach.* Translated by Thomas Bendyshe. London: Longman, Green, Longman, Roberts & Green, 1865.

———. *De generis humani varietate nativa.* 3rd ed. Göttingen, Germany: Vandenhoek & Ruprecht, 1795.

Boltwood, Scott. "Dion Boucicault: From Stage Irishman to Staging Nationalism." In *A Companion to Irish Literature*, 2 vols., edited by Julia M. Wright, 1:460–75. Chichester, West Sussex, UK: Wiley-Blackwell, 2010.

———. "'The Ineffaceable Curse of Cain': Race, Miscegenation, and the Victorian Staging of Irishness." *Victorian Literature and Culture* 29, no. 2 (September 2001): 383–96.

Boucicault, Dion. "The Art of Dramatic Composition. Part I." *North American Review* 126, no. 260 (January/February 1878): 40–52.

———. *The Colleen Bawn; or, The Brides of Garryowen. A Domestic Drama, in Three Acts.* New York: Samuel French, n.d. [1860].

———. *The Octoroon; or, Life in Louisiana.* 1859. Edited by Sarika Bose. Peterborough, Ontario: Broadview, 2014.

———. "*The Octoroon.* To the Editor of the Times" (letter). *Times* (London), 20 November 1862, 5.

Boulukos, George. *The Grateful Slave: The Emergence of Race in Eighteenth-Century British and American Culture.* Cambridge: Cambridge University Press, 2008.

Boyce, D. G. "'The Marginal Britons': The Irish." 1986. In *Englishness: Politics and Culture, 1880–1920*, edited by Robert Colls and Philip Dodd, 2nd ed., 255–78. London: Bloomsbury Academic, 2014.

Brantlinger, Patrick. *Dark Vanishings: Discourse on the Extinction of Primitive Races, 1800–1930.* Ithaca, NY: Cornell University Press, 2003.

The British Lion and the Irish Monkey. Punch, 8 April 1848, 147.

Broca, Paul. *On the Phenomena of Hybridity in the Genus Homo.* Edited by C. Carter Blake. London: Longman, Green, Longman & Roberts, 1864.

Brody, Jennifer DeVere. *Impossible Purities: Blackness, Femininity, and Victorian Culture*. Durham, NC: Duke University Press, 1998.
Brooks, Daphne A. *Bodies in Dissent: Spectacular Performances of Race and Freedom, 1850–1910*. Durham, NC: Duke University Press, 2006.
Brougham, Henry Peter. "From Lord Brougham." In *The Garies and Their Friends*, by Frank J. Webb, edited by William Huntting Howell and Megan Walsh, 39–40. Peterborough, Ontario: Broadview, 2016.
Brown, Malcolm. "Fenianism and Irish Poetry." *University Review* 4, no. 3 (Winter 1967): 241–49.
Brundage, David. *Irish Nationalists in America: The Politics of Exile, 1798–1998*. Oxford: Oxford University Press, 2016.
Burgess, Miranda J. "Violent Translations: Allegory, Gender, and Cultural Nationalism in Ireland, 1796–1806." *Modern Language Quarterly* 59, no. 1 (March 1998): 33–70.
Burke, Edmund. *A Philosophical Enquiry into the Origin of Our Ideas of the Sublime and Beautiful*. London: R. and J. Dodsley, 1757.
———. *Reflections on the Revolution in France*. London: J. Dodsley, 1790.
Burke, Mary. *Race, Politics, and Irish America: A Gothic History*. Oxford: Oxford University Press, 2022.
Byrd, Jodi A. *The Transit of Empire: Indigenous Critiques of Colonialism*. Minneapolis: University of Minnesota Press, 2011.
Calhoun, John C. *Speeches of John C. Calhoun, Delivered in the House of Representatives and in the Senate of the United States*. Vol. 4 of *The Works of John C. Calhoun*, edited by Richard K. Crallé. New York: D. Appleton, 1854.
Campbell, Matthew. *Irish Poetry under the Union, 1801–1924*. Cambridge: Cambridge University Press, 2013.
Cantrell, James P. *How Celtic Culture Invented Southern Literature*. Gretna, LA: Pelican, 2006.
Canuel, Mark. *Religion, Toleration, and British Writing, 1790–1830*. Cambridge: Cambridge University Press, 2002.
Carlyle, Thomas. *Chartism*. London: James Fraser, 1840.
———. *Latter-Day Pamphlets*. London: Chapman and Hall, 1850.
———. "Occasional Discourse on the Negro Question." *Fraser's Magazine for Town and Country* 40, no. 240 (December 1849): 670–79.
———. *Reminiscences of My Irish Journey in 1849*. London: Sampson, Low, Marston, Searle & Rivington, 1882.
———. "Repeal of the Union." *Examiner*, 29 April 1848, 275–76.
Carpenter, William Benjamin. *Zoology: A Systematic Account of the General Structure, Habits, Instincts, and Uses of the Principal Families of the Animal Kingdom*. 2 vols. London: William S. Orr, 1848.
Cassuto, Leonard. *The Inhuman Race: The Racial Grotesque in American Literature and Culture*. New York: Columbia University Press, 1997.
Chaffin, Tom. *Giant's Causeway: Frederick Douglass's Irish Odyssey and the Making of an American Visionary*. Charlottesville: University of Virginia Press, 2014.
Chander, Manu Samriti. *Brown Romantics: Poetry and Nationalism in the Global Nineteenth Century*. Lewisburg, PA: Bucknell University Press, 2017.

Chandler, James. "Edgeworth and Realism." In *Irish Literature in Transition, 1780–1830,* edited by Claire Connolly, 188–205. Cambridge: Cambridge University Press, 2020.

Chatterjee, Ronjaunee, Alicia Mireles Christoff, and Amy R. Wong. "Undisciplining Victorian Studies." *Los Angeles Review of Books,* 10 July 2020. https://lareviewofbooks.org/article/undisciplining-victorian-studies/#_edn3.

Child, Lydia Maria. Introduction to *Incidents in the Life of a Slave Girl, Written by Herself,* by Harriet Jacobs, 7–8. Boston: published for the author, 1861.

Chiu, Frances A. "Faulty Towers: Reform, Radicalism and the Gothic Castle, 1760–1800." *Romanticism on the Net,* no. 44 (November 2006). https://www.erudit.org/en/journals/ron/1900-v1-n1-ron1433/013996ar/.

Chuh, Kandice. *The Difference Aesthetics Makes: On the Humanities "After Man."* Durham, NC: Duke University Press, 2019.

Cima, Gay Gibson. *Performing Anti-Slavery: Activist Women on Antebellum Stages.* Cambridge: Cambridge University Press, 2014.

Clerk, Archibald. "Dissertation on the Authenticity of the Poems of Ossian." In *The Poems of Ossian in the Original Gaelic with a Literal Translation into English,* 2 vols., 1:i–lxvi. Edinburgh: William Blackwood and Sons, 1870.

Clukey, Amy. "Plantation Modernity: *Gone with the Wind* and Irish-Southern Culture." *American Literature* 85, no. 3 (September 2013): 505–30.

Coates, Ta-Nehisi. *We Were Eight Years in Power: An American Tragedy.* New York: One World, 2018.

Cohen, Ashley L. *The Global Indies: British Imperial Culture and the Reshaping of the World, 1756–1815.* New Haven, CT: Yale University Press, 2020.

———. "The Global Indies: Historicizing Oceanic Metageographies." *Comparative Literature* 69, no. 1 (March 2017): 7–15.

———. "Wage Slavery, Oriental Despotism, and Global Labor Management in Maria Edgeworth's *Popular Tales.*" *Eighteenth Century* 55, nos. 2–3 (Summer/Fall 2014): 193–215.

Colley, Linda. *Britons: Forging the Nation 1707–1837.* New Haven, CT: Yale University Press, 1992.

Cong. Globe. 32nd Cong., Appendix, 3d Sess. (1853).

Cong. Globe. 33rd Cong., 1st Sess. (1854).

Connolly, Claire. *A Cultural History of the Irish Novel, 1790–1829.* Cambridge: Cambridge University Press, 2012.

Conrad, Joseph. *Heart of Darkness.* 1899. Edited by Cedric Watts. Oxford: Oxford University Press, 2008.

Cooper Owens, Deirdre. *Medical Bondage: Race, Gender, and the Origins of American Gynecology.* Athens: University of Georgia Press, 2017.

Corfe, I. J. "'Erin go Bragh' in London: Irishness in the Nineteenth-Century English-Printed Street Ballad." *Studies in Romanticism* 58, no. 4 (Winter 2019): 505–23.

Coughlan, Ann. "Frederick Douglass, Arthur O'Connor, and the *Columbian Orator.*" In *Atlantic Crossings in the Wake of Frederick Douglass: Archaeology, Literature, and Spatial Culture,* edited by Mark P. Leone and Lee M. Jenkins, 65–82. Leiden, Netherlands: Brill Rodopi, 2017.

Cowper, William. *The Task: A Poem in Six Books.* London: J. Johnson, 1785.

Cromwell, Oliver. *Oliver Cromwell's Letters and Speeches with Elucidations.* Edited by Thomas Carlyle. 4 vols. New York: Charles Scribner's Sons, 1845.

Cugoano, Ottobah. *Thoughts and Sentiments on the Evil and Wicked Traffic of the Slavery and Commerce of the Human Species*. London, 1787.

Curtis, L. Perry, Jr. *Apes and Angels: The Irishman in Victorian Caricature*. Rev. ed. Washington, DC: Smithsonian Institution Press, 1997.

Cuvier, Georges. *The Animal Kingdom: Arranged in Conformity with its Organization*. 16 vols. London: George B. Whittaker, 1827–35.

Davis, Jefferson. *Jefferson Davis, Constitutionalist: His Letters, Papers and Speeches*. Edited by Dunbar Rowland. 10 vols. Jackson: Mississippi Department of Archives and History, 1923.

———. *The Papers of Jefferson Davis*. 14 vols. Baton Rouge: Louisiana State University Press, 1971–2015.

Davis, Thomas. "Ballad Poetry of Ireland." In *Literary and Historical Essays*, edited by Charles Gavan Duffy, 220–31. Dublin: James Duffy, 1846.

———. *The Poems of Thomas Davis*. Dublin: James Duffy, 1846.

"Davis and Wilde." *Selma Times*, 27 June 1882, 2.

Deane, Seamus. *A Short History of Irish Literature*. 1986. Notre Dame. IN: University of Notre Dame Press, 1994.

———. *Strange Country: Modernity and Nationhood in Irish Writing since 1790*. Oxford: Clarendon, 1997.

Defoe, Daniel. *Roxana: The Fortunate Mistress*. 1724. Edited by David Blewett. London: Penguin, 1982.

Delahanty, Ian. "The Transatlantic Roots of Irish American Anti-Abolitionism, 1843–1859." *Journal of the Civil War Era* 6, no. 2 (June 2016): 164–92.

DeLamotte, Eugenia. "White Terror, Black Dreams: Gothic Constructions of Race in the Nineteenth Century." In *The Gothic Other: Racial and Social Constructions in the Literary Imagination*, edited by Ruth Bienstock Anolik and Douglas L. Howard, 17–31. Jefferson, NC: McFarland, 2004.

de Nie, Michael. "'A Medley Mob of Irish-American Plotters and Irish Dupes': The British Press and Transatlantic Fenianism." *Journal of British Studies* 40, no. 2 (April 2001): 213–40.

Dickerson, Vanessa D. *Dark Victorians*. Urbana: University of Illinois Press, 2008.

Dillon, William. *Life of John Mitchel*. 2 vols. London: Kegan Paul, Trench, 1888.

Dimock, Wai Chee. "Introduction: Genres as Fields of Knowledge." *PMLA* 122, no. 5 (October 2007): 1377–88.

Diouf, Sylviane A. *Dreams of Africa in Alabama: The Slave Ship* Clotilda *and the Story of the Last Africans Brought to America*. Oxford: Oxford University Press, 2007.

Dolan, Jay P. *The Irish Americans: A History*. London: Bloomsbury, 2008.

Donoghue, John. "The Curse of Cromwell: Revisiting the Irish Slavery Debate." *History Ireland* 25, no. 4 (July/August 2017): 24–28.

Douglass, Frederick. "The Color Line." *North American Review* 132, no. 295 (June 1881): 567–77.

———. *The Frederick Douglass Papers, Series One: Speeches, Debates, and Interviews*. Edited by John W. Blassingame. 5 vols. New Haven, CT: Yale University Press, 1979–92.

———. "The Hutchinson Family.—Hunkerism." *North Star*, 27 October 1848, 2.

———. "Letters from Frederick Douglass, No. III." *Liberator*, 24 October 1845, 170.

———. *Life and Times of Frederick Douglass, Written by Himself. His Early Life as a Slave, His Escape from Bondage, and His Complete History to the Present Time.* Hartford, CT: Park Publishing, 1881.

———. *My Bondage and My Freedom.* New York: Miller, Orton & Mulligan, 1855.

———. *Narrative of the Life of Frederick Douglass, an American Slave.* Boston: Anti-Slavery Office, 1845.

Doyle, Laura. *Freedom's Empire: Race and the Rise of the Novel in Atlantic Modernity, 1640–1940.* Durham, NC: Duke University Press, 2008.

"A Drama with Variations." *Examiner*, 14 December 1861, 788.

"The Dual Form of Labour." *Russell's Magazine* 6, no. 1 (October 1859): 1–18.

Du Bois, W. E. B. *Black Reconstruction in America.* 1935. New York: Free Press, 1998.

———. *The Philadelphia Negro: A Social Study.* 1899. Edited by Henry Louis Gates Jr. Oxford: Oxford University Press, 2007.

———. *The Souls of Black Folk.* 1903. Edited by Brent Hayes Edwards. Oxford: Oxford University Press, 2007.

Duffy, Charles Gavan. *Four Years of Irish History, 1845–1849.* London: Cassell, Petter, Galpin, 1883.

———. *Young Ireland: A Fragment of Irish History, 1840–1850.* London: Cassell, Petter, Galpin, 1880.

Dwan, David. *The Great Community: Culture and Nationalism in Ireland.* Dublin: Field Day, 2008.

Eagleton, Terry. *Scholars and Rebels in Nineteenth-Century Ireland.* Oxford: Blackwell, 1999.

Earls, Brian. "Bulls, Blunders and Bloothers: An Examination of the Irish Bull." *Béaloideas* 56 (1988): 1–92.

Easton, Hosea. *A Treatise on the Intellectual Character, and Civil and Political Condition of the Colored People of the U. States; and the Prejudice Exercised Towards Them.* Boston: Isaac Knapp, 1837.

Edgeworth, Maria. *Popular Tales.* 3 vols. London: J. Johnson, 1804.

———. *Tales of Fashionable Life.* 6 vols. London: J. Johnson, 1812.

Edgeworth, Maria, and Richard Lovell Edgeworth. *Practical Education.* 2 vols. London: J. Johnson, 1798.

Edgeworth, Richard Lovell, and Maria Edgeworth. *Essay on Irish Bulls.* London: J. Johnson, 1802.

"Editor's Table." *Southern Literary Messenger* 23 (new series vol. 2) (October 1856): 306–14.

Egan, Timothy. *The Immortal Irishman: The Irish Revolutionary Who Became an American Hero.* Boston: Houghton Mifflin Harcourt, 2016.

Eglinton, John (William Kirkpatrick Magee). *Bards and Saints.* Dublin: Maunsel, 1906.

Ellmann, Richard. *Oscar Wilde.* New York: Vintage, 1988.

Engle, Anna. "Depictions of the Irish in Frank Webb's *The Garies and Their Friends* and Frances E. W. Harper's *Trial and Triumph*." *Melus* 26, no. 1 (Spring 2001): 151–71.

Erkkila, Betsy. "The Poetics of Whiteness: Poe and the Racial Imaginary." In *Romancing the Shadow: Poe and Race*, edited by J. Gerald Kennedy and Liliane Weissberg, 41–74. Oxford: Oxford University Press, 2001.

Evans, Brad. *Before Cultures: The Ethnographic Imagination in American Literature, 1865–1920.* Chicago: University of Chicago Press, 2005.

Fanon, Frantz. *Black Skin, White Masks*. 1952. Translated by Richard Philcox. New York: Grove, 2008.
Fawkes, Richard. *Dion Boucicault: A Biography*. London: Quartet, 1979.
Ferreira, Patricia J. "Frederick Douglass in Ireland: The Dublin Edition of His *Narrative*." *New Hibernia Review* 5, no. 1 (Spring 2001): 53–67.
Ferris, Ina. *The Romantic National Tale and the Question of Ireland*. Cambridge: Cambridge University Press, 2002.
Festa, Lynn. *Sentimental Figures of Empire in Eighteenth-Century Britain and France*. Baltimore, MD: Johns Hopkins University Press, 2006.
Fielder, Brigitte. *Relative Races: Genealogies of Interracial Kinship in Nineteenth-Century America*. Durham, NC: Duke University Press, 2020.
Fields, Karen E., and Barbara J. Fields. *Racecraft: The Soul of Inequality in American Life*. London: Verso, 2012.
"The Five Act Drama—The Octoroon." Review. *New York Daily Tribune*, 7 December 1859, 5
Flanagan, Thomas. "Rebellion and Style: John Mitchel and the Jail Journal." *Irish University Review* 1, no. 1 (Autumn 1970): 1–29.
Flynn, Joyce. "Sites and Sights: The Iconology of the Subterranean in Late Nineteenth-Century Irish-American Drama." *Melus* 18, no. 1 (Spring 1993): 5–19.
Fogarty, L. *Father John Kenyon: A Patriot Priest of Forty-Eight*. Dublin: Mahon's Printing Works, n.d. [1921].
Foreman, P. Gabrielle. "Who's Your Mama? 'White' Mulatta Genealogies, Early Photography, and Anti-Passing Narratives of Slavery and Freedom." *American Literary History* 14, no. 3 (Autumn 2002): 505–39.
Foster, R. F. *The Irish Story: Telling Tales and Making It Up in Ireland*. London: Allen Lane, Penguin, 2001.
———. *Paddy and Mr Punch: Connections in Irish and English History*. London: Allen Lane, Penguin, 1993.
———. *Words Alone: Yeats and His Inheritances*. Oxford: Oxford University Press, 2012.
Foster, Travis M. *Genre and White Supremacy in the Postemancipation United States*. Oxford: Oxford University Press, 2019.
Fox, Renée. "Realism's Irish Forms: Queering the Fog in Charles Dickens's *Bleak House* and Emily Lawless's *Grania*." *Victorian Studies* 61, no. 4 (Summer 2019): 559–81.
Freedgood, Elaine. *Worlds Enough: The Invention of Realism in the Victorian Novel*. Princeton, NJ: Princeton University Press, 2019.
Freeman, Edward Augustus. *Some Impressions of the United States*. New York: Henry Holt, 1883.
Friedman, David M. *Wilde in America: Oscar Wilde and the Invention of Modern Celebrity*. New York: Norton, 2014.
Fuentes, Marisa J. *Dispossessed Lives: Enslaved Women, Violence, and the Archive*. Philadelphia: University of Pennsylvania Press, 2016.
Fuess, Claude M. *The Life of Caleb Cushing*. 2 vols. New York: Harcourt, Brace, 1923.
[Fuller, Margaret.] "Entertainments of the Past Winter." *Dial* 3, no. 1 (July 1842): 46–72.
Gallagher, Catherine. *The Industrial Reformation of English Fiction: Social Discourse and Narrative Form 1832–1867*. Chicago: University of Chicago Press, 1985.
Galton, Francis. *Inquiries into Human Faculty and Its Development*. London: Macmillan, 1883.

"*The Garies and Their Friends.*" Review. *Athenæum,* 24 October 1857, 1320.
"*The Garies and Their Friends.*" Review. *Daily News* (London), 9 October 1857, 2.
"*The Garies and Their Friends.*" Review. *Frederick Douglass' Paper,* 4 December 1857, 1–2.
"*The Garies and Their Friends.*" Review. *Literary Gazette and Journal of Archæology, Science, and Art for the Year 1857* (26 September 1857): 917–19. London, 1857.
"*The Garies and Their Friends.*" Review. *Morning Post* (London), 6 October 1857, 7.
"*The Garies and Their Friends.*" Review. *Observer* (London), 21 September 1857, 7.
Garrison, William Lloyd. "The Irish Address on American Slavery." *Liberator,* 8 April 1842, 54.
———. Preface to *Narrative of the Life of Frederick Douglass, an American Slave,* by Douglass, iii–xii. Boston: Anti-Slavery Office, 1845.
Gates, Henry Louis, Jr. *Figures in Black: Words, Signs, and the "Racial" Self.* Oxford: Oxford University Press, 1989.
Gibbons, Luke. *Gaelic Gothic: Race, Colonization, and Irish Culture.* Galway: Arlen House, 2004.
Gillespie, Niall. "Irish Jacobin Gothic, c. 1796–1825." In *Irish Gothics: Genres, Forms, Modes, and Traditions, 1760–1890,* edited by Christina Morin and Gillespie, 58–73. Basingstoke, Hampshire, UK: Palgrave Macmillan, 2014.
Gilley, Sheridan. "English Attitudes to the Irish in England, 1780–1900." 1978. In *Immigrants and Minorities in British Society,* edited by Colin Holmes, 81–110. London: Routledge, 2016.
Gilroy, Paul. *The Black Atlantic: Modernity and Double Consciousness.* Cambridge, MA: Harvard University Press, 1993.
Gleeson, David T. *The Green and the Gray: The Irish in the Confederate States of America.* Chapel Hill: University of North Carolina Press, 2013.
———. *The Irish in the South, 1815–1877.* Chapel Hill: University of North Carolina Press, 2001.
Glenn, Evelyn Nakano. *Unequal Freedom: How Race and Gender Shaped American Citizenship and Labor.* Cambridge, MA: Harvard University Press, 2002.
Goddu, Teresa A. *Gothic America: Narrative, History, and Nation.* New York: Columbia University Press, 1997.
———. "Rethinking Race and Slavery in Poe Studies." *Poe Studies/Dark Romanticism* 33, nos. 1–2 (2000): 15–18.
———. *Selling Antislavery: Abolition and Mass Media in Antebellum America.* Philadelphia: University of Pennsylvania Press, 2020.
Godwyn, Morgan. *The Negro's and Indians Advocate, Suing for their Admission into the Church.* London: printed for the author by J. D., 1680.
Goldberg, David Theo. *The Racial State.* Malden, MA: Blackwell, 2002.
———. *Racist Culture: Philosophy and the Politics of Meaning.* Oxford: Blackwell, 1993.
Gonzales, Ambrose E. *The Black Border: Gullah Stories of the Carolina Coast.* Columbia, SC: State Company, 1922.
Goyal, Yogita. *Runaway Genres: The Global Afterlives of Slavery.* New York: New York University Press, 2019.
Grayson, William J. *The Autobiography of William John Grayson* (Continued). Edited by Samuel Gaillard Stoney. *South Carolina Historical and Genealogical Magazine* 51, no. 1 (January 1950): 29–44.
———. *The Hireling and the Slave, Chicora, and Other Poems.* Charleston: McCarter, 1856.

"Great Debate between Lincoln and Douglas at Ottawa." *Chicago Daily Press and Tribune*, 23 August 1858, 1, 4.

Greiner, Rae. *Sympathetic Realism in Nineteenth-Century British Fiction.* Baltimore, MD: Johns Hopkins University Press, 2012.

Griffith, Arthur. Headnote to "The Famine Year." In *Jail Journal*, by John Mitchel, edited by Griffith, 421. Dublin: M. H. Gill & Son, 1913.

———. Preface to *Jail Journal*, by John Mitchel, ix–xvi. Dublin: M. H. Gill & Son, 1913.

Gross, Ariela J. "Litigating Whiteness: Trials of Racial Determination in the Nineteenth-Century South." *Yale Law Journal* 108, no. 1 (October 1998): 109–88.

Hack, Daniel. *Reaping Something New: African American Transformations of Victorian Literature.* Princeton, NJ: Princeton University Press, 2017.

Hadley, Elaine. *Melodramatic Tactics: Theatricalized Dissent in the English Marketplace, 1800–1885.* Stanford, CA: Stanford University Press, 1995.

Hale, Anthony R. "Martyrs for Contending Causes: John Mitchel, David Walker, and the Limits of Liberation." In *The Black and Green Atlantic: Cross Currents of the African and Irish Diasporas*, edited by Peter D. O'Neill and David Lloyd, 197–212. Basingstoke, Hampshire, UK: Palgrave Macmillan, 2009.

Hall, Kim F. "Reading What Isn't There: 'Black' Studies in Early Modern England." *Stanford Humanities Review* 3, no. 1 (1993): 23–33.

———. *Things of Darkness: Economies of Race and Gender in Early Modern England.* Ithaca, NY: Cornell University Press, 1996.

———. "'Troubling Doubles': Apes, Africans, and Blackface in *Mr. Moore's Revels.*" In *Race, Ethnicity, and Power in the Renaissance*, edited by Joyce Green MacDonald, 120–44. Madison, NJ: Fairleigh Dickinson University Press, 1997.

Hall, Stuart. "New Ethnicities." In *Stuart Hall: Critical Dialogues in Cultural Studies*, edited by David Morley and Kuan-Hsing Chen, 441–49. London: Routledge, 1996

Hamm, Charles. *Yesterdays: Popular Song in America.* New York: Norton, 1979.

Hankins, Laurel. "What the Folk Printed: Verse Culture and the Black Press in 1865 New Orleans." *African American Review* 45, no. 4 (Winter 2012): 527–40.

Hannah-Jones, Nikole. "Democracy." In *The 1619 Project: A New Origin Story*, edited by Hannah-Jones, Caitlin Roper, Ilena Silverman, and Jake Silverstein, 7–36. New York: One World, 2021.

Hansord, Katie. "Eliza Hamilton Dunlop's 'The Aboriginal Mother': Romanticism, Anti Slavery, and Imperial Feminism in the Nineteenth Century." *Journal of the Association for the Study of Australian Literature* 11, no. 1 (2011): n.p. (12 pp.).

Harper, Frances E. W. *Iola Leroy, or Shadows Uplifted.* Philadelphia: Garrigues Brothers, 1893.

Harris, Jonathan Gil. "Introduction: Forms of Indography." In *Indography: Writing the "Indian" in Early Modern England*, edited by Harris, 1–20. New York: Palgrave Macmillan, 2012.

Hartman, Saidiya V. *Scenes of Subjection: Terror, Slavery, and Self-Making in Nineteenth-Century America.* Oxford: Oxford University Press, 1997.

Haslam, Richard. "Irish Gothic: A Rhetorical Hermeneutics Approach." *Irish Journal of Gothic and Horror Studies* 2 (March 17, 2007): n.p. https://irishgothichorror.files.wordpress.com/2018/03/richard-haslam.pdf.

Hayot, Eric. *The Hypothetical Mandarin: Sympathy, Modernity, and Chinese Pain.* Oxford: Oxford University Press, 2009.

Hazlitt, William. *Lectures on the English Poets*. London: Taylor and Hessey, 1818.
Hébert, Keith S. *Cornerstone of the Confederacy: Alexander Stephens and the Speech That Defined the Lost Cause*. Knoxville: University of Tennessee Press, 2021.
Hemenway, Mark. "Gothic Sociology: Charles Chesnutt and the Gothic Mode." *Studies in the Literary Imagination* 7, no. 1 (Spring 1974): 101–19.
Heneghan, Bridget T. *Whitewashing America: Material Culture and Race in the Antebellum Imagination*. Jackson: University Press of Mississippi, 2003.
Heng, Geraldine. *Empire of Magic: Medieval Romance and the Politics of Cultural Fantasy*. New York: Columbia University Press, 2003.
——— . *The Invention of Race in the European Middle Ages*. Cambridge: Cambridge University Press, 2018.
Hensley, Nathan K. *Forms of Empire: The Poetics of Victorian Sovereignty*. Oxford: Oxford University Press, 2016.
Hoffman, John. "Kant's Aesthetic Categories: Race in the *Critique of Judgment*." *Diacritics* 44, no. 2 (2016): 54–81.
Hogan, Liam, Laura McAtackney, and Matthew C. Reilly. "The Irish in the Anglo-Caribbean: Servants or Slaves?" *History Ireland* 24, no. 2 (March-April 2016): 18–22.
Hogan, Robert. *Dion Boucicault*. New York: Twayne, 1969.
——— , ed. *The Macmillan Dictionary of Irish Literature*. London: Macmillan, 1980.
hooks, bell. "Essentialism and Experience." *American Literary History* 3, no. 1 (Spring 1991): 172–83.
Horrocks, Ingrid. "More Than a Gravestone: *Caleb Williams, Udolpho,* and the Politics of the Gothic." *Studies in the Novel* 39, no. 1 (Spring 2007): 31–47.
Horsman, Reginald. "Origins of Racial Anglo-Saxonism in Great Britain Before 1850." *Journal of the History of Ideas* 37, no. 3 (July-September 1976): 387–410.
Howard, Benjamin C. *Reports of Cases Argued and Adjudged in the Supreme Court of the United States, December Term, 1856*. Washington, DC: William M. Morrison, 1857.
Howe, LeAnne, and Padraig Kirwan, eds. *Famine Pots: The Choctaw-Irish Gift Exchange, 1847–Present*. East Lansing: Michigan State University Press, 2020.
Howell, William Huntting, and Megan Walsh. Introduction and "A Note on the Text" to *The Garies and Their Friends*, by Frank J. Webb, edited by Howell and Walsh, 11–25, 29. Peterborough, Ontario: Broadview, 2016.
Howes, Marjorie. "Melodramatic Conventions and Atlantic History in Dion Boucicault." *Éire-Ireland* 46, nos. 3 and 4 (Fall/Winter 2011): 84–101.
Hutcheson, Francis. *A Short Introduction to Moral Philosophy, in Three Books; Containing the Elements of Ethicks and the Law of Nature*. Translated from Latin. Glasgow: Robert Foulis, 1747.
Ignatiev, Noel. *How the Irish Became White*. New York: Routledge, 1995.
Ingelbien, Raphaël. "Realism, Allegory, Gothic: The Irish Victorian Novel." In *Irish Literature in Transition, 1830–1880*, edited by Matthew Campbell, 238–56. Cambridge: Cambridge University Press, 2020.
"The Insurrection in Jamaica." *Nation* (Dublin), 25 November 1865, 211–12.
"Insurrection in One of the British Dependencies." *Nation* (Dublin), 4 November 1865, 173.
"Ireland." *Times* (London), 25 June 1852, 5.
"Ireland." *Times* (London), 14 March 1854, 11.

Jackson, J. W. "The Race Question in Ireland." *Anthropological Review* 7, no. 24 (January 1869): 54–76.
Jackson, Spencer. "A Black Tory Abolitionist in Early America: Phillis Wheatley's Republican Poetics." *Postcolonial Studies* 23, no. 3 (September 2020): 371–88.
Jacobs, Edward. "Ann Radcliffe and Romantic Print Culture." In *Ann Radcliffe, Romanticism and the Gothic*, edited by Dale Townshend and Angela Wright, 49–66. Cambridge: Cambridge University Press, 2014.
Jacobs, Harriet. *The Harriet Jacobs Family Papers*. Edited by Jean Fagan Yellin. 2 vols. Chapel Hill: University of North Carolina Press, 2008.
———. *Incidents in the Life of a Slave Girl, Written by Herself*. Edited by L. Maria Child. Boston: published for the author, 1861.
Jacobson, Matthew Frye. *Whiteness of a Different Color: European Immigrants and the Alchemy of Race*. Cambridge, MA: Harvard University Press, 1998.
Jaffe, Audrey. *Scenes of Sympathy: Identity and Representation in Victorian Fiction*. Ithaca, NY: Cornell University Press, 2000.
Jameson, Fredric. *The Political Unconscious: Narrative as a Socially Symbolic Act*. Ithaca, NY: Cornell University Press, 1981.
Jarrett, Thomas D. "The Literary Significance of William J. Grayson's *The Hireling and the Slave*." *Georgia Review* 5, no. 4 (Winter 1951): 487–94.
Jefferson, Joseph. *The Autobiography of Joseph Jefferson*. London: T. Fisher Unwin, 1889.
Jerng, Mark C. *Racial Worldmaking: The Power of Popular Fiction*. New York: Fordham University Press, 2018.
"John Mitchel." *New York Freeman's Journal and Catholic Register*, 24 June 1865, 4.
"John Mitchell vs. Daniel O'Connell." *Liberator*, 27 January 1854, 1.
Johnson, James. *A Tour in Ireland; With Meditations and Reflections*. London: S. Highley, 1844.
Johnson, Walter. "The Slave Trader, the White Slave, and the Politics of Racial Determination in the 1850s." *Journal of American History* 87, no. 1 (June 2000): 13–38.
———. "To Remake the World: Slavery, Racial Capitalism, and Justice." *Boston Review* 42, no. 1 (Winter 2017): 11–31.
Jones, Douglas A., Jr. "Slave Evangelicalism, Shouting, and the Beginning of African American Writing." *Early American Literature* 53, no. 1 (2018): 69–95.
Jones, John Bush, and Priscilla Shaw. "Artists and 'Suggestors': The *Punch* Cartoons, 1843–1848." *Victorian Periodicals Newsletter* 11, no. 1 (March 1978): 2–15.
Jordan, Don, and Michael Walsh. *White Cargo: The Forgotten History of Britain's White Slaves in America*. New York: New York University Press, 2008.
Kaplan, Sidney. "*The Octoroon*: Early History of the Drama of Miscegenation." *Journal of Negro Education* 20, no. 4 (Autumn 1951): 547–57.
Keneally, Thomas. *The Great Shame: A Story of the Irish in the Old World and the New*. London: Chatto & Windus, 1998.
Kennedy, J. Gerald. "'Trust No Man': Poe, Douglass, and the Culture of Slavery." In *Romancing the Shadow: Poe and Race*, edited by Kennedy and Liliane Weissberg, 225–57. Oxford: Oxford University Press, 2001.
Kenny, Kevin. *The American Irish: A History*. 2000. Abingdon, Oxon, UK: Routledge, 2014.
———. "The Irish in the Empire." In *Ireland and the British Empire*, edited by Kenny, 90–122. Oxford: Oxford University Press, 2004.

Kerr-Ritchie, Jeffrey R. "Samuel Ward and the Gordon Rebellion." *Journal of Caribbean History* 50, no. 1 (2016): 36–51.
Kettner, James H. *The Development of American Citizenship, 1608–1870*. Chapel Hill: University of North Carolina Press, 1978.
Key, Francis Scott. "The Star-Spangled Banner." In *American Melodies*, edited by George P. Morris, 232–33. Philadelphia: Henry F. Anners, 1840.
Kiely, Robert. *The Romantic Novel in England*. Cambridge, MA: Harvard University Press, 1972.
Killeen, Jarlath. *The Emergence of Irish Gothic Fiction: History, Origins, Theories*. Edinburgh: Edinburgh University Press, 2014.
Kinealy, Christine. *Black Abolitionists in Ireland*. Abingdon, Oxon, UK: Routledge, 2020.
———. *Daniel O'Connell and the Anti-Slavery Movement: "The Saddest People the Sun Sees."* London: Routledge, 2016.
———, ed. *Frederick Douglass and Ireland: In His Own Words*. 2 vols. Abingdon, Oxon, UK: Routledge, 2018.
Kingsley, Frances E. *Charles Kingsley: His Letters and Memories of His Life*. 2nd ed. 2 vols. London: Henry S. King, 1877.
Knox, Robert. *The Races of Men: A Fragment*. Philadelphia: Lea & Blanchard, 1850.
Larrissy, Edward. "Moore's Romantic Neoclassicism." In *Thomas Moore and Romantic Inspiration: Poetry, Music, and Politics*, edited by Sarah McCleave and Brian G. Caraher, 59–71. New York: Routledge, 2018.
"Law Reports. The Octoroon War: An Irrepressible Conflict between the Manager and Stage Director of the Winter Garden." *New York Times*, 26 December 1859, 2–3.
Leavell, Lori. "Poe's Steadfast Servant in the Aftermath of Walker's *Appeal*." *Mississippi Quarterly* 66, no. 4 (Fall 2013): 539–64.
Lecourt, Sebastian. *Cultivating Belief: Victorian Anthropology, Liberal Aesthetics, and the Secular Imagination*. Oxford: Oxford University Press, 2018.
Lee, Julia Sun-Joo. *The American Slave Narrative and the Victorian Novel*. Oxford: Oxford University Press, 2010.
Leerssen, Joep. "Ossian and the Rise of Literary Historicism." In *The Reception of Ossian in Europe*, edited by Howard Gaskill, 109–25. London: Thoemmes Continuum, 2004.
———. "Ossianic Liminality." In *From Gaelic to Romantic: Ossianic Translations*, edited by Fiona Stafford and Howard Gaskill, 1–16. Amsterdam: Rodopi, 1998.
———. *Remembrance and Imagination: Patterns in the Historical and Literary Representation of Ireland in the Nineteenth Century*. Cork, Ireland: Cork University Press, 1996.
Lemire, Elise. *"Miscegenation": Making Race in America*. Philadelphia: University of Pennsylvania Press, 2002.
Lepore, Jill. "The Long Blue Line: Inventing the Police." *New Yorker*, 20 July 2020, 64–69.
———. *These Truths: A History of the United States*. New York: Norton, 2018.
Levine, Caroline. *Forms: Whole, Rhythm, Hierarchy, Network*. Princeton, NJ: Princeton University Press, 2015.
———. "From Nation to Network." *Victorian Studies* 55, no. 4 (Summer 2013): 647–66.
Levine, George. *The Realistic Imagination: English Fiction from Frankenstein to Lady Chatterley*. Chicago: University of Chicago Press, 1981.

Levine, Robert S. "Disturbing Boundaries: Temperance, Black Elevation, and Violence in Frank J. Webb's *The Garies and Their Friends*." *Prospects: An Annual Journal of American Cultural Studies* 19 (1994): 349–74.

Lewis, Matthew Gregory. "The Anaconda: An East-Indian Tale." In *Romantic Tales*, 4 vols., 2:1–114. London: Longman, Hurst, Rees, and Orme, 1808.

———. *Journal of a West India Proprietor, Kept during a Residence in the Island of Jamaica*. London: John Murray, 1834.

"The Life of Arthur Murphy, Esq. By Jesse Foote, Esq. his Executor." Review. *Critical Review: or, Annals of Literature*, 3rd ser., 23, no. 3 (July 1811): 253–63.

The Lincoln-Douglas Debates: The First Complete, Unexpurgated Text. Edited by Harold Holzer. New York: Fordham University Press, 2004.

Lindfors, Bernth. "'Mislike Me Not for My Complexion. . .': Ira Aldridge in Whiteface." In *Ira Aldridge: The African Roscius*, edited by Lindfors, 180–90. Rochester, NY: University of Rochester Press, 2007.

Lloyd, David. "Black Irish, Irish Whiteness and Atlantic State Formation." In *The Black and Green Atlantic: Cross-Currents of the African and Irish Diasporas*, edited by Peter D. O'Neill and Lloyd, 3–19. Basingstoke, Hampshire, UK: Palgrave Macmillan, 2009.

———. "The Indigent Sublime: Specters of Irish Hunger." In *Memory Ireland*, vol. 3, *The Famine and the Troubles*, edited by Oona Frawley, 17–58. Syracuse, NY: Syracuse University Press, 2014.

———. *Nationalism and Minor Literature: James Clarence Mangan and the Emergence of Irish Cultural Nationalism*. Berkeley: University of California Press, 1987.

———. *Under Representation: The Racial Regime of Aesthetics*. New York: Fordham University Press, 2019.

Lootens, Tricia. "Looking Beyond (and Before) *Ancient Ballads*: Toru Dutt's *Sheaf* and the Force of Abolition Time." *Victorian Studies* 61, no. 2 (Winter 2019): 268–77.

Lorimer, Douglas. "Reconstructing Victorian Racial Discourse: Images of Race, the Language of Race Relations, and the Context of Black Resistance." In *Black Victorians/Black Victoriana*, edited by Gretchen Holbrook Gerzina, 187–207. New Brunswick, NJ: Rutgers University Press, 2003.

Lott, Eric. *Love and Theft: Blackface Minstrelsy and the American Working Class*. 1993. Twentieth-anniversary ed. Oxford: Oxford University Press, 2013.

Lowe, Lisa. *The Intimacies of Four Continents*. Durham, NC: Duke University Press, 2015.

Lyons, F. S. L. *John Dillon: A Biography*. Chicago: University of Chicago Press, 1968.

Mabbott, Thomas Ollive. "Introduction to the Poems" and "Index of Names and Titles." In *Collected Works of Edgar Allan Poe*, vol. 1: *Poems*, xxiii–xxx and 601–27, edited by Mabbott. Cambridge, MA: Belknap Press, 1969.

MacDonald, Joyce Green. "Acting Black: *Othello*, *Othello* Burlesques, and the Performance of Blackness." In *Ira Aldridge: The African Roscius*, edited by Bernth Lindfors, 135–56. Rochester, NY: University of Rochester Press, 2007.

MacGregor, Patrick. "Preliminary Dissertation." In *The Genuine Remains of Ossian, Literally Translated*, 1–120. London: Smith, Elder; Edinburgh: William Tate, 1841.

MacKenzie, Clayton G. "Thomas Carlyle's 'The Negro Question': Black Ireland and the Rhetoric of Famine." *Neohelicon* 24, no. 2 (September 1997): 219–36.

Macpherson, James. *The Poems of Ossian, in the Original Gaelic, with a Literal Translation into Latin, by the Late Robert Macfarlan, A.M., Together with a Dissertation on the Authenticity of the Poems, by Sir John Sinclair, Bart.* 3 vols. London: W. Bulmer, 1807.

———. *The Works of Ossian, the Son of Fingal.* 3rd ed. 2 vols. London: T. Becket and P. A. Dehondt, 1765.

Makdisi, Saree. *Making England Western: Occidentalism, Race, and Imperial Culture.* Chicago: University of Chicago Press, 2014.

Malchow, H. L. *Gothic Images of Race in Nineteenth-Century Britain.* Stanford, CA: Stanford University Press, 1996.

Malenas, Ellen. "Reform Ideology and Generic Structure in Matthew Lewis's *Journal of a West India Proprietor.*" *Studies in Eighteenth-Century Culture* 35 (2006): 27–51.

Malouf, Michael G. "The Poe Test: Global English and 'The Gold Bug.'" *Cambridge Journal of Postcolonial Literary Inquiry* 7, no. 1 (January 2020): 35–49.

———. *Transatlantic Solidarities: Irish Nationalism and Caribbean Poetics.* Charlottesville: University of Virginia Press, 2009.

Martin, Amy E. *Alter-Nations: Nationalisms, Terror, and the State in Nineteenth-Century Britain and Ireland.* Columbus: Ohio State University Press, 2012.

———. "Blood Transfusions: Constructions of Irish Racial Difference, The English Working Class, and Revolutionary Possibility in the Work of Carlyle and Engels." *Victorian Literature and Culture* 32, no. 1 (March 2004): 83–102.

———. "Fenian Fever: Circum-Atlantic Insurgency and the Modern State." In *The Black and Green Atlantic: Cross-Currents of the African and Irish Diasporas,* edited by Peter D. O'Neill and David Lloyd, 20–32. Basingstoke, Hampshire, UK: Palgrave Macmillan, 2009.

———. "Representing the 'Indian Revolution' of 1857: Towards a Genealogy of Irish Internationalist Anticolonialism." *Field Day Review* 8 (2012): 126–47.

———. "Victorian Ireland: Race and the Category of the Human." *Victorian Review* 40, no. 1 (Spring 2014): 52–57.

Martin, Bonnie. "Neighbor-to-Neighbor Capitalism: Local Credit Networks and the Mortgaging of Slaves." In *Slavery's Capitalism: A New History of American Economic Development,* edited by Sven Beckert and Seth Rockman, 107–21. Philadelphia: University of Pennsylvania Press, 2016.

Marx, Karl. *Dispatches for the New York Tribune: Selected Journalism of Karl Marx.* Edited by James Ledbetter. London: Penguin, 2007.

———. *Grundrisse.* 1857–58. Translated by Martin Nicolaus, London: Penguin, 1993.

Marx, Karl, and Friedrich Engels. *On Colonialism.* Moscow: Progress, 1974.

Maume, Patrick. Introduction to *The Last Conquest of Ireland (Perhaps),* by John Mitchel, ed. Maume, ix–xxx. Dublin: University College Dublin Press, 2005.

Maurer, Sara. *The Dispossessed State: Narratives of Ownership in Nineteenth-Century Britain and Ireland.* Baltimore, MD: Johns Hopkins University Press, 2012.

McCarter, Thomas N. *Memorial of John McCarter and His Descendants.* Newark, NJ: Baker Printing, 1900.

McFeely, Deirdre. *Dion Boucicault: Irish Identity on Stage.* Cambridge: Cambridge University Press, 2012.

McGovern, Bryan P. *John Mitchel: Irish Nationalist, Southern Secessionist.* Knoxville: University of Tennessee Press, 2009.

McKee, Clayton Tyler. "Translation and Audience: Edgar Allan Poe's 'The Gold-Bug.'" *International Journal of Comparative Literature & Translation Studies* 5, no. 4 (October 2017): 1–10.
McKenna, Neil. *The Secret Life of Oscar Wilde*. New York: Basic, 2005.
Meer, Sarah. "Boucicault's Misdirections: Race, Transatlantic Theatre and Social Position in *The Octoroon*." *Atlantic Studies* 6, no. 1 (April 2009): 81–95.
Mehta, Uday Singh. *Liberalism and Empire: A Study in Nineteenth-Century British Liberal Thought*. Chicago: University of Chicago Press, 1999.
Melville, Herman. "Hawthorne and His Mosses" (first of two parts). *Literary World* 7, no. 185 (August 17, 1850): 125–27.
Mendelssohn, Michèle. *Making Oscar Wilde*. Oxford: Oxford University Press, 2018.
Merrill, Lisa. "'May She Read Liberty in Your Eyes?': Beecher, Boucicault and the Representation and Display of Antebellum Women's Racially Indeterminate Bodies." *Journal of Dramatic Theory and Criticism* 26, no. 2 (Spring 2012): 127–44.
Michael, John S. "Nuance Lost in Translation: Interpretations of J. F. Blumenbach's Anthropology in the English Speaking World." *NTM Zeitschrift für Geschichte der Wissenschaften, Technik und Medizin* 25, no. 3 (September 2017): 281–309.
Mill, John Stuart. *England and Ireland*. London: Longmans, Green, Reader, and Dyer, 1868.
———. "The Negro Question." *Fraser's Magazine for Town and Country* 41, no. 241 (January 1850): 25–31.
"The Missing Link." *Punch, or the London Charivari* 43 (18 October 1862): 165.
"Miss Sarah P. Remond." *Liberator*, 23 September 1859, 150.
Mitchel, John. *Jail Journal; Or, Five Years in British Prisons*. New York: Office of the 'Citizen,' 1854.
———. *Jail Journal [. . .] With an Introductory Narrative of Transactions in Ireland*. Dublin: M. H. Gill & Son, 1913.
———. "June in the Famine Year." Reprinted in *Irish Monthly* 14, no. 156 (June 1886): 289–96.
———. *The Last Conquest of Ireland (Perhaps)*. Author's ed. Glasgow: R. & T. Washbourne, n.d. [1882].
———. Letter. *New York Daily News*, 14 June 1865, 4.
———. "Letter to the Protestant Farmers, Labourers, and Artizans, of the North of Ireland. No. II." *United Irishman*, 13 May 1848, 209.
———. "Poetic Politics." *United Irishman*, 29 April 1848, 186.
Mitchell, Margaret. *Gone with the Wind*. 1936. London: Vintage, 2019.
———. *Margaret Mitchell's "Gone with the Wind" Letters, 1936–1949*. Edited by Richard Harwell. New York: Macmillan, 1976.
"Moore." *Irish Quarterly Review* 6 (June 1852): 382–460.
Moore, Jane. "'Transatlantic Tom': Thomas Moore in North America." In *Ireland and Romanticism: Publics, Nations and Scenes of Cultural Production*, edited by Jim Kelly, 77–93. Basingstoke, Hampshire, UK: Palgrave Macmillan, 2011.
Moore, Thomas. *The Poetical Works of Thomas Moore, Collected by Himself*. 10 vols. London: Longman, Orme, Brown, Green, & Longmans, 1840–41.
Moran, Patrick Francis. *Historical Sketch of the Persecutions Suffered by the Catholics of Ireland under the Rule of Cromwell and the Puritans*. Dublin: M. H. Gill and Son, 1884.
Morgan, Sydney. "Prefatory Address" to *The Wild Irish Girl*, rev. ed., vii–xlii. London: Henry Colburn, 1850.

Morin, Christina. "'Gothic' and 'National'? Challenging the Formal Distinctions of Irish Romantic Fiction." In *Ireland and Romanticism: Publics, Nations and Scenes of Cultural Production*, edited by Jim Kelly, 172–87. Basingstoke, Hampshire, UK: Palgrave Macmillan, 2011.

———. *The Gothic Novel in Ireland, c. 1760–1829*. Manchester, UK: Manchester University Press, 2018.

Morrison, Matthew D. "Race, Blacksound, and the (Re)Making of Musicological Discourse." *Journal of the American Musicological Society* 72, no. 3 (Fall 2019): 781–823.

Morrison, Toni. *Playing in the Dark: Whiteness and the Literary Imagination*. New York: Vintage, 1993.

———. *The Source of Self-Regard: Selected Essays, Speeches, and Meditations*. New York: Vintage, 2020.

Mouton Kinyon, Chanté. "'I'm Apparently Not Famous Anymore': Appropriating Dion Boucicault's Octoroon and Reckoning with Racial Violence in America." In *Transnationalism in Irish Literature and Culture*, edited by Cóilín Parsons. Cambridge: Cambridge University Press, forthcoming.

Moynahan, Julian. *Anglo-Irish: The Literary Imagination in a Hyphenated Culture*. Princeton, NJ: Princeton University Press, 1995.

Mufti, Nasser. "Hating Victorian Studies Properly." *Victorian Studies* 62, no. 3 (Spring 2020): 392–405.

Mullen, Mary L. "How the Irish Became Settlers: Metaphors of Indigeneity and the Erasure of Indigenous Peoples." *New Hibernia Review/Iris Éireannach Nua* 20, no. 3 (Autumn 2016): 81–96.

———. *Novel Institutions: Anachronism, Irish Novels and Nineteenth-Century Realism*. Edinburgh: Edinburgh University Press, 2019.

Mulvey-Roberts, Marie. *Dangerous Bodies: Historicising the Gothic Corporeal*. Manchester, UK: Manchester University Press, 2016.

"Municipal Corporations (Ireland)." *Times* (London), 11 April 1837, 3–4.

Murphy, Arthur. *No One's Enemy but His Own: A Comedy in Three Acts*. London: P. Vaillant, 1764.

Murphy, James H. *Irish Novelists and the Victorian Age*. Oxford: Oxford University Press, 2011.

Murray, Amelia M. *Letters from the United States, Cuba and Canada*. New York: G. P. Putnam, 1856.

Nadler, Susannah. "The Equation of Consent and Coercion in M. G. Lewis's *The Monk*." *Gothic Studies* 18, no. 2 (November 2016): 18–36.

Nally, David P. *Human Encumbrances: Political Violence ant the Great Irish Famine*. Notre Dame, IN: University of Notre Dame Press, 2011.

Nast, Thomas. *The Ignorant Vote—Honors Are Easy*. Harper's Weekly: A Journal of Civilization, 9 December 1876, cover.

Nelson, Bruce. *Irish Nationalists and the Making of the Irish Race*. Princeton, NJ: Princeton University Press, 2012.

Neocleous, Mark. "Gothic Fascism." *Journal for Cultural Research* 9, no. 2 (April 2005): 133–49.

Nicholson, Asenath. *Annals of the Famine in Ireland, in 1847, 1848, and 1849*. New York: E. French, 1851.

Ní Mhunghaile, Lesa. "Ossian and the Gaelic World." In *The International Companion to James Macpherson and "The Poems of Ossian,"* edited by Dafydd Moore, 26–38. Glasgow: Scottish Literature International, 2017.

Noddings, Nel. *Caring: A Relational Approach to Ethics and Moral Education.* 1984. 2nd ed. Berkeley: University of California Press, 2013.

Noori, Margaret. "Bicultural before There Was a Word for It." *Women's Review of Books* 25, no. 2 (March/April 2008): 7–9.

Norris, Claire. "The Big House: Space, Place, and Identity in Irish Fiction." *New Hibernia Review/Iris Éireannach Nua* 8, no. 1 (Spring 2004): 107–21.

Nott, J. C., and George R. Gliddon. *Types of Mankind: or, Ethnological Researches, Based upon the Ancient Monuments, Paintings, Sculptures, and Crania of Races, and upon Their Natural, Geographical, Philological, and Biblical History.* Philadelphia: Lippincott, Grambo; and London: Trübner, 1854.

Nowatzki, Robert. "Blurring the Color Line: Black Freedom, Passing, Abolitionism, and Irish Ethnicity in Frank J. Webb's *The Garies and Their Friends*." *Studies in American Fiction* 33, no. 1 (Spring 2005): 29–58.

———. *Representing African Americans in Transatlantic Abolitionism and Blackface Minstrelsy.* Baton Rouge: Louisiana State University Press, 2010.

Nyquist, Mary. *Arbitrary Rule: Slavery, Tyranny, and the Power of Life and Death.* Chicago: University of Chicago Press, 2013.

O'Byrne, M. L. (Emolibie De Celtis). *Leixlip Castle: A Romance of the Penal Days of 1690.* Dublin: M. H. Gill and Son, 1883.

O'Connell, Daniel. *Daniel O'Connell upon American Slavery: With Other Irish Testimonies.* New York: Anti-Slavery Society, 1860.

———. *The Select Speeches of Daniel O'Connell, M.P.* Edited by John O'Connell. 2 vols. Dublin: James Duffy, 1865.

"O'Connell and the Abolitionists." *Pilot* (Boston), 5 February 1842, 46.

"The Octoroon." *New York Times*, 15 December 1859, 4.

"'The Octoroon.' A Disgrace to the North, a Libel on the South." *Spirit of the Times; A Chronicle of the Turf, Agriculture, Field Sports, Literature and the Stage*, 17 December 1859, 529.

"The Octoroon Gone Home: Letters from Mr. Bourcicault." *New York Times*, 9 February 1860, 2.

O'Grady, Standish James. *History of Ireland: Cuculain and His Contemporaries.* London: Sampson, Low, Searle, Marston & Rivington, 1880.

O'Halloran, Clare. "Irish Re-Creations of the Gaelic Past: The Challenge of Macpherson's Ossian." *Past and Present* 124 (August 1989): 69–95.

O'Malley, Patrick R. "'It May Be Remembered': Spatialized Memory and Gothic History in *The Mysteries of Udolpho*." *Eighteenth Century* 59, no. 4 (Winter 2018): 493–512.

———. *Liffey and Lethe: Paramnesiac History in Nineteenth-Century Anglo-Ireland.* Oxford: Oxford University Press, 2017.

O'Neill, Peter D. *Famine Irish and the American Racial State.* London: Routledge, 2017.

———. "Memory and John Mitchel's Appropriation of the Slave Narrative." *Atlantic Studies* 11, no. 3 (September 2014): 321–43.

Onkey, Lauren. *Blackness and Transatlantic Irish Identity: Celtic Soul Brothers.* New York: Routledge, 2010.

Orr, Jennifer. "Enlightened Ulster, Romantic Ulster: Irish Magazine Culture of the Union Era." In *Irish Literature in Transition, 1780–1830*, edited by Claire Connolly, 148–69. Cambridge: Cambridge University Press, 2020.
"Oscar Wilde." *New Orleans Daily Picayune*, 25 June 1882, 11.
"Oscar Wilde: Arrival of the Great Esthete and His Lecture." *Atlanta Constitution*, 5 July 1882, 8.
Osterweis, Rollin G. *Romanticism and Nationalism in the Old South*. New Haven, CT: Yale University Press, 1949.
O'Toole, James M. *Passing for White: Race, Religion, and the Healy Family, 1820–1920*. Amherst: University of Massachusetts Press, 2002.
Owenson, Sydney. *The Wild Irish Girl: A National Tale*. 1806. Edited by Kathryn Kirkpatrick. Oxford: Oxford University Press, 1999.
Painter, Nell Irvin. *The History of White People*. New York: Norton, 2010.
———. "How We Think about the Term 'Enslaved' Matters." *Guardian*, 14 August 2019 (revised 21 August 2019). https://www.theguardian.com/us-news/2019/aug/14/slavery-in-america-1619-first-ships-jamestown/.
The Parliamentary Debates from the Year 1803 to the Present Time. Vol. 22. London: Longman, Hurst, Rees, Orme, and Brown, 1812.
The Parliamentary Debates. New series, Vol. 10. London: printed by T. C. Hansard, 1824.
Patterson, Orlando. *Slavery and Social Death: A Comparative Study*. Cambridge, MA: Harvard University Press, 1982.
Peeples, Scott. "Love and Theft in the Carolina Lowcountry." *Arizona Quarterly: A Journal of American Literature, Culture, and Theory* 60, no. 2 (Summer 2004): 33–56.
Pendergrast, Mark. *Uncommon Grounds: The History of Coffee and How It Transformed Our World*. Rev. ed. New York: Basic, 2010.
Pepper, Robert D. Introduction to *Irish Poets and Poetry of the Nineteenth Century*, by Oscar Wilde, 3–23. San Francisco: Book Club of California, 1972.
Person, Leland S. "Poe's Philosophy of Amalgamation: Reading Racism in the Tales." In *Romancing the Shadow: Poe and Race*, edited by J. Gerald Kennedy and Liliane Weissberg, 205–24. Oxford: Oxford University Press, 2001.
Phillips, Wendell. "Letter from Wendell Phillips, Esq." In *Narrative of the Life of Frederick Douglass, an American Slave*, by Douglass, xiii–xvi. Boston: Anti-Slavery Office, 1845.
———. *Speeches, Lectures, and Letters*. 2nd ser. Boston: Lee and Shepard, 1891.
Pinto, Samantha. *Infamous Bodies: Early Black Women's Celebrity and the Afterlives of Rights*. Durham, NC: Duke University Press, 2020.
Pittock, Murray. "'My Country Takes Her Place among the Nations of the Earth': Ireland and the British Archipelago in the Age of Union." In *Irish Literature in Transition, 1780–1830*, edited by Claire Connolly, 323–41. Cambridge: Cambridge University Press, 2020.
Poe, Edgar Allan. *The Annotated Poe*. Edited by Kevin J. Hayes. Cambridge, MA: Belknap Press of Harvard University Press, 2015.
———. "The Gold-Bug." 1843. In *Tales*, 1–36. New York: Wiley and Putnam, 1845.
———. "Letter to B—." *Southern Literary Messenger* 2, no. 8 (July 1836): 501–3.
———. *Literary Theory and Criticism*. Edited by Leonard Cassuto. Mineola, NY: Dover, 1999.
———. "Longfellow's Poems." *Aristidean: A Magazine of Reviews, Politics, and Light Literature* 1, no. 2 (April 1845): 130–42.

Pollard, Edward A. *The Lost Cause: A New Southern History of the War of the Confederates.* New York: E. B. Treat, 1866.

———. *The Lost Cause Regained.* New York: G. W. Carleton; London: S. Low, Son, 1868.

Pollin, Burton R. "Light on 'Shadow' and Other Pieces by Poe; Or, More of Thomas Moore." *ESQ* 18 (third quarter 1972): 166–73.

Price, Fiona. "The Politics of Fear: Gothic Histories, the English Civil War and Walter Scott's *Woodstock.*" *Yearbook of English Studies* 47 (2017): 110–24.

Price, Leah. *The Anthology and the Rise of the Novel from Richardson to George Eliot.* Cambridge: Cambridge University Press, 2000.

Prichard, James Cowles. *The Eastern Origin of the Celtic Nations.* London: Sherwood, Gilbert, and Piper, 1831.

———. *Researches into the Physical History of Mankind.* 3rd ed. 5 vols. London: Sherwood, Gilbert, and Piper, 1836–47.

The Public Statutes at Large of the United States of America. 8 vols. Boston: Charles C. Little and James Brown, 1845–67.

Quinlan, Kieran. *Strange Kin: Ireland and the American South.* Baton Rouge: Louisiana State University Press, 2005.

Quinn, Arthur Hobson. *Edgar Allan Poe: A Critical Biography.* 1941. Baltimore, MD: Johns Hopkins University Press, 1998.

Quinn, James. "An Exiled History: Young Ireland from Mitchel to O'Leary." In *Irish Literature in Transition, 1830–1880,* edited by Matthew Campbell, 162–78. Cambridge: Cambridge University Press, 2020.

———. "Southern Citizen: John Mitchel, the Confederacy and Slavery." *History Ireland* 15, no. 3 (May-June 2007): 30–35

Rai, Amit S. *Rule of Sympathy: Sentiment, Race, and Power, 1750–1850.* New York: Palgrave, 2002.

Rezek, Joseph. "The Racialization of Print." *American Literary History* 32, no. 3 (Fall 2020): 417–45.

———. "Transatlantic Influences and Futures." In *Irish Literature in Transition, 1780–1830,* edited by Claire Connolly, 381–401. Cambridge: Cambridge University Press, 2020.

Riach, Douglas C. "Blacks and Blackface on the Irish Stage, 1830–60." *Journal of American Studies* 7, no. 3 (December 1973): 231–41.

———. "Daniel O'Connell and American Anti-Slavery." *Irish Historical Studies* 20, no. 77 (March 1976): 3–25.

Richards, Shaun. "Dion Boucicault and the Globalised Irish Stage." In *Irish Literature in Transition, 1830–1880,* edited by Matthew Campbell, 280–98. Cambridge: Cambridge University Press, 2020.

Rifkin, Mark. *Beyond Settler Time: Temporal Sovereignty and Indigenous Self-Determination.* Durham, NC: Duke University Press, 2017.

Rigney, Ann. *The Afterlives of Walter Scott: Memory on the Move.* Oxford: Oxford University Press, 2012.

Roach, Joseph. *Cities of the Dead: Circum-Atlantic Performance.* New York: Columbia University Press, 1996.

Rodgers, Nini. *Ireland, Slavery and Anti-Slavery: 1612–1865.* Basingstoke, Hampshire, UK: Palgrave Macmillan, 2007.

Roediger, David R. *The Wages of Whiteness: Race and the Making of the American Working Class*. Rev. ed. London: Verso, 2007.

Rosenthal, Caitlin. *Accounting for Slavery: Masters and Management*. Cambridge, MA: Harvard University Press, 2018.

Rousey, Dennis C. "Friends and Foes of Slavery: Foreigners and Northerners in the Old South." *Journal of Social History* 35, no. 2 (Winter 2001): 373–96.

Rudy, Jason R. "Beyond Universalisms: Individuation, Race and Sentiment in Colonial New South Wales." In *Eliza Hamilton Dunlop: Writing from the Colonial Frontier*, edited by Anna Johnston and Elizabeth Webby, 93–104. Sydney, Australia: Sydney University Press, 2021.

Runcie, John. "'Hunting the Nigs' in Philadelphia: The Race Riot of August 1834." *Pennsylvania History: A Journal of Mid-Atlantic Studies* 39, no. 2 (April 1972): 187–218.

Ryan, Abram. *Father Ryan's Poems*. Mobile: John L. Rapier, 1879.

Ryan, Thomas. "Erin Go Bragh." *Charleston Daily Courier*, 13 January 1862, 2.

Sancho, Ignatius. *Letters of the Late Ignatius Sancho, An African*. 2 vols. London: printed by J. Nichols, 1782.

Sartre, Jean-Paul. "Black Orpheus." Translated by John MacCombie. *Massachusetts Review* 6, no. 1 (Autumn 1964–Winter 1965): 13–52.

Scarry, Elaine. "The Difficulty of Imagining Other People." In *For Love of Country?*, edited by Martha C. Nussbaum and Joshua Cohen, 98–110. Boston: Beacon, 2002.

Schaffer, Talia. *Communities of Care: The Social Ethics of Victorian Fiction*. Princeton, NJ: Princeton University Press, 2021.

Schneer, Jonathan. "Anti-Imperial London: The Pan-African Conference of 1900." In *Black Victorians/Black Victoriana*, edited by Gretchen Holbrook Gerzina, 175–86. New Brunswick, NJ: Rutgers University Press, 2003.

Schuller, Kyla. *The Biopolitics of Feeling: Race, Sex, and Science in the Nineteenth Century*. Durham, NC: Duke University Press, 2018.

Sedgwick, Eve Kosofsky. *The Coherence of Gothic Conventions*. New York: Methuen, 1986.

Shanahan, Jim. "Imperial Minds: Irish Writers and Empire in the Nineteenth Century—Charles Gavan Duffy, Thomas Moore, Charles Lever and *Kim*." In *Irish Literature in Transition, 1830–1880*, edited by Matthew Campbell, 143–61. Cambridge: Cambridge University Press, 2020.

Sharpe, Christina. *In the Wake: On Blackness and Being*. Durham, NC: Duke University Press, 2016.

Shelley, Percy Bysshe. "A Defence of Poetry." In *Essays, Letters from Abroad, Translations and Fragments*, 2 vols., edited by Mary Shelley, 1:1–57. London: Edward Moxon, 1840.

Simpson, John. "Vengeance and the Shores of Manhattan." James Joyce Online Notes. http://www.jjon.org/joyce-s-allusions/vengeance/.

Simpson, John Hawkins. *Poems of Oisin, Bard of Erin*. London: Bosworth & Harrison; Edinburgh: John Menzies; Dublin: M'Glashan and Gill, 1857.

Smallwood, Stephanie E. *Saltwater Slavery: A Middle Passage from Africa to American Diaspora*. Cambridge, MA: Harvard University Press, 2007.

Smart, Robert. "The 'Vital Blood' of Irish Colonials in America and the Formation of the New Nation." In *Irish Famines before and after the Great Hunger*, edited by Christine Kinealy and Gerard Moran, 49–60. Hamden, CT: Quinnipiac University Press, 2020.

Smith, Adam. *The Theory of Moral Sentiments*. 1759. 2nd ed. London: A Millar; Edinburgh: A. Kincard and J. Bell, 1761.

Somerville, Alexander. *Letters from Ireland during the Famine of 1847.* Edited by K. D. M. Snell. Dublin: Irish Academic Press, 1994.
Sonstegard, Adam. "Performing Remediation: The Minstrel, The Camera, and *The Octoroon*." *Criticism* 48, no. 3 (Summer 2006): 375–95.
Spillers, Hortense J. "Moving on Down the Line." *American Quarterly* 40, no. 1 (March 1988): 83–109.
Spires, Derrick R. "Imagining a State of Fellow Citizens: Early African American Politics of Publicity in the Black State Conventions." In *Early African American Print Culture*, edited by Lara Langer Cohen and Jordan Alexander Stein, 274–89. Philadelphia: University of Pennsylvania Press, 2012.
Stancliff, Michael. *Frances Ellen Watkins Harper: African American Reform Rhetoric and the Rise of a Modern Nation State.* New York: Routledge, 2011.
"State of the Country." *Freeman's Journal*, 11 February 1863, 3.
Stevens, Anne H. *British Historical Fiction before Scott.* Basingstoke, Hampshire, UK: Palgrave Macmillan, 2010.
Stocking, George W., Jr. *Victorian Anthropology.* New York: Free Press, 1987.
"Stop My Pilot!" *Pilot* (Boston), 5 May 1877, 4.
Stowe, Harriet Beecher. Preface to *The Garies and Their Friends*, by Frank J. Webb, edited by William Huntting Howell and Megan Walsh, 41–42. Peterborough, Ontario: Broadview, 2016.
Strode, Hudson. *Jefferson Davis, Tragic Hero.* New York: Harcourt, Brace & World, 1964.
Sturgis, Matthew. *Oscar: A Life.* London: Apollo, 2019.
Sullivan, Alexander Martin. *The Story of Ireland; or, A Narrative of Irish History, From the Earliest Ages to the Present Time.* Dublin: A. M. Sullivan, 1867.
[Sullivan, Timothy Daniel, and Denis Baylor Sullivan, eds.] *"Guilty or Not Guilty?": Speeches from the Dock, or Protests of Irish Patriotism.* Dublin, 1867.
Swarns, Rachel L. *The 272: The Families Who Were Enslaved and Sold to Build the American Catholic Church.* New York: Random House, 2023.
Swift, Jonathan. *A Modest Proposal for Preventing the Children of Poor People from being a Burthen to their Parents, or Country, and for Making Them Beneficial to the Publick.* Dublin: S. Harding, 1729.
Taine, Hippolyte Adolphe. *History of English Literature.* Translated by H. van Laun. 2 vols. Edinburgh: Edmonston and Douglas, 1871.
Temple, Kathryn. "Imagining Justice: Gender and Juridical Space in the Gothic Novel." In *Illicit Sex: Identity Politics in Early Modern Culture*, edited by Thomas DiPiero and Pat Gill, 68–85. Athens: University of Georgia Press, 1997.
Tennyson, Alfred. *Poems.* 2 vols. London: Edward Moxon, 1842.
Teukolsky, Rachel. *Picture World: Image, Aesthetics, and Victorian New Media.* Oxford: Oxford University Press, 2020.
"The Theatres." Review. *Illustrated London News*, 14 December 1861, 597.
Times (London), 2 April 1849, 4.
Todorov, Tzvetan. "The Origin of Genres." Translated by Richard M. Berrong. *New Literary History* 8, no. 1 (Autumn 1976): 159–70.
Townshend, Dale. *Gothic Antiquity: History, Romance, and the Architectural Imagination, 1760–1840.* Oxford: Oxford University Press, 2019.
Trent, William P. *William Gilmore Simms.* Boston: Houghton, Mifflin, 1895.

Trumpener, Katie. *Bardic Nationalism: The Romantic Novel and the British Empire*. Princeton, NJ: Princeton University Press, 1997.

Tuck, Eve, and K. Wayne Yang. "Decolonization Is Not a Metaphor." *Decolonization: Indigeneity, Education & Society* 1, no. 1 (2012): 1–40.

Tucker, Irene. "Historicizing the Theorization of Race: A Nineteenth-Century Story." *Criticism* 61, no. 4 (Fall 2019): 527–49.

Twain, Mark. *Life on the Mississippi*. London: Chatto & Windus, 1883.

Vail, Jeffery. "Thomas Moore: After the Battle." In *A Companion to Irish Literature*, 2 vols., edited by Julia M. Wright, 1:310–25. Chichester, West Sussex, UK: Wiley-Blackwell, 2010.

Vara-Dannen, Theresa. Appendix 1 in *The African-American Experience in Nineteenth-Century Connecticut: Benevolence and Bitterness*, 161–62. Lanham, MD: Lexington, 2014.

Vaughan, Alden T. *Roots of American Racism: Essays on the Colonial Experience*. Oxford: Oxford University Press, 1995.

Vizenor, Gerald. *Fugitive Poses: Native American Indian Scenes of Absence and Presence*. Lincoln: University of Nebraska Press, 1998.

Walters, Alisha R. "The 'Sallow Mr. Freely': Sugar, Appetite, and Unstable Forms of Whiteness in George Eliot's 'Brother Jacob.'" *Victorian Literature and Culture* 50, no. 3 (Fall 2022): 431–60.

"The War about Theatres: Mr. Dion Bourcicault and Rev. Henry Ward Beecher—Interesting Controversy." *New York Daily Times*, 15 May 1857, 3.

Ward, Samuel Ringgold. *Autobiography of a Fugitive Negro: His Anti-Slavery Labours in the United States, Canada, & England*. London: John Snow, 1855.

Wardrop, Daneen. "'What Tangled Skeins Are the Genealogies of Slavery!': Gothic Families in Harriet Jacobs' *Incidents in the Life of a Slave Girl*." *Literary Griot* 14, nos. 1 and 2 (Spring/Fall 2002): 23–43.

Watson, G. J. "Yeats, Macpherson and the Cult of Defeat." In *From Gaelic to Romantic: Ossianic Translations*, edited by Fiona Stafford and Howard Gaskill, 216–25. Amsterdam: Rodopi, 1998.

Watt, James. *Contesting the Gothic: Fiction, Genre and Cultural Conflict, 1764–1832*. Cambridge: Cambridge University Press, 1999.

Webb, Frank J. *The Garies and Their Friends*. London: G. Routledge, 1857.

———. *The Garies and Their Friends*. 1857. Edited by William Huntting Howell and Megan Walsh. Peterborough, Ontario: Broadview, 2016.

Weheliye, Alexander G. *Habeas Viscus: Racializing Assemblages, Biopolitics, and Black Feminist Theories of the Human*. Durham, NC: Duke University Press, 2014.

Weissberg, Liliane. "Black, White, and Gold." In *Romancing the Shadow: Poe and Race*, edited by J. Gerald Kennedy and Weissberg, 127–56. Oxford: Oxford University Press, 2001.

Werner, Winter Jade. *Missionary Cosmopolitanism in Nineteenth-Century British Literature*. Columbus: Ohio State University Press, 2020.

West, Cornel. *Race Matters*. 1993. 25th anniversary ed. Boston: Beacon, 2017.

Wester, Maisha L. *African American Gothic: Screams from Shadowed Places*. New York: Palgrave Macmillan, 2012.

Whalen, Terence. "Average Racism: Poe, Slavery, and the Wages of Literary Nationalism." In *Romancing the Shadow: Poe and Race*, edited by J. Gerald Kennedy and Liliane Weissberg, 3–40. Oxford: Oxford University Press, 2001.

———. *Edgar Allan Poe and the Masses: The Political Economy of Literature in Antebellum America*. Princeton, NJ: Princeton University Press, 1999.
Wheeler, Roxann. *The Complexion of Race: Categories of Difference in Eighteenth-Century British Culture*. Philadelphia: University of Pennsylvania Press, 2000.
"White Slavery in Connecticut." *Arkansas State Gazette and Democrat*, 12 September 1857, 2.
Whitfield, James M. "The North Star." *North Star*, 21 December 1849, 4.
Wickramasinghe, Chandima S. M. "The Abolition of Colonial and Pre-Colonial 'Slavery' from Ceylon (Sri Lanka)." *Cultural and Social History* 7, no. 3 (2010): 315–35.
Wilde, Oscar. *The Complete Letters of Oscar Wilde*. Edited and with notes by Merlin Holland and Rupert Hart-Davis. New York: Henry Holt, 2000.
———. *Irish Poets and Poetry of the Nineteenth Century: A Lecture Delivered in Platt's Hall, San Francisco on Wednesday, April Fifth, 1882*. Edited by Robert D. Pepper. San Francisco: Book Club of California, 1972.
Wilderson, Frank B., III. *Afropessimism*. New York: Liveright, 2020.
———. *Red, White & Black: Cinema and the Structure of U.S. Antagonisms*. Durham, NC: Duke University Press, 2010.
Wilentz, Sean. *Chants Democratic: New York City and the Rise of the American Working Class, 1788–1850*. 20th anniversary ed. Oxford: Oxford University Press, 2004.
Williams, Linda. *Playing the Race Card: Melodramas of Black and White from Uncle Tom to O. J. Simpson*. Princeton, NJ: Princeton University Press, 2001.
Williams, Maggie M. *Icons of Irishness from the Middle Ages to the Modern World*. New York: Palgrave Macmillan, 2012.
Williams, Patricia J. *The Alchemy of Race and Rights*. Cambridge, MA: Harvard University Press, 1991.
Winn, T. S. *Emancipation; or Practical Advice to British Slave-Holders: with Suggestions for the General Improvement of West India Affairs*. London: sold by W. Phillips, 1824.
Wong, Edlie L. *Neither Fugitive nor Free: Atlantic Slavery, Freedom Suits, and the Legal Culture of Travel*. New York: New York University Press, 2009.
Wright, Julia M. *Ireland, India, and Nationalism in Nineteenth-Century Literature*. Cambridge: Cambridge University Press, 2007.
———. "Lewis's 'Anaconda': Gothic Homonyms and Sympathetic Distinctions." *Gothic Studies* 3, no. 3 (December 2001): 262–78.
———. *Representing the National Landscape in Irish Romanticism*. Syracuse, NY: Syracuse University Press, 2014.
Wynter, Sylvia. "Unsettling the Coloniality of Being/Power/Truth/Freedom: Towards the Human, After Man, Its Overrepresentation—An Argument." *CR: The New Centennial Review* 3, no. 3 (Fall 2003): 257–337.
Yao, Xine. *Disaffected: The Cultural Politics of Unfeeling in Nineteenth-Century America*. Durham, NC: Duke University Press, 2021.
Yeats, William Butler. *The Death of Synge, and Other Passages from an Old Diary*. Dublin: Cuala, 1928.
Yuhl, Stephanie E. "Hidden in Plain Sight: Centering the Domestic Slave Trade in American Public History." *Journal of Southern History* 79, no. 3 (August 2013): 593–624.

INDEX

abolitionism, 12–18, 22, 66–67, 93–95, 109, 111–12, 210, 246n41; Dion Boucicault's ambivalence regarding, 196–99, 212; Irish support for, 12–14, 113–14, 167, 183, 229–30, 267n24. *See also* anti–abolitionism; Haughton, James; Madden, Richard Robert; O'Connell, Daniel

Act of Union, 13, 14, 66, 68, 72, 164, 194. *See also* Repeal Association

Agamben, Giorgio, 178

Aldridge, Ira, 259n68, 265n51

Allen, Theodore W., 45–46. See also *Invention of the White Race, The* (Allen)

American Indian, 33, 60–61, 116–29, 175, 194; Choctaw donation to Famine–era Ireland, 122; fantasized absence of, 116–29

"Anaconda, The" (Lewis), 69, 76–80, 257n33, 258n55

analogy as ruse, 14, 17, 26, 31, 52, 63, 185, 195. *See also* Wilderson III, Frank B.

anti–abolitionism, 25, 62, 96–129, 167, 182–83, 198–99, 202, 205–7, 210, 218, 224–26, 267n24. *See also* Grayson, William J.; Hughes, John Joseph; Kenyon, John; Mitchel, John

anti–amalgamationism, 34, 36, 263n20

Appiah, K. Anthony, 24

Arkansas State Gazette and Democrat, 60–61

Arnold, Matthew, 9–10, 43–44, 118, 122–23. See also *On the Study of Celtic Literature* (Arnold); Ossian

Arrah–na–Pogue (Boucicault), 195, 215

"Art of Dramatic Composition, The" (Boucicault), 189, 201–3, 220,

Athenæum, 133–36, 146

Atlanta Constitution, 2, 6

Bailyn, Bernard, 156

ballad, 23, 60, 98, 234, 237. *See also* genre

Ballad Poetry of Ireland, The (Duffy), 98, 261n37

bardic poem, 22, 96–129. *See also* genre

Bassett, John Spencer, 173

Baudelaire, Charles, 84–85

Beddoe, John, 34

Beecher, Henry Ward, 211–13

Bell, Bernard W., 154, 157–58

Berry, Daina Ramey, 180

blackface, Irish, 87–88, 145–46, 258–59n68. *See also* minstrelsy

Black Republican, 23

Blair, James, 8–9

Blight, David W., 14–16

{301}

Blumenbach, Johann Friedrich, 37–44, 128, 250n36, 251n56. *See also* race science; monogenism
Boltwood, Scott, 193–95, 209
Boucicault, Dion, 19, 22, 26, 70, 132, 189–222, 242, 270n25, 270n38. *See also Arrah-na-Pogue* (Boucicault); "The Art of Dramatic Composition" (Boucicault); *Colleen Bawn, The* (Boucicault); *Octoroon, The* (Boucicault); *Shaughraun, The* (Boucicault)
Boulukos, George, 74
Boyce, D. G., 231
boycotting, as Irish American tactic, 225
Brantlinger, Patrick, 29, 34, 40, 79–80, 119–21
Broca, Paul, 41–42
Brody, Jennifer DeVere, 208, 210
Brooks, Daphne A., 192–93, 210–11, 219
Brown, Malcolm, 161
Brundage, David, 225, 246n41
Burke, Edmund, 9, 149, 221–22, 273n105, 274n29. *See also Reflections on the Revolution in France* (Burke)
Burke, Mary, 80, 249n88, 275nn40–41, 276n71
Buxton, Thomas Fowell, 13, 182
Byrd, Jodi A., 120, 126–27
Byron, George Gordon, Lord, 52–53, 61, 76

Calhoun, John C., 51–52
Campbell, Matthew, 122, 124
Canning, George, 74–75
Cantrell, James P., 232, 240, 275n47
capitalism, 100, 104, 121, 157, 179–82, 184–85, 187, 233–34, 268n58. *See also* racial capitalism
caricatures, of Irish and Black people, 36–37, 44–47, 49–50, 252n81
Carlyle, Thomas, 34–36, 48–49, 55, 64–65, 100–102, 108–10, 121–22, 127, 178, 179–82, 186–88, 217, 221, 225–26, 228, 268n54, 269n71; as source for Irish nationalist rhetoric, 165–68, 170. *See also Chartism* (Carlyle); *Latter-Day Pamphlets* (Carlyle); "Occasional Discourse on the Negro Question"; "The Repeal of the Union"
Carpenter, William Benjamin, 42
Cassuto, Leonard, 81
Catholic Emancipation, 14–15, 52–54, 68, 92
Catholicism, 13, 29, 45–46, 54–55, 63, 69–71, 79, 108–9, 113, 124, 150–51, 152, 161, 167, 175, 176–77, 205–8, 224, 228, 231, 232–33, 234–36, 249n88, 267n29
Caucasian, term, 37–40, 42–44, 51, 127–28, 253n94. *See also* Indo-European
Celticism, 3, 9–10, 29, 31, 33–37, 40–45, 48–50, 52, 64, 70, 98, 115–18, 121–24, 127–28, 156, 165–66, 173, 186–87, 194–95, 226–27, 236–37. *See also* Arnold, Matthew; Ossian
Chander, Manu Samriti, 113, 202–3
Chandler, James, 138–39
Chartism (Carlyle), 35, 268n54
Chartism (political movement), 35, 68
Chatterjee, Ronjaunee, 12
Chicago Press and Tribune, 175
"Chicora" (Grayson), 97, 115–17, 123–29
Child, Lydia Maria, 90, 192, 211
Chiu, Frances A., 69
chivalry, 6–11, 166, 217, 241–43. *See also* Lost Causism
Christoff, Alicia Mireles, 12
Christy's Minstrels, 114
Cima, Gay Gibson, 195–96, 203, 271n51
Citizen, 175
Civil Rights Act (1875), 227
Civil War, American, 2–3, 9, 18, 25, 32, 47, 66, 194, 195, 223–43, 248n81, 275n36

Clark, Eliza, 235
class, intersection with race, 46, 103–5, 153–57, 177–78, 187–88, 191, 195
Clukey, Amy, 233–34, 237
Coates, Ta-Nehisi, 148–49, 186
Cohen, Ashley L., 79, 185
Colleen Bawn, The (Boucicault), 193–95, 215, 270n25
Colley, Linda, 135
color line, the (concept of), 47, 48, 136, 145–47, 151–52, 158, 166, 229, 252n78. *See also* Douglass, Frederick
"Color Line, The" (Douglass), 136, 201, 252n78, 263n12
Colquhoun, Patrick, 150–51
Columbian Orator, 15–16
Confederacy, 1–8, 11–12, 18, 23, 60, 66–67, 126, 177, 181, 223–43, 246n32. *See also* Lost Causism
Congressional Globe, 104
Connolly, Claire, 71
Conrad, Joseph, 50
Cooper Owens, Deirdre, 254n112
Corfe, I. J., 23
"Cornerstone Speech" (Stephens), 177–78
Cromwell, Oliver, 10, 36, 55, 60, 235, 253n107, 275n53
Cugoano, Quobna Ottobah, 64–65
Curtis, L. Perry, Jr., 29, 36–37, 44–45, 251n66
Cushing, Caleb, 51–52

Daily News (London), 133–34, 141,
Davis, Jefferson, 1–12, 18, 51–52, 80, 185–86, 205, 223, 246n32
Davis, Thomas, 98–99, 161, 232
Deane, Seamus, 25, 70
Defoe, Daniel, 26, 253n101. *See also Roxana* (Defoe)

Delahanty, Ian, 25
de Nie, Michael, 29–30, 48
Derozio, Henry, 113
Dial, 144
dialect (as index of race or ethnicity), 23, 78, 81, 84–85, 88–89, 146, 148, 194, 209, 240, 276n67. *See also* minstrelsy
Dickens, Charles, 86, 138, 141, 264n36
Dickerson, Vanessa D., 49
Dillon, John Blake, 99, 231, 274n35
Dimock, Wai Chee, 20
Dolan, Jay P., 25
Donahoe, Patrick, 205. See also *Pilot*
Douglas, Stephen A., 51, 128, 175
Douglass, Frederick, 27, 47, 66, 111–12, 136, 144–45, 147, 149, 174, 201, 219, 252n78, 259n83, 263n12; and gothic, 89–92; on Ireland and the Irish, 14–18, 19, 20, 26, 29, 62–66, 92–94, 130–31, 151–53, 218, 224, 227–28, 247n53; Irish reception of, 17, 22; on John Mitchel, 161–63. *See also* "Color Line, The" (Douglass); "This Decision Has Humbled the Nation" (Douglass); *My Bondage and My Freedom* (Douglass); *Narrative of the Life of Frederick Douglass* (Douglass); "Nation in the Midst of a Nation, A" (Douglass); "Our Composite Nationality" (Douglass)
Doyle, Laura, 259n89
Dred Scott v. Sanford, 173–74
Du Bois, W. E. B., 130, 149–51, 252n78, 264n37
Duffy, Charles Gavan, 25, 98–99, 163, 172–73, 218, 261n37. *See also Ballad Poetry of Ireland, The* (Duffy); *Nation* (Irish nationalist newspaper)
Dunbar, William, 156
Dunlop, Eliza Hamilton, 12
Dwan, David, 221–22

Eagleton, Terry, 179–81
Earls, Brian, 88
Easton, Hosea, 27, 59, 119, 174
Edgeworth, Maria, 23, 54, 73–74, 76, 89, 138–39, 276n65. See also *Essay on Irish Bulls* (Edgeworth and Edgeworth); "Grateful Negro, The" (Edgeworth); *Practical Education* (Edgeworth and Edgeworth)
Edgeworth, Richard Lovell, 23, 54, 89. See also *Essay on Irish Bulls* (Edgeworth and Edgeworth); *Practical Education* (Edgeworth and Edgeworth)
Eglinton, John (William Kirkpatrick Magee), 160
elegy, 23, 248n81; proleptic, 119–23, 126. See also genre
Elgee, John Kingsbury, 235
Ellmann, Richard, 6
empathy, 207, 271n51. See also sympathy
Engels, Friedrich, 58–59
Engle, Anna, 156–57
epigraph as literary device, 85–89, 99–103, 113, 258n60
Equiano, Olaudah, 12–13, 22, 53
"Erin go Bragh," 23, 60
Essay on Irish Bulls (Edgeworth and Edgeworth), 89
ethnicity, term, 41, 63, 143–44
Examiner, 216

Fanon, Frantz, 131–32, 188, 256n16
Fenianism, 25, 46, 115, 193, 215, 229–30
Ferreira, Patricia J., 15, 22
Ferris, Ina, 237–38
Festa, Lynn, 61, 208, 239
Fielder, Brigitte, 20–21, 255n134, 263n20, 264n33
fire companies, Philadelphia, Irish centrality to, 146

Flying Horses Riot (1834), 265n56
Foster, R. F., 44–46, 165–66. See also race science
Foster, Stephen, 114, 146
Foster, Travis M., 23–24
Frederick Douglass' Paper, 133, 141
Freedgood, Elaine, 137
Freeman, Edward Augustus, 47–48, 65. See also *Some Impressions of the United States* (Freeman)
Friedman, David M., 1, 245n18
Fuentes, Marisa J., 272n82
Fugitive Slave Act (1850), 136, 162,
Fuller, James Cannings, 14
Fuller, Margaret, 144–45

Gallagher, Catherine, 100, 255n128, 268n54
Garies and Their Friends, The (Webb), 26, 130–58, 193, 196
Garrison, William Lloyd, 14, 62, 66–67, 93–94, 266n9. See also *Liberator*
Gates, Henry Louis, Jr., 259n76
gender, 155, 173, 191, 210–11, 265n68
genre, 4–5, 16–17, 19–24, 26–27, 32, 51–52, 65–67, 68–70, 73, 75, 81, 87, 97, 98, 110, 112, 128, 138–39, 154, 160, 162–63, 218, 233, 237–39, 242, 248n81, 259n76, 276n71. See also *specific genres*
gentleman, use of term, 155–57, 242
Georgetown College, sale of enslaved people by, 235–36, 276n54
Gibbons, Luke, 70
Gillespie, Niall, 70
Gilley, Sheridan, 50–51
Gilroy, Paul, 268n58
Gleeson, David T., 223, 225, 234–35
Glenn, Evelyn Nakano, 173, 267n37
Goddu, Teresa A., 75, 81, 89–90, 91–92, 111–12, 128–29
Godwyn, Morgan, 57–59

Goldberg, David Theo, 46–47, 181, 217, 221, 246n33, 250n38, 273nn103–4
"Gold-Bug, The" (Poe), 80–89
Gone with the Wind (Mitchell), 19, 231–43, 275n36, 275–76n53
Gonzales, Ambrose E., 88
gothic, 68–95, 107–8, 248n67, 256n20, 256n24, 259nn76–77, 259n85, 259n89; Ireland as gothic, 69–73. *See also* genre
Goyal, Yogita, 20
"Grateful Negro, The" (Edgeworth), 73–74
Grayson, William J., 96–129, 132, 169, 181, 198, 204–5, 207, 224, 242. *See also* "Chicora"; "The Hireling and the Slave"
Great Famine, 16, 25, 32, 35, 55–56, 63, 68, 71–72, 102, 108, 112, 120–22, 128, 164, 166, 169, 179, 218, 234, 249n88, 256n12, 268n50; as act of genocide, 164
Greeley, Horace. *See New York Daily Tribune*
Greiner, Rae, 137, 202
Griffith, Arthur, 73, 159–60, 163. *See also* Sinn Féin
Gross, Ariela J., 24, 61, 210, 272n68
Grundrisse (Marx), 220

Hadley, Elaine, 201
Hale, Anthony R., 172,
Hamm, Charles, 114
Hankins, Laurel, 23
Hannah-Jones, Nikole, 57
Harper, Frances Ellen Watkins, 226–27, 253n94
Hartman, Saidiya, 92, 145, 207–9, 214, 264n48
Haughton, James, 167, 183–84, 218, 246n41, 266n9, 267n24
Healey, T. M., 230–31
Healy, Michael, 235
Healy, Patrick, 235
Hemenway, Mark, 73, 75, 256n16, 259n77

Heneghan, Bridget T., 84
Heng, Geraldine, 32
"hireling and slave," conventional contrast between, 99, 260n17
"Hireling and the Slave, The" (Grayson), 96–129, 181, 224
History of English Literature (Taine), 21
Hogan, Liam, 57
Hogan, Robert, 189–90, 193
Horsman, Reginald, 40
Howes, Marjorie, 189–91, 194
Hughes, John Joseph, 108–9, 224
Hutcheson, Francis, 270n42

Ignatiev, Noel, 30, 45, 62, 65, 150, 151, 265n62
Illustrated London News, 44, 215–16
India, analogy with Ireland, 43, 46, 231, 255n141, 257n34; British slavery in, 53; Irish civil and military service in, 274n34; *Nation*'s attention to 1857 Indian Revolution, 274n28; *Nation* uses as example of savagery, 228–29. *See also* "Anaconda, The" (Lewis); Derozio, Henry.
Indigeneity. *See* American Indian
Indo-European, term, 43–44. *See also* Caucasian
Invention of the White Race, The (Allen), 45–46
Irish Citizen, 175
Irish Melodies (Moore), 54–55, 86, 113, 146
Irishness, designated white, 30–32, 39–43, 47–52, 59, 61–67, 97, 101–2, 106–7, 128–29, 131–32, 151–52, 175, 230, 236–37, 239–43, 252n81, 254n120
"Irish Poets and Poetry of the Nineteenth Century" (Wilde), 3, 115, 161, 245n9
"Irish slavery" myth. *See* slavery as metaphor
Irish Tribune, 186

Jackson, J. W., 43, 50. *See also* race science
Jackson, Spencer, 111
Jacobs, Edward, 86
Jacobs, Harriet, 1, 26–27, 68, 101, 136, 183, 200, 214–15, 242, 272n83; and the gothic, 89–95; on Irish starvation, 95; on John Mitchel, 161–63
Jacobson, Matthew Frye, 31–32, 33–34, 128, 143–44
Jaffe, Audrey, 208, 211
Jail Journal (Mitchel), 10, 20, 73, 159–60, 163, 164, 166–67, 169–72, 176, 179, 181–82, 186, 217, 221, 222
Jameson, Fredric, 247n63
Jarrett, Thomas D., 110
Jefferson, Joseph, 197, 199
Jerng, Mark C., 4, 20, 276n71
Johnson, James, 46,
Johnson, Walter, 157, 209–10
Jolson, Al (in *The Jazz Singer*), 143–44
Jones, Douglas A., Jr., 111
Journal of a West India Proprietor (Lewis), 76, 99–100
"June in the Famine Year" (Mitchel), 72–73

Kansas-Nebraska Act (1854), 104, 205
Kenny, Kevin, 108–9, 224, 274n34
Kenyon, John, 167, 177, 181–83, 267n24
Key, Francis Scott, 99
Kiely, Robert, 75
Killeen, Jarlath, 70
Kinealy, Christine, 12, 22, 246–47n41, 253n102, 268n42
Kingsley, Charles, 50–51
Knox, Robert, 33–36, 40–44, 48, 49, 53, 110, 128, 165–66, 173, 186–87. *See also* polygenism, race science; *Races of Men, The* (Knox)

Lady of the Lake, The (Scott), 66
Last Conquest of Ireland (Perhaps), The (Mitchel), 11, 160, 164–70, 174, 177–78, 179, 186–87, 241, 257n34
Latter-Day Pamphlets (Carlyle), 48–49, 100, 109
Lawson, Henry, 202–3
Lecourt, Sebastian, 32, 44, 250n40, 251n62
Leerssen, Joep, 21, 116, 122, 173
Lepore, Jill, 150–51
Levine, Caroline, 19–20, 22
Levine, George, 137, 141, 264n36
Levine, Robert S., 263n17
Lewis, Matthew Gregory, 75–80, 83, 99–100, 256n28, 257n33, 258n55. *See also* "Anaconda, The" (Lewis); *Journal of a West India Proprietor* (Lewis)
Liberator, 14, 266n9. *See also* Garrison, William Lloyd
Lincoln, Abraham, 49, 175; comparison to Cromwell, 60, 235, 275n53
Literary Gazette, 133, 137–38, 153–54, 156
Lloyd, David, 30, 49–50, 160–61, 180, 249n16
Lombard Street Riot (1842), 149–50
Longfellow, Henry Wadsworth, 116, 192, 257n47
Lootens, Tricia, 19
Lorimer, Douglas, 24
Lost Cause, The (Pollard), 6–7
Lost Cause Regained, The (Pollard), 7–8
Lost Causism, 6–11, 18–19, 23, 223–43, 275n36; relationship to Irish rhetoric, 9–12
Lott, Eric, 144, 146, 264n48, 265n50
Lowe, Lisa, 78, 127, 220–21
Lyons, F. S. L., 231, 274n35

INDEX   307

Mabbott, Thomas Ollive, 86
Macpherson, James, 10, 114–17, 226, 261n42, 261n49. *See also* Ossian
Madden, Richard Robert, 12–14, 18
Malchow, H. L., 74–75
Malouf, Michael G., 84, 228–29
Mangan, James Clarence, 3, 80, 161, 233
manifest destiny, 126, 190
Martin, Amy E., 31, 46, 228–30, 255n141
Martin, Bonnie, 180–81
Martin, Egbert, 113
Marx, Karl, 58, 179–80, 182, 184–85, 220, 273n104. *See also* Engels, Friedrich; *Grundrisse* (Marx)
Maturin, Charles Robert, 22, 70, 86
Maume, Patrick, 166
Maurer, Sara, 179
McAtackney, Laura, 57
McGovern, Bryan P., 45, 72, 172
McKee, Clayton Tyler, 84
Meagher, Thomas Francis, 25, 218, 224, 273n6
Meaher, Timothy, 235–36
Meer, Sarah, 198
Mehta, Uday Singh, 134–35, 219–21, 271n60
Meiners, Christoph, 40–41
melodrama, 20, 140–41, 264n33, 264n36; stage melodrama, 189–222. *See also* genre
Mendelssohn, Michèle, 4, 235, 245n18
Meriwether's Weekly, 1–2
Merrill, Lisa, 211, 213
Mill, John Stuart, 64–65, 103, 134–35, 217, 220, 221, 255n141
minstrelsy, 20, 23, 80–89, 114, 143–49, 157, 193, 209, 265nn50–51. *See also* blackface, Irish; Christy's Minstrels; Foster, Stephen; Fuller, Margaret;
Mitchel, John, 3–4, 9, 10–13, 18, 20, 22, 25, 26, 45–46, 65–66, 67, 72–73, 159–88, 217–22, 223–24, 231, 233, 241, 242, 246n32, 257n34, 266n14, 266n21, 267n28, 273n104. *See also Jail Journal* (Mitchel); "June in the Famine Year" (Mitchel); *Last Conquest of Ireland (Perhaps), The* (Mitchel)
Mitchell, Margaret, 19, 231–43, 275n36, 275nn40–41, 275n47, 275n53. *See also Gone with the Wind* (Mitchell)
Modest Proposal, A (Swift), 121
monogenism, 38–39. *See also* race science
Moore, Jane, 114
Moore, Thomas, 3, 54–55, 74, 86, 97, 98, 113–15, 118, 128, 146, 233, 261n37, 261n41, 261n45. *See also Irish Melodies* (Moore); Ossian
Moran, Patrick Francis, 55, 61
Morant Bay Rebellion, 228–29, 274n29
Morgan, Sydney, Lady, 114, 237–40, 276n59. *See also Wild Irish Girl, The* (Morgan)
Morin, Christina, 70, 248n67
Morning Post, 133, 141
Morrison, Matthew D., 144–46
Morrison, Toni, 68–69, 73, 76, 81, 88, 126, 128, 131, 155–57, 185
Moynahan, Julian, 69
Mufti, Nasser, 29
Mullen, Mary L., 123, 138–39, 248n78
Murphy, Arthur, 87–88
Murray, Amelia M., 100–102
My Bondage and My Freedom (Douglass), 16

Narrative of the Life of Frederick Douglass (Douglass), 15, 22, 90–93, 219
Nast, Thomas, 252n81
Nation (Irish nationalist newspaper), 2, 12, 25, 61–62, 99, 123–24, 161, 163, 165, 172–73, 175, 186, 228–29, 260n24, 267n24
national tale, 19, 112, 223–43, 276n65. *See also* genre

"Nation in the Midst of a Nation, A" (Douglass), 63, 130
Naturalization Act (1790), 30, 173–74
New Orleans Daily Picayune, 2, 197, 205
New York Daily News, 67, 223
New York Daily Tribune, 184, 197
New York Freeman's Journal and Catholic Register, 223–24
New York Herald, 196–97, 202–3, 218–19, 270n32, 270n38
New York Times, 194, 198
Nicholson, Asenath, 55–57, 61, 71, 260n23
Noddings, Nel, 203
Noori, Margaret, 117
North American Review, 201
North British Review, 42
Northern Star (Chartist newspaper), 16. *See also* O'Connor, Feargus
Northern Star (United Irish newspaper), 16
North Star, 16, 111–12. *See also* Douglass, Frederick
Nott, Josiah, 40, 42
Nowatzki, Robert, 143–44, 265n56

Observer, 133–35
O'Byrne, M. L. (Emolibie De Celtis), 55, 61
"Occasional Discourse on the Negro Question" (Carlyle), 34–35, 64–65
O'Connell, Daniel, 11, 13–16, 18, 25–26, 45, 54, 62, 93–94, 163–64, 167, 184, 205–6, 218–19, 229–30, 246n41, 263n20
O'Connor, Arthur, 15–16
O'Connor, Feargus, 16, 68
Octoroon, The (Boucicault), 26, 189–222, 269n21, 270n25, 270n38, 271n66
O'Grady, Standish James, 112
O'Neill, Peter D., 30, 170, 224–25, 273n13
On the Study of Celtic Literature (Arnold), 9–10, 43–44, 123–24. *See also* Ossian

O'Reilly, John Boyle, 229–30. *See also Pilot*
Orr, James, 12
Ossian, 9–10, 11, 70, 97, 114–18, 122–24, 128, 226, 261n45. *See also* Macpherson, James
O'Sullivan, John Louis, 126. *See also* manifest destiny
"Our Composite Nationality" (Douglass), 227
Owenson, Sydney. *See* Morgan, Sydney

Painter, Nell Irvin, 33, 37, 39, 61
Peeples, Scott, 81
Person, Leland S., 81–82
Phillips, Wendell, 13, 196, 219
Pilot, 205–8, 229–30
Pinto, Samantha, 111
Pittock, Murray, 237
plantation, transnational concept, 186–87, 233–39, 257n34
Poe, Edgar Allan, 3, 75, 80–89, 92, 95, 97, 242, 257–58n47, 259n83. *See also* "Gold-Bug, The" (Poe)
poetry, Irish nationalist, 3, 98; abolitionist, 12, 111–12
Police forces, relationship to Irishness, 150–51, 224–25, 230–31, 265n62, 272n9
political polemic, 4, 12, 20, 96–97, 112, 159–88, 218. *See also* genre
Pollard, Edward A., 6–10, 239. *See also Lost Cause, The* (Pollard); *Lost Cause Regained, The* (Pollard)
Pollin, Burton R., 86
polygenism, 38–40, 44, 110, 250n38, 250n40. *See also* race science
poverty, Irish, 31, 55–58, 71–73, 97, 104–10, 112, 179, 193, 227–28. *See also* Great Famine
Practical Education (Edgeworth and Edgeworth), 23, 54

Prichard, James Cowles, 43–44. *See also* Indo-European; monogenism; race science
Punch, 36–37, 44–46, 49

Quinlan, Kieran, 54, 224, 232, 233, 273n9
Quinn, James, 25

race; citizenship and, 25–26, 30–31, 51–52, 63, 94–95, 143–45, 163, 173–77, 184, 188, 218, 241, 268n43; construction of, 29–67, *passim;* history of term, 32–33, 41–42; "master race," use by William J. Grayson, 97, 110
race science, 32–52, 64, 98, 110, 128, 194–95, 227
Races of Men, The (Knox), 33–36, 40, 48, 166
racial capitalism, 147, 157
racial extinction, 120–22. *See also* American Indian, fantasized absence of; Great Famine
Racialization. *See* race, construction of
racial violence, white, Irish participation in, 130–58, 224–25
Radcliffe, Ann, 85, 87, 258n60
Rai, Amit S., 202–3, 259n76, 271n54
realism, 20, 132, 136–41, 153, 154, 157, 193, 263n21, 263n29. *See also* genre
Reconstruction, 25, 227, 236, 241–42
Reflections on the Revolution in France (Burke), 9, 149, 221–22, 274n29
Reilly, Matthew C., 57
Remond, Charles Lenox, 22, 246–47n41
Remond, Sarah P., 196
Repeal Association, 25, 163–64. *See also* O'Connell, Daniel
"Repeal of the Union" (Carlyle), 35, 48
Rezek, Joseph, 21, 22, 26, 54, 74, 261n41
Richards, Shaun, 195

Richardson, Samuel, 138
Rifkin, Mark, 120
Roach, Joseph, 190, 193
Robertson, Agnes, 194, 198, 208, 210–11
Rodgers, Nini, 12–13, 246n25
Roediger, David R., 18, 51, 106, 255n128, 260n17, 265n63
Rosenthal, Caitlin, 180
Roxana (Defoe), 26
Rudy, Jason R., 12
"Rule, Britannia" (Thomson), 134–35, 146
Russell's Magazine, 102, 108
Ryan, (Father) Abram, 22, 225–26, 233
Ryan, Thomas, 60, 235, 254n124, 275n53

Sancho, Ignatius, 22, 30–31
Sartre, Jean-Paul, 187–88
Scarry, Elaine, 220
Schaffer, Talia, 203, 216
Schneer, Jonathan, 230–31, 274n33
Schoolcraft, Henry, 116–17
Schoolcraft, Jane Johnston (Obahbahm-wawageezhagoquay), 117
Schuller, Kyla, 211
Scott, Walter, 66, 85. See also *Lady of the Lake, The* (Scott)
Scottishness, 66, 70, 74, 116, 134–35
Sedgwick, Eve Kosofsky, 90, 259n85
Selma Times, 2, 5
sentimental novel, 22, 130–58. *See also* genre
sermon, 22–23, 248n81. *See also* genre
Shanahan, Jim, 261n37
Sharpe, Christina, 136
Shaughraun, The (Boucicault), 195
Shelley, Mary, 74–75
Sheridan, Richard Brinsley, 15–16, 89, 106–7, 247n53,
Simpson, John, 123–24
Sinn Féin, 73, 159

slave narrative, 22, 170, 259n76. *See also* Douglass, Frederick; genre; Jacobs, Harriet

slavery, *passim;* chattel slavery, 12, 17, 26, 54, 57, 76, 89–95, 136, 211, 214, 217, 219, 239, 242, 253n107; Irish enslavers, 8–9, 165, 186, 234–36, 246n25, 254n124; as metaphor/analogy, 6–7, 14, 19, 20, 35, 54–57, 60–62, 66, 99–106, 108–10, 126, 167–72, 176–78, 179, 181–86, 191, 197–200, 206, 210, 212–14, 255n128

Slavery Abolition Act (1833), 53

Slave Trade Act (1807), 53, 78, 239

Smith, Adam, 201–4, 208, 213–14, 270nn41–42, 271n51. *See also* sympathy

Some Impressions of the United States (Freeman), 47–48, 252n81

Somerville, Alexander, 71

Southern Citizen 11, 168, 174, 175, 183. *See also* Mitchel, John

Southern Literary Messenger, 86–87, 97–99, 110–13, 126.

Spirit of the Times, 196, 199, 218

Stancliff, Michael, 226–27

Stanhope, Charles, Lord, 53–54

Stephens, Alexander, 11, 177–78. *See also* "Cornerstone Speech"

Stocking, George, Jr., 38–39, 40, 42

Stowe, Harriet Beecher, 92, 110, 133–38, 198. *See also Uncle Tom's Cabin* (Stowe)

Sullivan, Alexander Martin, 124, 160

Sullivan, Denis Baylor, 160

Sullivan, Timothy Daniel, 160

Swift, Jonathan, 96, 121, 159–60, 250n31. *See also Modest Proposal, A* (Swift)

sympathy, 2, 15, 104, 129, 130, 182, 183–84, 189–222, 270nn41–42, 271n51, 271nn54–55, 272n82. *See also* empathy; Smith, Adam

Taine, Hippolyte Adolphe, 21

Taney, Roger B. See *Dred Scott v. Stanford*

Tara (as iconic Irish symbol), 232, 236–37, 275n37

Teutonism, 43, 47, 50, 263n12

Thackeray, William Makepeace, 138, 141, 264n36

"This Decision Has Humbled the Nation" (Douglass), 29, 227

Thompson, Mary, 168, 181

Thomson, James, 134–35, 146

Times (London), 120–21, 123–24, 164, 197–99, 214, 228, 266n14

Todorov, Tzvetan, 4

Trent, William Peterfield, 97

Trumpener, Katie, 112–14.

Tuck, Eve, 127

Tucker, Irene, 33

Twain, Mark, 66

Uncle Tom's Cabin (Stowe), 110, 137, 141, 198, 202, 209

Union, language for United States and United Kingdom, 66–67, 206, 233. *See also* Act of Union; Civil War, American

United Irishman (newspaper), 11, 25, 161, 170–71, 186

United Irishmen Uprising (1798), 12, 68, 104,

Vail, Jeffery, 113

Vaughan, Alden T., 39, 57, 58

Vizenor, Gerald, 119–20

Walsh, Mike, 104, 205, 260n19

Walters, Alisha R., 38

Ward, Samuel Ringgold, 22, 64–65, 268n42, 274n29

Wardrop, Daneen, 91

Watson, G. J., 10

Webb, Alfred, 274n33
Webb, Frank J., 20, 22, 26, 130–58, 193, 196, 211, 243, 264n33, 265n56, 265n68. See also *Garies and Their Friends, The* (Webb)
Webb, Richard Davis, 246n41
Weheliye, Alexander G., 178
Weissberg, Liliane, 88
Wellesley, Marquess, 53, 55, 61
Wester, Maisha L., 75, 89–91
Whalen, Terence, 81, 257–58n47
Wheatley, Phillis, 111
Wheeler, Roxann, 32–33
"white slavery" myth, 60–62, 106, 210, 253n101, 255n128. See also slavery as metaphor/analogy
white supremacy, 3, 7–8, 18, 23, 26, 27, 45, 62–64, 66, 89, 97, 99, 119, 125–26, 130–32, 141–42, 143, 151–53, 157, 158, 162, 173, 177–78, 188, 226, 231, 241–42, 254n121
Wilde, Jane Francesca (Elgee), 2, 12, 115. See also Wilde, Oscar

Wilde, Oscar, 1–12, 18, 21–22, 25, 47, 70, 80, 89, 98, 115, 161, 205, 235, 246n32; compares Ireland to Confederacy, 2–4. See also "Irish Poets and Poetry of the Nineteenth Century" (Wilde)
Wilderson III, Frank B., 14, 31, 52, 118, 195, 254n121. See also analogy as ruse
Wild Irish Girl, The (Morgan), 114, 237–40
Williams, Linda, 191
Williams, Patricia J., 211
Williams, Richard D'Alton, 186
Winn, T. S., 8
Wong, Amy R., 12
Wong, Edlie L., 268n43
Wright, Julia M., 77–80
Wynter, Sylvia, 249n13

Yang, K. Wayne, 127
Yao, Xine, 201, 202
Yeats, William Butler, 159–60
Young Ireland, 25, 98, 165, 167, 173, 175, 224, 232, 248n85, 261n37
Young Irelander Rebellion (1848), 25, 161

www.ingramcontent.com/pod-product-compliance
Lightning Source LLC
Chambersburg PA
CBHW030807230426
43667CB00008B/1110